TOPICS IN
C
PROGRAMMING

TOPICS IN
C
PROGRAMMING

Stephen G. Kochan and Patrick H. Wood
Pipeline Associates, Inc.

HAYDEN BOOKS
A Division of Howard W. Sams & Company
4300 West 62nd Street
Indianapolis, Indiana 46268 USA

International Standard Book Number: 0-672-46290-7
Library of Congress Catalog Card Number: 87-60647

Acquisitions Editor: *Therese Zak*
Editor: *Maureen Connelly*
Cover: *Visual Graphic Services, Indianapolis*
    Design by Jerry Bates
    Illustration by Robert Pitcher
Typesetting: *Pipeline Associates, Inc.*

This entire text was edited and processed under UNIX. The text was formatted using `troff`, with the assistance of `tbl` for the tables. The figures were created with MacDraw on an Apple Macintosh and then merged with the `troff` input. The `troff` output was converted to PostScript using `devps`. The camera ready copy was printed on an Apple LaserWriter Plus, with no pasteup required.

Printed in the United States of America

C O N T E N T S

To my daughter, Julia May
            S. G. K.

To my wife, Leslie
            P. H. W.

1

INTRODUCTION

This book is an intermediate to advanced level book on the C programming language. Its purpose is to teach you about various topics related to C programming. The book assumes that you have completed an introductory C programming text (such as *Programming in C*, Hayden Books, 1983), or have equivalent experience.

Since working with structures and pointers is the most difficult aspect of the C language, we decided to cover this area in detail in Chapter 2. Not only are the basics reviewed, but the more advanced aspects of working with structures and pointers are also described in detail. The structures section of the chapter focuses on operations on structures, structures and functions, arrays of structures, and complex structures.

The pointers section of Chapter 2 reviews the preliminaries of working with pointers from a conceptual point of view and also from an implementation point of view. After reviewing the basics, you'll learn about pointers and functions, pointers to structures, pointers to arrays, and character strings. Here we emphasize the often-confused distinction between character arrays, constant character strings, and character pointers. We then discuss the distinction between two-dimensional arrays and arrays of pointers. This is followed by detailed descriptions of pointer arithmetic, the relationship between pointers and arrays, how pointers are used to work with more complex data structures like linked lists and trees, pointers to pointers, and last, pointers to functions. A practical example of pointers to functions—setting up a dispatch table—is shown.

Chapters 3-5 cover the various C libraries provided under the UNIX system. Chapters 3 and 4 cover the Standard C Library and the Standard I/O Library. These libraries can be found on many non-UNIX systems as well. Chapter 5 describes the UNIX system calls. The functions described here are part of the UNIX system's kernel and therefore may not be available on non-UNIX systems.

One of the easiest ways to waste time and effort is to write a function that was already written by someone else. Yet experience shows that this happens time and again simply because programmers are unaware of the functions available in the various libraries and/or how to use them. Chapters 3-5 give you a good overview of these libraries by describing in detail many of the popularly-used functions from the Standard C, Standard I/O, and UNIX System Interface Libraries (and even some of the not so popular ones).

The routines in each chapter are logically grouped by the type of function they serve. For example, in the Standard C chapter, you'll see headings for functions that do character testing, data conversion, string handling, memory access, dynamic memory allocation, date and time conversion, data encryption, password and group file processing, process control, and table and tree management. In most cases, the description of a particular routine is followed by a complete working program example, so you can see how it's actually used.

As noted, Chapter 4 covers the Standard I/O Library. The chapter begins with an overview of the Library. Next, we review the concepts of *standard input* and *standard output* and we describe the functions that read from standard input and write to standard output. This section includes a thorough review of `printf` and the finicky `scanf`. Working with files is covered next, followed by a discussion of functions to perform *random I/O*, create and manage temporary files, give command lines to the UNIX system's shell for execution, control the buffering scheme, handle errors, and obtain miscellaneous types of information.

We mentioned that Chapter 5 describes the UNIX system calls. The chapter begins with an overview of these calls. We then describe the various calls, beginning with the I/O calls to open and close files, read and write data, perform random I/O, create and use pipes, and control terminal I/O.

The I/O calls are followed by a treatment of the file manipulation calls: calls for creating, removing, and linking files, and changing file attributes. This in turn is followed by a description of the process control routines. This includes discussions on creating new processes with `fork`, executing programs with `exec`, sending data between two programs over pipes, and getting and setting process information. Chapter 5 concludes with a description of the signal handling routines, and some miscellaneous system information routines.

The best reference source for the material described in Chapters 3-5 is *The UNIX Programmer's Reference Manual* (AT&T Bell Laboratories, Inc.). This book doesn't replace the manual but teaches you how to use many of the functions summarized there. You should keep a copy of the manual at your side while reading this book. At the start of Chapter 3 in this text you'll see a discussion on how the manual is organized, how to find function descriptions in it, and how to interpret the descriptions once you've found them.

Unfortunately, there is is no standard way to tell a terminal how to do a hardware-related function like clear the screen or move the cursor to the top left corner of the screen (i.e., "home" it). Historically, each different terminal type recognized its own unique codes to do these functions. So to clear a screen on say an Digital Equipment VT-52 terminal, you send the characters *Escape* H whereas on a Hewlett-Packard 2621 you need to send the characters *Escape* H *Escape* J. Consider the plight of a programmer trying to write a screen-oriented application like a screen editor, a spreadsheet, or a menu-driven system. Just trying to write the code to clear the screen could be an enormous task if your program is to allow the user to run it from any possible terminal type.

Luckily, the UNIX system has adopted a convention by the creation of a database known as `terminfo`[†] that describes how to perform the various functions for many different terminal types. The `curses` library contains functions that know how to work with this database. So to clear the screen on the terminal, you don't have to know what codes to send to the particular terminal. Instead, you call the `curses` function `clear` and let it figure out the necessary codes. Chapter 6 teaches you how to write terminal-independent programs using the `curses` library. Many current UNIX applications have been written with the aid of this library. If your application is a screen-oriented program, you will find the `curses` package invaluable.

Chapter 7 discusses the `make` command. This command allows you to easily manage generation of programs, particularly those that have been divided into many different files. `make` will keep track of which files have been changed and will automatically issue the commands to regenerate the program, doing as little work as possible. So, for example, if your C program is divided into five source files and you edit two of them, `make` will only recompile those two, recognizing that the object files from the other three are still okay. It will then link the two newly created objects with these three to produce a new executable object. This approach saves you the headache of trying to remember which files you changed and which have to be recompiled. In the case where your program is divided into more files and depends upon other files like `include` files and libraries, `make` becomes an even more valuable tool.

It's too bad that programs never run error-free the first time they're executed. Fortunately, a variety of powerful tools are available under UNIX for debugging C programs. The last chapter in the book talks about these tools in detail. Here you'll learn about the `lint` program, a sort of C compiler that takes a closer look at your C program than the compiler does to detect potential bugs and nonportable code usage. Then you'll see how the C preprocessor can be used effectively to control the inclusion of debugging statements in your program. With the techniques described here you'll be able to compile in or out all of your debugging code by simply giving an option to the `cc` command. You'll also learn how to set up your program so that different levels of debug output can be obtained at runtime.

The `ctrace` command, which provides automatic trace output of your program as it executes, was added to the UNIX system as of System V Release 2. You'll see how this command can be used to easily trace your program's execution.

The last tool covered in this chapter is the most powerful: `sdb`. This program is an interactive *symbolic* debugger that allows you to trace your program's execution and to examine and set variables while it executes. Its symbolic nature allows you to examine structure members, array elements, character strings, and variables by using standard C notation. The only unfortunate thing about `sdb` is that it is not available on all UNIX implementations.

---

† This database is called `termcap` on AT&T UNIX prior to System V, and on XENIX and BSD systems.

Included in the appendixes is a description on how to write your own `termcap` and `terminfo` entries (for use with `curses`) in case you have a terminal that's not already described there. Also summarized for reference purposes in Appendix B are all of the functions in the `curses` library.

We recommend that you read Chapter 2, Structures and Pointers, first. This will give you a solid foundation for the remaining chapters. Chapters 3 through 5, on the libraries, should be read in order. Chapters 6 through 8, which cover fairly independent topics (`curses`, `make`, and debugging) can be read in any order, either before or after the other chapters.

We think examples are the best way to teach, whether they're showing how to use a library function or an interactive debugging tool like `sdb`. So you shouldn't be surprised to find a large number of actual working examples throughout the book. You should try these examples on your system. Then modify them to test other options or to increase their usefulness. You'll also notice that exercises appear at the end of each chapter. You should try these to test your knowledge of the material.

The source code for all programs listed in this book is obtainable free of charge from Pipeline Associates, Inc., to any user with an electronic mail address that has access to USENET. To get the programs, simply send UNIX mail to one of the following addresses:

```
ihnp4!bellcore!phw5!topics
harpo!bellcore!phw5!topics
```

Lines beginning with

```
SEND_PROGRAMS_TO:
```

are parsed automatically, and the programs are sent in a *shell archive* (which contains information about how to unpack it) as UNIX mail to the electronic mail address listed on the rest of the line. All addresses must be specified relative to either `ihnp4` or `harpo`.

The following causes the program archive to be mailed to the user `joe` on the system `ihnp4!ucbvax!galaxy`:

```
$ mail ucbvax!ihnp4!bellcore!phw5!topics
SEND_PROGRAMS_TO: ihnp4!ucbvax!galaxy!joe
.
$
```

Note that the address is used literally, so addresses of the form

```
joe@outer.space.UUCP
```

will *not* work.

This text is based on UNIX System V Release 2. However, most of the programs will run unaltered under XENIX III, XENIX V, and Berkeley BSD UNIX. Some programs in the UNIX System Interface and `curses` chapters may require minor modification for XENIX and BSD systems. If you're programming in C on a different operating system, then you will still find much of the material applicable. All of Chapter 2 will be applicable, and many of the functions described in Chapters 3 and 4 may be available on your system. Chapters 5-8 are more UNIX specific, but even here you may find that some of the routines and programs described are available on your system.

We would like to acknowledge Dick Fritz for doing such a thorough technical review (as usual), and Marc Rochkind for reviewing the first few chapters. We'd also like to thank Therese Zak and Maureen Connelly, formerly of Hayden Book Company, for their work and contributions to all of the books (including this one) in Hayden's UNIX Library. Finally, we want to thank Jim Hill, Jennifer Ackley, Wendy Ford, and Lou Keglovits of Howard W. Sams & Co. for their cooperation and support.

C H A P T E R
2

STRUCTURES AND POINTERS

I n this chapter you'll learn about structures and pointers in detail. We'll cover how to define structures and structure variables, how to initialize them, the types of operations that you can perform on them, how they work with functions, and how to define and work with arrays of them.

The second part of the chapter discusses the most difficult aspect of C: pointers. You'll learn here how to define pointers, how to indirectly access the values they point to, what types of arithmetic operations are allowed on them, how to work with pointers to arrays, pointers to structures, pointers to pointers, pointers to functions, and how pointers can be used to create sophisticated data structures like linked lists and dispatch tables.

· Structures ·

Defining

A structure is a set of values that can be referenced collectively. It differs from an array in that elements of the structure (known as the structure's *members*) do not necessarily have to be of the same type, and that elements are also referenced differently.

To use a structure variable in your program, you first have to tell the C compiler what the structure "looks" like. This involves defining what the members are called and what their data types are.

The general format of a structure definition is:

```
struct sname {
    member-declaration
    member-declaration
    ...
};
```

This defines a structure called *sname* with the indicated members. Each
member-declaration takes the following general form:

```
type    member-name;
```

Once you have defined a structure to the C compiler, you can then go
ahead and declare variables to be of that particular structure type. Note that a
structure definition does not in itself cause *any* storage to be allocated by the C
compiler. Not until variables are declared will storage be reserved.

As an example, suppose you need to store several dates inside your program. It might be a good idea to define a structure called `date` that could be
used for storing such dates. If the date is to be represented in the program as
three integers indicating the month, day, and year, then the following structure
definition would do the trick:

```
struct date {
    int   month;
    int   day;
    int   year;
};
```

This defines a structure called `date` that contains three members: an integer
called `month`, another called `day`, and a third called `year`. Once again,
remember that here you're only telling the C compiler what a `date` structure
looks like; you're not reserving any space. In a sense, you have defined a template for a `date` structure as shown in Fig. 2-1.

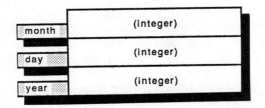

Fig. 2-1. Defining a structure

The template that's shown here has three member names listed on the left. These tell the C compiler which of the three integers of a `date` structure is referred to by the name `month`, which by the name `day`, and which by the name `year`. These member names are *not* stored with your values inside a structure variable—they only exist while your program is being compiled.

Declaring Variables

Now that you've told the C compiler what a `date` structure looks like, you're ready to go ahead and declare variables to be of this structure type:

```
struct date today;
```

This tells the compiler to reserve space for a variable called `today`, which is of type `struct date` (Fig. 2-2).

struct date today;

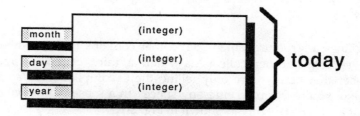

Fig. 2-2. Declaring a structure variable

Assigning Values to Structure Variables

Now that you have a variable declared, you can store values in it. To assign a value to one of the members of a structure variable, you use the format

```
variable.member = value
```

The structure variable is followed by the structure member operator "." which then must be followed by a valid member of that structure. In the case of our `date` structure variable `today`, valid members would be `month`, `day`, or `year`.

So to store the date March 13, 1987 inside the `today` variable, you could write the three statements:

```
today.month = 3;
today.day = 13;
today.year = 1987;
```

Now the three members of the variable `today` will be set as shown in Fig. 2-3.

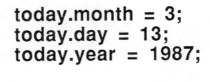

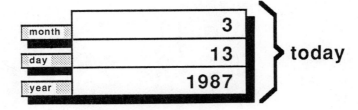

Fig. 2-3. Assigning values to a structure variable

Program 2-1 is a short program that summarizes the discussion thus far.[†]

Inside `main`, the variable `today` is declared to be of type `struct date` and then its three members `month`, `day`, and `year` are set equal to the three integers `3`, `13`, and `1987`, respectively. After that, the values stored in the structure are retrieved and passed to `printf` to be displayed.

Note that the `date` structure is defined outside of `main`. Here it makes no difference, but in some cases it does matter *where* you define your structures. Structure definitions, like variable declarations have *scope* associated with them. If a structure is defined in a function, then only that function knows of its definition—this is a *local* structure definition. On the other hand, if the structure is defined outside of any function (typically at the beginning of the file), then its definition is *global*, meaning that any functions subsequently defined in the file can use this structure definition.

---

† The programs in this book do not declare a return type for `main`. On some non-UNIX systems, `main` must be declared `void` to prevent the compiler from complaining about the absence of a `return` statement inside `main`.

Program 2-1

```
struct date {
    int month;
    int day;
    int year;
};

main ()
{
    struct date today;

    today.month = 3;
    today.day = 13;
    today.year = 1987;

    printf ("%d/%d/%d\n", today.month, today.day,
            today.year - 1900);
}

$ a.out
3/13/87
```

(Recall that under the UNIX system the excutable object file is called a.out by default.)

Structure Initialization

Structure variables can be assigned initial values at the time they are declared, provided such variables are either global or static. In other words, you can't assign initial values to automatic structure variables. You will recall that static variables differ from automatic ones in that they retain their values through function calls and have default initial values of zero. Also recall that automatic arrays, like structures, cannot be initialized.

The general format for initializing a structure variable is:

```
struct sname   variable = { val1, val2, ... };
```

So to initialize the variable today from the previous program in its declaration, you can write

```
static struct today = { 3, 13, 1987 };
```

Note the keyword static is required here since, as noted, automatic structure variables cannot be initialized. If you omit the keyword static, then the compiler will issue an error message.

Operations on Structures

One of the few operations supported with structures is the ability to assign one structure variable to another, *provided they are both of the same structure type.*[†] So if you want to copy the date stored in the `date` structure variable `today` to another `date` structure variable called `tomorrow`, you simply write

```
tomorrow = today;
```

You can't do much else with structures as a whole, except pass them and return them to and from functions (more on that soon).[‡] So don't try to test two structures for equality with a statement like

```
if ( today == tomorrow )
    ...
```

because it won't work. You have to compare them member by member:

```
if ( today.month == tomorrow.month && today.day == tomorrow.day
        && today.year == tomorrow.year )
    ...
```

When you reference a particular member of a structure, the resulting type of that expression is that of the member you're referencing. So when you write

```
today.year
```

the type of this expression is the type of the member `year`: `int`. `today.year` can now be used like a normal `int`: you can pass it to a function that expects an `int` as argument, you can add one to it with the `++` operator, and so on. Writing the statement

```
century = today.year / 100 + 1;
```

results in an integer division being performed between `today.year` and 100. (Recall that dividing two integers in C results in an integer result, with the fractional remainder discarded.)

Structures and Functions

You can pass an entire structure as an argument to a function simply by writing the variable in the argument list when calling the function. So if you have a function called `juliandate` that calculates the Julian date from a date stored in a `date` structure, then you can pass the entire structure to the function as a single argument as follows:

---

† Note that this feature is not supported on Version 7 and BSD 4.1 systems.
‡ This too is not supported on Version 7 and BSD 4.1 systems.

```
    julian = juliandate (today);
```

The function must make the appropriate declaration in the function header to tell the compiler that an argument of type `struct date` is expected:

```
    int juliandate (caldate)
    struct date caldate;
    {
        int result;
        ...
        return (result);
    }
```

This says that `juliandate` is a function that returns an `int` and takes a single argument called `caldate` that's of type `struct date`.

Remember that C passes arguments by value. Therefore, any time you pass a structure to a function, the function cannot make any permanent changes to the variable itself. It can only change a copy that is created when the function is called. So in the previous example, `juliandate` cannot make any changes to the variable `today`, whose value is passed to the function; it can only change a *copy* of `today` that is placed in the variable `caldate` when the function is called.

You are permitted to return an entire structure from a function, provided you make the appropriate return type declaration. Suppose you write a function called `nextday` whose purpose is to take a `date` structure passed as its argument and calculate the day after that date. You'd like to return an entire `date` structure representing the new date. The `nextday` function should look like this:

```
    struct date nextday (now)
    struct date now;
    {
        ...
        return (now);
    }
```

This tells the C compiler that `nextday` is a function that returns a value of type `struct date` and that takes a single argument of the same type. The function presumably updates the variable `now` and then *returns* the modified structure back to the calling routine by executing the statement

```
    return (now);
```

Note that the type of the value being returned is consistent with the return type declared for the function: `struct date`.

Back in the calling routine, you can take the date structure that is returned by nextday and assign it to a date structure variable with a statement like

```
tomorrow = nextday (today);
```

This is just an extension of the ability to assign structures of the same type.

The following program illustrates the nextday function plus some support routines necessary to determine tomorrow's date based upon today's.

Program 2-2

```
struct date {
    int month;
    int day;
    int year;
};


/* find the day after the one given as the argument */

struct date nextday (now)
struct date now;
{
    if ( now.day == month_days (now) )
        if ( now.month == 12 )  {   /* end of year */
            now.day = 1;
            now.month = 1;
            ++now.year;
            }
        else {                      /* end of month */
            now.day = 1;
            ++now.month;
            }
    else                                /* not end of month */
        ++now.day;

    return (now);
}
```

```c
/* find the number of days in a month */

int month_days (now)
struct date now;
{
        static int days_per_month[] =
            { 31, 28, 31, 30, 31, 30, 31, 31, 30, 31, 30, 31 };

        if ( now.month == 2  &&  leapyear (now.year) )
                return (29);
        else
                return (days_per_month[now.month - 1]);
}


/* Determine if it's a leap year */

int leapyear (year)
int year;
{
        if ( (year % 4 == 0  &&  year % 100 != 0)  ||
          year % 400 == 0 )
                return (1);
        else
                return (0);
}


main ()
{
        static struct date  d1 = { 7, 30, 1985 };
        static struct date  d2 = { 12, 31, 1983 };
        static struct date  d3 = { 2, 28, 1988 };
        static struct date  d4 = { 2, 28, 1987 };
        struct date         next;

        next = nextday (d1);
        printf ("%d, %d, %d\n", next.month, next.day, next.year);

        next = nextday (d2);
        printf ("%d, %d, %d\n", next.month, next.day, next.year);

        next = nextday (d3);
        printf ("%d, %d, %d\n", next.month, next.day, next.year);

        next = nextday (d4);
        printf ("%d, %d, %d\n", next.month, next.day, next.year);
}
```

```
$ a.out
7, 31, 1985
1, 1, 1984
2, 29, 1988
3, 1, 1987
```

The date structure definition is made global so that all subsequent functions will know about it.

The nextday function first checks to see if we're at the end of a month by calling the function month_days. This function takes a date structure as its argument and finds the number of days in the month stored in that argument. month_days checks to see if it's February of a leap year (as determined by the leapyear function) and, if it is, returns the value 29. Otherwise, the function looks up the month in the days_per_month array and returns the corresponding value.

If we're at the end of a month, then a test has to be made to see if we're at the end of the year (December 31). If we are, then the new date is set to January 1 of the following year. If we're not at the end of the year, then the new date is set to the first day of the next month.

If we're not at the end of a month, then the new date is calculated by simply incrementing the current day by one.

Inside main, four date structures d1 through d4 are declared and set to different dates to test the nextday function. Since nextday is defined before it's called in the program, it's not necessary to declare its return type. However, remember that any function that doesn't return an int must be declared before it's called unless it is defined in the file first. So if nextday were defined *after* main, or in another source file, then a declaration statement like

```
struct date nextday ();
```

would have been required in the program to alert the C compiler of the fact that nextday doesn't return an int.

Arrays of Structures

An array of structures is defined just like any other array; in this case each element of the array is a structure:

```
struct date holidays[100];
```

This defines an array of 100 elements called holidays. Each element of the holidays array is of type struct date (see Fig. 2-4).

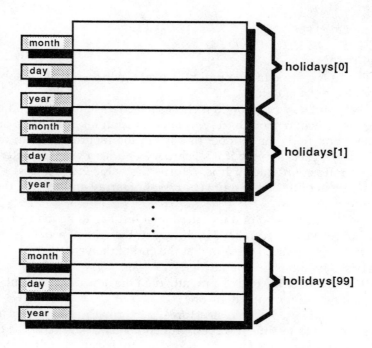

Fig. 2-4. Arrays of structures

An element of an array of structures is accessed in the normal fashion, simply by writing

```
array[index]
```

The type of such an expression is the type defined for the elements of the array, so

```
holidays[1]
```

is of type `struct date`; its value is that of the second `date` structure stored inside the `holidays` array. To reference a member of one of these structures, you simply tack on the structure member operator `.` followed by the member name, using the general format

```
array[index].member
```

The array element reference operator `[ ]` and the structure member operator `.` have the same precedence but associate from left to right, thus the particular array element will be correctly accessed *before* the member of the structure is referenced.

As an example, writing

```
holidays[0].month
```

references the `month` member of the first `date` structure stored in the `holidays` array, and

```
++holidays[0].month;
```

adds one to it. The statements

```
holidays[0].month = 7;
holidays[0].day = 4;
holidays[0].year = 1987;
```

set the first element of `holidays` to July 4, 1987 (see Fig. 2-5).

Since the type of an element of `holidays` is `struct date`, you can use it wherever a `date` structure can appear:

```
for ( i = 0; i < 100; ++i )
    holidays[i] = nextday (holidays[i]);
```

This will pass each holiday to the `nextday` function, and store the day after each holiday back into the `holidays` array.

Arrays of structures can be initialized by combining the techniques you learned for initializing arrays and initializing structures. The declaration

```
static struct dates[] = {
    {11, 3, 1983}, {7, 16, 1955}, {7, 25, 1987},
    {2, 4, 1988}, {9, 1, 1986}
};
```

declares an array of `date` structures called `dates` like before. The absence of a size specification tells the C compiler to set it to the number of initial values, 5. `dates[0]` is set to November 3, 1983, `dates[1]` to July 16, 1955, and so on. Remember that `dates` must be made `static` if declared inside a function.

holidays[0].month = 7;
holidays[0].day = 4;
holidays[0].year = 1987;

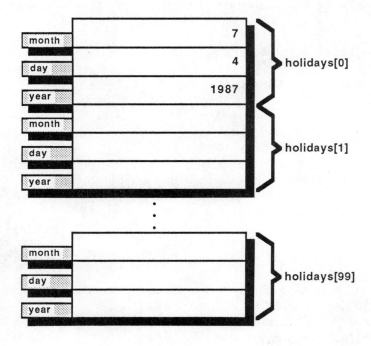

Fig. 2-5. Working with arrays of structures

More Complex Structures

The members of a structure can be any of the basic data types like `ints`, `floats`, or `chars`, or they can be *derived* data types like arrays or other structures. If you have a structure called `time` that is used to store times in your program in hours, minutes, and seconds, then its definition might look like this:

```
struct time {
    int  hours;
    int  mins;
    int  secs;
};
```

Suppose you need to record events in your program, where an event is noted by the date and the time that it occurred. Given the `date` and `time` structure definitions as previously shown, you can make a `date_time` structure definition whose members are themselves structures as follows:

```
struct date_time {
    struct date  sdate;
    struct time  stime;
};
```

Here `date_time` is defined as a structure containing two members. The first is called `sdate` and is of type `struct date`. The second is called `stime` and is of type `struct time`. You declare a variable to be of type `struct date_time` in the normal fashion:

```
struct date_time event;
```

You can set the `sdate` member of `event` to July 4, 1988 with the statements

```
event.sdate.month = 7;
event.sdate.day   = 4;
event.sdate.year  = 1987;
```

and the `stime` member can be set to noon with the statements

```
event.stime.hours = 12;
event.stime.mins  = 0;
event.stime.secs  = 0;
```

The statement

```
event.sdate.month = 7;
```

uses two structure member operators. Since this operator associates from left to right, it is correctly evaluated as

```
(event.sdate).month = 7;
```

The expression

```
event.sdate
```

references the `sdate` member of the `date_time` structure variable `event`. It is of type `struct date`. So if you wanted to update this date, you could pass it as an argument to `nextday` as shown:

```
event.sdate = nextday (event.sdate);
```

Once again, our data types are consistent: `nextday` expects to see an argument of type `struct date`—which is what you're supplying when you write `event.sdate`. Similarly, `nextday` returns a value of type `struct date`, which is why the assignment is made to `event.sdate`. The first step in writing correct statements in C is to figure out the data types that you're dealing with and then to write the expressions that produce values of these data types.

The `date_time` structure variable `event` can be initialized using techniques previously described:

```
static struct date_time event = {
    {7, 4, 1988}, {12, 0, 0}
};
```

The inner sets of braces are not needed, but they aid in the readability of the assignment.

Naturally, you can define an array of `date_time` structures as follows:

```
struct date_time events[100];
```

You could initialize the first two elements of this array to March 13, 1987, 10:30 A.M., and to August 8, 1988, 7:03 P.M., respectively, with the following declarations:

```
static struct date_time events[100] = {
    { {3, 13, 1987}, {10, 30, 0} },
    { {8,  8, 1988}, {19,  3, 0} }
};
```

To calculate the day after the first date in `events` and put it back into the array, you could use the `nextday` function with a call as shown:

```
events[0].sdate = nextday (events[0].sdate);
```

To increment the seconds field of this element you would write:

```
++events[0].stime.secs;
```

Table 2-1 summarizes various expressions and their data types when working with the `events` array.

TABLE 2-1. Arrays of structures

Expression	Data Type
events	struct date_time *
events[i]	struct date_time
events[i].sdate	struct date
events[i].stime	struct time
events[i].sdate.month	int
events[i].stime.hours	int

According to the table, the expression `events` produces a value of type "pointer to `struct date_time`." This is something we'll be discussing in more detail shortly.

An Employee Data Structure

Suppose you had to create a data base that contained information about the employees in your company. You might want to record each employee's name, room number, job level, salary, and starting date. Assume that employees are paid an annual salary.

Dealing with the various information about an employee can be handled in C by defining an appropriate structure definition:

```
struct emprec {
    char        name[25];
    char        room[10];
    int         joblevel;
    long int    salary;
    struct date startdate;
};
```

The first member of the `emprec` structure is called `name` and is an array of 25 characters. This will be used to store the employee's name. The second member is called `room` and will contain the employee's room number (it's not an `int` because we'll assume room numbers are noninteger designations like 3A-331).

The third member is an integer that identifies the employee's job level. This is followed by the employee's salary, and the last member of the structure—called `startdate`—is a `date` structure that contains the employee's starting date.

If you're creating a data base of information for employees in your company, then it might not be unreasonable to want to have an array of `emprec` structures in your program. For instance, you can set up an array large enough to store information about 1000 employees by writing

```
#define NUMEMPLOYEES   1000

struct emprec employees[NUMEMPLOYEES];
```

If you wanted to hard-code the information for three employees into your program, you could do it like this:

```
static struct emprec employees[NUMEMPLOYEES] = {
    { "Elvida Ippolito", "4B-208", 10, 35400, {6, 1, 1984} },
    { "John Musa",       "3G-711", 5, 25000, {1, 9, 1966} },
    { "Steven Levy",     "2D-928", 12, 65500, {9, 15, 1977} }
};
```

Inside employees[0] we're storing information about an employee named Elvida Ippolito. Her room is 4B-208, job level is 10, salary is $35,400, and starting date is June 1, 1984. The information on the other two employees, John Musa and Steven Levy, is handled similarly.

To change Elvida's salary to $38,000, you would write

```
employees[0].salary = 38000;
```

To change her room to 7F-544, you could write

```
employees[0].room[0] = '7';
employees[0].room[1] = 'F';
employees[0].room[2] = '-';
employees[0].room[3] = '5';
employees[0].room[4] = '4';
employees[0].room[5] = '4';
employees[0].room[6] = '\0';
```

Or, more concisely, you could copy the new room in with strcpy (described in the next chapter):

```
strcpy (employees[0].room, "7F-544");
```

Table 2-2 summarizes various expressions and their data types when dealing with the employees array. In later chapters we'll return to this emprec data structure. You'll see how to create a database, write it to a file, and subsequently scan the database to update information for a particular employee.

TABLE 2-2. Working with complex structures

Expression	Data Type
employees	struct emprec *
employees[i]	struct emprec
employees[i].name	char *
employees[i].name[0]	char
employees[i].startdate	struct date
employees[i].startdate.month	int

Variations on a Theme

You may recall that there are a couple of options available when defining a structure. One is that you can also declare variables at the same time, simply by listing them in front of the terminating semicolon. So the statement

```
struct date {
    int  month;
    int  day;
    int  year;
} today, tomorrow;
```

not only defines to the compiler what a date structure is, but also declares two variables, today and tomorrow, to be of that structure type. Naturally, you can even initialize such a variable at the same time:

```
static struct date {
    int  month;
    int  day;
    int  year;
} today = { 7, 10, 1987 };
```

This does three things: it defines a date structure, declares a variable called today, and sets its initial value to July 10, 1987.

If you're going to use this format and will be declaring *all* of the variables of this structure type at the same time, then you don't have to name your structure. So if today is the only variable in your program that will be used to store a date, you can write the previous declaration as

```
static struct {
    int   month;
    int   day;
    int   year;
} today = { 7, 10, 1987 };
```

As noted, since the structure is not named, you can not subsequently declare variables to be of this structure type.

This concludes (for now) our discussion on structures. In the next section of this chapter we'll return to them when we talk about pointers to structures.

▪ Pointers ▪

Defining

There are two different ways to look at pointers. The first way is from a conceptual point of view; the second is from an implementation point of view. We'll talk about pointers from both standpoints, since one may prove to be more enlightening or easier to understand than the other.

From a conceptual point of view, a pointer variable in C is one that "points" to another variable or to a function. A pointer itself does not directly contain a value like an `int` or a `float`, but it points to another variable that does. When you access this value through the pointer variable, you are *indirectly* accessing the value.

In order to produce a pointer to a variable, the unary `&` operator is placed immediately before the variable. We'll talk here about `int`s and pointers to them, although the discussion applies equally to other data types.

If a variable called `int1` is of type `int`, then the expression

```
&int1
```

produces a pointer to `int1` and is of type *pointer to* `int` (written as `int *`).

The pointer produced by applying the `&` operator can be stored inside a variable that has been appropriately declared to be of the correct pointer type. This is done by putting a `*` in front of the variable name when it is declared:

```
int   *int_ptr;
```

Here `int_ptr` is declared to be not of type `int`, but of type pointer to `int`. Therefore, `int_ptr` won't be used to store an integer value, but rather a pointer to another variable that contains one.

HOWARD W. SAMS & COMPANY

Bookmark

DEAR VALUED CUSTOMER:

Howard W. Sams & Company is dedicated to bringing you timely and authoritative books for your personal and professional library. Our goal is to provide you with excellent technical books written by the most qualified authors. You can assist us in this endeavor by checking the box next to your particular areas of interest.

We appreciate your comments and will use the information to provide you with a more comprehensive selection of titles.

Thank you,

Vice President, Book Publishing
Howard W. Sams & Company

COMPUTER TITLES:

Hardware
☐ Apple 140   ☐ Macintosh 101
☐ Commodore 110
☐ IBM & Compatibles 114

Business Applications
☐ Word Processing J01
☐ Data Base J04
☐ Spreadsheets J02

Operating Systems
☐ MS-DOS K05   ☐ OS/2 K10
☐ CP/M K01   ☐ UNIX K03

Programming Languages
☐ C L03   ☐ Pascal L05
☐ Prolog L12   ☐ Assembly L01
☐ BASIC L02   ☐ HyperTalk L14

Troubleshooting & Repair
☐ Computers S05
☐ Peripherals S10

Other
☐ Communications/Networking M03
☐ AI/Expert Systems T18

ELECTRONICS TITLES:
☐ Amateur Radio T01
☐ Audio T03
☐ Basic Electronics T20
☐ Basic Electricity T21
☐ Electronics Design T12
☐ Electronics Projects T04
☐ Satellites T09

☐ Instrumentation T05
☐ Digital Electronics T11

Troubleshooting & Repair
☐ Audio S11   ☐ Television S04
☐ VCR S01   ☐ Compact Disc S02
☐ Automotive S06
☐ Microwave Oven S03

Other interests or comments: _____

_____

_____

Name_____

Title _____

Company _____

Address _____

City _____

State/Zip _____

Daytime Telephone No. _____

A Division of Macmillan, Inc.
4300 West 62nd Street
Indianapolis, Indiana 46268

46290

Bookmark

HOWARD W. SAMS
& COMPANY

HOWARD W. SAMS & COMPANY
HAYDEN BOOKS

Exploring the UNIX® System
Stephen G. Kochan and Patrick H. Wood
ISBN: 0-8104-6268-0, $22.95

UNIX® Shell Programming
Stephen G. Kochan and Patrick H. Wood
ISBN: 0-8104-6309-1, $24.95

UNIX® System Security
Patrick H. Wood and Stephen G. Kochan
ISBN: 0-8104-6267-1, $34.95

UNIX® Text Processing
Dale Dougherty and Tim O'Reilly
ISBN: 0-672-46291-5, $26.95

UNIX® System Administration
David Fielder and Bruce H. Hunter
ISBN: 0-8104-6289-3, $24.95

The Waite Group's UNIX® Communications
Bart Anderson, Bryan Costales, Harry Henderson
ISBN: 0-672-22511-5, $26.95

The Waite Group's UNIX® Primer Plus
Mitchell Waite, Donald Martin, Stephen Prata
ISBN: 0-672-22028-8, $22.95

The Waite Group's UNIX® Shell Programming Language
Rod Manis and Marc H. Meyer
ISBN: 0-672-22497-6, $24.95

The Waite Group's UNIX® System V Primer, Revised Edition
Mitchell Waite, Donald Martin, Stephen Prata
ISBN: 0-672-22570-0, $22.95

The Waite Group's Tricks of the UNIX® Masters
Russell G. Sage
ISBN: 0-672-22449-6, $24.95

The Waite Group's UNIX® Papers
The Waite Group
ISBN: 0-672-22578-6, $26.95

The Waite Group's UNIX® System V Bible
Stephen Prata and Donald Martin
ISBN: 0-672-22562-X, $24.95

The Waite Group's Advanced UNIX®—A Programmer's Guide
Stephen Prata
ISBN: 0-672-22403-8, $24.95

The Waite Group's Inside XENIX®
Christopher L. Morgan
ISBN: 0-672-22445-3, $24.95

To order, return the card below, or call 1-800-428-SAMS. In Indiana call (317) 298-5699.

- -

Please send me the books listed below.

Title	Quantity	ISBN #	Price

☐ Please add my name to your mailing list to receive more information on related titles.

Name (please print) _____

Company _____

City _____

State/Zip _____

Signature _____
(required for credit card purchase)

Telephone # _____

Subtotal _____
Standard Postage and Handling **$2.50**
All States Add Appropriate Sales Tax _____
TOTAL _____

Enclosed is My Check or Money Order for $_____

Charge my Credit Card: ☐ VISA ☐ MC ☐ AE

Account No. _____ Expiration Date _____
☐☐☐☐ ☐☐☐☐ ☐☐☐☐ ☐☐☐☐

46290

HOWARD W. SAMS & COMPANY

Dept. DM
4300 West 62nd Street
Indianapolis, IN 46268-2589

Using Pointers

Pointers are useless unless they're set pointing to something. If `int1` is declared with

```
int   int1 = 100;
```

then `int_ptr` can be set pointing to `int1` by writing the statement

```
int_ptr = &int1;
```

This stores inside `int_ptr` not the value of `int1`, but rather a *pointer* to the variable `int1` (see Fig. 2-6).

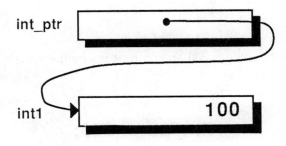

```
int   *int_ptr;
int   int1 = 100;

int_ptr = &int1;
```

Fig. 2-6. Pointer to `int`

You'll recall that the expression

```
&int1
```

produces a pointer to `int1`. Its type is pointer to `int`, meaning that it can be stored inside a variable declared to be of type pointer to `int`.

To retrieve the value contained inside `int1`, you can simply write

```
int1
```

This would have the value 100 according to our example, and would be of type `int`.

To retrieve the same value indirectly *through* the pointer variable `int_ptr` you don't write the expression

```
int_ptr
```

since this has as its value the pointer stored inside `int_ptr`, and is of type pointer to `int`. By placing the unary indirection operator `*` before a pointer variable, you tell the compiler not to retrieve the value of the pointer itself, but to retrieve *what the pointer points to*. So writing

```
*int_ptr
```

says to fetch what `int_ptr` points to. Since you set `int_ptr` pointing to `int1`, it's the value stored inside `int1` that's retrieved: 100.

To generalize, if a variable called `x` is of type y, then the expression `&x` produces a pointer to `x` and is of type pointer to y.

If `ptrx` is a variable of type pointer to y and has been set pointing to a variable of type y, then the expression `*ptrx` has as its value whatever is stored in the variable that `ptrx` points to. It is of type y. In other words, if `ptrx` is of type pointer to y, then `*ptrx` is of type y.

If you want to change the value stored in the variable pointed to by `int_ptr` to, say, 200, you write

```
*int_ptr = 200;
```

This says to take the integer 200 and store it inside the variable that `int_ptr` points to (see Fig. 2-7).

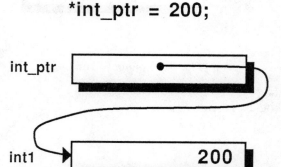

Fig. 2-7. Changing values indirectly

The constant 200 is of type `int`, and so is the expression `*int_ptr`, which is why this assignment works (remember once again the importance of matching types as a guide to writing expressions correctly in C).

The next program example illustrates the two fundamental pointer operators `&` and `*`. This time we're dealing with a pointer to a character.

Program 2-3

```
main ()
{
    char  c = 'X';
    char  *char_ptr;

    /* set char_ptr pointing to c */
    char_ptr = &c;
    printf ("%c\n", *char_ptr);

    *char_ptr = 'A';
    printf ("%c\n", *char_ptr);

    printf ("%c\n", c);
}


$ a.out
X
A
A
```

The character variable `c` is declared and set to the character `'X'`. Next the character pointer variable `char_ptr` is declared and set pointing to the variable `c`. Since automatic variables can be initialized to expressions that include previously declared variables, you could have declared `char_ptr` and set it pointing to `c` with the single statement

```
    char  *char_ptr = &c;
```

The following statements in the program show how the value of the variable `c` can be indirectly accessed and changed through the pointer variable `char_ptr`.

Now let's talk about pointers from an implementation point of view. When your program is executing, your variables reside at various locations—called addresses—in the computer's memory. When you write the expression

```
&int1
```

we noted that you are producing a pointer to the variable `int1`. More precisely, you're taking the address of the variable `int1` in memory (that's why the `&` operator is called the *address* operator). When you write the statement

```
int_ptr = &int1;
```

you're telling the C compiler to generate code to take the address of the variable `int1` and to store that address in the variable `int_ptr`. So when you declare `int_ptr` with

```
int   *int_ptr;
```

you're telling the C compiler that `int_ptr` is a variable that will be used to store memory addresses.

Suppose you write a program that contains the following declarations as seen previously:

```
int   *int_ptr;
int   int1 = 100;
```

When your program is executing, the variables `int_ptr` and `int1` will reside at some locations in memory. Assume that `int_ptr` is assigned to memory location 1000 and `int1` to location 1200 (see Fig. 2-8).

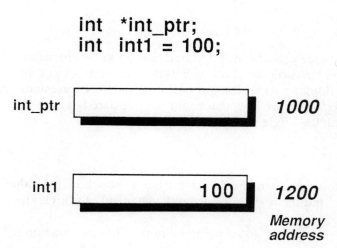

Fig. 2-8. Variables and memory addresses

When you write the expression

```
int_ptr = &int1;
```

you're saying to take the address of `int1` and store it inside `int_ptr`. Since we know that `int1` is at memory location 1200, that's what actually gets stored inside `int_ptr` (see Fig. 2-9).

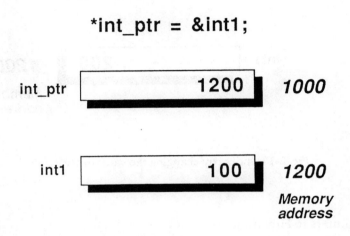

Fig. 2-9. Setting a pointer variable

When you write the expression

```
*int_ptr
```

you're saying to take the value stored inside `int_ptr` and treat it as a memory address. You're also saying that at that memory address you'll find an `int` (that's because you declared `int_ptr` to be of type pointer to `int`). The integer stored there is then retrieved and that's the value of the expression.

When you write the statement

```
*int_ptr = 200;
```

you're saying to take the integer 200 and store it at the memory location specified by `int_ptr`. In our example, since `int_ptr` contains 1200, the value 200 will then be stored at memory location 1200, thus indirectly changing the value of the variable `int1` from 100 to 200 (see Fig. 2-10).

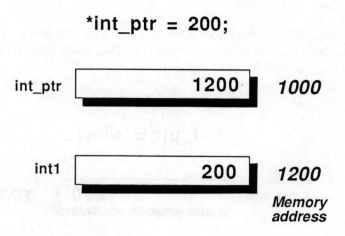

Fig. 2-10. Indirectly changing the value of a variable

Passing Pointers to Functions

In C, arguments are passed to functions by value. This means that if you call the sqrt function to calculate the square root of the variable x with a call like

```
sqrt (x)
```

it is the value stored inside x that will get passed to the function. The sqrt function itself can't change the value of x; all it can change is a copy of x that is made when the function is called.

As you know, functions in C can only return a single value (although that value can be a structure). Sometimes you need to have a function set more than one value. One way to do that is to make the variables you want the function to modify global, and then the function can explicitly change those variables. Another approach is to pass *pointers* to the variables you want to modify. While the function won't be able to permanently modify these pointers, it can modifiy *what the pointers point to.*

As an example, consider the task of trying to write a function to exchange the values of two integer variables passed as arguments. A first attempt might be as shown:

Program 2-4

```
void exchange (d1, d2)
int d1, d2;
{
    int  temp;

    temp = d1;
    d1 = d2;
    d2 = temp;
}

main ()
{
    int x1 = 100, x2 = 200;

    printf ("%d %d\n", x1, x2);
    exchange (x1, x2);
    printf ("%d %d\n", x1, x2);
}


$ a.out
100 200
100 200
```

The exchange function takes two integer arguments and exchanges them—using a temporary variable called temp to store one of the values while the switch is being made. The main routine declares two integers x1 and x2 with initial values of 100 and 200, respectively. These two values are displayed and the exchange function is called with x1 and x2 as arguments. When the function returns, the values of x1 and x2 are once again displayed. Notice that exchange was unable to switch the values stored inside x1 and x2. This is because when exchange is called, the values stored inside x1 and x2 are passed to the function. These values of 100 and 200 are stored inside the local variables d1 and d2 in the exchange function. Any changes made to d1 and d2 therefore affect only these local variables and have no effect whatsoever on x1 and x2. Like all automatic local variables, d1 and d2 "disappear" when exchange finishes execution.

The correct way to write the exchange function is so that it takes not two integers as arguments but *pointers* to them instead. In this way, we *can* permanently change the values of the variables x1 and x2.

Program 2-5

```
void exchange (p1, p2)
int *p1, *p2;
{
    int  temp;

    temp = *p1;
    *p1 = *p2;
    *p2 = temp;
}

main ()
{
    int x1 = 100, x2 = 200;

    printf ("%d %d\n", x1, x2);
    exchange (&x1, &x2);
    printf ("%d %d\n", x1, x2);
}


$ a.out
100 200
200 100
```

exchange is defined to take two arguments called p1 and p2, which are of type pointer to int. The exchange is then made, once again using temp as a temporary holding place. The values that are switched are not the values of p1 and p2 themselves—these are pointers. Rather, it's the values that p1 and p2 *point to* that are switched.

The main routine calls exchange, this time passing pointers to the variables x1 and x2, which is consistent with the type of arguments expected by exchange (pointer to int). You can see from the output that the new version of exchange successfully switched the two values of x1 and x2.

Understanding this small program example is critical to your understanding of how arguments are passed to functions and how pointers work. Let's review this example once more to see precisely what happens when exchange is called.

Let's assume that x1 and x2 have been assigned to memory addresses 500 and 504, respectively (see Fig. 2-11).

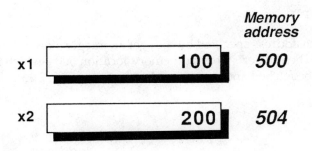

Fig. 2-11. x1 and x2 in memory

The call

```
exchange (&x1, &x2);
```

passes the addresses of x1 and x2 to exchange as the arguments. Inside exchange, these two values of 500 and 504 are stored in the local variables p1 and p2, respectively (see Fig. 2-12).

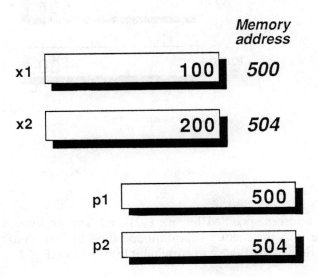

Fig. 2-12. Assignment to variables p1 and p2

So `p1` points to the variable `x1` and `p2` points to `x2`. After `temp` is declared, the statement

```
temp = *p1;
```

says to go to the address specified by `p1`, get an integer stored there, and store it inside `temp`. The integer stored at memory location 500—which is the value of `x1` (100)—will be fetched and stored inside `temp` (see Fig. 2-13).

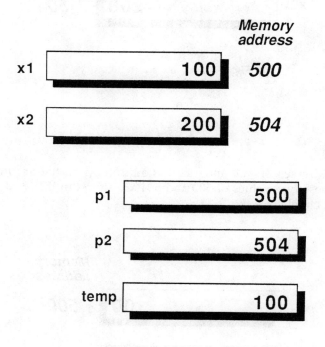

Fig. 2-13. `temp = *p1;`

The next statement

```
*p1 = *p2;
```

says to go the address specified by `p2` (504), retrieve an integer stored there (200), and store it at the memory location specified by `p1` (500). This has the effect of taking the value of `x2` and copying it into `x1` (see Fig. 2-14).

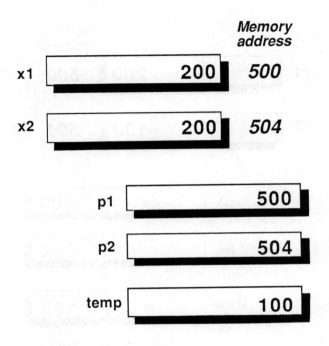

Fig. 2-14. `*p1 = *p2;`

The last statement in `exchange`

    *p2 = temp;

says to take the value of `temp` (100) and store it at the memory location specified by `p2` (504). This will change the value of `x2` to 100, thus completing the exchange (see Fig. 2-15).

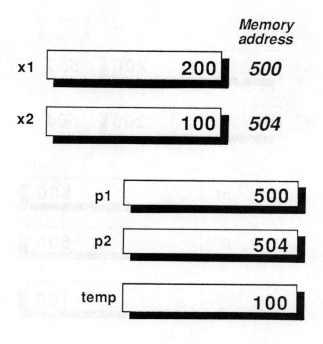

Fig. 2-15. `*p2 = *temp;`

scanf and Pointers

The `scanf` function in the Standard I/O Library needs to be able to make changes to variables. That's why when you call it you have to pass pointers to the variables. So to read in an integer and store it in the variable `count` you write

```
scanf ("%d", &count);
```

`scanf` sees the `%d` and expects its next argument to be a pointer to an integer variable. The memory location specified by that argument is where the integer that `scanf` reads will be stored.

If the integer variable `count` has been set to zero, and you make the common programming mistake of omitting the `&` in front of the variable when calling `scanf`, as in

```
scanf ("%d", count);
```

then `scanf` will try to store the integer that it reads into memory location zero! Under UNIX, this typically results in abnormal termination of your progam with a `Memory Fault--core dumped` or `Bus Error--core dumped` message printed at your terminal.

Pointers to Structures

Recall the `date` structure from previous examples:

```
struct date {
    int month;
    int day;
    int year;
};
```

If `today` is a `date` structure variable declared as follows:

```
static struct date today = {3, 16, 1987};
```

then you can declare a variable called `dateptr` which can be used to point to the variable `today` with the statement

```
struct date *dateptr;
```

Remember, in C it doesn't suffice to say that a variable is of type pointer. It has to point to something, so the type of the variable `dateptr` is actually of type pointer to `struct date`.

To set `dateptr` pointing to `today`, you apply the `&` address operator to the latter, assigning the result to the former:

```
dateptr = &today;
```

Since `today` is of type `struct date`, placing an `&` in front of it produces a value of type pointer to `struct date`, which is precisely the type declared for the variable `dateptr`.

The link that has now been made between `dateptr` and `today` is depicted in Fig. 2-16.

static struct date today = { 3, 16, 1987};
struct date *dateptr;

dateptr = &today;

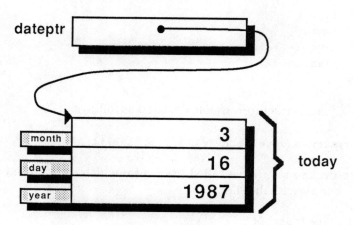

Fig. 2-16. Pointer to date structure

To access the structure that dateptr points to, you apply the indirection operator as you'd expect:

```
*dateptr
```

Since dateptr is of type pointer to struct date, applying the indirection operator produces a value of type struct date. So you could update the date structure that dateptr points to with nextday by using the following statement:

```
*dateptr = nextday (*dateptr);
```

Remember that nextday returns a value of type struct date. That's why you write

```
*dateptr
```

to the left of the = and not

```
dateptr
```

which is of type pointer to `struct date`.

To access one of the members of the structure that `dateptr` points to, you first apply the indirection operator to get at the `date` structure, and then use the structure member operator to access the particular member of the structure. So

```
(*dateptr).day = 21;
```

will store 21 in the `day` member of the `date` structure pointed to by `dateptr`. Note that the parentheses are needed here, since the `.` operator has higher precedence than the `*`. Without them, the expression would be evaluated as

```
*(dateptr.day) = 21;
```

which is incorrect (`dateptr` isn't itself a `date` structure, so you can't access one of its members).

Luckily, C provides a special operator to avoid this precedence problem: the `->` operator (the dash followed by the greater-than character). Writing

```
structptr->member
```

is equivalent to writing

```
(*structptr).member
```

The first form is easier to write and to read. Thus you can do the same operation on that `date` structure shown previously by writing

```
dateptr->day = 21;
```

Remember that the only thing that can appear to the left of the `->` operator is a structure pointer, and not a structure.

To increment the day member of the `date` structure pointed to by `dateptr` you write

```
++dateptr->day;
```

This works since `++` has lower precedence than `->`. This means that the `day` member gets incremented, not the pointer variable.

Pointers to Arrays

Pointers are probably most often used to point to elements in an array. There are several reasons for this that will be noted in this section.

If you want to use a pointer to an array, you don't declare the pointer variable to be of type pointer to array. Rather, you declare it to be of type "pointer to the type of element contained in the array." So if you have an array of `ints` called `data`, and you want to declare a pointer to work with that array, you declare it to be of type pointer to `int`:

```
int *int_ptr;
```

To set the pointer variable pointing to a particular element in the array, the `&` operator is applied to that element in the normal way:

```
int_ptr = &data[4];
```

Here we are taking the address of the fifth element of the `data` array and assigning it to `int_ptr`.

To set `int_ptr` pointing to the first element of `data`, you can write

```
int_ptr = &data[0];
```

or you can simply write

```
int_ptr = data;
```

and take advantage of the fact that *whenever an array name is not followed by a subscript, a pointer to the first element in the array is produced.* So the expression `data` is equivalent to `&data[0]`. This implies that the expression `data` is of type pointer to `int`. This is precisely the case, and explains why the above assignment works.

Figure 2-17 shows a five element array of integers called `data` and an integer pointer variable `int_ptr` that has been set pointing to the first element of the `data` array.

```
int  *int_ptr;
static int data[5] = {1, 2, 3, 4, 5};

int_ptr = data;
```

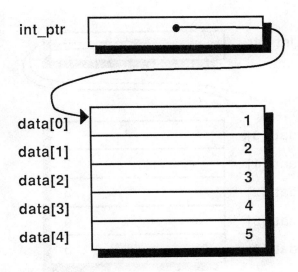

Fig. 2-17. Pointer to element in data array

Once a pointer has been set pointing to an element of an array, the increment and decrement operators can be applied to the pointer. The result of applying the ++ operator is that the pointer variable will be set pointing to the next element of the array *no matter what type of element is contained in the array.* In the case of the −− operator, the pointer will be set pointing to the previous element of the array, once again regardless of the particular type of element in the array (see Fig. 2-18).

When incrementing and decrementing pointers, it's your responsibility to ensure that the resulting pointer still points to a valid element of the array. If your pointer goes past the bounds of an array, and you try to use that pointer, your program may terminate abnormally with a "Memory Fault" or "Bus Error" diagnostic under UNIX. Or you may simply end up overwriting other data inside your program (or other code if the code section of your program isn't write-protected!).

int   *int_ptr;
static int data[5] = {1, 2, 3, 4, 5};

int_ptr = data;
++int_ptr;

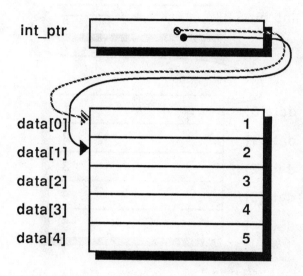

Fig. 2-18. Incrementing a pointer to an array element

The following program shows how a simple `for` loop can be used with a pointer variable to provide sequential access to the elements of an array.

Program 2-6

```
main ()
{
    static int data[5] = {1, 2, 3, 4, 5};
    int        *int_ptr;

    for ( int_ptr = data; int_ptr <= &data[4]; ++int_ptr )
        printf ("%d ", *int_ptr);

    printf ("\n");
}

$ a.out
1 2 3 4 5
```

The `for` loop that starts

```
for ( int_ptr = data; int_ptr <= &data[4]; ++int_ptr )
```

says to set `int_ptr` pointing to the beginning of the array; to continue execution of the loop as long `int_ptr` still points to a valid element of the array (i.e., is less than or equal to the address of the last element in the array—`data[4]`); and to set `int_ptr` pointing to the next element in the array each time through the loop.

The body of the loop consists of a single `printf` call to display the integer that `int_ptr` points to.

The output of the program confirms that each of the five elements of the `data` array were successfully accessed and displayed.

The question that may arise here is: "I can do the same thing with array indexing, so why should I bother using pointers?"

One good reason is that, depending upon the machine the program is compiled on, using pointers may result in code that is smaller and executes faster. Consider a program that does the same thing except uses array indexing. The `for` loop in this case would go like this:

```
for ( i = 0; i <= 4; ++i )
    printf ("%d\n", data[i]);
```

Suppose that integers occupy four bytes on the machine on which this program is run. Accessing the contents of `data[i]` would then probably entail the following steps:

1.   Fetch the value of `i`.

2.   Multiply `i` by the size of an integer (4).

3.   Add the result to the starting address of the `data` array.

4.   Fetch the integer stored at that address.

So each time through the loop, we have to do two memory fetches (assuming here that `i` is not a register variable), a multiplication, and an addition.

Now consider the loop that uses pointers instead:

```
for ( int_ptr = data; int_ptr <= &data[4]; ++int_ptr )
    printf ("%d ", *int_ptr);
```

Each time through this loop all that has to be done is two memory fetches (one to get the address stored in `int_ptr` and the second to get the integer at that address). Thus we save a multiplication (very expensive on most machines) and an addition.[†] (The expression `&data[4]` is evaluted before execution and is therefore treated as a constant in the `for` loop.) For small arrays like `data`, this savings is insignificant. However, when dealing with larger arrays and when performing multiple accesses to the elements of an array from inside a loop, this savings can be substantial. Once again, such savings depend upon your particular machine and on how good a job your compiler does at optimizing code (the standard UNIX C compiler doesn't fare well in this respect, making working with pointers more attractive).

Pointers to Character Arrays

If `buf` is an array of 81 characters declared as follows:

```
char buf[81];
```

and `char_ptr` is a pointer to `char` declared with the statement

```
char *char_ptr;
```

then `char_ptr` can be set pointing to the first character in `buf` in the expected way:

```
char_ptr = buf;
```

If `buf` contains a sequence of characters terminated by a null character—sometimes called a character *string*—then you can write a loop to sequence through all of the characters in `buf` with a `for` loop that begins

```
for ( char_ptr = buf;  *char_ptr != '\0'; ++char_ptr )
    . . .
```

Recall that `'\0'` is the null character—a character whose value is zero. C programmers often take advantage of the fact that its value is zero to more succinctly write statements like that shown above as

```
for ( char_ptr = buf;  *char_ptr; ++char_ptr )
    . . .
```

The second expression in the `for` loop is tested to see if it's *true* (nonzero) or *false* (zero). In the former case the loop continues; in the latter case the loop is terminated. In the example, the expression will be false when `*char_ptr` evaluates to zero, that is, when it accesses the terminating null character in the string.

---

† We recognize that the multiplication by 4 in this case may actually be done as a shift operation, which is far less expensive. We also recognize that a good optimizing compiler may produce code that avoids the multiplication in other cases as well.

The following program shows some basic operations with character arrays.

Program 2-7

```
main ()
{
    static char word[] = { "hello" };
    char  *char_ptr;

    for ( char_ptr = word; *char_ptr != '\0'; ++char_ptr )
        printf ("%c", *char_ptr);

    printf ("\n");

    printf ("%s\n", word);
}

$ a.out
hello
hello
```

Recall that the declaration

```
static char word[] = { "hello" };
```

stores the characters 'h', 'e', 'l', 'l', and 'o', *plus a terminating null character* into the word array. The lack of a size specification tells the compiler to compute it from the number of initializers, which is six, once again including that terminating null.

The for loop passes each character in turn to printf to be displayed. When the null character is reached, the loop is exited and a newline character is printed.

The last printf takes advantage of the fact that a character string can be printed by using the %s conversion characters. In such a case, printf expects to see a corresponding argument of type pointer to character. That's precisely what's passed, since specifying the expression word produces a pointer to the first character in word and is of type pointer to character.

The pointer that is passed to printf could have been pointing anywhere in the array before the terminating null. This should explain the output from the following program.

Program 2-8

```
main ()
{
    static char word[] = { "hello" };

    printf ("%s\n", &word[1]);
    printf ("%s\n", &word[3]);
}

$ a.out
ello
lo
```

So you see, `printf` just expects to see a pointer that points into a character array; it's not necessary that it point to the beginning of the array.

Constant Character Strings

Whenever you code a constant character string in your program such as

```
"a constant character string"
```

you are writing an expression that, like all expressions in C, has a value and a type associated with it. The C compiler automatically allocates space in your program to store this constant character string. Think of it as defining an *unnamed* array of characters and assigning values to the elements of this array. The value that's produced is a pointer to the first character in this unnamed array. The type is pointer to `char`.

So when you call `printf` with the statement

```
printf ("a constant character string\n");
```

what you're actually passing to the function is a pointer to the first character in an unnamed character array. In fact, all that `printf` requires as its first argument is a pointer to a `char`. This explains the output from the following program.

Program 2-9

```
main ()
{
    static char word[] = { "print this out\n" };
    static char format[] = { "x = %d\n" };
    int  x = 100;
```

```
    printf (word);
    printf (format, x);
}

$ a.out
print this out
x = 100
```

Don't confuse character arrays and character pointers. If `char_ptr` is of type `char *`, and `word` is an array of `char`, then you can write the statement

```
char_ptr = "point to me";
```

anywhere in your program, but you can't write the statement

```
word = "you can't do this";
```

The first statement says to allocate an unnamed character array, fill it with the characters "point to me" (plus the terminating null), and store a pointer to the first character in this array in the variable `char_ptr`. The second statement says to allocate an unnamed array, fill it with the characters "you can't do this", and store a pointer to it in `word`. That last part is what makes the statement illegal. In fact, an array name by itself can never be assigned a value; it's considered a constant by the compiler. Think about writing the equivalent statement

```
&word[0] = "you can't do this";
```

which more clearly shows that the assignment is invalid.

The next program shows how character pointers can be initialized and used in a program to point to constant character strings. Note that `char_ptr` doesn't have to be declared `static`, since it's not an array but a pointer.

Program 2-10

```
main ()
{
    char *char_ptr = "print this\n";

    printf (char_ptr);

    char_ptr = "followed by this\n";
    printf (char_ptr);

    char_ptr = "and end it with this";
    printf ("%s\n", char_ptr);
}
```

```
$ a.out
print this
followed by this
and end it with this
```

Figure 2-19 shows what's happening when `char_ptr` is declared and initialized in the preceding program. Study the program example and the accompanying figure until you understand the use of character pointers in this context and how they differ from character arrays.

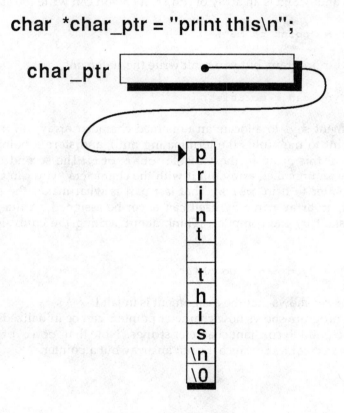

Fig. 2-19. Pointer to constant character string

Some String Copying Functions

Now we'd like to describe three functions for copying a character string. These three functions are each called copystr and they take two arguments: the first is the character array where the copied string is to be placed (the destination array), and the second is the array of characters to be copied (the source array). Assume that the characters in the source array are terminated by a null character, and that the destination array is big enough to accommodate the string to be copied into it.

Following is the first version of copystr that treats the two arguments as arrays of characters:

```
/* copy a character string from 'from' to 'to' */

void copystr (to, from)
char to[], from[];
{
    int i = 0;

    while ( from[i] ) {
        to[i] = from[i];
        ++i;
        }

    to[i] = '\0';
}
```

copystr declares the two arguments—the destination and source arrays—as arrays of characters. Recall that it's not necessary to declare the sizes of the arrays; all the C compiler is concerned with is the fact that it expects to see two character arrays as arguments, and couldn't care less about their sizes. Even if you specify a size, it will be ignored anyway.

After the local variable i is declared and set to zero, a while loop is entered. This loop continues execution until the character referenced from the source array (from[i]) is the null character. As long as from[i] is not equal to the null, it is copied into the corresponding position of the destination array. Then the index variable i is incremented.

The loop terminates when the terminating null character is encountered. However, the loop is exited immediately upon encountering this null, before it has a chance to be copied. That's why the statement

```
to[i] = '\0';
```

is needed.

The second version of copystr is written to use pointers instead of array indexing. In this case, the two arguments to the function are declared to be of type pointer to char.

```
/* copy a character string from 'from' to 'to' */

void copystr (to, from)
char *to, *from;
{
    while ( *from ) {
        *to = *from;
        ++from;
        ++to;
        }

    *to = '\0';
}
```

As noted, the arguments to the function should be pointers to the destination and source arrays, respectively.

As long as the character pointed to by from is not null, the while loop continues execution. Inside the loop, the character pointed to by from is copied to the one pointed to by to. Then the from pointer is incremented to set it pointing to the next character to be copied, and the to pointer incremented to set it pointing to the next location in the destination array where the character is to be placed. As before, when the loop exits, the null character has to be put into the destination array.

The final version of copystr is similar to the previous one, except it is presented in a form that optimizes execution speed and program size.

```
/* copy a character string from 'from' to 'to' */

void copystr (to, from)
register char *to, *from;
{
    while ( *to++ = *from++ )
        ;
}
```

to and from are declared to be register variables. This tells the compiler to keep these pointers inside registers if possible, thus providing faster access to their values.

The expression inside the while loop is doing several things at once. The expression to the right of the = operator,

```
*from++
```

says to fetch the character that from points to and then increment the pointer. This works this way because the * and ++ operators have equal precedence but associate from right to left, meaning it gets evaluated as

```
* (from++)
```

So the subexpression

```
from++
```

says to first use the value of `from` in the expression and *then* increment it. Applying the indirection operator to the result will therefore fetch the character that `from` points to before it gets incremented.

On the left hand side of the = operator, a similar discussion applies:

```
*to++
```

means to use the value of the variable `to` in the expression and then increment it.

After the character has been assigned, it is tested by the `while` (the value of an assignment operation is the actual value that is assigned).

To review the sequence of steps involved in evaluating the statement

```
while ( *to++ = *from++ )
    ;
```

here's what happens:

1. The character pointed to by `from` is fetched, and then the pointer variable `from` is incremented.

2. The character that was fetched is stored into the location pointed to by `to`, then the pointer variable `to` is incremented.

3. The character that was assigned is tested. If it's nonzero (non-null), then the loop continues execution. If it's zero (null), then the loop terminates.

Note that in this version of `copystr` the null character gets copied into the destination array in the loop, thus obviating the need for an extra statement after the loop terminates.

The reasons for illustrating this third version of `copystr` are twofold: First, it shows that the programmer does have some control over the efficiency of the code that gets generated for a program—the loop in this last version of `copystr` can produce as few as *three* machine language instructions on machines that have fetch-and-increment instructions. While in many cases, efficiency considerations like these may not be important, there are many applications where they are. The process of copying a character string is so fundamental to many programming applications that it does pay to have a function that's optimized as much as possible.

The second reason for showing this program is that these types of expressions are used by programmers in practice. If you have to support other people's code, you have to understand precisely what's going on here.

Now that we've discussed these three versions of `copystr`, let's see a `main` routine to test them out.

Program 2-11

```
main ()
{
    char        *str1 = "string one";
    static char str2[] = { "string two" };
    char        buf[80];

    copystr (buf, str1);
    printf ("%s\n", buf);

    copystr (buf, str2);
    printf ("%s\n", buf);

    copystr (buf, "string three");
    printf ("%s\n", buf);
}

$ a.out
string one
string two
string three
```

In all three calls to `copystr` the first argument is the same: `buf`. This is the destination array for the copied string.

The first call passes the value of the expression `str1` as the second argument. The variable is defined to be of type pointer to `char`, so this is the type of the expression.

The second call passes the value of the expression `str2`. This is the name of a character array. The value produced by this expression is a pointer to the first character in the array, and is of type pointer to `char`.

The third call to `copystr` passes the value of the expression `"string three"`. Recall that this value is a pointer to the first character in the unnamed character array `"string three"` and is of type pointer to `char`.

So all three calls to `copystr` pass the same argument type as the second argument: pointer to `char`. This is important for you to understand, and reinforces an earlier discussion concerning the first argument to `printf`.

Wherever a pointer to a character is expected, you can write the name of a character pointer variable, the name of a character array, or a literal character string. They each produce the same data type. The only exception to be noted is to the left of an assignment operator. In that case, only a pointer variable is allowed.

You should note that *any* of the three versions of copystr can be used in this program, *and the calling sequence and results will be the same!* This implies that when the C compiler sees the first version of copystr, which begins:

```
void copystr (to, from)
char to[], from[];
    ...
```

it knows that what's really being passed are not entire arrays of characters but rather pointers to them. This is precisely the case, and it starts to shed some light on the relationship between pointers and arrays in C, a topic we'll be getting to in more detail shortly.

The fact that pointers to arrays are what get passed to functions, rather than the elements in them, explains why a function can make a permanent change to an element in an array. This is illustrated in the following short program example.

Program 2-12

```
void foo (arr)
int arr[];
{
    arr[0] = 100;
}

main ()
{
    static int vals[] = {1, 2, 3};

    printf ("%d\n", vals[0]);
    foo (vals);
    printf ("%d\n", vals[0]);
}


$ a.out
1
100
```

foo could have modified any element in the array passed as argument, since it's not the elements in `vals` that was passed but rather a *pointer* to the first element in the array (remember that's what happens when you write the name of an array not followed by a subscript).

The Relationship Between Pointers and Arrays

Let's backtrack a second to try to deduce the relationship between pointers and arrays in C. First, recall that if `intptr` is set pointing into an array of `ints`, and you write

```
++intptr
```

then `intptr` will be set pointing to the next `int` in the array. Suppose that integers occupy four bytes on the machine that you're compiling your program on, and that the array `values` has been assigned consecutive memory locations starting at 1000. When you write

```
intptr = values;
```

`intptr` is set to the address of the first element of `values`. This address is 1000 in our example (see Fig. 2-20).

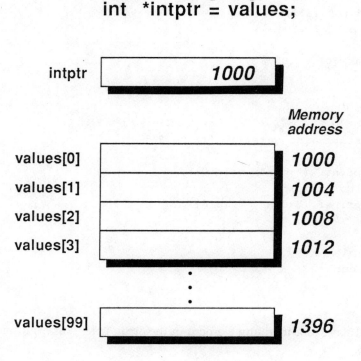

Fig. 2-20. Pointer to array

When you write

```
++intptr;
```

you set `intptr` pointing to the next element of `values`. Here the value of `intptr` can't be incremented by one, since that would set it to 1001, whereas the next element of `values`, `values[1]`, is at location 1004. In order for this to work correctly, what actually has to get added to `intptr` is not one, but four. This is in fact what happens (see Fig. 2-21).

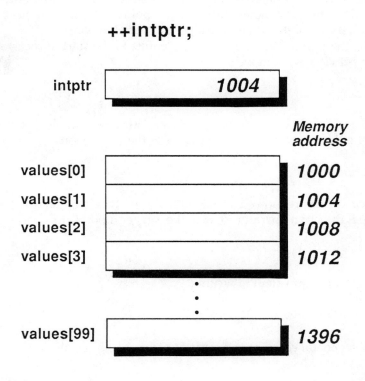

Fig. 2-21. Incrementing a pointer to an array

In C, whenever *any* pointer gets incremented, what gets added to the pointer is not one, but the *size of the data type that the pointer points to.*
Since `++intptr;` is the same as writing

```
intptr = intptr + 1;
```

it follows that the same type of adjustment has to be made when adding an integer and a pointer. In fact, if `intptr` is of type pointer to `int` and `i` is an integer, then the expression

```
intptr + i
```

is also of type pointer to `int`. What gets added to `intptr` is not the value of `i`, but instead the value of `i` multiplied by the size of an integer (`i * sizeof (int)`).

And as to be expected, this applies to pointers to any data type in C. Integers can be added to and subtracted from pointers, and the result is still a pointer. The actual value that gets added or subtracted is automatically adjusted to reflect the size of the element the pointer points to. That's another reason you have to tell the compiler what type a pointer variable points to.

Now the plot thickens. If `intptr` points to the start of the `values` array as shown previously, then the expression

```
intptr + 1
```

will produce a pointer to element number 1 (the second element) of `values`, and has the same type and the same value as the expression

```
&values[1]
```

Since the expression `intptr + 1` is of type pointer to `int`, you can apply the indirection operator to fetch the integer it points to:

```
*(intptr + 1)
```

This is therefore equivalent to writing

```
values[1]
```

In the general case, the expression

```
intptr + i
```

is equivalent to

```
&values[i]
```

and the expression

```
*(intptr + i)
```

is equivalent to

```
values[i]
```

Since `intptr` was set pointing to `values` with the statement

```
intptr = values;
```

let's simply substitute `values` for `intptr` in the previous expressions. So you can write

```
values + 1
```

to produce a pointer to `values[1]`; this is equivalent to writing

```
&values[1]
```

Generalizing, you find that the expression

```
values + i
```

is equivalent to the expression

```
&values[i]
```

and the expression

```
*(values + i)
```

is the same as

```
values[i]
```

It's mandatory that you understand these generalizations to fully understand the relationship between pointers and arrays. In fact, because of the equivalences just noted, the compiler doesn't care whether a pointer is used like an array (i.e., with a following subscript), or an array name like a pointer (with the indirection operator `*`). This means you can also write the expression

```
intptr[i]
```

to access element number $i + 1$ of the `values` array (assuming once again that `intptr` has been previously set pointing to the start of `values`)!

Table 2-3 summarizes the various relationships between pointers to arrays and arrays. It assumes the following declaration has been made:

```
int   values[100], *intptr = values, i;
```

TABLE 2-3. Pointers and arrays

Expression	Value

`&values[0]`
`values`
`intptr`
	pointer to first element of `values`

`values[0]`
`*values`
`*intptr`
	first element of `values`

`&values[i]`
`values + i`
`intptr + i`
	pointer to element i+1 of `values`

`values[i]`
`*(values + i)`
`*(intptr + i)`
`intptr[i]`
	element i+1 of `values`

Pointer Operations

The valid operations on pointers seen so far are: applying the `*` operator (and the `->` operator for structure pointers); assigning them to other pointers (generally of the same pointer type); adding and subtracting integers to and from them; and comparing them. In the last case, any relational operator (`==`, `!=`, `<`, `<=`, `>` and `>=`) can be used to compare two pointers. This is usually done between two pointers to elements in the same array.

Two pointers into the same array can also be subtracted. The result is an integer that represents the *number* of elements that separate them. So given the following statements:

```
int values[100], *intptr;

intptr = &values[100];
```

the expression

```
intptr - values
```

gives the result of 100. Recall that in this case this is the same as writing

```
&values[100] - &values[0]
```

In order for this to produce a result of 100, it's implied that this expression really gets evaluated as

```
(&values[100] - &values[0]) / sizeof (int)
```

The C compiler automatically divides the result of the subtraction by the size of the element they point to. This means that you can only subtract two pointers of the same type.

This technique of subtracting two pointers provides a quick way to convert a pointer into an array into a corresponding subscript. If `intptr` and `intptr2` both point to elements in `values`, then the expression

```
intptr2 - intptr
```

yields an integer that represents the number of elements that separate them. For example, given the following two statements

```
intptr  =  &values[20];
intptr2 = &values[80];
```

the result of the subtraction

```
intptr2 - intptr
```

is 60.

A last point about valid operations on pointers: adding them does not produce a meaningful result.

Linked Lists

This section discusses how to use pointers to build more sophisticated data structures like linked lists and trees. It's beyond the scope of this book to go into the motivations for using such data structures; we just want to illustrate the mechanisms involved.

The first step in creating a linked list is to decide what each entry of the list is to look like. Once that decision has been made, you define a structure that describes such a list entry. You also have to reserve one or more members of the structure to point to other list entries. The number of such members depends on the type of data structure you're working with. For singly linked lists, just one pointer member suffices. For doubly linked lists or trees, two or more such members are needed.

For example purposes, we'll work with a singly linked list. Only two members will appear in each entry of this list: a value field, which will be an integer, and a pointer field, which will point to the next entry in the list. The declaration

```
struct listrec {
    int value;
    struct listrec *next;
};
```

defines a structure called `listrec`. Note the second member of `listrec` (called `next`): it's a *pointer to another `listrec` structure* (see Fig. 2-22).

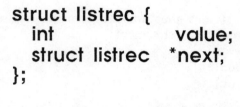

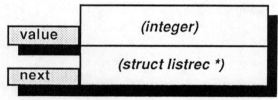

Fig. 2-22. Defining a linked list entry

To show how this structure can be used, we'll start by constructing a small linked list that has two entries. To start with, we declare two variables to be of the appropriate structure type:

```
struct listrec  x1, x2;
```

To make a link between `x1` and `x2`, you set the `next` member of `x1` pointing to `x2`:

```
x1.next = &x2;
```

When working with linked lists in general, the end of the list is frequently marked in much the same manner as the end of a variable length character string is marked with a null character. In this case, a *null pointer* is used. The null pointer is simply a pointer with a value of zero, since the language guarantees that no valid pointer in C can ever have a value of zero.

To add readability to programs that deal with null pointers, the following preprocessor definition is frequently made:

```
#define   NULL   0
```

If you include the header file `stdio.h` in your program, then you'll find that NULL has already been defined for you.

Getting back to our small two-element linked list, you can mark the end of the list by writing the statement

```
x2.next = (struct listrec *) NULL;
```

The integer 0 (remember that's what NULL is defined to be) is typecast to be of type pointer to `struct listrec` so that a pointer of the correct type is assigned to `x2.next`. Omitting the typecast operation shouldn't affect operation of the program but may cause a warning diagnostic to be issued by your compiler (UNIX compilers complain here about "different levels of indirection").

Our small linked list that contains a terminating null pointer is illustrated in Fig. 2-23. Here the null pointer is indicated by the hatched box.

In practice, elements of a linked list are not allocated statically, but instead dynamically while the program is executing. We'll return to this point in the next chapter when we talk about dynamic memory allocation in detail.

```
struct listrec  x1, x2;

x1.value = 100;
x1.next = &x2;

x2.value = 200;
x2.next = (struct listrec *) NULL;
```

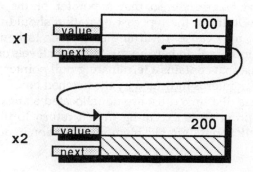

Fig. 2-23. Linked list with terminating null pointer

Adding an Element to a List

There are several common operations associated with working with lists: adding an element to the list, removing an element from the list, and searching the list.

One of the advantages lists have over arrays is that operations like adding and removing elements are simply a matter of pointer adjustment.

To add a new element x3 in between elements x1 and x2 of your linked list, you set x3's pointer field pointing to the element that x1 points to. Then you set x1 pointing to the new element, x3. This is accomplished with two statements in C:

```
x3.next = x1.next;
x1.next = &x3;
```

Note that x1.next must be accessed and stored into x3.next *before* it is overwritten with the address of x3. The process of adding an element to a list is depicted in Fig. 2-24.

$$x3.value = 150;$$
$$x3.next = x1.next;$$

$$x1.next = \&x3;$$

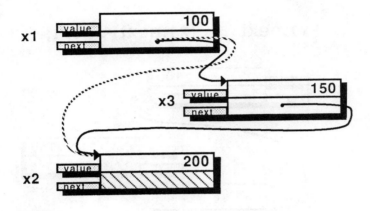

Fig. 2-24. Adding an element to a list

Unlike arrays, the elements of a list do not typically occupy consecutive memory locations; they don't have to since they are linked together through their pointer fields.

Removing an Element from a List

Removing an element from a list is also straightforward once you understand the technique. If you want to remove the element *after* x1 in your three element list, then you can do so independent of the name of that element with the statement

```
x1.next = (x1.next)->next;
```

Let's pick this one apart. First, the expression

```
x1.next
```

yields a pointer to the entry linked to x1 (which is x3). Then the -> operator is applied (remember that x1.next is a pointer, so the -> operator is required) to get the corresponding pointer from that entry. So in our example if x1 points to x3, then x1.next has as its value the address of x3, and the expression (x1.next)->next has as its value what's stored in the next member of x3: the address of x2 (the third element in the list).

Assigning this pointer to x1.next therefore sets x1 pointing to what x3 points to: x2. Note that nothing points to x3 now, so it has been effectively removed from the list (although the memory allocated for it still exists). The operation of removing an element from a list is depicted in Fig. 2-25.

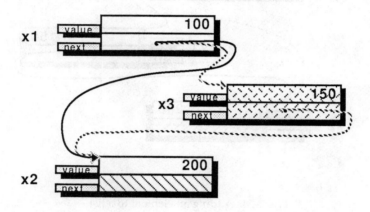

Fig. 2-25. Removing an element from a list

Note that parentheses are not required around the expression

    x1.next

since . and -> have the same precedence and associate from left to right.

You should study the operations of adding and removing elements from a list until you feel comfortable with the principles involved. Work out an example with paper and hypothetical memory addresses to see what's happening to the pointers in each case.

Searching a List

Once you have built a larger linked list in your program, you'll probably have some other variables associated with the list to make operations faster. One may be a pointer to the start of the list; another may be a pointer to the end of the list (useful if you're often adding elements to the end of the list). Figure 2-26 shows a linked list with a pointer to the start (often called the *head*) of the list. Also note that the last entry of the list is marked with a null pointer (as indicated by the hatched box).

struct listrec   *listhead;

listhead = &x1;

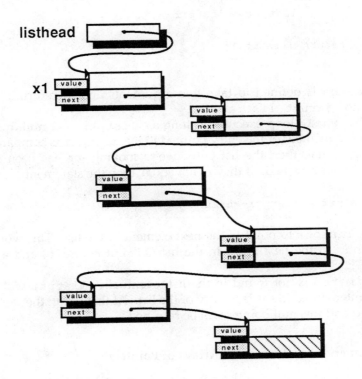

Fig. 2-26. Linked list with list pointer

    Another common operation on linked lists is searching them. Let's write a function called `search` that takes as arguments a pointer to the start of a linked list and an integer value to be found in that list. The function will search the list for the given integer value and, if found, will return a pointer to the matching entry. If the value is not found in the list, then the null pointer will be returned. Here is such a function:

```
/* search linked list for specified value */

struct listrec *search (listptr, match)
struct listrec *listptr;
int match;
{
    while ( listptr != (struct listrec *) NULL )
        if ( listptr->value == match )
            break;
        else
            listptr = listptr->next;

    return (listptr);
}
```

search is defined to take two arguments and to return a value of type pointer to struct listrec.

The while loop executes as long as listptr isn't null. Inside the loop, the value member of the entry pointed to by listptr is compared to match. If they're equal, then the list entry we're looking for has been found, and a pointer to it is returned. If they're not equal, then the statement

```
listptr = listptr->next;
```

adjusts listptr to point to the next element in the list. This works by getting the pointer to the next entry in the list (listptr->next) and assigning it to listptr.

If match is not found in the list, eventually listptr will be set to the null pointer stored in the last entry of the list. At that point, the while loop will be exited and this null pointer will be returned.

Two-Dimensional Arrays and Arrays of Pointers

Suppose you had to store the names of the days of the week inside your program. One approach would be to declare a two-dimensional character array called days that contains seven rows. Each row of the array would contain the name of a day of the week. In order to decide how much space to reserve for the number of columns, you would have to determine which day of the week has the longest name. That's simple enough: Wednesday. So to store this day's name (plus the terminating null), you'd have to reserve 10 columns in your two-dimensional matrix.

The statement

```
static char days[7][10] = {
    "Sunday", "Monday", "Tuesday", "Wednesday",
    "Thursday", "Friday", "Saturday"
    };
```

declares days to be a two-dimensional array of characters containing seven rows and ten columns. The first row of the array (row zero) is initialized to the characters 'S', 'u', 'n', 'd', 'a', 'y', and '\0', and so on for the remaining six rows. The layout of days in memory is depicted in Fig. 2-27.

	[0]	[1]	[2]	[3]	[4]	[5]	[6]	[7]	[8]	[9]
days[0]	S	u	n	d	a	y	\0			
days[1]	M	o	n	d	a	y	\0			
days[2]	T	u	e	s	d	a	y	\0		
days[3]	W	e	d	n	e	s	d	a	y	\0
days[4]	T	h	u	r	s	d	a	y	\0	
days[5]	F	r	i	d	a	y	\0			
days[6]	S	a	t	u	r	d	a	y	\0	

Fig. 2-27. `char days[7][10]`

Each row of days is actually an array of characters. So the expression

    days[0]

has as its value a pointer to the first character in the first row of days, and is of type pointer to char. To display the name of the first day of the week you could write

    printf ("%s\n", days[0]);

The expression

    days[0][0]

fetches the first character in the first row of days—the character S.

Following from the previous discussions on pointers and arrays, you can write

    *days[0]

to also retrieve the first character in the first row of days.

Verify that the following two loops could both be used to display the characters in `days[0]` a single character at a time:

```
int  i;

for ( i = 0;  days[0][i] != '\0';  ++i )
    printf ("%c", days[0][i]);
```

and

```
char *charptr;

for ( charptr = days[0]; *charptr != '\0'; ++charptr )
    printf ("%c", *charptr);
```

There is another often-used way to store the days of the week in your program. Rather than defining a two-dimensional array, you can define a single dimensional array, where each element of the array points to the corresponding name of the day of the week. In other words, each element of the array is of type pointer to `char`. This is achieved with the following declaration:

```
static char *days[7] = {
    "Sunday", "Monday", "Tuesday", "Wednesday",
    "Thursday", "Friday", "Saturday"
    };
```

This `days` array contains only seven elements; the previous one contained 70 (7 * 10). Each element of `days` is a pointer to an unnamed array of characters as depicted in Fig. 2-28.

To print the name of the first day of the week, you can write, just like before,

```
printf ("%s\n", days[0]);
```

To get the first character from the character array pointed to by `days[0]`, you can still write either

```
*days[0]
```

or

```
days[0][0]
```

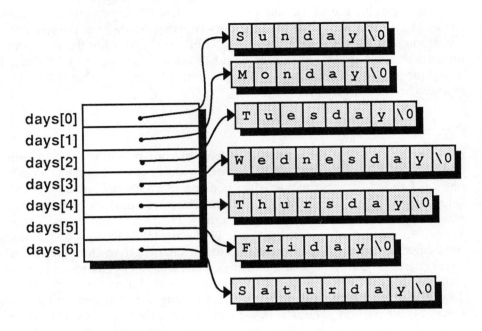

Fig. 2-28. `char *days[7]`

One of the reasons for using arrays of pointers rather than two dimensional arrays is that in many cases it can save you space. For example, suppose you have to read in 1000 lines from a file and store them in your program. If the maximum size of each line is 256 characters, and you decide to use the two-dimensional array approach, then your array declaration might appear as shown:

```
char linetab[1000][257];
```

(Here we reserve 257 characters per line, and not 256, to store a terminating null character at the end of each line.) If characters occupy a single byte on your machine (as they do on most), then you'd have to set aside a little more than 1/4 megabyte of memory for this array alone! And if the average size of each line you'd be reading is, say, 64 characters, then you'd be wasting about 257,000 - 65,000 = 192,000 bytes of storage!

If you instead define `linetab` to be an array of character pointers:

```
char *linetab[1000];
```

then you can use dynamic memory routines to allocate just enough space for each line from the file *as it is read in*. Pointers to each line can then be stored in linetab. In this way, your total memory consumption will be the space for the 1,000 pointers (assume 4,000 bytes for 32-bit pointers), plus the space for the lines themselves (65,000 bytes), or about 69,000 bytes instead of 257,000. This technique outlined for reading in lines and dynamically allocating space for them is shown in the next chapter.

Command Line Arguments

If you want to access the arguments typed to your program on the command line, then you have to know how to work with arrays of pointers. Recall that main is handed two arguments when your program begins execution. The first is an integer called argc, by convention. This represents the number of arguments typed on the command line, with the name of the program itself counting as one. So argc is always at least one. Under the UNIX system, an argument is considered a sequence of characters up to a *whitespace* character, where a whitespace character is either a space, tab, or newline character. Quotes can be used to group words into a single argument, but that's beyond the scope of this text.

The second argument to main is an array of character pointers called argv, by convention. The first pointer in argv, argv[0], points to the name of the program being executed. Successive locations in the array, argv[1], ..., argv[argc - 1], contain pointers to the arguments typed after the program name.

As an example, consider execution of a program called nroff. If the following command line is typed:

```
nroff -mm -TXR memo1
```

then the first argument to main will be the integer 4 (the program name plus the three arguments that follow) and the second argument will be an array of character pointers. The first element of the array will point to the string "nroff" (the name of the program), the second to "-mm", the third to "-TXR", and the fourth to "memo1". This is depicted in Fig. 2-29.

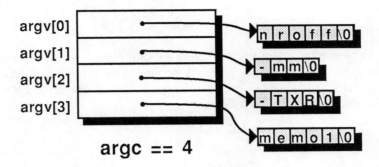

Fig. 2-29. Command line arguments

The program that follows takes its command line arguments and writes them to the terminal, one per line:

Program 2-13

```
main (argc, argv)
int argc;
char *argv[];
{
    int  i;

    for ( i = 0; i < argc; ++i )
        printf ("%s\n", argv[i]);
}


$ a.out one two three 125
a.out
one
two
three
125
```

Remember that the arguments passed to a program are represented as character strings. So in the example, the last value in the `argv` array is a pointer to the character string `"125"`, and is not the number 125. If you needed to use this argument as a number, you would have to convert it. You can use a function like `sscanf` or `atol` from the Standard C Library for such a purpose. These functions are described in the next chapter.

Pointers to Pointers

Pointers can be used to point to other pointers. Suppose `int1` is an integer containing the value 100, and `int_ptr` is a pointer to an integer that has been set pointing to `int1`. A variable called `ptr_ptr` can be declared to be of type "pointer to pointer to `int`" as follows:

```
int  **ptr_ptr;
```

The `**` means that `ptr_ptr` doesn't point to an integer, but instead points to another pointer that points to an integer. To set `ptr_ptr` pointing to `int_ptr`, you apply the `&` operator to `int_ptr` as usual:

```
ptr_ptr = &int_ptr;
```

Now `ptr_ptr` points to `int_ptr`, which in turn points to `int1` (see Fig. 2-30).

To access the value contained in `int1` (100), you naturally can write

```
int1
```

or to access the same value indirectly through `int_ptr`, you can write

```
*int_ptr
```

Finally, to access the same value through `ptr_ptr`, you can write

```
**ptr_ptr
```

`ptr_ptr` is of type pointer to pointer to `int`. Applying the indirection operator to this expression (`*ptr_ptr`) results in one of type pointer to `int`. Applying it once again (`**ptr_ptr`) yields an expression of type `int`. You could change the value of `int1` to 200 through `ptr_ptr` by writing

```
**ptr_ptr = 200;
```

```
int   *int_ptr;
int   **ptr_ptr;
int   int1 = 100;

int_ptr = &int1;
ptr_ptr = &int_ptr;
```

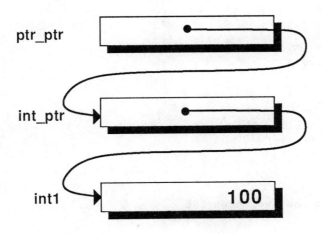

Fig. 2-30. Pointers to pointers

If you wanted to set `int_ptr` pointing to a different integer, say, `int2`, then you could write

```
int_ptr = &x2;
```

or you could make the change indirectly through `ptr_ptr` by writing

```
*ptr_ptr = &x2;
```

Pointers can go to as many levels as you like. Just make sure you use the correct number of asterisks in the declaration and when accessing the value that the pointer ultimately points to.

One common use of pointers to pointers is when dealing with the command line argument vector `argv`. Some programmers prefer to treat `argv` as a pointer to a pointer to a character, rather than as an array of character pointers.

This is often reflected in the declaration of `argv`:

```
main (argc, argv)
int argc;
char **argv;
{
    ...
}
```

As in the last program, the following program prints the command line arguments, but it uses pointers to pointers to reference elements from `argv`.

Program 2-14

```
main (argc, argv)
int argc;
char **argv;
{
    while ( argc-- > 0 ) {
        printf ("%s\n", *argv);
        ++argv;
        }
}

$ a.out one two three 125
a.out
one
two
three
125
```

`argv` points to a pointer to a character. Recalling what `argv` looks like (refer back to Fig. 2-29), the expression `*argv` gives the first pointer in the `argv` array. (Remember that `*argv` is equivalent to `argv[0]` anyway). After `argv` is incremented the first time, it then points to the second pointer in the argument vector (the old `argv[1]`).

To get the first character of the program name (`a.out` in the example), for instance, you would write the expression

```
**argv
```

And to get the first character of the first argument (the o in one in the example), you could write

```
*(*argv + 1)
```

Admittedly, working with pointers to pointers is confusing. And since such a small percentage of a typical C program's time is spent processing its command line arguments, it's hard to cite efficiency as the reason for treating `argv` this way. You're better off sticking to the convention of declaring and accessing `argv` as an array of character pointers as shown previously.

Pointers to Functions

Since functions occupy an area of memory, the C language allows you to have pointers to them. Recall our `leapyear` function from an earlier example. That function returns an integer indicating whether or not the integer year given as its argument is a leap year.

You can produce a pointer to any function simply by writing the name of the function *without* any following parentheses. So simply writing

```
leapyear
```

produces a pointer to the `leapyear` function. The C compiler *must* know that `leapyear` is a function before such an expression can be written. This is satisfied either by previously defining the function or by declaring the function and its return type:

```
int leapyear ();
```

As noted, when you write the expression `leapyear` you get a pointer to the function produced. Such an expression is of type "pointer to function that returns an `int`." In order to take this pointer and store it in a variable, you must declare the variable accordingly:

```
int (*fnptr)();
```

This declares `fnptr` to be a pointer to a function that returns an `int`. The parentheses around `*fnptr` are needed because the function call operator `()` (yes, its an operator) has higher precedence than the indirection operator. Without the parentheses, the statement

```
int *fnptr();
```

mistakenly declares `fnptr` to be a function that returns a pointer to an `int`. As you can see, operator precedence matters even when making declarations! With the proper declaration of `fnptr` in hand, you can now write a statement like

```
fnptr = leapyear;
```

to store a pointer to the `leapyear` function in the variable `fnptr`.

The declaration and assignment of a function pointer variable are depicted in Fig. 2-31.

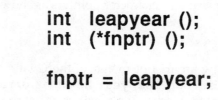

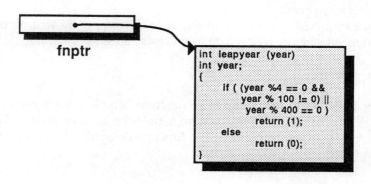

fnptr

Fig. 2-31. Pointer to function returning `int`

To make sure you understand the declaration for `fnptr`, Table 2-4 shows some function declarations and corresponding declarations for `fnptr` to be used to point to these functions.

TABLE 2-4. **Pointers to functions**

Function declaration	*Function pointer declaration*
`double sqrt ();`	`double (*fnptr)();`
`void init ();`	`void (*fnptr)();`
`struct date nextday ();`	`struct date (*fnptr)();`
`struct listrec *search ();`	`struct listrec *(*fnptr)();`

Once you have stored a pointer to a function inside a variable, the next step is indirectly calling that function through the variable. To make such a call, you apply the indirection operator to the variable, and follow it with a parenthetical list of arguments to be passed to the function.

Since `leapyear` takes only a single argument, you would write

```
result = (*fnptr)(2000);
```

to test if the year 2000 is a leap year and to assign the answer to the variable `result`. Once again, parentheses are required around `*fnptr` because the `()` operator has higher precedence than the `*`.

Pointers to functions are useful for two reasons: you can't pass a function itself as an argument to another function, but you can pass a pointer to one. Second, you can't store a function in an array or structure, but once again, you can store a pointer to one.

The `qsort` function in the Standard C Library takes as one of its arguments a pointer to a function. `qsort` uses the *quick sort* algorithm to sort an array of data elements. The function can be used to sort an array of *any* data type. In order to be able to do this, `qsort` needs some help. First, it must be told the number of elements in the array. Second, it must be told the size of each element in the array. Third, it has to be given a pointer to a user-supplied function. This function will be called by `qsort` whenever it has to determine whether one of two elements in the array is less than, equal to, or greater than the another. So whenever `qsort` has to decide whether two elements are out of place (to see if they should be swapped), it calls the function. It passes to the function *pointers* to the two elements to be compared. By convention, the function returns a negative value if the element pointed to by the first argument is less than the element pointed to by the second argument, zero if the two elements are equal, and a positive value if the first element is greater than the second element.

`qsort` is described in more detail in the next chapter, where you'll see how to use it in practice.

Pointers to functions are often used to implement so-called "dispatch" tables. For example, suppose you have an integer variable called `index`, and stored in that variable is one of ten possible values, zero through nine. Assume that if the value of `index` is 0, you want to call the function `fn0`; if its value is 1, you want to call `fn1`, and so on, down to a value of 9, which will cause the function `fn9` to be called.

Rather than executing a large `if` or `switch` statement to test the value of `index` and to call the corresponding function, you can instead set up an array of function pointers. The first element of the array can be set pointing to `fn0`, the second element to `fn1`, and so on. The following statements set up such an array:

```
int   fn0 (), fn1(), fn2 (), fn3 (), fn4 (),
      fn5 (), fn6 (), fn7 (), fn8 (), fn9 ();

static int (*dispatch) () [] = {
    fn0, fn1, fn2, fn3, fn4, fn5, fn6, fn7, fn8, fn9
    };
```

dispatch is declared to be an array whose elements are of type pointer to function that returns an int. To call the function indicated by the variable index (assume here that functions fn0 through fn9 take no arguments), you write

```
(*dispatch[index]) ()
```

If index has the value 2, then the function pointed to by dispatch[2], which is fn2, will be called.

As another example of this sort, suppose that you are writing an interactive data base manager. Assume that the program reads a command from the terminal and then calls a corresponding function to carry out the operations associated with that command. The following table lists the recognized commands and the names of the corresponding functions to be called:

Command	Function
add	addentry ()
calc	calcvals ()
delete	delentry ()
list	listdb ()
quit	quit ()
update	updentry ()

So if the user types in add, you want to call the addentry function; if the user types calc, you want to call calcvals, and so on.

You can define a data structure called command that contains two members. The first member can be a pointer to the name of the command; the second can be a pointer to the corresponding function to call:

```
struct command {
    char  *name;
    int   (*function) ();
};
```

Now you can proceed to set up a table containing all of your command names and corresponding functions to be called:

```
static struct command dispatch[] = {
    {  "add",     addentry  },
    {  "calc",    calcvals  },
    {  "delete",  delentry  },
    {  "list",    listdb  },
    {  "quit",    quit  },
    {  "update",  updentry  }
};
```

Now when you read the command from the terminal, you can search the dispatch table until you find the command. When found, you can then call the corresponding function. The following function named execute takes a character pointer as its argument. This presumably points to a command read from the terminal. The function searches the dispatch table until it finds a match, and then calls the corresponding funtion. execute returns the value returned by that function as its return value as well. If no match is found, then execute returns UNKNOWNCMD (assume here that none of the functions called by execute will return a value of UNKNOWNCMD).

The function also takes the dispatch table and the number of entries in the table as arguments.

```
#define  UNKNOWNCMD   -1

int execute (typedcmd, dispatch, numcmds)
char *typedcmd;
struct command dispatch[];
int  numcmds;
{
    int  i, fnresult = UNKNOWNCMD;

    for ( i = 0; i < numcmds; ++i )
        if ( strcmp (typedcmd, dispatch[i].name) == 0 ) {
            fnresult = (*dispatch[i].function) ();
            break;
        }

    return (fnresult);
}
```

The function performs a linear search of the table. If the table is large, then a more sophisticated search algorithm is in order. For example, if the command names are sorted in the table, then a binary search would be appropriate.

Inside the for loop, the command name pointed to by typedcmd is compared to that pointed to by dispatch[i].name. The Standard C Library's strcmp function is used to make the comparison—it returns 0 if the two strings passed as arguments are identical, nonzero otherwise. If the two strings match, the corresponding function from the dispatch table is called, and the result of the function call is stored in `fnresult`.

When the loops exits, the value of `fnresult` is returned. If no match is found in the table, then the value `UNKNOWNCMD` (assigned to `fnresult` when the function began execution) is returned.

The following test program declares the `dispatch` table shown previously, reads in commands from the terminal, and calls `execute` to carry out the command. For this example, we've merely supplied dummy routines that display a simple message to verify the proper function is being called. The `quit` function returns a value of `QUITCMD` (999) so that we can know in the `main` routine when the `quit` command was typed.

Program 2-15

```
#define   QUITCMD          999
#define   OKCMD            0
#define   UNKNOWNCMD       -1

struct command {
    char   *name;
    int    (*function) ();
};

main ()
{
    char buf[81];

    int    status;
    int    addentry (), calcvals (), delentry (),
           listdb (), quit (), updentry ();

    static struct command dispatch[] = {
        { "add",    addentry   },
        { "calc",   calcvals   },
        { "delete", delentry   },
        { "list",   listdb     },
        { "quit",   quit       },
        { "update", updentry   }
    };

    int    entries = sizeof (dispatch) / sizeof (struct command);
```

```
        do {
                printf ("\nEnter your command: ");
                scanf ("%s", buf);
                status = execute (buf, dispatch, entries);

                if ( status == UNKNOWNCMD )
                        printf ("Unknown command: %s\n", buf);
        }
        while ( status != QUITCMD );
}

int addentry () { printf ("in addentry\n"); return OKCMD; }

int calcvals () { printf ("in calcvals\n"); return OKCMD; }

int delentry () { printf ("in delentry\n"); return OKCMD; }

int listdb   () { printf ("in listdb\n"); return OKCMD; }

int quit     () { printf ("in quit\n");  return QUITCMD;  }

int updentry () { printf ("in updentry\n"); return OKCMD; }


$ a.out

Enter your command: add
in addentry

Enter your command: delete
in delentry

Enter your command: replace
Unknown command: replace

Enter your command: quit
in quit
$
```

The program prompts the user to enter a command and then reads the command with scanf, storing it in buf. Then execute is called. The arguments passed are the typed command, the dispatch table, and the number of entries in the table (entries). This last value is computed by the statement

```
entries = sizeof (dispatch) / sizeof (struct command);
```

which says to divide the size of the entire table (`sizeof (dispatch)`) by the size of each entry in the table (`sizeof (struct command)`), giving the number of entries.

`execute` searches `dispatch` for the command, calls the corresponding function if found, and returns the value returned by that function. If the command is not found in the table, then `UNKNOWNCMD` is returned. This causes the program to print an "Unknown command" message.

When the user types `quit`, the `quit` function is called by `execute`. `quit` displays the message `in quit` and then returns the value `QUITCMD`. This causes the `do` loop in `main` to be exited.

As you can see, pointers to functions are useful for these types of applications. In Chapters 3 and 5 we'll take a look at some functions that take pointers to functions as arguments.

E X E R C I S E S

1. Write a function called `lenstr` that takes as its argument a pointer to a null terminated string. Have the function return an integer value which represents the number of characters in the string, excluding the terminating null. Write the function using pointers and use the following program to test it out.

```
main ()
{
    char *charptr = "Count me please.";

    printf ("%d\n", lenstr ("hello"));
    printf ("%d\n", lenstr (charptr));
    printf ("%d\n", lenstr (""));  /* null string */
}

$ a.out
5
16
0
```

2. What does the following function called `x` do?

```
int x (ptr)
char *ptr;
{
    char *saveptr = ptr;

    while ( *ptr++ != '\0' )
        ;

    return (ptr - saveptr - 1);
}
```

3. Write a function called `searchstr` which takes two character pointers as arguments and which returns a character pointer. Have the function search the first string to see if it contains the second string. If it does, return a pointer to where the second string is located inside the first string; if it doesn't, return a null pointer.

With `charptr` and `sptr` declared as

```
char *charptr = "A string to be searched", *sptr;
```

The call

```
sptr = searchstr (charptr, "be");
```

should return a pointer to where the string "be" begins inside the string pointed to by `charptr`. The call

```
sptr = searchstr (charptr, "nosuch");
```

should return a null character pointer, since the string "nosuch" is not present in the first string.

Write the function using pointer variables exclusively. Be careful with boundary conditions, and make sure that calls like

```
searchstr ("/dev/ttty10", "tty")
searchstr ("end of str", "string")
```

produce the correct results.

4. Write a function called `listsize` that takes a pointer to the start of a linked list and returns the number of elements in the list. Assume entries in the list are of type `struct listrec` as defined in this chapter.

5. Write the declaration for a pointer variable called `fnptr` that could be used to point to a function that returns a pointer to an `int`.

6. The `qsort` function in the Standard C Library sorts an array containing any type of data. The arguments to `qsort` are: a pointer to the aray to be sorted, the number of elements in the array, the size of each element in the array, and a pointer to a function that returns an `int`. Page 77 describes how this function pointer is used by `qsort`.

    Here is how `qsort` would be called to sort an array of 100 integers called `values`:

```
int compare ();
...
qsort ( (char *) values, 100, sizeof (int), compare);
```

    `qsort` expects its first argument—which points to the start of the array—to be a character pointer. This explains the need for the typecast in the above call.

    Write `qsort` using any sort algorithm you desire.

3

THE STANDARD C LIBRARY

▪ Introduction to the Libraries ▪

The *UNIX Programmer's Reference Manual* is divided into several sections. These sections are numbered as follows:

Section 2   UNIX system interface calls

Section 3   UNIX system library calls

Section 4   UNIX system file formats

Section 5   Miscellaneous descriptions of macro packages, character sets, etc.

The routines in Section 2 talk directly to the UNIX system kernel. They're described in detail in Chapter 5 of this book. Because these routines are generally UNIX-specific, it is wise to avoid using them if you want to write a program that will run on operating systems other than UNIX (like MS-DOS, TSO, or VMS).

Section 3 contains descriptions of routines in the so-called "Standard C Library." It also contains descriptions of routines in the Math Library, Fortran Library, and various "specialized" libraries. These routines are generally ordered alphabetically. They are distinguished from one another by a special letter that designates the particular library the routine belongs to:

C   Standard C Library

S   Standard I/O Library

M   Math Library

F   Fortran Library

X   Specialized Libraries

You may be interested in using a routine from any library except the Fortran Library (although you *can* call a Fortran routine, you usually don't want or need to).

The Standard C and Standard I/O Libraries are automatically searched by the link editor when your program is compiled. This means that to use any routine from the library, you just go ahead and call it from your C program. No special option is needed for the `cc` command when the program is compiled:

```
$ cat prog1.c
main ()
{
    char buf[81],

    strcpy (buf, "Copy me please");
    printf ("%s\n", buf);
}
$ cc prog1.c
$ a.out
Copy me please
$
```

`strcpy` and `printf` are found by the linker because of its automatic search of the Standard C and Standard I/O Libraries.

To use a routine from the Math Library or from any of the Specialized Libraries, however, a special link editor option must be supplied. To use any function from the Math Library, you need to specify the `-lm` option to the `cc` command:

```
$ cc trigfuncs.c -lm
```

Note that the `-lm` option must *follow* the file name on the command line because the linker resolves external references from left to right. By listing `trigfuncs.c` first, the linker knows which routines to extract from the Math Libray when it subsequently searches it.

The manual page (often called the "man page") that describes a routine from one of the Specialized Libraries will also mention the appropriate command line option that is required in order to use the function.

Locating a Man Page Description

While on the topic of the man pages, it's worthwhile discussing how to use your manual. The first step is locating the correct man page that describes the function you're looking for. Since the functions are organized alphabetically, this is usually straightforward: you turn to section 3 of the manual and flip through the pages until you find the function listed at the top of the page. Unfortunately, not all of the functions are listed separately in the manual. For example, if you want to find out more about the string copy function `strcpy`, you'll notice that it doesn't appear as a separate entry. When this happens, the best thing to do is to turn to the *Permuted Index* that appears at the front of the manual. Locate the function you're interested in in the second column. On the corresponding line in the third column you'll find the appropriate man page entry that describes the function.

Looking up `strcpy` in the second column of the Permuted Index shows the following line:

/strncat, strcmp, strncmp,   strcpy, strncpy, strlen,/ .... string(3C)

The third column shows that `strcpy` is described on the page headed by "string." The "3C" says that it's a Section 3 routine and is part of the Standard C Library.

Be careful when looking up routines—make sure that you find the one you're looking for. For instance, suppose you need to take the square root of a number. You know the name of the routine is `sqrt` but want to find out more about it. So you look up `sqrt` in Section 3 and find that it's alphabetically listed. However, if you read further you'll quickly realize that the square root function being described is from the Fortran Library. The quickest way to tell is by the fact that the header page lists the function as `SQRT(3F)`. To find the one you need, go to the Permuted Index, where you'll find it's listed under the man page `EXP(3M)`.

Reading the Man Page

The description of a particular function is itself divided into several sections. Some of these appear for every function, while other sections (like **BUGS**) are only used when needed. Let's take a look at a sample man page. Figure 3-1 shows one for the function `abs`, which takes the absolute value of an integer. The **NAME** section lists the name of the function and a brief description of its purpose. The **SYNOPSIS** section summarizes how to use the function. If a special header file is needed by the function, it will be listed here. For example, the man page entry for `sqrt` shows that the header file `<math.h>` needs to be included in the program in order to use the function. You should always include the recommended header files. In some cases, the function call will not work at all without them. That's because some functions like `islower` and `getchar` are actually defined as *macros* inside the header files. At the very least, these header files will often include return type declarations for functions that don't

---

ABS(3C)   ABS(3C)

NAME

     abs – return integer absolute value

SYNOPSIS

     int abs (i)
     int i;

DESCRIPTION

     Abs returns the absolute value of its integer operand.

BUGS

     In two's-complement representation, the absolute value of
     the negative integer with largest magnitude is undefined.
     Some implementations trap this error, but others simply
     ignore it.

SEE ALSO

     floor(3M).

Fig. 3-1. Man page for abs Function

return integers, thus sparing you the chore of having to declare them yourself.

    After the required header files are listed, the type of value returned by the function, and the number of arguments expected by the function and their types are summarized. For example, the **SYNOPSIS** section looks like this:

```
int abs (i)
int i;
```

This says that abs returns an int, and that it takes one argument also of type int.

The **DESCRIPTION** section describes in more detail what the function does. In our simple example, a single sentence suffices; more sophisticated functions can take up to several pages to describe.

The **BUGS** section—not always present—describes known problems or caveats that exist with the function.

The **SEE ALSO** section is a cross reference listing of other functions you may want to check. These functions might be listed because they serve a similar purpose, or because the one you're reading about actually uses it.

The man page may also contain a **FILES** section which lists files that are used by the function. A **WARNINGS** section will describe special precautions you should be aware of. A **DIAGNOSTICS** section is sometimes present to detail how error conditions are handled or reported by the function.

You should note that the organization of the *XENIX Programmer's Reference* manual is different from what's been described. Specifically, the manual combines Sections 2 and 3 into a single section. Also, all routines are classified as "System Service" routines and not as Standard I/O, Standard C, Math, or System Interface routines.

▪ What's in the Standard C Library? ▪

The routines in the Standard C Library can be categorized according to the type of function they serve:

- Character testing
- Data conversion
- String handling
- Memory functions
- Dynamic memory allocation
- Date and time processing
- Group, password, and utmp file processing
- Data encryption
- Process control and information
- Table and tree manipulation
- Random number generation
- Miscellaneous routines

Also included in the Standard C Library are routines for performing I/O operations. These routines are separately categorized under the Standard I/O Library—the topic of the next chapter.

The following sections in this chapter describe functions in the Standard C Library as of UNIX System V Release 2. Each section describes routines that perform related tasks, like character testing, string operations, or dynamic memory allocation. At the start of the section is a list of the functions covered in that section and a brief description of what each function does.

• Character Testing •

`isalnum`	TRUE if arg is an alphanumeric (i.e., alphabetic or numeric) character
`isalpha`	TRUE if arg is a letter
`isascii`	TRUE if arg is less than octal 0200
`iscntrl`	TRUE if arg is octal 0177 (delete) or less than octal 040
`isdigit`	TRUE if arg is a digit character
`isgraph`	TRUE if arg is octal 041-0176, inclusive
`islower`	TRUE if arg is a lowercase letter
`isprint`	TRUE if arg is octal 040-0176, inclusive
`ispunct`	TRUE if arg is a punctuation character (not a control or alphanumeric char)
`isspace`	TRUE if arg is a space character (space, tab, carriage return, newline, vertical tab, or formfeed)
`isupper`	TRUE if arg is an uppercase letter
`isxdigit`	TRUE if arg is a hexadecimal digit character (0-9, A-F, or a-f)

These routines each take a single character as argument and return a nonzero value if the result of the test is TRUE, a zero result otherwise. All require that the special header file `ctype.h` be included in your program, since they're actually defined as macros.

`isgraph` checks to see if the character given as argument is a "graphic" character (i.e., if it will show up on the display when printed). Notice that `isprint` does a similar test, except it also includes octal 40, a space character, in its test.

The definition of a punctuation character to `ispunct` is simplistic: anything that's not a control character or alphanumeric character satisfies this function.

Note that functions that mention specific character values are with respect to the ASCII character set. In non-ASCII environments, these functions have most likely been redefined.

In the manual, all of these functions are grouped together on the page headed **CTYPE(3C).**

The following program shows how these routines can be used. We're only going to show the use of one routine here, since they're all used similarly. The program reads in a line from standard input and then scans the line to identify all characters that aren't lowercase. Each such character is written to standard output.

Program 3-1

```
/* islower */

#include <ctype.h>

main ()
{
    char buf[81], *bufptr;

    gets (buf);

    /* Flag all chars in buf that
       aren't lowercase letters */

    for ( bufptr = buf; *bufptr != '\0'; ++bufptr )
        if ( ! islower (*bufptr) )
            printf ("%c not lowercase!\n", *bufptr);
}
```

```
$ a.out
Here's a line!
H not lowercase!
' not lowercase!
  not lowercase!
  not lowercase!
! not lowercase!
```

(Remember to include the header file ctype.h in your program.)

The program reads a line from standard input into the character array buf using the gets function. This function is part of the Standard I/O Library and is discussed in greater detail in the next chapter. Note here that the function does not store the newline character inside the array but does put a terminating null at the end of the string.

After the line has been read, a loop is set up to sequence through each character in the array until the terminating null is found. Rather than using array indexing, a pointer variable called `bufptr` is used to sequentially access the contents of `buf`. (We wouldn't want you to forget what you learned from the last chapter already.)

`bufptr` is set pointing to the first character in `buf` when the `for` loop is entered. The loop continues as long as what `bufptr` points to is not the null character. This character is given as the argument to `islower`, and the result negated with the logical negation operator (`!`). Thus, the `if` will succeed if the character pointed to by `bufptr` is *not* lowercase (note how well the `if` statement reads).

If the character is in fact not lowercase, then it is displayed. The next character in the array is then examined.

• Data Conversion •

`a64l`	converts base 64 to long (password processing)
`atof`	converts string to double
`atoi`	converts string to integer
`atol`	converts string to long
`ecvt`	converts floating point to ASCII, with rounding
`fcvt`	converts floating point to ASCII, with rounding to specified place
`gcvt`	converts floating point to ASCII (in *f* or *e* format)
`l3tol`	converts three-byte integers into longs
`l64a`	converts long to base 64 (password processing)
`ltol3`	converts longs to three-byte integers
`strtod`	converts string to double
`strtol`	converts string (representing number in specified base) to long
`toascii`	converts integer to valid ASCII character
`tolower`	converts uppercase letter to lowercase
`_tolower`	converts uppercase letter to lowercase (requires uppercase arg)
`toupper`	converts lowercase letter to uppercase
`_toupper`	converts lowercase letter to uppercase (requires lowercase arg)

atof, atoi, atol, strtol, and strtod

atof converts a number stored in a string to its floating point representation. It scans the character string given as its argument, ignoring any leading whitespace characters, until it finds a digit, plus sign, or minus sign. Scanning of the string continues until a character that is not a valid part of the number is encountered, or the end of the string is reached. The number is then converted and the value returned.

atoi works like atof except that it converts a number in a string to an int, which it returns. atol converts and returns a long int. strtol is like atol, only more sophisticated; it allows a base to be specified for the number and also returns a pointer to the character in the string that terminated the scan. strtod works like atof except it, too, returns a pointer to the character that terminated the scan.

These conversion routines are particularly handy for converting command line arguments—which as you recall are passed to main as character strings. Program 3-2 shows a program called calc that takes three command line arguments; the first and last are floating point values, and the second is an operator that specifies an operation to be performed on them.

atof must be declared before it's called, since it doesn't return an int. The program checks to ensure that the correct number of command line arguments are typed; if not, a message is displayed and the program exits. The exit function is actually a part of the UNIX system interface. It takes as its argument an integer that is returned to the UNIX system as the program's *exit status*. An exit status of zero is used to indicate success, nonzero failure. This exit status can be tested by another program such as the shell, which provides access to the exit status through the special variable $?.

If the correct number of arguments is supplied, then atof is called twice to convert the numbers pointed to by argv[1] and argv[3] into floating point values. A switch statement then tests the character pointed to by argv[2] to determine the operator that was typed. The corresponding result is then calculated and displayed using the format conversion characters %g. These conversion characters—described in more detail in the next chapter—display the result in either floating or exponential format.

The second time calc is executed shows that atof recognizes numbers expressed in exponential notation.

You have to be careful when converting strings since, as noted, the routines atoi, atol, atof, strol, and strtod terminate their scan upon the first occurrence of an invalid character. In fact, a value of 0 is returned even if no number is present at the start of the string. This explains the last set of output. The functions strtod and strtol can be used to determine if a value is successfully converted or not (by checking the pointer that comes back to see if any characters were matched). Check your manual for details.

Program 3-2

```
/* atof */

main (argc, argv)
int argc;
char *argv[];
{
    double  f1, f2, atof ();

    if ( argc < 4 ) {
            printf ("Bad argument count\n");
            exit (1);
    }

    f1 = atof (argv[1]);
    f2 = atof (argv[3]);

    switch (*argv[2]) {
            case '+':
                printf ("%g\n", f1 + f2);
                break;
            case '-':
                printf ("%g\n", f1 - f2);
                break;
            case '*':
                printf ("%g\n", f1 * f2);
                break;
            case '/':
                if ( f2 != 0 )
                    printf ("%g\n", f1 / f2);
                else
                    printf ("Division by zero!\n");
                break;
            default:
                printf ("Unknown operator: %c\n", *argv[2]);
    }

    exit (0);
}


$ calc 12.7 + 17.6
30.3
$ calc 5.9e+20 / 7.7e+8
7.66234e+11
$ calc xx - yy
0
```

tolower, _tolower, toupper, and _toupper

Each of these conversion routines requires the header file `ctype.h` (like the "is" functions, they're really defined as macros in that header file). Notice that there are two routines to convert from upper to lower case, and two that convert from lower to upper case. The difference between them is that the underscored version of the routine requires, in the case of `_tolower`, that *the argument be an uppercase letter*. In the case of `_toupper`, it is required that *the argument be a lowercase letter*. If you give these two functions any other type of argument, the result will be undefined.

So, for example, if you know that your character is a lowercase letter and you want to convert it to uppercase, you can use the `_toupper` function:

```
c = _toupper (c);
```

Execution of `_toupper` will be faster than `toupper`. If you're not sure about the particular character and want to convert it to uppercase, use `toupper`, as it *leaves any nonlowercase letter alone*. A similar recommendation applies to `_tolower` and `tolower`.

The following program reads a line from standard input (like the program from the previous section) and converts all lowercase letters in the line to uppercase. Since a test is not made prior to the conversion, `toupper` is used instead of `_toupper`.

Program 3-3

```
/* toupper */

#include <ctype.h>

main ()
{
    char buf[81], *bufptr;

    gets (buf);

    for ( bufptr = buf; *bufptr != '\0'; ++bufptr )
        *bufptr = toupper (*bufptr);

    printf ("%s\n", buf);
}


$ a.out
Here's a line
HERE'S A LINE
```

Note that since `_toupper` and `_tolower` (and on some UNIX systems, `toupper` and `tolower`) are implemented as macros, you've got to be careful not to use the increment or decrement operator inside the macro call:

```
c = tolower (*bufptr++);
```

This reads as though `bufptr` will be incremented once after the character it points to is converted, when in reality it would be incremented *two or three* times given these macro definitions:

```
#define  isupper(x)     ((x) >= 'A'  &&  (x) <= 'Z')
#define  _tolower(x)    ((x) - 'A' + 'a')
#define  tolower(x)     (isupper(x) ? _tolower(x) : (x))
```

Always be careful when using `++`, `--`, or when calling another function inside a macro call.

• String Handling •

`strcat`	concatenates two strings
`strncat`	concatenates at most *n* characters from one string to the end of another string
`strcmp`	compares two character strings
`strncmp`	compares at most *n* characters from two character strings
`strcpy`	copies a character string
`strncpy`	copies at most *n* characters from a character string
`strlen`	returns number of characters in a string (excluding null)
`strchr`	finds first occurrence of a specified character in a string
`strrchr`	finds last occurrence of a specified character in a string
`strpbrk`	finds first occurrence of any character from a set in a string
`strtok`	parses a character string into tokens

strcspn   returns number of characters in a string that consist
                 entirely of characters not found in a specified set

strspn   returns number of characters in a string that consist
                 entirely of characters from a specified set

These string functions are all listed under **STRING(3C)** in the manual. Most of them return values of type `char *`. Therefore, be sure to declare their return types as appropriate. Better yet, include the file `string.h` in your program to have the functions automatically declared.

The string functions are probably among the most often used functions from the Standard C Library, particularly `strcat`, `strcpy`, `strcmp`, and `strlen`. Similar versions of the first three functions exist with similar names, except the letter *n* appears after the characters "str." These functions take an extra argument that specifies the maximum number of characters to be concatenated (`strncat`), copied (`strncpy`), or compared (`strncmp`). They're quite handy for dealing with character arrays that are *not* null terminated, or for limiting the number of characters involved in the operation.

strcat and strncat

`strcat` takes two arguments, both character pointers. These must point to null-terminated character arrays (i.e., character strings). The function takes the character string pointed to by the second argument and copies it to the *end* of the character string pointed to by the first argument. Warning: It's your responsibility to ensure that enough space is provided in the destination character array to accommodate the string to be copied!

`strncat` is like `strcat` except that it takes a third argument. This is an integer specifying the maximum number of characters to be copied from the second character string. If the null character is encountered before the specified number of characters have been copied, then the copying stops right there. Whether or not the null is encountered, a null character is inserted at the end of the destination string.

Program 3-4 shows how `strcat` and `strncat` are used. The first call

```
strcat (s1, s2);
```

says to copy the character string pointed to by `s2` ("tests") to the end of the string pointed to by `s1` ("Some string "). Care was taken when dimensioning `s1` to ensure that space was reserved at the end of the array to copy some extra characters in. After `strcat` does its thing, the `s1` array is displayed by `printf`. As you can deduce, `strcat` puts a terminating null at the end of the destination array.

Program 3-4

```
/* strcat and strncat */

#include <string.h>

main ()
{
    static char s1[50] = { "Some string " };
    static char s2[] = { "tests" };

    strcat (s1, s2);
    printf ("%s\n", s1);
    printf ("%s\n", strcat (s1, " again"));
    printf ("%s\n", strncat (s1, " again", 3));
}


$ a.out
Some string tests
Some string tests again
Some string tests again ag
```

The next call to `strcat` takes advantage of the fact that the function returns a value—namely its first argument. This pointer is then handed directly to `printf`. As you can see from the second call to `printf`, this `strcat` call had the effect of copying the literal character string " again" to the end of the character string stored inside `s1`.

The `strncat` function is then called. The third argument specifies that at most three characters are to be concatenated to the end of the destination string. The output verifies that just the first three characters from the literal character string " again" were copied to `s1`.

strcmp and strncmp

These functions take two character strings as arguments and compare them character by character. If the two character strings are identical, then the value zero is returned. Otherwise, if the first character string is "less than" the second, a value less than zero is returned; if the first is "greater than" the second, a value greater than zero is returned.

On an ASCII machine, the string "a" (octal 141) will be less than the string "b" (octal 142) but greater than the string "A" (octal 101). Ignoring the problem with case distinction, this comparison works well for alphabetizing words; that is, the word "agate" will compare less than the word "zygote," but greater than the word "abracadabra."

Program 3-5

```
/* strcmp and strncmp */

#include <string.h>

main ()
{
    char *s1 = "string1";
    char *s2 = "string3";

    printf ("%d\n", strcmp (s1, s2));
    printf ("%d\n", strcmp (s2, s1));
    printf ("%d\n", strcmp (s1, "string1"));
    printf ("%d\n", strncmp (s1, s2, 6));
}


$ a.out
-2
2
0
0
```

In that last case, strncmp is used to compare just the first six characters of the strings pointed to by s1 and s2. Since the first six characters of "string1" and "string2" are identical, strncmp returns the value 0.

As a last point, don't write

```
if ( strcmp (s1, s2) )
    ...
```

when what you mean to write is

```
if ( strcmp (s1, s2) == 0 )
    ...
```

Remember, strcmp returns a nonzero value when the strings are *not* equal, a zero value when they're equal.

strcpy and strncpy

These functions copy character strings from the array pointed to by the second argument to that pointed to by the first. As with strcat, it's your responsibility to ensure that enough space exists in the destination array to accommodate the copied string.

Both functions return the first argument as their value.

Program 3-6

```
/* strcpy and strncpy */

#include <string.h>

main ()
{
    static char s1[] = { "Some string" }, s2[25];

    strcpy (s2, s1);
    printf ("%s\n", s2);

    strncpy (s2, s1, 4);
    s2[4] = '\0';
    printf ("%s\n", s2);

    printf ("%s\n", strncpy (s2, s1, 20));
}
```

```
$ a.out
Some string
Some
Some string
$
```

The call to `strcpy` says to copy the characters in `s1` (up to and including the terminating null) to `s2`. The `printf` that follows verifies that the copy succeeded.

The call

```
strncpy (s2, s1, 4);
```

says to copy 4 characters from `s1` to `s2`. The null character is copied into `s2` only if it's encountered in the process of copying the specified number of characters from `s1`. That's why it was necessary to explicitly insert a null character into `s2[4]`.

If you ask `strncpy` to copy more characters than are contained in the string, then it will pad the destination array with null characters (remember, it always places the exact number of characters specified into the destination array, even if it has to pad the destination array with nulls to fulfill its obligation).

The last call to strncpy says to copy 20 characters from s1 to s2 and
then passes the returned value (s2) directly to printf. Since strncpy will
encounter the null character in s1 after copying 11 characters, it will copy nine
nulls to s2.

strlen

This function returns an integer representing the number of characters in the
character string given as its argument. It does *not* include the terminating null
character in its count.

Program 3-7

```
/* strlen */

#include <string.h>

main ()
{
    static char s1[50] = { "Some string" };

    printf ("%d\n", strlen (s1));
    printf ("%d\n", strlen (""));
    printf ("%d\n", strlen ("\007\n"));
}
```

```
$ a.out
11
0
2
$
```

The second call to strlen shows the length of the null character string is zero.
The third call verifies that escape sequences are single characters.

Be careful to remember that the null is not included in the character count.
This is an important concern when doing something like dynamically allocating
space for a character string. In that case, you have to remember to allocate space
for that terminating null. See the discussion on the dynamic memory allocation
routines later in this chapter for an example.

strchr, strrchr, and strpbrk

strchr and strrchr take two arguments: the first is a character string, and the second is a character to locate in that string. In the case of strchr, the first occurrence of the character in the string is located, whereas in the case of strrchr it's the last occurrence of the character that's found. A pointer to precisely where the character can be found in the string is returned by either routine. If the character doesn't exist in the string, then the null pointer is returned.

strpbrk works similarly, except that the second argument is not a single character but instead a character string. This function searches the string given as the first argument for the first occurrence of *any* of the characters contained in the second string, returning a pointer to it when found.   strpbrk returns the null pointer if none of the characters is found.

Program 3-8

```
/* strchr, strrchr and strpbrk */

#include <string.h>
#define   NULLCHARPTR     (char *)  0

main ()
{
    char *teststring = "Here is a string of text";
    char *textptr;

    /* find first 's' in teststring */

    if ( (textptr = strchr (teststring, 's')) != NULLCHARPTR )
        printf ("%s\n", textptr);

    /* find last 's' in teststring */

    if ( (textptr = strrchr (teststring, 's')) != NULLCHARPTR )
        printf ("%s\n", textptr);

    /* find first 'Z' in teststring */

    if ( (textptr = strchr (teststring, 'Z')) == NULLCHARPTR )
        printf ("Z not found in string\n");

    /* find first  'a', 'g', or 'x' in teststring */

    if ( (textptr = strpbrk (teststring, "agx")) != NULLCHARPTR )
        printf ("%s\n", textptr);
}
```

```
$ a.out
s a string of text
string of text
Z not found in string
a string of text
```

The first call to strchr says to search the string pointed to by teststring ("Here is a string of text") for the character 's' (remember that the second argument to strchr and strrchr is a character). The pointer that is returned is assigned to textptr. If this pointer is nonnull, then the character was found in the string. The printf will display the character string from the point in the string that the match begins through to the end.

The program then calls strrchr to find the last occurrence of 's' in the same string. This causes a pointer to the second 's' in the string to be returned.

In the next to last case, strchr is asked to find the first occurrence of the character 'Z' in the string. Since it doesn't exist, the null pointer is returned, causing the printf function to be called.

The last case calls strpbrk to find the first occurrence of either an 'a', 'g', or 'x' in teststring.

strchr, strrchr, and strpbrk are useful for parsing character strings. For example, if you have a directory name such as /usr/george/bin stored in a character array called buf, then the expression

```
strrchr (buf, '/') + 1
```

will give a pointer to the basename of the directory path ("bin").

And if you have a string of directories separated by colons (like the PATH) stored in buf (like "/usr/bin:/bin:/usr/lbin"), then the expression

```
strchr (buf, ':')
```

will return a pointer to the first colon in buf, and

```
textptr = strchr (buf, ':');
strncpy (dirname, buf, textptr - buf);
```

will copy the first directory path name ("/usr/bin") to dirname (you may want to work this one through to verify for yourself that this is in fact what will happen). Of course, when doing this sort of thing on your own you always should check the pointer that comes back from strchr and strrchr before you do anything with it. Giving the null pointer to a function that expects to see a valid pointer (like strncpy) may result in abnormal termination of your program.

strtok

More sophisticated parsing of a character string can be accomplished with the strtok function. This function parses a string into its *tokens*, where a token is simply considered a sequence of characters up to a *token-delimiter* (or the terminating null) character that you specify.

Operation of strtok is a little tricky, but if you need to parse command lines, it can prove quite useful.

First let's take a look at an example and then we'll describe the function in detail.

Program 3-9

```
/* strtok */

#include <string.h>
#define   NULLCHARPTR     (char *)  0

main ()
{
    char buf[81];
    char *tokptr, *strptr = buf;

    gets (buf);

    while ( (tokptr = strtok (strptr, " \t")) != NULLCHARPTR ) {
        printf ("%s\n", tokptr);
        strptr = NULLCHARPTR;
        }
}


$ a.out
   Here is        a        line    of           text
Here
is
a
line
of
text
```

Like strpbrk, strtok takes two character strings as arguments. The first is a pointer to the character string to be parsed; the second specifies the token delimiters. strtok must be called repeatedly to process all of the tokens in a string. Each time it's called, it locates the next token in the string and returns a pointer to it. When no tokens are left in the string, strtok returns a null pointer.

In the example, the first argument to `strtok` is the line of text as read from the terminal and pointed to by `strptr` (notice that `strptr` was set pointing to `buf`), and the second is a character string containing a space and tab character.

`strtok` searches `buf` until it finds a nondelimiter character (the character `'H'` in the example). Then it continues scanning the string until either a delimiter character (space or tab) or the terminating null is encountered. At that point, `strtok` *inserts a null character at the end of the token in the string* and returns a pointer to the start of the token. This pointer is given to `printf` so that the token can be displayed. The program then sets the pointer variable `strptr` to the null character pointer. This must be supplied as the first argument to `strtok` for all calls to the function but the first. As you recall, the first time `strtok` is called, the first argument has to point to the string to be parsed. Giving it a null first argument on subsequent calls tells `strtok` to continue scanning in the string from where it left off the last time it was called—`strtok` keeps track of this information internally.

When no tokens are left in `buf` (i.e., when it encounters the terminating null), `strtok` returns a null pointer, causing the `while` loop to terminate.

Realize that `strtok` makes permanent changes to the character string you're parsing (it inserts nulls at the end of each token). If this presents a problem, then make a copy of the character string first before you begin calling the function. Also note that `strtok` can be used only to parse one string at a time.

strspn and strcspn

These two functions count characters: the first counts the number of consecutive characters in the first argument string that consist *entirely* of characters specified in the second argument string. Counting starts with the first character in the string.

`strcspn` works like `strspn` except that the sense of how the characters in the second argument string are interpreted is reversed. That is, starting from the beginning of the first character string argument, `strcspn` counts the number of consecutive characters in the string that consist of characters *not* included in the second argument string. Some examples will clarify their operation.

Program 3-10

```
#include <string.h>

main ()
{
    char *teststr  = "self-explanatory program";
    char *teststr2 = "123 is the number";
    int  count;

    /* count number of inital lowercase letters */

    count = strspn (teststr, "abcdefghijklmnopqrstuvwxyz");
    printf ("%d\n", count);

    /* count number of initial digits */

    count = strspn (teststr2, "0123456789");
    printf ("%d\n", count);

    /* count number of initial characters up to a space */

    count = strcspn (teststr, " ");
    printf ("%d\n", count);
}



$ a.out
4
3
16
```

The output from this program should be self-explanatory. In the last case, strcspn is used to count the characters in the string up to the first space.

▪ Memory Functions ▪

memccpy   copies characters until specified character is copied or count reached

memchr   searches an area of memory for specified character

memcmp   compares characters in memory

| `memcpy` | copies a specifed number of characters |
| `memset` | sets an area of memory to a specified value |

These routines perform operations on characters in memory. Unlike the string functions, which they resemble, they have no concept of a terminating null byte. That's why they all require an additional argument that specifies a character count.

Since characters usually occupy a single byte on a machine, these memory routines can also be used to perform operations on other types of data arrays. They can be used to move chunks of data from one place to another, search an area of memory for a specified byte, and so forth.

The memory functions are written to be as efficient as possible, sometimes coded in assembler language to take advantage of special machine instructions (like block move or memory search instructions).

You should include the header file `memory.h` in your program when using any of these routines. Program 3-11 shows how to use the various memory routines.

Since you're already familiar with the string routines, understanding the operation of three of the memory routines should be straightforward: `memchr` works like `strchr`, `memcpy` like `strcpy`, and `memcmp` like `strcmp`. The only differences, as noted, are that the memory routines ignore null characters and require a third argument specifying exactly how many characters to examine, copy, or compare (recall that a routine like `strncmp` specifies the *maximum* number of characters to compare, since the function will stop after a null character is encountered; `memcmp` will continue right past that null, until either the corresponding characters compare unequal or exactly the specified number of characters have been compared.)

In the program example, `memcpy` is used to copy the characters in `buf1` to `buf2`. The number of characters to copy is specified by the expression

```
sizeof (buf1)
```

which will be equal to the number of bytes in the array, including the terminating null. The number of bytes in the array will be equal to the number of characters in the array if characters occupy a single byte on your machine (which is the case for most machines). If you are compiling your program on a machine that uses more than a byte for storing a character, then the expression

```
sizeof (buf1) / sizeof (char)
```

should be used instead to calculate the length of `buf1` in characters, recalling that the mem*xxx* functions take *character* and not *byte* count arguments.

Next, `memcpy` is called again to show how it can be used to copy something other than a character array. Since `memcpy` expects to see character pointers as the first two arguments, the pointers `data1` and `data2` are coerced to the appropriate type with the type cast operator.

Program 3-11

```c
/* Illustrate various memory routines */

#include <memory.h>

main ()
{
    static char buf1[] = {"I am to be copied"};
    char buf2[25], *strptr;
    static int data1[5] = {1, 2, 3, 4, 5};
    int data2[5], i;

    /* copy characters from buf1 to buf2 */

    memcpy (buf2, buf1, sizeof(buf1));
    printf ("%s\n", buf2);

    /* copy data1 array to data2 */

    memcpy ( (char *) data2, (char *) data1, sizeof(data1));
    for ( i = 0; i < 5; ++i )
        printf ("%d ", data2[i]);

    printf ("\n");

    /* scan buf1 for character 't' */

    strptr = memchr (buf1, 't', sizeof (buf1));
    printf ("%s\n", strptr);

    /* compare buf1 to buf2 */

    printf ("%d\n", memcmp (buf1, buf2, sizeof (buf1)));

    /* set the buf2 array to all 'x' characters */

    memset (buf2, 'x', sizeof (buf2));
    for ( i = 0; i < sizeof (buf2); ++i )
        printf ("%c", buf2[i]);

    printf ("\n");
}
```

```
$ a.out
I am to be copied
1 2 3 4 5
to be copied
0
xxxxxxxxxxxxxxxxxxxxxxxxx
```

As noted, `memchr` works just like `strchr`, except that it will scan right past any null characters until either the character is found (second argument) or the specified number of characters have been examined (third argument). This is particularly useful for scanning an area in memory for a particular value (a byte). In the example, it's used just like `strchr` to look for the first occurrence of the character `'t'` in the array `buf1`. As with `strchr`, it returns a pointer to the matching character if found, or a null pointer if the character is not found.

The program next calls `memcmp` to compare the first `sizeof (buf1)` characters from `buf1` and `buf2`. The return value is the same as `strcmp`: less than zero if a character from the first array is less than the corresponding character from the second; zero if the two arrays are identical up to the specified number of characters; and greater than zero if a character from the first array is greater than the corresponding character from the second array.

As you might expect, `memcmp` can be used to compare any two areas of memory. For example, with `data1` and `data2` as declared previously, the expression

```
memcmp ((char *) data1, (char *) data2,  sizeof (data1));
```

will return zero if the two integers arrays have identical contents, nonzero if they don't.

`memset` is useful for setting an area of memory to a specified character, like setting all characters in an array to blanks (or to `xs`, as shown in the example).

The only memory function left is `memccpy`. This works like `memcpy` except that it takes an added argument: a character that will be used to terminate the copy if encountered before the specified number of characters have been copied. This character is given as the third argument, and is followed by the count.

So the call

```
memccpy (buf2, buf1, '\0', 25);
```

will copy 25 characters from `buf1` to `buf2`, stopping earlier if a null character is encountered (which will get copied). In this case, it's like writing

```
strncpy (buf2, buf1, 25);
```

except that, as you'll recall, the latter function will always copy exactly 25 characters, even if it has to insert extra nulls to fulfill the request.

Remember these memory functions the next time you write a program. Since they're written with efficiency in mind, they can save your program some execution time.

· Dynamic Memory Allocation ·

`malloc`	allocates storage
`calloc`	allocates storage initialized to all zeroes
`realloc`	changes size of allocated storage
`free`	frees storage allocated by `malloc` or `calloc`

These routines enable you to obtain chunks of memory *dynamically*; that is while your program is executing. As you know, when you declare an array in your program you have to tell the compiler how many elements to reserve for the array. If you know this number in advance, then you're in good shape. However, things are not always that simple. You may not know how many elements to reserve because it may be based upon other factors. For instance, if you wanted to read all of the lines from a file and store them in your program, the amount of storage needed would depend upon the size of the file. And if this size could vary widely, then you'd have to reserve enough space to accommodate the largest possible file size. This is wasteful, particularly if the files you deal with are generally small.

Allocating the maximum amount of space for your data structures increases the size of your program. In a multitasking environment such as is provided under UNIX, you're always competing for free memory space. If your program is unnecessarily wasteful of space, it means that fewer processes will be able to occupy memory. Furthermore, when your task has to be swapped in and out, it will require longer to do so, since there will be more data to transfer to and from the disk.

malloc and calloc

With `malloc` and `calloc`, you can allocate space for your data after you have determined how much space you need. And if your estimate proves to be too high or low, you can change the size of your allocated space with `realloc`. Finally when you're done with your allocated space, the `free` function can be called to release it for subsequent use by `malloc`, `calloc`, and `realloc`.

`malloc` and `calloc` allocate new space for you. The first one takes one argument—the number of *bytes* of storage to allocate, and the second one takes two—the number of data items to allocate followed by the size of each such item. `calloc` guarantees that the space allocated is initialized to all zeroes, whereas `malloc` does not.

malloc and calloc return character pointers that point to the newly allocated data space.   As an example, if you have an array of characters called buf,
and you want to allocate space for a new character array and copy the entire contents of buf into that space, then you would write

```
char buf[81], *charptr, *malloc ();
   ...
charptr = malloc (sizeof(buf));

if ( charptr != (char *) 0 )
    memcpy (charptr, buf, sizeof(buf));
else {
    printf ("malloc failed\n");
    exit (1);
}
```

malloc, calloc, and realloc all return null pointers if for some reason your
allocation request cannot be fulfilled (there simply may not be enough memory
space left). That's why you should always check the pointer that is returned
before you use it.

Since the allocation routines allocate space by bytes, the sizeof operator
is perfect for calculating the number of such bytes to reserve in a machine
independent way.

The previous example allocates space for 81 characters. The pointer to the
newly allocated space as returned by malloc is stored in the character pointer
variable charptr. After ensuring that the allocation was successful, memcpy is
called to copy the contents of buf to the allocated storage area pointed to by
charptr.

If you wanted to reserve just enough space for a null terminated string
stored in buf, and copy just that, you would write instead

```
char buf[81], *charptr, *malloc ();
   ...
charptr = malloc (strlen(buf) + 1);

if ( charptr != (char *) 0 )
    strcpy (charptr, buf);
else {
    printf ("malloc failed\n");
    exit (1);
}
```

Be careful here and remember that strlen doesn't count the terminting null in
the string, but strcpy does copy it! That's why one was added to the value
returned by strlen and that result handed to malloc.

If you will be storing something other than characters in the allocated space, then you should type cast the pointer that is returned by the allocation functions into a pointer to the data type you'll be storing in that space.   malloc, calloc, and realloc guarantee that the pointer returned will be properly aligned so that any type of data can be stored at that memory address (for example, on some machines integers must be stored starting at an even memory address).

Suppose you want to allocate space for 500 integers in your program. Here's the way to do it:

```
char *malloc ();
int  *intptr;

intptr = (int *) malloc (500 * sizeof (int));

if ( intptr == (int *) 0 ) {
    printf ("Couldn't allocate space\n");
    exit (1);
}
```

The expression

```
500 * sizeof (int)
```

represents the number of bytes needed to store 500 integers. This is given to malloc, and the pointer returned is type cast to be of type pointer to int. Next, a check is made to ensure that the allocation succeeded.

If you wanted the space for your 500 integers all preset to zero, you would replace the previous call to malloc with the following call to calloc:

```
intptr = (int *) calloc (500, sizeof (int));
```

This tells calloc to allocate space for 500 elements, where each element is the size of an int.

Whether you use malloc or calloc (or even realloc), realize that the returned pointer points to an area of memory that has been reserved for your use. So in the previous example, enough space will exist for 500 integers to be stored in memory, starting at the location pointed to by intptr.   intptr can now be used *just as if it points to the start of an array of 500 integers*. So, for instance, the expression

```
*intptr = 1;
```

will store the value 1 at the first location in your newly allocated array, and

```
++intptr;
```

will set `intptr` pointing to the second element of the array. If `iptr` is also an integer pointer, then the loop

```
for ( iptr = intptr; iptr < intptr + 500;   ++iptr)
    *iptr = -1;
```

will set all 500 locations to -1. In fact, based upon discussions in the previous chapter, `intptr` can be used with indexing just like any other array, so the loop

```
for ( i = 0; i < 500; ++i )
    intptr[i] = -1;
```

can also be used to set all locations of the allocated array to -1.

Suppose you need to read all of the lines from a file into your program. Let's assume that you set a maximum size on the number of lines that your program can handle at, say, 1000.[†] If the maximum size of a line is, say, 256 characters, then using a conventional approach to storage allocation, you'd have to declare an array to store the largest possible file as shown:

```
char lines[1000][257];
```

This will reserve space for 1000 lines of 256 characters each (including a terminating null at the end of each line), or 257,000 characters (¼ MB)! Suppose that you know that the average length of each line from the file you're going to read in is 65 characters, then your actual storage requirements for the array is $1,000 \times 66$ or 66,000 characters. Therefore, your program would be wasting 257,000 - 66,000 or 191,000 characters!

A much better approach is to declare an array of 1,000 character *pointers*. As each line is read from the file, you can then allocate space dynamically for the precise number of characters contained in the line, storing the pointer to it in the array. Now to store 1,000 lines from a file in your program, where the average size of each line is 65 characters, you'd need $1,000 \times 66 + 1,000 \times 4$ (assuming 4 bytes/pointer), or 70,000 bytes instead of 257,000!

The following program example reads lines from standard input, storing them with the technique as discussed. After all of the lines have been read and stored, the program simply writes them back out in reverse order.

---

† It's left as an exercise for you to see how even this constraint can be avoided using the dynamic memory routines. (Hint: See the discussion on `realloc` coming up shortly.)

Program 3-12

```
/* reverse lines on standard input */

#define  NULLCHARPTR    (char *) 0
#define  MAX            100

main ()
{
    char *linetab[MAX], *gets(), *malloc(), buf[257];
    int  i;

    for ( i = 0; i < MAX  &&  gets(buf) != NULLCHARPTR; ++i ) {
        linetab[i] = malloc (strlen(buf) + 1);

        if ( linetab[i] == NULLCHARPTR ) {
            printf ("malloc failed!\n");
            exit (1);
        }

        strcpy (linetab[i], buf);
    }

    /* now print out the lines in reverse order */

    while ( --i >= 0 )
        printf ("%s\n", linetab[i]);
}


$ a.out
This is just a test to
show how more efficient use of
storage can be made with dynamic memory allocation
routines malloc and calloc.
CTRL-d
routines malloc and calloc.
storage can be made with dynamic memory allocation
show how more efficient use of
This is just a test to
```

(Note the return type declarations for gets and malloc, both of which
return character pointers.) As each line is read by the program into the buffer
buf, space is allocated to accommodate the line and the pointer to the allocated
space is stored inside linetab. Then the line is copied to the newly allocated
space. Remember that the statement

```
strcpy (linetab[i], buf);
```

is not copying the string stored in buf into linetab[i], but rather to the area in memory pointed to by linetab[i] (that's the area just allocated by malloc).

When the last line has been read, gets returns a null character pointer, thus causing the while loop to exit. At that point the lines are displayed in reverse order.

Dynamic memory allocation is often used for building data structures like linked lists. Recall the discussion on linked lists from the previous chapter. There we defined a structure called listrec that represented an entry in a linked list:

```
struct listrec {
    int             value;
    struct listrec *next;
};
```

To dynamically allocate a listrec structure, you could use malloc, type casting the resulting pointer to be of type pointer to struct listrec:

```
listptr = (struct listrec *) malloc (sizeof (struct listrec));
```

Here we assume that listptr is a listrec structure pointer variable, and that it will be tested immediately afterward to see if it's null or not.

The following program builds a linked list with values read in from standard input. It uses scanf to read in each integer. Since scanf returns the number of values successfully read and assigned, when this value is no longer equal to one, we know that the last integer has been read (or an invalid number was typed).

The program traverses the list after it has been built, simply displaying the value of each entry. As with many program examples in this text, this program is more instructional than practical.

Program 3-13

```c
/* simple list building with malloc */

struct listrec {
    int         value;
    struct listrec *next;
};

#define  NULLPTR        (struct listrec *) 0


struct listrec *build_list ()
{
    struct listrec  *liststart = NULLPTR, *listend, *newentry;
    int  val;

    while ( scanf ("%d", &val) == 1 ) {
        newentry = (struct listrec *)
                    malloc (sizeof (struct listrec));

        if ( newentry == NULLPTR ) {
            printf ("malloc failed!\n");
            exit (1);
        }

        if ( liststart == NULLPTR )
            /* first entry in list */
            liststart = listend = newentry;
        else {
            /* link new entry into list */
            listend->next = newentry;
            listend = newentry;
        }

        listend->value = val;
    }

    /* mark end of list */

    listend->next = NULLPTR;

    return (liststart);
}
```

```
void  visit_list (listptr)
struct listrec *listptr;
{
    while ( listptr != NULLPTR ) {
        printf ("%d\n", listptr->value);
        listptr = listptr->next;
    }
}


main ()
{
    struct listrec  *liststart;

    liststart = build_list ();
    visit_list (liststart);
}


$ a.out
100 -95 17 33
12 2 6
CTRL-d
100
-95
17
33
12
2
6
```

The `build_list` function creates a linked list from the integers read from standard input. The function continually reads integers from standard input until `scanf` returns a value other than one. `malloc` is then called to allocate space for a new entry in the list, and the resulting pointer is type cast and assigned to `newentry`. After ensuring that the allocation succeeded, the function then checks to see whether or not this is the first entry in the list. This test is made by checking the value of the `listrec` pointer variable `liststart`, whose value is initially set null. If it's still null, then this is the first entry in the list, so the value of `newentry` is saved in `liststart` and is also assigned to `listend`.

If it's not the first entry in the list, then the statement

```
listend->next = newentry;
```

sets the current last entry in the list pointing to the newly allocated entry. The statement that follows

```
listend = newentry;
```

sets `listend` pointing to the new end of the list. The integer read by `scanf` is then stored in the new list entry with the statement

```
listend->value = val;
```

When the `while` loop exits, the end of the list is marked with the null pointer, and then the function returns a pointer to the start of the list.

The `visit_list` function visits each entry in the list, simply displaying the value of each entry along the way. This is the same algorithm used by the `search` function from the previous chapter. You'll recall that that function searched the linked list for a specified value.

realloc

Even with dynamic memory allocation, it's not always possible to predetermine the precise amount of storage to allocate. To handle this situation, `realloc` is available. This function allows you to change the size of a previously allocated chunk of memory. You can either shrink its size or expand it.

The first argument to `realloc` is a pointer to the *start* of some previously allocated memory. This is important: the pointer must be a value that was returned by a previous call to `malloc`, `calloc`, or `realloc`. Giving this function anything else will yield undefined results.

The second argument to `realloc` is the new total size of the allocated area, once again either smaller or larger than the original allocated space.

`realloc` returns a pointer to the start of the allocated space, which will be the same as the pointer given as the first argument when you're asking that the space be shrunk, but which may be *different* from the original pointer if you're asking that the space be expanded. This is because the allocation routines always allocate contiguous storage cells. If you ask for a larger size, and that much contiguous space is not available, then `realloc` will have to find some place in memory where enough contiguous space is available. When it does, it will copy your data to the new place, and return a pointer to it. This is an important consideration if you have variables that point to your allocated space and then you call `realloc` to expand it. If `realloc` has to move the space, then your pointers will now be pointing into *deallocated* space, space that may be reclaimed with a subsequent call to `malloc`, `calloc`, or `realloc`. It's your responsibility to check the pointer that is returned by `realloc` and to adjust your pointer variables if the data area has been moved.

As some simple examples of `realloc`, let's say you allocated space for 500 integers with `malloc` and assigned the pointer to the `int` pointer variable `intptr`:

```
intptr = (int *) malloc (500 * sizeof (int));
```

If you later discover that you instead need space for 1,000 integers, then the following call to `realloc` will do the trick:

```
intptr = (int *) realloc (intptr, 1000 * sizeof (int));
```

(As with `malloc` and `calloc`, `realloc` returns a null pointer if the allocation fails, which should be tested by your program.) Once again remember that since you're expanding your data area here, `intptr` may not be equal to the old value of `intptr`.

Shrinking your memory space is just as easy. To deallocate the space taken for all but the first 100 integers in your storage area:

```
intptr = (int *) realloc (intptr, 100 * sizeof (int));
```

free

This function takes a single argument that points to the start of a previously allocated area (just like with `realloc`, it's critical that this pointer be a value that was returned by a previous call to `malloc`, `calloc`, or `realloc`). The entire storage area is deallocated and can be reused by subsequent allocation calls. If you're doing a lot of allocation in your program, then giving back storage when you're done with it can help keep your program from growing larger and larger (although your program will never get smaller using `free`—that is, `free` will not "shrink" the size of a process).

So to remove the entire array of integers pointed to by `intptr`, the call

```
free ( (char *) intptr);
```

can be used.

The following function, called `delete_entry`, takes a pointer to a linked list entry and removes the entry *after* it in the list. (Why can't the function be written to remove the entry pointed to by the argument?)

```
void delete_entry (one_before)
struct listrec *one_before;
{
    struct listrec *one_to_remove;

    one_to_remove = one_before->next;

    if ( one_to_remove != (struct listrec *) 0 ) {
        one_before->next = one_to_remove->next;
        free ( (char *) one_to_remove);
    }
}
```

The pointer to the entry to be removed is obtained from the `next` member of the list entry pointed to by `one_before`. If this pointer is null, then we're already at the end of the list. If it's not null, then the entry is logically removed from the list by taking the `next` member of `one_before` and setting it pointing to what `one_to_remove->next` points to. The space taken up by the list entry is then deallocated by calling `free`.

You may want to think about how you can use `delete_entry` to remove the *first* entry in the linked list.

Incidentally, `free` does not return a value.

• Time Functions •

clock	returns CPU time (in microseconds) used since first call to `clock`
ctime	converts long integer to ASCII time representation
asctime	converts `tm` structure to ASCII time representation
localtime	converts long integer to `tm` structure format
gmtime	converts long integer to `tm` structure in Greenwich Mean Time (GMT)
tzset	sets time zone variables

These routines allow you to internally time execution of your program (`clock`) and to gain access to the system clock for the date and the time (the rest of the functions). If you use `asctime`, `localtime`, or `gmtime`, then you should include the header file `time.h` in your program.

`clock`

This routine takes no arguments and returns a long integer representing the number of CPU microseconds that have elapsed since the first time the routine was called. By sandwiching statements in your program between calls to `clock`, you can accurately measure the CPU time taken to execute those statements:

Program 3-14

```
/* Timing execution with clock */

main ()
{
    long  clock (), cputime;

    clock ();
    foo ();
    cputime = clock ();

    printf ("foo took %.2f secs.\n",  cputime / 1.0e+6);
}

foo ()
{
    long i;

    for ( i = 0; i < 1000000L; ++i )
        ;
}
```

```
$ a.out
foo took 5.84 secs.
```

The purpose of this program is to show how execution of `foo` can be timed. The first call to `clock` sets the baseline.[†] The function `foo` is then called. When it returns, `clock` is called again and the result assigned to `cputime`. This represents the number of CPU microseconds used since the first call to `clock` was made. By dividing this number by 10^6, you obtain the number of seconds taken to execute `foo` (displayed to two decimal places).

---

† Note that the return types of the routines described in this section may be declared in the header file `time.h`. Check your system to see if this is the case. If they are declared there, then you won't have to declare them yourself.

`ctime`

If you're simply interested in getting the date and time in a format suitable for printing at the top of a report, for example, then `ctime` is the function to use. Before you can use it, however, we must take a slight diversion to discuss how the time is internally represented on the UNIX system.

All dates and times on the UNIX system (like the last modification time of a file or the current clock time) are represented as a long integer value. This long integer expresses that date and time in terms of the *number of seconds since midnight, January 1, 1970*. This is the "creation" date of the UNIX system. Therefore, since 0 represents January 1, 1970, and there are

$$60 \text{ sec/min} \times 60 \text{ min/hr} \times 24 \text{ hr/day} = 86{,}400 \text{ sec/day}$$

the value 86,400 would therefore represent 0:00:00, January 2, 1970.

In order to obtain the current date and time from the system, you have to call a Section 2 routine named `time`. This function takes an argument that is a pointer to a long integer where the current date and time is to be stored. This same value is also returned by the function, so you can also supply a null pointer if you just want to use the return value and don't want it stored anywhere.

Once you have obtained the date and time from the system, you'll probably want to convert it into a more manageable format. `ctime` does just that:

Program 3-15

```
/* Print date and time using ctime */

#include <time.h>

main ()
{
    long  time (), now;
    char  *ctime ();

    time (&now);
    printf ("It's now %s\n", ctime (&now));
}
```

```
$ a.out
It's now Sat Aug  8 07:03:50 1987
```

`time` stores the current date and time in the variable pointed to by its argument (now). `ctime` also takes a *pointer* to a long integer representing the date and time. That value is converted to ASCII, and a pointer to the converted string is returned (that's why `ctime` has to be declared to return a character pointer).

This pointer is then handed to printf so that the results can be viewed. As you can see, ctime's format is similar to the output of the date command.

localtime and gmtime

These functions provide easy access to specific information about the current date and time. They do this by converting the long integer value returned by time into a data structure called tm, which is defined in the time.h header file. In fact, this is what that header file looks like:

```
struct tm {
    int    tm_sec;      /* time of day, seconds */
    int    tm_min;      /* time of day, minutes */
    int    tm_hour;     /* time of day, hours (24 hour clock) */
    int    tm_mday;     /* day of month (1-31) */
    int    tm_mon;      /* month of year (0-11) */
    int    tm_year;     /* year - 1900 */
    int    tm_wday;     /* day of week (Sunday = 0) */
    int    tm_yday;     /* day of year (0-365) */
    int    tm_isdst;    /* non-0 if DST in effect */
};
```

As you can see, there's quite a bit of information you can access. The members of the structure are self-explanatory. Just note that the month is an integer from 0 through 11, with January starting at 0; the year is represented as the actual year less 1900 (so 1987 is represented as 87); the days of the week are numbered 0 through 6, with 0 representing Sunday, 1 representing Monday, and so forth; tm_yday is the Julian date, where January 1 is day 0, through December 31, which is day 364 or 365 (leap year); and tm_isdst is nonzero if Daylight Savings Time is in effect.

On all UNIX systems, the time is internally expressed in Greeenwich Mean Time (GMT). To convert the time to a tm structure that expresses the date and time in accordance with your local time zone, use localtime; to convert it to a tm structure in GMT, use gmtime.

In the following program we're interested in writing the date in the familiar *mm/dd/yy* format. To do so, we convert the time returned by time into a tm structure in local time, and then access the appropriate members of the structure.

Both localtime and gmtime take as their argument a pointer to a long integer that represents the date and time as the number of seconds since January 1, 1970. They return pointers to a tm structure, where the converted data is placed.

Program 3-16

```
/* localtime -- print date in mm/dd/yy format */

#include <time.h>

main ()
{
    long int  time(), now;
    struct tm *tmstruct, *localtime();

    time (&now);
    tmstruct = localtime (&now);

    printf ("Today is %d/%d/%d\n", tmstruct->tm_mon + 1,
        tmstruct->tm_mday, tmstruct->tm_year);
}
```

```
$ a.out
Today is 5/8/87
```

The pointer returned by localtime is assigned to the pointer variable tmstruct. Then printf is called, with the appropriate members of the structure pointed to by tmstruct given as arguments (remember, you're dealing with a structure pointer here, so the -> operator is needed to access members of the structure). Since the month is represented as 0 through 11, one is added to the value to change it to a number from 1 through 12.

asctime, tzset, and Other Variables

asctime is used to convert a time expressed in a tm structure format into an ASCII string. The resulting format of the string is the same as that produced by ctime.

You can override the default time zone that is used by these functions with the tzset routine, or by setting an *environment variable* called TZ. Several external variables also provide access to the number of seconds that separate the current time zone from GMT as well as the name of the time zone. For more details, consult your manual under the heading **CTIME(3C)**.

• Group, Password, and Utmp File Processing •

getgrnam	gets group entry from /etc/group for specified group name
getgrgid	gets group entry from /etc/group for specified GID
getgrent	gets next group entry from /etc/group
setgrent	rewinds /etc/group file for subsequent processing with getgrent
endgrent	closes /etc/group file
fgetgrent	gets next group entry from specified stream
getpwnam	gets password entry from /etc/passwd for specified user name
getpwuid	gets password entry from /etc/passwd for specified UID
getpw	retrieves password file entry for specified UID (obsolete, shouldn't be used)
getpwent	gets next password entry from /etc/passwd
setpwent	rewinds /etc/passwd for subsequent getpwent calls
endpwent	closes /etc/passwd file
fgetpwent	reads password entry from specified stream
putpwent	writes password entry to specified stream
getutline	gets next utmp entry for specified device
getutid	gets next utmp entry of specified type
getutent	gets next entry from utmp file
setutent	rewinds utmp file
endutent	closes utmp file
pututline	writes utmp entry to file
utmpname	changes name of utmp file
ttyslot	finds index number of current user in /etc/utmp

The UNIX system maintains several master files that are certainly of interest to system administrators, and may be of interest to others as well. These files are /etc/passwd, /etc/group, and /etc/utmp. These files can be easily scanned (by users and administrators) or modified (by administrators) with the routines listed in this section.

Users of the UNIX system who are working on the same project may be put into the same *group* by the system administrator. Users can give access to one or more of their files to other users in the group by setting the appropriate access permissions on their files. In this way, only members of the group can read and/or write these files, while other users cannot. The routines listed above that contain the characters "gr" in their names (like `getgrnam` and `getgrgid`) are associated with processing of the group file. They are listed together in the manual under the heading **GETGRENT(3C)**

The `/etc/passwd` file is *the* master file on the UNIX system. Every user of the system will have an entry in this file. Each user's entry describes the user's name, password, user id number (UID), group id number (GID), home directory, and the name of the program to start up whenever the user logs in (the standard shell, `/bin/sh` is the default). The routines listed above that contain the characters "pw" in their names are associated with processing of the password file. With the exception of `getpw`, they are described in the manual on the page headed **GETPWENT(3C)**. `getpw` is an older function that may not be supported in future UNIX system releases; therefore, we advise against using it.

The file `/etc/utmp` is used by the `who` command to print out information about who logged in to what terminal and at what time. This file can be scanned and modified (once again, if you have write permission on the file) with the routines whose names contain the characters "ut." These routines are described under **GETUT(3C)**.

Since `/etc/passwd` is probably of most interest to both system administrators and regular users, and since the routines have consistent names and are used similarly, we'll talk only about the password file processing routines in this section.

The file /etc/passwd

`/etc/passwd` is a file that anyone on the system can read. Let's take a look at some typical lines from the file:

```
root:iUFcPQXyVNwK6:0:0:Admin(WH2244):/:
steve:TD.SnGT.bYxbg,M.IA:201:325:S LEVY (W514):/usr/steve:
pat:kdsjfkcn29ca8,L0j2:205:327:P WOOD (W552):/usr/pat:/usr/lbin/ksh
```

Each line from the file represents an entry. Each entry is divided into seven colon-delimited fields. The first field of the line is the user name. This field should be unique for each entry in `/etc/passwd`. The user name `root` is typically associated with a special user of the system—the *super-user*—who has access to any file on the system. The second entry is for a typical user called `steve`.

The second field in /etc/passwd is where the password for the user is kept. Don't worry, you can't make any sense of it because it's stored in an encrypted form (your password is never stored on the system in its unencrypted form.) After the thirteenth character in the password field there may be a comma. This comma can be followed by four characters known as your *aging* information. They describe whether or not you are allowed to change your password, and if so the minimum number of weeks that must elapse before successive changes, as well as the maximum number of weeks that must elapse before you will be required to change it again.† In case this information seems hard to decipher, it's because it's stored in a strange base: base 64! This base includes the digits 0-9, all of the upper and lowercase letters of the alphabet, and the special characters . and /. The special functions a64l and l64a in the Standard C Library exist solely for the purpose of converting numbers back and forth between long integers and base-64 character strings.

After the aging information, the next field in the password entry specifies the UID number. This number is generally a unique number assigned to you at the time your account is added to the system. File ownership is internally identified by the UID number. Whenever you execute an ls -l command, for example, ls looks up the UID number in /etc/passwd for each file you're listing and displays the corresponding user name as the file's owner.

After the UID field comes the group id (GID) number. This number identifies which group you belong to on the system. For each unique GID on the system, there should be a corresponding entry in the group file /etc/group that associates the GID with the name of the group, and provides other information about the group.

After the GID field comes a special field called the *comment* field. This field can contain strictly commentary information (like the user's full name) or can be used to store useful information that is needed by other programs (like the user's bin number if output is automatically sent to particular bins, or the user's account number for billing purposes).

After the comment field is the full path to the user's home directory. The shell automatically places the user in this directory whenever that user logs in.

Following the home directory field is a field that may or may not be filled in. If it's filled in, then it specifies the name of the program to be executed whenenver the user logs in. If it's empty, then the standard shell, /bin/sh, will be started automatically whenever the user logs in. This field is used for creating accounts on the system that run special programs (like network communication programs or programs that display system usage statistics) or for specifying an alternate shell to be used, like the Korn shell or the C shell.

Reviewing what we have discussed, the sample /etc/passwd entry for steve indicates his UID is 201, GID is 325, his home directory is /usr/steve, and he gets the standard shell on login.

---

† This information is described in more detail in [1] and [2].

The passwd Structure

Entries in the password file are described in terms of a data structure defined in the header file `pwd.h`. This structure, called `passwd`, contains members that correspond to the various fields in `/etc/passwd`. Here's what it looks like:

```
struct passwd {
    char  *pw_name;       /* login name */
    char  *pw_passwd;     /* encrypted pwd */
    int   pw_uid;         /* user ID */
    int   pw_gid;         /* group ID */
    char  *pw_age;        /* aging info */
    char  *pw_comment;
    char  *pw_gecos;
    char  *pw_dir;        /* home directory */
    char  *pw_shell;      /* startup program */
};
```

The field called `pw_gecos` is not used on most systems.

getpwnam

This function takes a single character string argument that specifies the name of a user on the system. It searches `/etc/passwd` for an entry corresponding to that user, converts it to a `passwd` structure format, and returns a pointer to the structure. If the specified user can not be found in `/etc/passwd`, the routine returns a null pointer.

Program 3-17, called `home`, takes a single command line argument which is presumably the name of a user on the system. The program then calls `getpwnam` to locate that user in the password file, and then displays that user's home directory.

After ensuring that a command line argument was typed, the program calls `getpwnam` to look up the user pointed to by `argv[1]` in `/etc/passwd`. The pointer returned by `getpwnam` is assigned to the `struct passwd` pointer variable `pwentry`. If this value is null, then no such user exists and an appropriate message is displayed. Otherwise, the lookup succeeded, so the user's home directory is obtained from the member `pw_dir` and is displayed.

Program 3-17

```
/*  Print home directory for user */

#include <pwd.h>

main (argc, argv)
int argc;
char *argv[];
{
    struct passwd *getpwnam(), *pwentry;

    if ( argc != 2 ) {
        printf ("Usage: home username\n");
        exit (1);
    }

    if ( (pwentry = getpwnam (argv[1])) == (struct passwd *) 0 )
        printf ("%s not in /etc/passwd\n", argv[1]);
    else
        printf ("home dir is %s\n", pwentry->pw_dir);
}
```

```
$ home steve
home dir is /usr/steve
$ home nosuch
nosuch not in /etc/passwd
```

getpwuid

This routine retrieves the first matching entry from /etc/passwd for the integer UID given as its argument. Like getpwnam, it converts the entry into a passwd structure and returns a pointer to it, or the null pointer if no such user with that UID exists on the system.

getpwent, setpwent, and endpwent

These routines provide access to all of the entries in /etc/passwd. getpwent is a function that takes no arguments but returns a pointer to the *next* entry from /etc/passwd. The first time it's called, it opens /etc/passwd and reads the first entry. From then on, it reads successive entries from the file. After the last entry has been read, it returns a null pointer.

If you want to reset the file pointer so that a subsequent call to `getpwent` starts from the beginning of the password file, you can call `setpwent`, which takes no arguments.

If you're done processing the password file, you can close it by calling `endpwent`.

The following function shows how sequential processing of the password file can be used to implement your own version of `getpwnam`:

```
/* using setpwent, getpwent and endpwent */

#include <pwd.h>

struct passwd *getpwnam (name)
char *name;
{
    static struct passwd  *passwd;
    struct passwd  *getpwent ();

    setpwent ();

    while ( (passwd = getpwent()) != (struct passwd *) 0 )
        if ( strcmp (passwd->pw_name, name) == 0 )
            break;

    endpwent ();
    return (passwd);
}
```

The function ensures that the password file is positioned at the beginning of the file by calling `setpwent`. Then it calls `getpwent` to retrieve the next entry from the file. If the pointer that's returned is nonnull, then the name given as the argument to `getpwnam` is compared to the user name retrieved from the password file. If they match, then the `break` terminates execution of the loop, at which point `/etc/passwd` is closed and a pointer to the matching entry is returned.

If `getpwent` returns a null pointer, then all entries have been read and the specified user does not exist in `/etc/passwd`. The password file is closed just the same, and the null pointer (the value that will be stored in `passwd` when the loop exits this way) is returned.

Note that the variable `passwd` must be declared static. If it's not, then the data stored in it may not be valid when the function returns, since space on the stack for automatic local variables is usually allocated when the function is entered and is deallocated when the function returns.

fgetpwent and putpwent

A system administrator may need to write programs to modify entries in /etc/passwd (for example, a program for managing and updating the password aging field). Since this file is so critical to proper operation of the system, modifying this file is not to be taken lightly. A technique that allows this file to be safely modified is outlined in [2]. The routine putpwent can be used to copy entries from the old password file to a temporary file. After the necessary changes have been made to the modified copy, the original copy of /etc/passwd can be replaced with the modified one (once again, check the referenced book for more details).

That concludes our discussions about these UNIX-specific routines. The next section will show how to write a program to verify someone's login password.

▪ Data Encryption ▪

crypt	performs password encryption given a key and two-character salt
setkey	sets the key for subsequent use with encrypt
encrypt	DES-encrypts/decrypts data

These routines give the programmer access to the National Bureau of Standards' (NBS) Data Encryption Standard (DES) algorithm for the encryption/decryption of data.

crypt

This routine returns a pointer to an encrypted password given a pointer to a two-character string called the *salt*, and a pointer to the password to be encrypted. crypt is the routine used by the login program to verify your typed-in password against your encrypted password stored in /etc/passwd. The special salt characters are used to make guessing someone's password more difficult. These salt characters are actually stored as the first two characters of your password entry in /etc/passwd.

Consider steve's password entry from before:

```
steve:TD.SnGT.bYxbg,M.IA:201:325:S. LEVY(WX5147):/usr/steve:
```

The salt characters are the characters TD, while the remaining characters up to the comma (.SnGT.bYxbg) are the encrypted password itself.[†]

---

† The salt characters increase the search space for someone attempting to find a password by scanning /etc/passwd. Encrypting a list of commonly used passwords and then searching /etc/passwd for a match won't work since the salt characters are encrypted together with the user's password to produce the encrypted password that is stored in the file. Therefore, the cracker would have to separately encrypt each password from the list with all possible two-character salts. See [2] for more details.

Whenever you log onto to the system, the following sequence occurs to validate your password:

1. You are prompted by the system to enter your user name and then your password.

2. The entry for your user name is found in `/etc/passwd`.

3. The first two characters of the encrypted password from this entry and the password you entered are given as arguments to `crypt`.

4. The encrypted password returned by `crypt` is compared to the one stored in `/etc/passwd`. If they match, you're allowed to log on; if they don't match, the message `Login incorrect` is displayed.

The following program prompts the user for a password and then compares the typed-in password against the one stored in the password file. If they match, the message `Proceed!` is displayed; if they don't match, the message `Incorrect password!` is displayed.

The program makes use of two other routines from the Standard C Library: `getlogin` and `getpass`. The former routine returns a pointer to a character string containing the name of the user executing the program.[†] The latter routine prompts the user for a password, turns off character echoing at the terminal, reads in the password, and returns a pointer to the entered password.

Program 3-18

```
/* Program to verify user's password */

#include <stdio.h>
#include <pwd.h>

main ()
{
    struct passwd *getpwnam (), *pwentry;
    char *username, salt[2], *typedpw, *crypt (), *getpass (),
        *getlogin (), *encryptedpw;

    /* get name of user */

    if ( (username = getlogin ()) == (char *) NULL ) {
        printf ("Error from getlogin\n");
        exit (1);
    }

    /* get user's entry from /etc/passwd */
```

---

† Be advised that this function can be fooled into thinking someone else is actually running the program. For more details, consult [2].

```
    if ( (pwentry = getpwnam (username)) == (struct passwd *) 0 ) {
        printf ("No passwd entry for %s\n", username);
        exit (2);
    }

    /* get password from user */

    if ( (typedpw = getpass ("Password: ")) == (char *) 0 ) {
        printf ("Not run a from terminal\n");
        exit (3);
    }

    /*
    ** use crypt to encrypt typed passwd
    ** and compare against password entry
    */

    salt[0] = * (pwentry->pw_passwd);
    salt[1] = * (pwentry->pw_passwd + 1);

    encryptedpw = crypt (typedpw, salt);

    if ( strcmp(encryptedpw, pwentry->pw_passwd) == 0 )
        printf ("Proceed!\n");
    else
        printf ("Incorrect password!\n");
}
```

```
$ a.out
Password: garbage
Incorrect password!
$ a.out
Password: stdc87
Proceed!
```

The pointer to the user's name as returned by getlogin is stored in the variable username. Then the program calls getpwnam to find that user in the password file. The pointer to the user's entry that is returned is stored in the variable pwentry.

Next, the program calls getpass to prompt for and read in the user's password. getpass uses its argument as the prompt message to be displayed. After displaying this prompt, the routine turns off character echo at the terminal so that all characters typed on the rest of the line by the user will not be displayed. When the user hits the *RETURN* key, getpass turns character echo back on and then returns a pointer to the entered password. `getpass` requires that the password be entered from a terminal (to prevent users from hard coding passwords into files). If the program's standard input is not coming directly from a terminal, then `getpass` returns a null pointer, in which case the program prints an appropriate message and exits.

Now we have to validate the user's typed-in password (pointed to by `typedpw`) against the encrypted password from the password file (pointed to by `pwentry->pw_passwd`). The first step is to extract the two salt characters from the password file entry and store them into a two-character array called `salt`. The statements

```
salt[0] = *(pwentry->pw_passwd);
salt[1] = *(pwentry->pw_passwd + 1);
```

do just this. As noted, `pwentry->pw_passwd` is a pointer to the user's encrypted password, and is of type pointer to `char`. Applying the indirection operator to the result gives the first character being pointed to. The next statement adds one to the pointer to retrieve the second character from the encrypted password.

After setting up the `salt` array, the `crypt` routine is called to encrypt the typed-in password. The pointer to the encrypted password that is returned is stored in `encryptedpw`.

Next, `strcmp` is used to compare the two encrypted passwords. If they're identical, then `strcmp` will return 0, and the message `Proceed!` will be displayed. Otherwise, the message `Password incorrect!` will be displayed.

In the sample output, the user apparently entered an incorrect password the first time (the italics indicate what was typed—remember, nothing will be echoed at the terminal), and the correct password the second time.

`crypt` is useful not only for validating a user's login password, but can verify other types of passwords as well. For example, suppose you have written an interactive data base program, and many users can access the data base but only privileged users can do administrative tasks (like remove data from it or clean it up). In order to distinguish a privileged user from a nonprivileged one, you can require that the former type in a special password before he or she is granted administrative privileges.

You can hard code a password into your program, and then simply compare that password to the one that is entered:

```
int get_adminpw ()
{
    static char *passwd = "The_Boss";
    char typedpw[81];

    printf ("Administrative password: ");
    gets (typedpw);
```

```
    if ( strcmp (passwd, typedpw) != 0 ) {
        printf ("Incorrect password!\n");
        return (0);
    }
    else {
        printf ("Entering Admininstration Mode\n");
        return (1);
    }
}
```

The function get_adminpw is presumably called when the user wants to enter administration mode. The routine has hard-coded the password The_Boss. It then prompts the user for the password, reads it in with gets, and then simply compares the two passwords. If they don't match, a message is displayed and zero returned. If they do match, a message is displayed and one returned.

There are several drawbacks to this approach. First, getpass should be used instead of printf and gets so that character echo will be turned off when the user is entering his password. Second, the password is hard-coded into the program, meaning anyone with read permission on the file can potentially discover the password by scanning the source or object files for character strings. It's better to store an *encrypted* version of the password in the file so that the password doesn't exist anywhere on the system in its unencrypted form.

In order to create an encrypted password to hard code into your program, you have to write a small program.

Program 3-19

```
/* Create an encrypted password */

main ()
{
    char  *passwd, *getpass (), *encryptedpw, *crypt ();

    passwd = getpass ("Password to encrypt: ");
    encryptedpw = crypt (passwd, "Kw");
    printf ("%s\n", encryptedpw);
}
```

$ a.out
Password to encrypt: *The_Boss*
KwruQeo1V605k

The program has hard-coded the salt characters Kw. If you like, you can prompt for these as well.

The encrypted password that comes out of this program can now be hard-coded into a much-improved version of the `get_adminpw` function:

```c
int get_adminpw ()
{
    static char *passwd = "KwruQeo1V605k";
    char salt[2], typedpw[81], *encryptedpw;

    typedpw = getpass ("Administrative password: ");

    salt[0] = *passwd;
    salt[1] = *(passwd + 1);
    encryptedpw = crypt (typedpw, salt);

    if ( strcmp (encryptedpw, passwd) != 0 ) {
        printf ("Incorrect password!\n");
        return (0);
    }
    else {
        printf ("Entering Admininstration Mode\n");
        return (1);
    }
}
```

Now if someone has read access to your source code or object files they won't be able to figure out the administrative password.

You should note that `crypt` only looks at the first two characters of its second argument. That means that the three statements

```c
salt[0] = *passwd;
salt[1] = *(passwd + 1);
encryptedpw = crypt (typedpw, salt);
```

can be replaced by

```c
encryptedpw = crypt (typedpw, passwd);
```

and the `salt` array eliminated entirely.

setkey and encrypt

These routines provide direct access to the DES encryption algorithm for encrypting/decrypting data. Unfortunately, their use is not so straightforward, and there's a fairly large amount of work you have to do to encrypt/decrypt data with these routines. However, if you need the safety afforded by DES encryption, it will be worthwhile.[†]

To encrypt some data in a file, you call `setkey` once with a character string that contains the *key* to be used for the subsequent encryption. Then the `encrypt` function is called to carry out the actual encryption. Here's where the work begins. `encrypt` only encrypts eight bytes of data at a time. Worse yet, it expects you to separate the eight bytes of data into its constituent bits and place those "bits" (either a zero or one value) into a 64-element array (so the first eight elements of the array will contain the first byte of the data, and so forth). This 64-element array is then passed to `encrypt` as the first argument. The second argument is the value zero, meaning that the data in the array is to be encrypted.

`encrypt` encrypts the data in the array in place. So when the encrypted array comes back, you've got to pack the bits together and then write the eight encrypted bytes out to a file. Then you start the process all over again with the next eight bytes to be encrypted.

Decryption of the data is similar. You call `setkey` initially, giving it the same key that was used to previously encrypt the data. Then you have to take the encrypted data eight bytes at a time. For each eight bytes, you must put the corresponding bits into a 64-element array, and pass the array as the first argument to `encrypt`. A nonzero value as the second argument instructs `encrypt` to decrypt the data in place. The resulting decrypted data must be repacked into eight bytes and then written out.

Rather than showing the code to DES encrypt/decrypt a file, you're respectfully referred to [2], which contains the complete source code for such a program.

▪ Process Control and Information ▪

`getlogin`	returns name associated with login terminal
`isatty`	TRUE if file is associated with a terminal
`ttyname`	returns terminal name
`getenv`	gets value of environment variable
`putenv`	sets value of environment variable
`sleep`	suspends execution for specified number of seconds
`getopt`	returns next matching option letter from argument vector

† The UNIX `crypt` command can be used to encrypt data but the algorithm used for the encryption is not as secure as that provided by DES.

`longjmp`	restores environment saved by last call to `setjmp`
`setjmp`	saves stack environment for later use by `longjmp`
`gsignal`	generates specified software signal
`ssignal`	sets action to be taken upon receiving specified software signal
`abort`	generates an IOT fault (normally aborts process)
`getcwd`	returns current working directory
`monitor`	controls execution profiling
`nlist`	gets entries from name list

These routines provide information about your process and also control over its execution. We won't describe all of the routines here; just those that are more commonly used or that we find particularly interesting. `getlogin` is familiar to you from the previous section.

getenv and putenv

The UNIX system maintains an *environment* for each process that is executed. This environment includes a list of variables and their associated values. These are not C variables that we're talking about here, but rather variables that are typically set by the UNIX system's shell. When you're programming in the shell, a variable becomes part of your environment when you export it. From that point on, any program subsequently executed can access the value of that variable. The routines `getenv` and `putenv` let you access your environment variables from inside a C program.

The `getenv` routine takes a character string as its argument. This string is the name of an environment variable whose value you want to access. The function returns a pointer to a character string that contains the value assigned to that variable, or a null pointer if the variable is not part of the current environment.

The following program shows how `getenv` is used to access the values of two commonly used environment variables, `PATH` (which contains a list of directories the shell searches when you type a command to execute) and `TERM` (which is usually set to your particular terminal type).

Program 3-20

```
/* getenv */

main ()
{
    char *value, *getenv ();

    value = getenv ("PATH");
    if ( value != (char *) 0 )
        printf ("%s\n", value);

    value = getenv ("TERM");
    if ( value != (char *) 0 )
        printf ("%s\n", value);
}
```

```
$ a.out
/bin:/usr/bin:/usr/lbin::
hp2621
```

From the example you see that the PATH of the user running the program is set to /bin:/usr/bin:/usr/lbin:: and the user's TERM variable is set to hp2621.

putenv allows you to add a variable to the current environment or to change the value of an existing one. Be aware, however, that changes to the environment can be carried down only to *child* processes, and will have no effect on the *parent* process.

In the next example, an environment variable DBDIR is set with putenv. getenv is then called to verify that the variable has been added to the environment. When the program has finished, you'll note that the variable is not known to the shell.

Program 3-21

```
/* putenv */

main ()
{
        char *getenv ();

        putenv ("DBDIR=/usr/steve/dbdir");
        printf ("%s\n", getenv("DBDIR"));
}
```

```
$ a.out
/usr/steve/dbdir
$ echo $DBDIR

$
```

The echo command verifies that DBDIR has no value when the program finishes execution. That's because the program is run as a child process of the shell, and therefore any changes made to the environment by the child disappear once the child finishes execution. Child processes are explained in greater detail in Chapter 5.

sleep

Sometimes you just want to kill some time in your program. For example, you may want to check periodically for something that's coming over the network. If you check once a minute, then you need to kill some time during each minute. Rather than executing a loop to consume time—which will unnecessarily also use CPU time—you can call the sleep function to ask that your process be *suspended* for a specified number of seconds. While your program is suspended, other processes on the system can run. As soon as your specified time period is up, your program will be automatically awakened and continued. For example, the call

```
sleep (60);
```

will suspend execution of your program for 60 seconds. Note that only full second increments can be specified; sleep takes an integer argument. The statements

```
tries = 0;

while ( ! check_file ()   &&   tries++ < 60 )
        sleep (60);
```

will cause the check_file function to be called once a minute until either the function returns a nonzero value (indicating that the file exists, for example), or until one hour has elapsed.

getopt

This function is for command line processing. It allows you to write UNIX-style commands and easily process the arguments and options to the command.

In order to use getopt to process your command line, you have to follow these conventions:

1. Command *options* are a single character preceded by a dash (e.g., -o).

2. If an option can be followed by an argument, then that argument must always be specified. A space is not needed between the option and its argument (so -o outfile or -ooutfile are both acceptable). Options can also be specified in any order.

3. Options can be "stacked"; that is, a single dash can precede a set of option letters (e.g., -wc is the same as writing -w -c). Only the last option in such a stacked list can be followed by an argument (e.g., -ro outfile is the same as -r -o outfile).

4. After all of the options (and respective arguments) have been listed on the command line, other arguments (like filenames) can follow.

The wc command is an example of a command that follows this format. As you know, wc takes three options: -w to count words, -c to count characters, and -l to count lines. Anything listed after the options is treated as a filename. Thus

```
wc -l -w /etc/passwd
wc -lw /etc/passwd
wc /etc/passwd
wc -w /usr/steve/docs/memo*
```

are all valid command lines, whereas

```
wc /etc/passwd -w
```

is not valid, since the options must precede the file names and

```
wc -x /etc/passwd
```

is also not valid, since -x is not a recognized option.

Let's see how to put getopt to work. For this example, let's suppose you are the one writing the UNIX cb command. This command automatically formats C programs so that they look nice. Its general format looks like this:

```
cb  [-s]  [-j]  [-l length]  [files...]
```

(Note that this is the System V version of cb). cb takes the files listed (or standard input if none are specified) and formats them in typical C programming style, writing the results to standard output. For example, given this input in the file ctest.c:

```
main () { int i;  i=0;while(i<10){printf("%d\n",i);++i;}}
```

here's the output after typing the command `cb ctest.c`:

```
main () {
    int i;
    i=0;
    while(i<10){
        printf("%d\n",i);
        ++i;
    }
}
```

(As you can see, this program is a boon to lazy programmers!)

The `-s` option tells `cb` to format the program along the coding styles of Kernighan and Ritchie's *The C Programming Language* (Prentice-Hall, 1978). The `-j` option says to join lines that are split where possible (normally `cb` will honor all of your line breaks). Finally, the `-l` option must be followed by a number that tells `cb` to break lines longer than that many characters.

Let's now see how we can write the code necessary to process the `cb` command line. First, you should know that `getopt` takes three arguments: the first is the argument count, the second is the argument vector, and the third is a character string that describes all of the valid options.

The first two arguments to `getopt` are usually the variables which are passed to `main` on startup: `argc` and `argv`. The third argument simply contains the option letters that are to be recognized by `getopt`. An option that takes an argument is followed by a colon. So the string `"sjl:"` would be used in our example, since `cb` takes options `-s`, `-j`, and `-l`, the last of which must be followed by an argument.

`getopt` is like the function `strtok` in that it must be called repeatedly to process successive command line arguments. It returns a character representing the next option recognized from your argument vector, the character `?` if it encounters an unknown option, or the value `EOF` (defined in the header file `stdio.h`) if it is done processing your arguments. This last event occurs either when there simply aren't any arguments left in your argument vector or when it encounters a value that's not preceded by a minus sign. (As noted, any arguments to your program that aren't option arguments must *follow* the options on the command line.) When `getopt` stops processing, it's up to you to take over and process the remaining arguments (if any) from the line.

When `getopt` matches an option that is followed by an argument, it returns the option letter matched, as noted, and also sets a globally defined character pointer variable called `optarg` pointing to the argument. The value of `optarg` should be stashed away in your program somewhere for later use.

`getopt` also keeps track of how far it has progressed in processing of your argument vector through the global `int` variable `optind`. This variable can be of use to you when you have to process the remaining command line arguments—it tells you precisely where `getopt` left off.

Finally, getopt automatically prints an error message when it encounters an option that it doesn't recognize or when it finds an option that's supposed to be followed by an argument yet isn't. You can disable this automatic error message generation by setting the global int variable opterr to a nonzero value.

Enough talk—let's take a look at a segment of the main program that will process cb's command line arguments:

Program 3-22

```
/* command line processing with getopt */

#include <stdio.h>

main (argc, argv)
int argc;
char *argv[];
{
    extern char    *optarg;
    extern int     optind;
    int            sopt = 0, jopt = 0, error = 0, c;
    long           length = 0;

    while ( (c = getopt (argc, argv, "sjl:")) != EOF )
        switch (c) {
            case 's':
                sopt = 1;
                break;
            case 'j':
                jopt = 1;
                break;
            case 'l':
                length = atol (optarg);
                if ( length <= 0 )  {
                    printf ("bad length!\n");
                    error = 1;
                }
                break;
            case '?':
                error = 1;
                break;
            default:
                printf ("bug\n");
                exit (1);
        }
```

```
        if ( error ) {
                printf ("Usage: mycb [-s] [-j] [-l len] [file...]\n");
                exit (2);
        }

        /*
        ** now format files left in argv or standard input if
        ** none specified (i.e., if optind == argc)
        */


}
```

Since the program needs to access the global `optind` and `optarg` variables, appropriate `extern` declarations are made in the program.

The variables `sopt` and `jopt` are flags initially set to zero. They're set to one if the respective `-s` or `-j` option is specified on the command line. The `long int` variable `length` is used both as a flag (with an initial value of zero) and to store the line length that is specified when the `-l` option is chosen.

The `while` loop calls `getopt` until the function returns the value `EOF`. The value that it does return is stored in the `int` variable `c`[†], and if it's not equal to `EOF`, the `switch` is executed.

The `switch` tests the value returned by `getopt`. If it's equal to the character `s`, then that means that the `-s` option was selected on the command line. In that case, the `sopt` variable is set to one. If the character is `j`, then the variable `jopt` is set to one. If the character is `l`, then the argument pointed to by `optarg` is converted to a `long int` with the help of `atol`. The result is stored in the variable `length`, whose value is then tested. If it's less than or equal to zero, then the program issues an error message and sets the flag variable `error` to one.

If `getopt` returns the character `?`, then that means the user selected an illegal option (like `-x`). In that case, `getopt` will automatically print a diagnostic message. The program then simply sets the `error` flag to one, to record the fact that an error occurred.

When the `while` loop exits, the `error` variable is tested. If it's not zero, then an error occurred. In that case, proper usage information is displayed and the program exits.

If no errors occurred in processing the command line, then the following will be true:

1.   The variable `sopt` will be equal to one if the `-s` option was specified.

2.   The variable `jopt` will be equal to one if the `-j` option was specified.

---

† This variable *must* be declared to be an `int` and not a `char`. The reason is the same as for the value returned by `getchar`, and is deferred until the next chapter where it is treated in detail.

3.   The variable `length` will be set to a nonzero value if the `-1` option was selected and was followed by a value greater than zero.

4.   The global variable `optind` will have as its value the index number of the argument in `argv` that caused the scan to terminate. If this value is equal to the total number of entries in `argv` (i.e., if it's equal to `argc`), then all of the command line arguments have been processed. That means that the user did not specify a file name and the program should read and format a C program from standard input. If `optind` is not equal to `optarg`, then some arguments remain in `argv`. Presumably, these are the names of the files to be formatted.

The example program can actually be executed to see how it works with sample command lines. We'll assume here that the program is named `mycb` and not `cb` (to avoid conflict with the standard UNIX command).

```
$ mycb -s -j ctest.c
$ mycb -js ctest.c ctest2.c
$ mycb -x
mycb: illegal option -- x
Usage: mycb [-s] [-j] [-l len] [file...]
$ mycb -l 72 ctest.c
$ mycb -l
mycb: option requires an argument -- l
Usage: mycb [-s] [-j] [-l len] [file...]
$ mycb -s -l0 ctest.c
bad length!
Usage: mycb [-s] [-j] [-l len] [file...]
$ mycb
$ mycb -s ctest.c -j
$
```

The first two examples select the `-s` and `-j` options. In the first case, `optind` will be equal to three when `getopt` encounters `ctest.c`, which will terminate its scan. Since this value won't be equal to `argc` (which will have a value of four), the program will know that there's a file name to be processed in `argv[3]`.

In the second example, `optind` will be equal to two when `getopt` returns EOF. `argc - optind` will have the value two, meaning that two file names remain to be processed by the program (in `argv[2]` and `argv[3]`).

The third example shows the error message that `getopt` displays when it encounters an invalid option letter.

The next two examples illustrate processing of option letters followed by arguments. In the second case, no argument follows `-l` on the command line, so `getopt` complains.

The command

```
mycb -s -10 ctest.c
```

specifies a value of zero as the length, which the program detects and reports.

The next to last example shows that giving this program no arguments at all is valid use (no options are selected and standard input is to be formatted).

The last case shows that getopt is not perfect. Once again, remember that getopt stops processing your command line when it encounters something other than a dash-prefaced option (possibly followed by an argument). So here getopt stops when it hits ctest.c, leaving optind set to two. Your program will then think that it has two files to format: ctest.c and -j. The same sort of thing happens to other commands that rely on getopt. For instance, if you type

```
wc -c /etc/passwd -l
```

wc will try to count the characters in the files /etc/passwd and -l!

setjmp and longjmp

As you may know, whenever you execute a goto in C (and hopefully it's something you don't do very often), the target of the goto has to be a label located in the same function as the goto. There's no way to branch directly to a label defined in a different function. The function pair setjmp and longjmp do implement such a capability. setjmp "marks" a particular spot in your program, and longjmp can be called from anywhere to make an immediate branch to such a marked location.

You may want to resort to using setjmp or longjmp in the following circumstances:

1. You detect an error in a deeply nested function and want to branch back several levels (e.g., back to main) to continue processing.

2. Your program receives an interrupt (see signal described in detail in Chapter 5), and after processing the interrupt you want to branch to a specified location in your program.

To use setjmp and longjmp, you include the header file setjmp.h in your program. Inside that header file a special data type called a jmp_buf is defined. In order to mark your spot as the subsequent target of a longjmp call, you call setjmp, supplying as its argument a variable declared to be of type jmp_buf. The function returns the value zero to tell you that the spot has been marked. When you need to branch to that marked spot, you call longjmp, giving it two arguments: the first is the jmp_buf variable that was used to mark the spot with setjmp, and the second is an integer that must have a nonzero value. Now here's the tricky part. longjmp returns the value that you specify as the second argument. But it returns it *indirectly* through setjmp. In other words, setjmp returns a value of zero when it's called to mark the spot. It returns a nonzero value when it's returning through a longjmp call. So setjmp is actually called once yet returns twice: once when you mark the spot, and again when you call longjmp. The actual spot you're marking is therefore the point where setjmp returns.

An example will best illustrate the operation of setjmp and longjmp. This is shown in Program 3-23.

The global jmp_buf variable env is defined (it's a good idea to make this variable global rather than passing it down the line to any function that may want to execute a longjmp). Inside main a local integer variable called i is declared and given an initial value of 1. The purpose of this variable is to illustrate the effect that longjmp has on the values of variables.

The checkpoint messages are included in this program so that you can trace its execution. The first checkpoint message is followed by an if statement that begins

```
if ( setjmp (env) != 0 ) {
```

This calls the setjmp function to mark the spot for a subsequent longjmp call. The jmp_buf variable env is used by setjmp to record the current state of your environment. After that's done, the function returns the value zero, which causes all of the statements in the block that follows the if to be skipped.

Next, the variable i is assigned the value two, and its value is displayed, followed by the second checkpoint message. This, in turn, is followed by a call to the function foo1.

The foo1 function prints checkpoint 3 and then calls foo2. foo2 prints checkpoint 5 and then executes an unconditional longjmp call (in practice this will be based upon some condition occurring, like an error or an interrupt). The argument to longjmp is the jmp_buf variable env which tells longjmp where to branch to. The second argument (which must be nonzero) is the value to return. longjmp will then return immediately to the marked spot, which, as you'll remember, will be precisely at the point where the setjmp function returns:

```
if ( setjmp (env) != 0 ) {
```

This time, setjmp returns the value given to longjmp, or one in this case. Realize once again that setjmp is returning twice: once with a value of zero when the spot was marked and again when the branch was made via a call to longjmp.

Program 3-23

```
/* setjmp and longjmp  */

#include <setjmp.h>

jmp_buf env;

main ()
{
    int    val;
    int    i = 1;

    printf ("checkpoint 1\n");

    if ( setjmp (env) != 0 ) {
        printf ("longjmp call made\n");
        printf ("i = %d\n", i);
        exit (1);
    }

    i = 2;
    printf ("i = %d\n", i);
    printf ("checkpoint 2\n");
    foo1 ();
    exit (0);
}


foo1 ()
{
    printf ("checkpoint 3\n");
    foo2 ();
    printf ("checkpoint 4\n");
}


foo2 ()
{
    printf ("checkpoint 5\n");
    longjmp (env, 1);
    printf ("checkpoint 6\n");
}
```

```
$ a.out
checkpoint 1
i = 2
checkpoint 2
checkpoint 3
checkpoint 5
longjmp call made
i = 2
$
```

Since the value returned by setjmp is nonzero, the body of the if is executed. This displays the message longjmp call made followed by the value of i. Notice here that i has the value two, and not one. That's the value it had at the time that the longjmp call was executed. In general, the value of any variable is the value it had when the longjmp was executed, not the value that it had when setjmp was called.

The program then exits, although it's not necessary to do so. Typical applications might continue processing. For example, suppose you have written an interpreter and detect an error on an input line way down in some function. You can execute a longjmp call to dig yourself out, and then continue processing with the next input line.

You should note that longjmp leaves the stack okay. Therefore, even if you have your functions very deeply nested, longjmp will clean things up on the stack when the branch is made.

You can mark different locations in your program to branch to simply by calling setjmp at each such location, using a different jmp_buf variable for each call. Just give the corresponding variable as the argument to longjmp to branch to your required spot.

You can also execute several different longjmp calls, each with the same first argument, to return to the same spot. By using a different value as the second argument in each case, you'll be able to determine which longjmp branch was made.

Finally, be advised that like the infamous goto, setjmp and longjmp are easily abused routines and can result in programs that are hard to follow. Use them only when they're really needed.

• Tables and Trees: Sorting, Searching, and Managing •

bsearch   performs a binary search of a sorted table

hcreate   allocates space for hash table

`hdestroy`	destroys hash table
`hsearch`	finds (and optionally adds) an entry in a hash table
`lfind`	performs a linear search of a table
`lsearch`	performs a linear search of a table, and adds data if not found
`qsort`	performs a quick-sort
`tdelete`	deletes a node from a binary tree
`tfind`	searches a binary tree
`tsearch`	searches a binary tree, adding the data if not found
`twalk`	traverses a binary tree

These routines allow you to work with more sophisticated data structures like binary trees and hash tables. The function `bsearch` can be used to perform a binary search on a sorted table that contains *any* type of data. The routines that begin with the letter 'h' allow you to create, search and destroy hash tables. The routines that begin with the letter 'l' perform linear searches of tables, with `lsearch` automatically adding the data to the table if it's not found. Finally, the routines that begin with the letter 't' allow you to create, search, maintain and destroy binary trees. In this section, we'll just take a closer look at the `qsort` function, which can be used to sort an array of data of any type.

qsort

This function does a "quick sort" of your data. It takes four arguments: the first is a pointer to the start of the table to be sorted (and if this points to anything but a character then it should be type cast into a character pointer); the second argument is the number of elements in the array; the third argument specifies the size of each such element (use the `sizeof` operator here to keep it machine independent); and the fourth argument to `qsort` is a pointer to a function that returns an `int`. This function must be supplied by you and is called whenever `qsort` needs to compare two elements in your array. It calls the function with pointers to the two elements to be compared. Your function must then compare the two elements and return a value less than, equal to, or greater than zero based upon whether the first element is less than, equal to, or greater than the second element.

Here is a small sample program showing how `qsort` can be used. In this example, `qsort` is called to sort an array of 10 integers.

Program 3-24

```
/* qsort */

main ()
{
    int compareint (), i;
    static int data[10] =
        { 77, 10, 5, 6, 33, 2, -1, 19, 0, -4 };

    qsort ((char *) data, 10, sizeof (int), compareint);

    for ( i = 0; i < 10; ++i )
        printf ("%d ", data[i]);

    printf ("\n");
}


int compareint (i1, i2)
int *i1, *i2;
{
    if ( *i1 < *i2 )
        return (-1);
    else if ( *i1 == *i2 )
        return (0);
    else
        return (1);
}

$ a.out
-4 -1 0 2 5 6 10 19 33 77
```

Inside `main`, `compareint` is declared to be a pointer to a function that returns an `int`. You'll recall that this declaration is needed even though the function returns an `int`, since we will be creating a pointer to it later in the program by writing its name without any following parentheses.

The static array `data` is declared and set equal to 10 arbitrary values. Then the `qsort` function is called with the statement

```
qsort ((char *) data, 10, sizeof (int), compareint);
```

The first argument is a pointer to the start of the array to be sorted. As noted, this pointer should be turned into a "generic" pointer by typecasting it to a character pointer.

The second argument is the number of elements in the array, followed by the size of each element. The last argument is a pointer to a function that returns an `int`.

The `compareint` function is defined to take two arguments, `i1` and `i2`, which are *pointers* to integers. Remember, `qsort` passes pointers to the elements to your function and not the actual elements themselves.

The integer pointed to by `i1` is compared to the integer pointed to by `i2`. If the former is less than the latter, -1 is returned; if the two are equal, 0 is returned; and if the former is greater than the latter, 1 is returned. If you invert these values (i.e., return 1 if the first is less than the second, 0 if they're equal, and -1 if the first is greater than the second), then `qsort` will end up sorting your data in *descending* order, as opposed to *ascending* order as it does here.

Let's see how `qsort` can be used to sort an array containing more complex data, like the `date` structures that we defined in the last chapter. First, recall what a `date` structure looks like:

```
struct date {
    int   month;
    int   day;
    int   year;
};
```

Suppose you want to sort an array called `birthdays` that contains 100 such `date` structures and is declared as follows:

```
struct date birthdays[100];
```

The call to `qsort` is straightforward:

```
qsort ((char *) birthdays, 100, sizeof(struct date), compdates);
```

The only tricky part here is writing the comparison function `compdates` to compare two dates. We'll assume we want the dates sorted in chronological order. So the function should return a value less than zero if the first date is chronologically less than the second, equal to zero if the two dates are equal, and greater than zero if the first date is chronologically greater than the second. Here's such a comparison function:

```
int compdates (d1, d2)
struct date *d1, *d2;
{
    long l1 = d1->year * 10000 + d1->month * 100 + d1->day;
    long l2 = d2->year * 10000 + d2->month * 100 + d2->day;

    if ( l1 < l2 )
       return (-1);
    else if ( l1 == l2 )
       return (0);
    else
       return (1);
}
```

Rather than comparing the two date structures pointed to by d1 and d2 member by member, the function converts the two dates into long integers l1 and l2. Then l1 and l2 are compared. If l1 is less than l2, then the date pointed to by d1 must be less than the date pointed to by d2, so the value -1 is returned. If l1 and l2 are equal, then the two dates are equal, so the value 0 is returned. Otherwise, the date pointed to by the d1 must be greater than that pointed to by d2, so the value 1 is returned. It's left as an exercise for you to verify that the logic of this function works as described.

Although not described here, bsearch—which performs a binary search of an array of sorted data—is so similar in operation to qsort (it only takes one extra argument, which is the item you're searching for in the table), that you should be able to figure out how to use it simply by looking under **BSEARCH(3C)** in your manual.

▪ Random Numbers ▪

rand	returns random number (see srand)
srand	resets random number generator to random starting point (see rand)
drand48	returns nonnegative floating point random number in range [0,1)
erand48	returns nonnegative floating point random number in range [0,1) (needs arg)
irand48	returns nonnegative long random number in range [0, arg-1] (for use on machines without floating point)

`jrand48`	returns long random number in range $[-2^{31}, 2^{31})$ (needs arg)
`krand48`	returns nonnegative long random number in range [0, arg-1] (needs arg; for use on machines without floating point)
`lcong48`	initializes 48-bit value, multiplier, and addend value for random number generators
`lrand48`	returns nonnegative long random number in range $[0, 2^{31})$
`mrand48`	returns long random number in range $[-2^{31}, 2^{31})$
`nrand48`	returns nonnegative long random number in range $[0, 2^{31})$ (needs arg)
`seed48`	sets 48-bit seed for random number generators
`srand48`	sets initial seed for `drand48`, `lrand48`, or `mrand48`

As you can see, there are a large number of routines that can be used for generating random numbers. Basically, they're divided into two groups: `rand` and `srand`, and the routines whose last two characters are `48`.

srand and rand

These routines provide for seeding the random number generator (`srand`) and for generating a random number in the range from 0 to $2^{15}-1$ (`rand`). `rand` uses a "multiplicative congruential" algorithm, and according to the description in the manual, the random numbers that are generated leave "a great deal to be desired." Nevertheless, if you're not too concerned about how random your random numbers really are, these two routines are easy to use.

To seed the random number generator, you call `srand` with an integer argument. By default, the random number generator is automatically seeded to 1. Supplying the same seed each time your program is run will result in the same sequence of random numbers. Supplying a different seed each time will give different sequences. Of course, you can reseed the generator at any time during program execution by calling `srand`.

The following program takes a seed from the command line and generates 10 random numbers.

Program 3-25

```
/* srand and rand */

main (argc, argv)
int argc;
char *argv[];
{
    int  seed, i;

    seed = atoi (argv[1]);
    srand (seed);

    for ( i = 0; i < 10; ++i )
        printf ("%d ", rand());

    printf ("\n");
}
```

```
$ a.out 1
16838 5758 10113 17515 31051 5627 23010 7419 16212 4086
$ a.out 1
16838 5758 10113 17515 31051 5627 23010 7419 16212 4086
$ a.out 716
30371 12963 1711 4240 5312 20069 22481 11689 24252 25650
```

The program converts the string pointed to by argv[1] to an integer and supplies that as the seed to srand. rand is then called 10 times to generate 10 random numbers, whose values are displayed.

If you want to automatically seed the random number generator with a different value each time your program is executed, you can call a function like time that returns the current date and time as a long integer, typecast the result to an int, and give that as the argument to srand:

```
long int  time ();
    ...
srand ( (int) time ((long int *) 0) );
```

Recall that if the argument to time is a null pointer, then the resulting time is not stored but is simply returned.

The "*48" Routines

These functions are all grouped under **DRAND48(3C)** in the manual, and they generate random numbers that are "more random" than those generated by `rand`. They use a "linear congruential" algorithm and 48-bit arithmetic to generate the numbers. They also allow you to save the state of the random number generator so that the sequence can be continued at a later time. Another feature allows for multiple independent streams of random numbers to be generated.

The functions are well-documented in the manual, so we won't go into details here. However, if you're just interested in the simplest use of these routines, the following program shows how to call `lrand48` to generate five random numbers.

Program 3-26

```
main ()
{
    long   lrand48(), time ();
    int    i;

    srand48 (time ((long int *) 0));

    for ( i = 0; i < 5; ++i )
        printf ("%ld ", lrand48 ());
}
```

```
$ a.out
23111392 422561 433820718 1073 3332712
```

`srand48` takes a *long* integer as its argument to seed the random number generator. `lrand48` returns long random integers in the range $[0, 2^{31})$.

If you want double floating point random numbers, then use `drand48` instead. If you need long random numbers in the range $[-2^{31}, 2^{31})$, then use `mrand48`. Anything more sophisticated than that requires use of one of the functions that takes an argument. That argument for all but the `lcong48` routine is an array of three `short ints` that contains a 48-bit value (16-bits per element). Once again, for more details, consult your manual.

• Miscellaneous Routines •

abs	returns absolute value of an integer
dial	establishes a connection with a terminal line (with or without modem control)
frexp	floating point manipulation function
ftok	returns key for use with subsequent Inter-Process Communication (IPC) system calls
ftw	recursively descends a directory hierarchy
getpass	reads password from terminal
ldexp	floating point manipulation function
mktemp	creates temporary file name
modf	floating point manipulation function
perror	writes description of last error to standard error
swab	swaps pairs of bytes
undial	disconnects terminal connection established with dial

These routines are grouped here because they didn't seem to fit well under any of the other section headings. We'll talk about only two routines in this section: ftw, and perror. You'll recall that getpass was described in detail earlier in this chapter under the heading **Data Encryption**. mktemp is discussed briefly under **Temporary Files** in the next chapter.

ftw

The ftw function is useful for recursively descending your file system hierarchy. This *file tree walker* takes three arguments. The first specifies the name of a directory from which the descent is to begin. The second is a pointer to a function that returns an int. This user-supplied function is called for each and every file that ftw encounters while traversing your directory tree. The last argument to ftw is a number that specifies the maximum number of files that ftw can keep open while doing its thing. This integer should be between 1 and 17. The best choice is the maximum depth of your directory tree. In other words if you're asking ftw to start scanning from a directory that go three levels deep, then give the value 3 as the last argument. In any case, this value is only an optimization parameter, so a value of 1 will work in all cases. Just be aware that this value plus the number of open files you have (see the next chapter for more on this) cannot exceed 20.

As mentioned, the function that you specify as the second argument will be called by `ftw` every time a new file is visited. The function will be passed three arguments: the first a pointer to the name of the file that's being visited, the second a pointer to a special data structure—called a `stat` structure—that contains detailed information about the file, and the third an integer that tells a bit more about the file.

The `stat` structure—described in more detail in Chapter 5—tells you things like who owns the file (the UID number of the owner), its type, when the file was last modified, what its size is, and what its access permissions are. This structure is defined in the header file `ftw.h`, which should be included in your program whenever you use `ftw`.

The integer value that is the third argument passed to your function will have one of the values listed in Table 3-2. These identifiers are defined in `ftw.h`:

TABLE 3-2. ftw values

Value	Meaning
FTW_D	File is a directory
FTW_DNR	File is a directory, but you can't read it
FTW_F	File is a nondirectory file
FTW_NS	File could not be stated

The last value, `FTW_NS`, means that the `stat` system call failed for the file. This call is described in Chapter 5.

When your function has done whatever it wants to do with the file (which may be nothing), then it returns a zero or nonzero value. A zero value tells `ftw` to continue its scan; a nonzero value tells it that you've seen enough and you want it to stop (for example, you may have found a file you've been using `ftw` to locate).

Here is a program that recursively descends a directory specified on the command line. For each file that it visits, it simply displays some information about the file. The program is called `myfind`, and it is similar in operation to the `find` command with the `-print` option.

Program 3-27

```c
#include <ftw.h>

main (argc, argv)
int argc;
char *argv[];
{
    int prfile ();

    if ( argc != 2 ) {
        printf ("Usage: myfind dir\n");
        exit (1);
    }

    ftw (argv[1], prfile, 5);
}


int prfile (fname, statptr, flag)
char *fname;
struct stat *statptr;
int flag;
{
    switch (flag) {
        case FTW_F:
            printf ("%s\n", fname);
            break;
        case FTW_D:
            printf ("[%s]\n", fname);
            break;
        case FTW_DNR:
            printf ("[%s]: Can't read\n", fname);
            break;
        case FTW_NS:
            printf ("%s: Can't stat\n", fname);
            break;
    }

    return (0);
}
```

```
$ myfind /usr/steve
[/usr/steve]
[/usr/steve/foo]: Can't read
[/usr/steve/C]
/usr/steve/C/C.CPM
/usr/steve/C/casting
/usr/steve/C/init
/usr/steve/C/DEBUG
/usr/steve/C/Cbooks
/usr/steve/C/ANSI
/usr/steve/C/breaks
/usr/steve/C/course
/usr/steve/C/VMS.redir
[/usr/steve/UNIX]
/usr/steve/UNIX/FIEDLER
/usr/steve/UNIX/UNIXREVIEW
/usr/steve/UNIX/drivers
[/usr/steve/bin]
   . . .
```

After ensuring that a command line argument was typed, ftw is called:

```
ftw (argv[1], prfile, 5);
```

The first argument, argv[1], points to the name of the file that the scan is to start from. The second argument, prfile, is a pointer to a function that will be called for each file visited. The third argument, 5, is an estimate of the maximum depth of the directory tree.

Each time prfile is called, it's passed a pointer to the *full* path name of the file being visited. The function enters a switch to test the third argument to the function, the integer flag. If flag is equal to FTW_F, then the file being visited is a nondirectory file, in which case the function simply displays the name of the file. If flag equals FTW_D then the file is a directory, which causes the name of the file to be displayed inside a pair of brackets (just an added extra touch here). If flag equals FTW_DNR then the file is a directory that can't be read, so a message to that effect is displayed. Finally, if flag is equal to FTW_NS then ftw couldn't stat the file.

The function unconditionally returns 0 to tell ftw to continue its scan. In this case, ftw will continue until it gets to the bottom of the directory tree.

The example shows myfind executed with the argument /usr/steve. As you can see from the output, the program starts scanning from that directory, displaying files encountered along the way.

Other uses of ftw might be to check the owner or permissions of all files in your directory, or simply to look for a particular file. For example, suppose you're looking for the file fopen.c, which you know is somewhere on the system, but you're not sure where. You can start ftw from the root directory with the call

```
ftw ("/", checkfile, 10);
```

and you can supply the following function called `checkfile` to check for the file `fopen.c`:

```
int checkfile (fname, statptr, flag)
char *fname;
struct stat *statptr;
int flag;
{
    if ( strcmp (strrchr(fname, "/") + 1, "fopen.c") == 0 ) {
        printf ("The full path is: %s\n", fname);
        return (1);
    }
    else
        return (0);
}
```

Since `ftw` passes the full path name to the file, you just want to check the last file name (the *basename*) against `fopen.c`. `strrchr` is used to find the location of the last / in the path name, and one is added to the resulting pointer to point to the character right after the /. `strcmp` then compares the two file names. If they're equal, the file has been located. In that case, the full path to the file is displayed, and the function returns 1 to tell `ftw` to terminate its scan. If the two file names are not equal, 0 is returned so that `ftw` will continue scanning.

perror

This is an extremely useful routine in the Library. It can be used to obtain a description of the last error produced from a library call. `perror` takes as its argument a string to be displayed. If the argument is not a null pointer, the string is written to standard error, followed by a description of the error.

By convention, library routines that detect an error during execution set a globally defined integer variable called `errno` to a value that identifies the particular error. This value is an index into an array of error messages called `sys_errlist`. `perror` takes the value of `errno` and displays the corresponding message from this error list. Another global integer variable called `sys_nerr` tells `perror` the number of entries in the `sys_errlist` table (it's conceivable for a new error number to be created without a corresponding message being added to the `sys_errlist` table).

Here is how you could write your own version of `perror`. This will help you understand how the actual routine in the library works.

```
/* perror function */

#include <stdio.h>

void perror (msg)
char *msg;
{
    extern int    errno, sys_nerr;
    extern char   *sys_errlist[];

    if ( msg != (char *) 0 )
        fprintf (stderr, "%s: ", msg);

    if ( errno < sys_nerr )
        fprintf (stderr, "%s\n", sys_errlist[errno]);
    else
        fprintf (stderr, "Unknown error\n");
}
```

fprintf is described in detail in the next chapter. It works like printf, except it can be used to write to places other than standard output. Here it's used to write to standard error (also described in detail in the next chapter).

Always bear in mind that errno is only changed when an error occurs in a library routine, and is not reset by a successful library call. So perror should only be called after you have verified that an error has in fact occurred. This is usually done by checking the return value from the library routine:

```
iptr = (int *)  malloc (TABSIZE * sizeof (int));

if ( iptr == (int *) 0 ) {
    perror ("malloc");
    exit (1);
}
```

Here if the allocation of TABSIZE integers fails, then perror is called to describe the cause of the error.

Most of the functions described in this chapter don't return an error value, so perror is probably more useful with the routines described in Chapters 4 and 5.

By now you should have a good understanding of the types of functions that are provided in the Standard C Library. You should also be able to put them to work in your own programs. In the next chapter, we'll discuss in detail that part of the Standard C Library known as the Standard I/O Libarary.

• Function Summary •

Table 3-3 summarizes the functions described in detail in this chapter. Each entry in the table lists the function's return value, its arguments, required include files, and provides a brief summary of its use.

The following notations are used for depicting argument types in the table:

Argument	Type
c	char
env	jmp_buf
fp	int (*()) (pointer to function returning int)
i	int
l	long int
*l	long int *
s, s1, s2	char *
tm	struct tm
u, u1, u2	unsigned int

TABLE 3-3. Summary of Standard C Library Routines

Function	Description (Include File)
`long a64l (s)`	Convert s from base 64 to long
`int abs (i)`	Absolute value of i
`char *asctime (tm)`	Convert structure tm to string (`time.h`)
`double atof (s)`	Convert s to double
`int atoi (s)`	Convert s to integer
`long atol (s)`	Convert s to long
`char *calloc (u1, u2)`	Allocate u1 * u2 bytes of storage, initialized to zero
`long clock ()`	Return number of milliseconds of CPU time used since first call
`char *crypt (s1, s2)`	Encrypt key s1 using salt array s2
`char *ctime (*l)`	Convert time l to string (`time.h`)
`void endpwent ()`	Close /etc/passwd file (`pwd.h`)
`void free (s)`	Release previously allocated space pointed to by s
`int ftw (s, fp, i)`	Walk file tree starting at s, calling fp for each file (i approximates maximum depth) (`ftw.h`)
`char *getenv (s)`	Get variable s from environment
`char *getlogin ()`	Get name associated with login terminal
`int getopt (argc, argv, s)`	Scan argv for next option letter as specified in s
`char *getpass ()`	Read password from terminal
`struct passwd *getpwent ()`	Get next entry from /etc/passwd (`pwd.h`)
`struct passwd *getpwnam (s)`	Look up user named s in /etc/passwd (`pwd.h`)
`struct passwd *getpwuid (i)`	Look up userid i in /etc/passwd (`pwd.h`)
`struct tm *gmtime (*l)`	Convert time l to tm structure (`time.h`)
`int isalnum (c)`	TRUE if c is alphanumeric (`ctype.h`)
`int isalpha (c)`	TRUE if c is alphabetic (`ctype.h`)
`int isascii (c)`	TRUE if c is ASCII (`ctype.h`)
`int iscntrl (c)`	TRUE if c is a control char (`ctype.h`)
`int isdigit (c)`	TRUE if c is a digit char (`ctype.h`)
`int isgraph (c)`	TRUE if c is a graphic char (`ctype.h`)
`int islower (c)`	TRUE if c is a lowercase letter (`ctype.h`)
`int isprint (c)`	TRUE if c is a printable char (`ctype.h`)
`int ispunct (c)`	TRUE if c is a punctuation char (`ctype.h`)
`int isspace (c)`	TRUE if c is a space char (`ctype.h`)
`int isupper (c)`	TRUE if c is an uppercase letter (`ctype.h`)
`int isxdigit (c)`	TRUE if c is a hexadecimal digit char (`ctype.h`)
`struct tm *localtime (*l)`	Convert time l to local time (`ctime.h`)
`void longjmp (env, i)`	Jump to location specified by jmp_buf var env, returning i (`setjmp.h`)
`long lrand48 ()`	Return random number
`char *malloc (u)`	Allocate u bytes of storage
`char *memccpy (s1, s2, c, i)`	Copy chars from s2 to s1 until i chars copied or c encountered (`memory.h`)
`char *memchr (s, c, i)`	Locate first occurence of c in s, examining up to i chars (`memory.h`)
`int memcmp (s1, s2, i)`	Compare up to i chars in s1 and s2 (`memory.h`)
`char *memcpy (s1, s2, i)`	Copy i chars from s2 to s1 (`memory.h`)
`char *memset (s, c, i)`	Set first i locations of s to c (`memory.h`)
`void perror (s)`	Write s to standard error followed by description of last error
`int putenv (s)`	Set environment variable

`void qsort (s, u1, u2, fp)`	Sort array pointed to by s, containing u1 elements each u2 bytes in length, using function fp for comparison
`int rand ()`	Return random number
`char *realloc (s, u)`	Change size of storage pointed to by s to u
`int setjmp (env)`	Store state of environment in `jmp_buf` var env (`setjmp.h`)
`void setpwent ()`	Reset `/etc/passwd` file to beginning (`pwd.h`)
`unsigned sleep (u)`	Suspend execution for u seconds
`void srand (u)`	Seed random generator with u
`void srand48 (l)`	Seed random generator with l
`char *strcat (s1, s2)`	Copy s2 to end of s1 (`string.h`)
`char *strchr (s1, c)`	Find first occurrence of c in s1 (`string.h`)
`int strcmp (s1, s2)`	Compare s1 to s2 (returns < 0 if s1 < s2, =0 if s1 == s2, >0 if s1 > s2) (`string.h`)
`char *strcpy (s1, s2)`	Copy s2 to s1 (`string.h`)
`int strcspn (s1, s2)`	Count number of chars at start of s1 consisting entirely of chars not in s2 (`string.h`)
`int strlen (s)`	Number of chars in s, excluding null (`string.h`)
`char *strncat (s1, s2, i)`	Copy at most i chars from s2 to end of s1 (`string.h`)
`int strncmp (s1, s2, i)`	Compare at most i chars from s1 and s2 (see `strcmp`) (`string.h`)
`char *strncpy (s1, s2, i)`	Copy at most i chars from s2 to s1 (`string.h`)
`char *strpbrk (s1, s2)`	Find first occurrence in s1 of any char from s2 (`string.h`)
`char *strrchr (s1, c)`	Find last occurrence of c in s1 (`string.h`)
`int strspn (s1, s2)`	Count number of chars at start of s1 consisting entirely of chars in s2 (`string.h`)
`char *strtok (s1, s2)`	Parse s1 using token delimiters in s2 (`string.h`)
`int toascii (c)`	Convert c to ASCII (`ctype.h`)
`int tolower (c)`	Convert c to lowercase letter (`ctype.h`)
`int _tolower (c)`	Convert uppercase letter c to lowercase (`ctype.h`)
`int toupper (c)`	Convert c to uppercase letter (`ctype.h`)
`int _toupper (c)`	Convert lowercase letter c to uppercase (`ctype.h`)

• References •

[1]   S. G. Kochan and P. H. Wood, *Exploring the UNIX System*, Hayden Books, Indianapolis, IN, 1984.

[2]   P. H. Wood and S. G. Kochan, *UNIX System Security*, Hayden Books, Indianapolis, IN, 1985.

E X E R C I S E S

1.   The UNIX system's `basename` command gives the base file name of its argument:

```
$ basename /etc/passwd
passwd
$ basename /usr/spool/uucppublic/steve
steve
$ basename data
data
```

Write the `basename` command.

2.   Write the `strtok` routine described on page 104.

3.   Modify the `search` function from page 66 so that if the value is not found in the list, a new entry with the specified value gets created and added to the end of the list. Dynamically allocate space for the new entry. Write a `main` program to test the function.

4.   Modify Program 3-12 to allocate space as needed for the `linetab` array in increments of 100. That is, initially allocate space to hold 100 character pointers and increase the size of the space by 100 pointers as needed. (Hint: Use the `realloc` routine.)

5.   Write a program called `tomorrow` to calculate tomorrow's date:

```
$ date        What's today's date?
Tue Apr 14 18:10:37 EST 1987
$ tomorrow
Wed Apr 15 1987
```

Make sure that boundary conditions like the end of the month (including the end of February in a leap year) and the end of the year are properly handled.

6.   Using `getopt`, write a program that processes the command line options for the UNIX system's `nroff` command. Consult your manual for the available `nroff` options.

7.   Write a program to sort an array of `date` structures into reverse chronological order using `qsort`. Refer to the `compdate` function presented on page 153.

8.   Using the random number generation routines described in this chapter, write a program that simulates the throw of a pair of dice.

9.   Write a program called `findfile` that takes two command line arguments: a starting directory and the name of a file. The program should recursively descend the file system from the starting directory in search of the specified file. If the file is located, have the program display the full directory path to the file and then exit. Here is some sample usage:

```
$ findfile / passwd
/etc/passwd
$ findfile /usr/steve amort.c
/usr/steve/src/amort.c
$ findfile /usr/steve nosuch
nosuch not found
```

Be sure to use the `ftw` function described in this chapter.

4

THE STANDARD I/O LIBRARY

W e noted in the previous chapter that the Standard I/O Library is actually part of the Standard C Library. Routines in the *UNIX Programmer's Reference Manual* that are part of the Standard I/O Library are designated as 3S in the manual.

· Overview of the Standard I/O Library ·

What's in the Library?

Inside the Standard I/O Library you will find a set of routines that do the following:

- Perform I/O operations with standard input and standard output
- Perform I/O directly with files
- Perform random I/O operations on files
- Create temporary files
- Execute commands by the shell
- Control the buffer managing scheme
- Handle errors
- Obtain miscellaneous information

Individual sections in this chapter take a close look at the routines according to these categories.

Buffered I/O

The Standard I/O Library consists of routines that perform *buffered* I/O operations. Buffering is a scheme that prevents excessive access to a physical I/O device like a disk or a terminal. Since access to I/O devices is generally the bottleneck in most systems, the less access that has to be made to the devices, the better the system will run.

In a nonbuffered I/O scheme, access to the device is done each and every time an I/O request is made. For example, if you're reading characters from a file into your program one character at a time, and the I/O operations are *not* buffered, then each and every time you read a character the system has to go to the disk to fetch the next character from the file. This involves an enormous amount of overhead, not to mention the relatively long time required to position the disk head at the precise spot on the disk that the character is to be read from, and to read and transfer the actual character from the disk to your program.

In a buffered I/O scheme, the system uses more intelligence. Rather than going to the device each time a character is read, the system will read in a whole slew of characters (a *buffer full*) the first time you ask for a character. Subsequent requests for characters from the file will therefore be retrieved from the buffer sitting in the computer's memory instead of physically from the disk. Then, when you've read all of the characters from the buffer, the system will automatically go to the disk to read in the next buffer full.

Buffering can be done not only for reading data but for writing data as well. Rather than physically writing each data item to a device as requested, the system can stash the data in a buffer in memory and then wait until the buffer is full before actually transferring the data to the device.

So you see, buffering provides for more efficient operation of a system. The UNIX system buffers I/O operations automatically. The Standard I/O Library routines actually provide a second level of buffering that makes I/O operations even more efficient.[†]

Using the Library

Like the routines described in the previous chapter, nothing special has to be specified to the `cc` command to have a routine from the Standard I/O Library linked with your program.

The `stdio.h` Header File

Just about every function from the Standard I/O Library relies on the header file `stdio.h` (`printf` and `scanf` are notable exceptions). You should therefore include this file in your program. Inside `stdio.h` several things are defined, among them:

---

† This is discussed in more detail in the next chapter.

- The default *streams* stdin, stdout, and stderr
- The identifier NULL (defined as 0); this is returned by many I/O routines to signal an error condition (and in some cases end of file)
- The identifier EOF (defined as -1); this is used by routines that return an integer to signal an end of file condition (and in some cases to signal an error)
- The identifier FILE; this is needed to perform I/O operations explicitly on files

A stream as it is used in the manual is simply a file that is open and has buffering associated with it.

stdin, stdout, and stderr

Whenever your program begins execution, you get three streams predefined for you: stdin, stdout, and stderr. All three of these are associated with your terminal by default.

stdin is the place functions like scanf and getchar get their input from. stdout is where routines like printf and putchar write their output to. stderr is where your error messages are usually written to by the standard UNIX commands like ls.

So, technically speaking, whenever you call printf to write a line of output, that output goes to standard output, which is associated with your terminal by default. And whenever you call scanf to read some data, that data will be read from the standard input stream, which is once again associated with your terminal by default.

This fact allows you to take full advantage of I/O redirection and pipes when your program executes under UNIX. For example, if your program reads in some data using any routine that reads from standard input, then that program can be made to read its input from a file instead of your terminal by redirecting standard input when the program is executed:

```
$ a.out < data
```

Here the program a.out reads its input from the file data instead of from your terminal.

The same applies to output: any routine in your program that writes output to a terminal will instead write that output to a file if you redirect output when you execute the program:

```
$ a.out > results
```

Here the standard output from the program will be written to the file results.

Standard error output can also be diverted to a file by using the notation
2> *file*. If your program writes errors to standard error (and you'll see how to do
that later in this chapter), then you can collect those errors in a file by redirecting
standard error:

```
$ a.out 2> errors
```

(Note that no space is permitted between the 2 and the >, but one or more are
permitted after the >.) The error messages here will be written to the file
errors.†

Naturally, you can specify multiple redirections on the command line:

```
$ a.out < data > results 2> errors
```

This is a very powerful technique. Here you're directing the program to take its
input from the file data, write its output to results, and its error messages to
errors. All of this happens unbeknownst to the program itself; the UNIX system (actually the shell) takes care of the redirection before it even starts execution
of the program. So you can now write programs to read data from a file and
write data to a file without doing anything more than what you've been doing all
along. Unfortunately, sometimes you may have to read from two files at once,
write results to more than one output file, or open a file in your program explicitly by its name. In these cases, programming with standard input and standard
output won't suffice. Furthermore, to take advantage of standard error you have
to do a bit more than what you've been doing.

Now we're ready to examine more closely the routines in the Standard I/O
Library. A good place to start is those routines that deal with standard input and
standard output.

▪ I/O with Standard Input and Standard Output ▪

printf	writes formatted output to standard output
sprintf	"writes" formatted output to a buffer
scanf	reads formatted data from standard input
sscanf	"reads" formatted data from a buffer
getchar	reads a character from standard input (macro)
putchar	writes a character to standard output (macro)

---

† The number 0 is the "file descriptor" for standard input, 1 for standard output, and 2 for standard
error. This is discussed in more detail in the next chapter.

gets   reads a line from standard input

puts   writes a line to standard output, followed by a newline

As noted, each of these routines (with the exceptions of sprintf and sscanf) reads data from standard input and writes data to standard output by default.

printf

You are no doubt fairly familiar with printf by now. In this section we'll take a look at some of its options that you may not be aware of.

The general format of a printf call is

```
printf (format, arg1, arg2, ...)
```

where *format* is a character string that describes how the remaining arguments (if any) are to be displayed. Characters inside the format string that are not preceded by % signs are written literally to standard output. Otherwise, a % sign is followed by one or more characters that describe in what format the corresponding argument to printf is to be displayed. The % sign and the following format characters are referred to as *conversion characters* in this text.

In general, therefore, for each % sign there must be a corresponding argument to printf that is the actual value to be displayed (the exception is the conversion characters %% which cause a single percent sign to be displayed). The type of the value that is displayed must be consistent with the type specified by the conversion characters (that is, if you're asking printf to display a float, then you have to give it a floating point value, and not an integer or character).

As a simple example, the printf call

```
printf ("The answer is %d\n", result);
```

calls printf to literally display the characters "The answer is ", followed by the value of an integer, followed by a newline character. The integer value that is displayed is specified by the next argument to printf: the value of the variable result.

Although not generally used by programmers, you should note that printf returns a value: the number of characters that were written.[†]

Table 4-1 summarizes all of the type conversion characters that printf recognizes.

---

† If you use lint to check your programs, then you'll notice that it will complain about printf calls with a message like "function returns value that is always ignored." That's because, as noted, printf does return a value, which most programmers choose to ignore. In Chapter 8 you'll see how the typecast operator can be used to "shut up lint."

TABLE 4-1. printf type conversion characters

Char	Use for printing
d	integers
u	unsigned integers
o	octal integers
x	hexadecimal integers, using a-f
X	hexadecimal integers, using A-F
f	floating pt numbers
e	floating pt numbers in exponential format using e before exponent
E	floating pt numbers in exponential format using E before exponent
g	floating pt numbers in f or e format
G	floating pt numbers in f or E format
c	single characters
s	null-terminated character strings
%	percent signs

The first five type conversion characters listed in the table—d, u, o, x, and X—are all used for displaying integers. Since characters and short ints are automatically converted to integers when passed to functions, these conversion characters can be used to display these data types as well.

The conversion characters %u can be used to display an unsigned integer, or to force a signed integer to be displayed as unsigned. By default, integers printed in octal or hexadecimal notation do *not* have a leading 0 or 0x, respectively, displayed in front of them. However, a special printf conversion *modifier* that we'll describe shortly does allow you to do this.

The only difference between %x and %X is that the former displays integers in hexadecimal using the lowercase letters a-f, whereas the latter uses the uppercase letters A-F.

The second five conversion characters listed in the table—f, e, E, g, and G—are all used to display floating point values. Since floats are automatically converted to doubles when passed to functions, these conversion characters can be used to display either floats or doubles.

The %f characters display a floating point value to six decimal places rounded by default. The characters %e display a value in exponential (scientific) notation, with a six decimal place mantissa, followed by a signed exponent of at least two digits. The only difference between %e and %E is that the former puts a lowercase e in front of the exponent while the latter puts an uppercase E.

For displaying floats, %g is probably the most useful. Here printf chooses between displaying the value in %f or %e format. The criteria used is based upon the value being displayed and the number of significant digits specified (more on this shortly): If the exponent is less than -4 or greater than the specified significant digits (six is the default), then the value is automatically displayed in `%e` format; otherwise it's displayed in `%f` format. When `%g` format is used, the resulting output is even cleaned up a bit: trailing zeroes are not displayed (they normally are when using `%f` or `%e` format), and if no digit follows the decimal point, then it too is not displayed.

The difference between the `%g` and `%G` formats is that the first chooses between `%f` and `%e` and the second between `%f` and `%E`.

The `%c` format character displays a single character, as in

```
char   c = 'A';

printf ("%c\n", c);
```

Naturally, an integer can be supplied as well since that's what `printf` gets anyway. So

```
printf ("%c\n", 7);
```

displays the character equivalent of the value 7, which is the ASCII bell character (beeps most terminals).

The conversion characters `%s` are used to display a null-terminated character array. `printf` simply starts displaying characters from the array until it reaches the null. If you forget to stick a null at the end of the array, `printf` displays whatever values are sitting in memory after the the element in the array until it finds a null (or until it causes your program to terminate abnormally with a "Memory Fault" or some such error message).

As you'll see shortly, `%s` *can* be used to display character arrays that aren't null-terminated.

The last conversion characters in the table are `%%` which cause a percent sign to be displayed. So the statement:

```
printf ("%d%% markdown\n", discount);
```

will produce the output

```
20% markdown
```

if `discount` has the value 20.

The `printf` function provides you with far greater flexibility than what is afforded simply by selecting a particular conversion character. This is done by specifying one or more conversion *modifiers* between the `%` and the type conversion character. These modifiers allow you to do things like specify the number of decimal places, the width of the field, and whether to left- or right-justify the value.

The general format of a `printf` conversion specification looks like this:

`% [flags] [width] [.prec] [l] type`

Optional fields are enclosed in brackets, so you see that all but the leading % and the *type* specification are optional. Optional fields that are selected must appear in the order as shown.

The meanings of the various modifiers are summarized in Table 4-2.

TABLE 4-2. printf conversion modifiers

Modifier		Meaning
flags	– + *(space)* #	left justify value precede value with + or – precede positive value with space character precede octal value with 0, hexadecimal value with 0x (or 0X); display decimal point for floats; leave trailing zeroes for g or G format
width		minimum size of field; * means take next argument as field width
prec		minimum number of digits to display for integers; number of decimal places for e or f formats; maximum number of significant digits to display for g; maximum number of characters for s format; * means take next argument as size
l		display long integer
type		type conversion character

The – flag—which left-justifies a value—is explained under the description of the *width* field.

printf normally displays a leading minus sign in front of negative numbers, and nothing in front of positive ones. The + flag forces a plus sign to appear before positive numbers, whereas a space (as in % d) causes a space to appear before positive values (rather than nothing).

The # flag has a different meaning depending upon the *type* character that it precedes: before o (as in %#o), it forces a leading zero to precede the integer displayed in octal; in front of x, it forces a leading 0x to precede the hexadecimal value; before X, it forces a leading 0X to precede the number. When placed before f, e, E, g, or G, it forces the decimal point to be displayed (see the meaning of the *prec* modifier). Finally, in front of g or G, it causes both the decimal point and trailing zeroes to be displayed.

Normally, printf displays only as many characters as it needs to. However, the *width* field can be used to override this. In such a case, if printf needs fewer characters to display the value than are specified, the value will be right-justified in the field by default. Leading spaces will be inserted in the output to satisfy the field width requirement. If the – flag is specified, then the value will be left-justified in the field, with trailing spaces added to satisfy the field width. In any case, if the field width is too small to accommodate the value being displayed, then `printf` *ignores* the *width* specification and simply displays as many characters as necessary.

As an example of a width specification, the call

```
printf (":%6d:\n", 100);
```

tells `printf` to display the value 100 right-justified in a field width of six characters, resulting in the output

```
:   100:
```

(The colons were used to show you more precisely what is actually displayed.) Here three leading spaces are output by `printf` to satisfy the field width specification.

If you add the left-justify flag:

```
printf (":%-6d:\n", 100);
```

then the output looks like this instead:

```
:100   :
```

Here three spaces are added after the value to satisfy the field width specification.

And as discussed, if your field width specification is too small, as in

```
printf (":1d:\n", 100);
```

it is simply ignored:

```
:100:
```

When displaying integer values, you should note that the field width includes the leading minus sign if the value is negative. For floats, it also includes the decimal point. In the case of exponential format, the letter e (or E), the sign of the exponent, and the exponent itself are also counted.

Character strings can also be displayed left- or right-justified within a field by putting a field width specification before the s conversion character.

If you like, you can specify the field width through an argument to `printf`. To do this, put a * instead of a number in the *width* field, and supply the actual width as the corresponding argument to `printf`. For example, if the integer variable `width` is set to 10, then the call

```
printf ("%*d", width, result);
```

will display the value of `result` right justified in a field width of 10 characters, and the call

```
printf ("%-*d", width, result);
```

will display it left-justified in the same size field. Note that the width argument precedes the actual value being displayed in the argument list.

The *prec* modifier is a decimal point followed by an integer value. This specifies the precision of the value being displayed and, like the `#` modifier, its exact meaning depends upon the *type* character it's modifying.

In front of any integer conversion character, the precision field specifies the *minimum* number of digits to display. If fewer digits are actually needed, then the number is padded with leading zeroes. So the call

```
printf ("%.6d\n", 100);
```

gives the following output

```
000100
```

In front of `f`, `e`, or `E` conversion characters, the *prec* modifier gives the number of decimal places to display the result to. The value is automatically rounded to the specified number of decimal places. So the call

```
printf ("%.2f\n", 100.1493);
```

produces this output

```
100.15
```

If the *prec* modifier is used in front of `g` or `G`, then it specifies the maximum number of significant digits to display.

Putting a precision modifier in front of the `s` conversion character causes only up to the specified number of characters to be displayed from the character string. Fewer are displayed if the null character is encountered first. So the call

```
printf ("%.4s\n", "abcdefghi");
```

says to display just the first four characters from the string, producing the output

```
abcd
```

This precision modifier is particularly useful for displaying character arrays that aren't null-terminated. For example, if `days` is an array defined as follows:

```
static char days [7][3] = {
    { 'S', 'u', 'n' },
    { 'M', 'o', 'n' },
    { 'T', 'u', 'e' },
    { 'W', 'e', 'd' },
    { 'T', 'h', 'u' },
    { 'F', 'r', 'i' },
    { 'S', 'a', 't' }
    };
```

then you can still use %s to display a day's name as shown:

```
printf ("Today is %.3s\n", days[i]);
```

(Here we assume i has the value 0 through 6.)

Like the *width* modifier, the precision can be specified as an argument to printf by putting a * where the precision value would normally appear and by supplying an integer argument at the appropriate point. So

```
printf ("The result is %.*f\n", places, result);
```

will display the value of result to places decimal places rounded.

Naturally, you can specify both the field width and precision as arguments, so

```
printf (":%*.*d:\n", 10, 6, 100);
```

says to display the value 100 right justified in a field width of 10 characters, and to display a minimum of 6 digits. This results in the output

```
:    000100:
```

The final modifier to be described is the letter l. This must precede any of the other integer type conversion characters when displaying the value of a long integer. So if lval is a long int, then the call

```
printf ("%lx\n", lval);
```

will display its value in hexadecimal.

As you can see, printf provides an enormous amount of power and flexibility for controlling output. With the width specification, it's easy to generate output that lines up in columns.

Before leaving the discussion on printf it might be helpful for you to see the various formatting options in use. The program that follows illustrates the various options for displaying integer values.

Program 4-1

```
/* printf: printing integers */

main ()
{
    int i = 2020, j = -55;
    long int k = 16000000L;

    printf ("%d %o %x %X\n", i, i, i, i);

    /* sign display */
    printf ("%+d %+d\n", i, j);

    /* space for pos value */
    printf ("% d % d\n", i, j);

    /* 0 before oct, 0x(X) before hex */
    printf ("%#o %#x %#X\n", i, i, i);

    /* long int */
    printf ("%ld\n", k);

    /* field width */
    printf ("%10d %10d\n", i, j);

    /* left justify */
    printf ("%-10d %-10d\n", i, j);

    /* min num digits to print */
    printf ("%.5d %10.5d\n", i, i);
}
```

```
$ a.out
2020 3744 7e4 7E4
+2020 -55
 2020 -55
03744 0x7e4 0X7E4
16000000
      2020         -55
2020       -55
02020      02020
```

The output here should be fairly self-explanatory, as it should be in the next example, which illustrates the various ways of displaying floating point numbers.

Program 4-2

```
/* printf: printing floats */

main ()
{
    float f1 = 123.456, f2 = 1.234e+5;

    /* f format */
    printf ("%f %f\n", f1, f2);

    /* e format */
    printf ("%e %e\n", f1, f2);

    /* g format */
    printf ("%g %g\n", f1, f2);

    /* dec pt specification */
    printf ("%.2f %.1e\n", f1, f2);

    /* field width */
    printf ("%10.2f %10.2e\n", f1, f2);

    /* variable dec pts */
    printf ("%.*f %*.*f\n", 0, f1, 20, 4, f1);
}

$ a.out
123.456001 123400.000000
1.234560e+02 1.234000e+05
123.456 123400
123.46 1.2e+05
    123.46    1.23e+05
123              123.4560
```

In the first line of output, you'll notice that 123.456 gets displayed as 123.456001. That's because floating point numbers can't always be represented internally on a computer as exact numbers (think about how the fraction one-third has to be represented).

This last program example illustrates how to display characters and strings with `printf`.

Program 4-3

```
/* printf: printing chars and strings */

main ()
{
    char c = 'X';
    char *s = "abcde";

    /* character */
    printf ("%c\n", c);

    /* null terminated string */
    printf ("%s\n", s);

    /* field width */
    printf ("%10s:%10s\n", s, s);

    /* left justify */
    printf ("%-10s:%-10s\n", s, s);

    /* char count */
    printf ("%.2s:%10.3s\n", s, s);
}

$ a.out
X
abcde
     abcde:     abcde
abcde     :abcde
ab:       abc
```

The last call says to first display the first two characters of s, followed by the first three characters of s right-justified in a field of 10 characters.

sprintf

This function actually doesn't perform any I/O, but it's so close to `printf` that it is included as part of the Standard I/O Library. The `sprintf` function takes an additional argument. This first argument points to a character array. `sprintf` "writes" the output into this character array instead of to standard output. This function is useful when you need to convert different data objects into a character string. It's often used to build up a command line inside an array and then hand that array line to the system for execution (you'll learn how to do that shortly).

The next example doesn't really show a practical application of sprintf. Nevertheless, it does show how it's used.

Program 4-4

```
main ()
{
    char buf[100], *cmd = "pr -w", *file = "/tmp/data";
    int  width = 80;

    sprintf (buf, "%s %d %s", cmd, width, file);
    printf ("%s\n", buf);
}


$ a.out
pr -w 80 /tmp/data
```

The sprintf call says to write the string pointed to by cmd, followed by a space, followed by the value of width, followed by another space, followed by the string pointed to by file into the character array buf. The printf that follows verifies what was written into the array. Typically, once a command like this has been "built," it will be given to the UNIX system for execution by calling system.

scanf

This routine allows formatted data to be read by a program. You're already familiar with the basic operation of scanf:

```
int count;

scanf ("%d", &count);
```

This says to read an integer from standard input and store it into the variable count. scanf requires that *all* of its arguments be pointers. Novice C programmers often forget the & before variables when calling scanf; after getting burned a few times, they quickly learn.

In general, each % sign specified in the format string (the first argument to scanf) requires a corresponding pointer to be supplied as an argument.

The valid conversion characters that can follow a % are summarized in Table 4-3.

TABLE 4-3. scanf conversion characters

Character	Use for reading
d	Integers
u	Unsigned integers
o	Octal integers
x	Hexadecimal integers
e, f, g	Floating point numbers
c	Single characters
s	Character strings terminated by whitespace
[...]	Character strings terminated by any character not listed inside brackets
[^...]	Character strings terminated by any character listed inside brackets
%	Percent signs

When reading numbers, if %o conversion is specified, then scanf assumes that the corresponding number that's read is expressed in octal notation. If %x is used, then the number is expressed in hexadecimal (you can use either lower- or uppercase letters a-f in the numbers).

Floating point numbers can be read with either %e, %f, or %g conversion characters. The number need not contain a decimal point, and can be expressed in exponential notation.

A character string can be read with %s, where a character string is defined as a sequence of characters up to a whitespace (space, tab, or newline) character. The corresponding argument to scanf must be a pointer to a character array that is large enough to store the string that is read, including the terminating null character that scanf will store.

If you're not happy with the defintion of a character string as far as scanf is concerned, then you can change it with the special [...] and [^...] conversion characters. In the first case, the characters listed between the [and the] define *all* of the valid characters in the string. scanf will start reading characters and will store them into your character array until one of the listed characters is encountered on input.

In the second case, the ^ character that immediately follows the [tells scanf that the remaining characters listed between the brackets are to be considered the string terminator characters. In other words, scanf will continue to read characters from standard input and store them in your array until it encounters any one of the characters listed in the brackets.

Ranges of characters can be abbreviated by placing a – between the first and last characters in the range. So, for example, the statements

```
char letters[100];

scanf ("%[a-z]", letters);
```

tell `scanf` to read characters from standard input and store them into the array `letters` until a nonlowercase letter is encountered. The call

```
scanf ("%[a-zA-Z]", letters);
```

is similar, except in this case `scanf` will read and store characters into `letters` until a nonalphabetic character is read.

The `scanf` call

```
scanf ("%[^,.;]", buf);
```

says to read characters until a comma, period, or semicolon is encountered, and to store all such characters read into `buf`. The call

```
scanf ("%[^\n]", line);
```

tells `scanf` that the only delimiter character for this read is a newline character. Therefore, `scanf` will read and store characters inside `line` until a newline is read (which will not be stored).

Like `printf`, `scanf` accepts conversion modifiers. In fact, the general format of a `scanf` conversion specification is

```
%[*][size][l][h]type
```

The meaning of these modifiers is summarized in the following table.

TABLE 4-4. `scanf` conversion modifiers

Modifier	Meaning
*	Field is to be skipped and not assigned
size	Maximum size of the input field
l	Value is to be stored in `long int` or `double`
h	Value to be read is to be stored in a `short int`
type	Conversion character

You must supply `scanf` with a pointer of the appropriate type. For instance, to read an integer into a `long int`, you have to specify `%ld` in the format string and give a pointer to a `long int` as the corresponding argument.

The asterisk says that `scanf` should read a value of the specified type but should not assign it to a variable. Therefore, `scanf` does *not* expect to see a corresponding pointer argument. The call

```
scanf ("%d %*s %d", &v1, &v2);
```

says to read an integer, followed by a string, followed by another integer. The `*` in front of the `s` says that the string that is read isn't to be stored; that's why only two pointer arguments follow the format string (and these are both presumably pointers to integers).

Remember that `scanf` returns the number of values *assigned* and not *read*. So in the previous example, `scanf` will return 2 and not 3 when it succeeds.

The *size* specification sets a maximum size on the input field. It's useful to ensure that character arrays don't overflow. For example, the following statements:

```
char word[10];
    ...
scanf ("%9s", word);
```

ensure that the `word` array won't overflow because only a maximum of 9 characters will be read (9 is specified and not 10, since `scanf` places a null at the end of the string).

The size specification is also useful to separate packed data fields. So the call

```
scanf ("%3d%2d", &part, &lot);
```

with the input

```
97623
```

causes the number 976 to be read and stored into `part` and the number 23 to be read and stored into `lot`.

For all conversion characters except `%c` and the bracket constructs, `scanf` automatically skips over any leading whitespace characters before reading the data. Once it finds a nonwhitespace character on the input it starts reading characters until the first character that's not valid for the data being read is encountered (for example, if `scanf` reads the character `x` when reading in an integer). At that point, reading of that value stops. Here's an important point (especially when reading characters or `[...]` strings): the next time `scanf` is called it will start reading from the character that stopped the previous scan. Some examples will clarify this.

Suppose you issue the following scanf call to read an integer and a string:

```
scanf ("%d %s", &val1, buf);
```

If you type this data:

```
        -123      test string
```

then scanf will skip the leading space characters on the line, and will then read the characters -, 1, 2, and 3. The space that appears after the 3 will cause scanf to stop its scan of the integer value, at which point it will store the number read (-123) into val1. scanf will then skip over all of the whitespace characters that follow until it finds the first t in test. It will then read characters until the first whitespace character, storing the result (test) into the character array pointed to by buf.

If you typed this line instead:

```
        -123test         string
```

then the same values would be assigned, as would be the case if you typed

```
        -123


                    test string
```

The following program example, which is run twice, shows how scanf can be used to read numbers. It's important to remember that scanf is not "record oriented"; it reads as many lines from the input as it has to. Furthermore, scanf always resumes scanning from the last point that it left off, so a call to scanf doesn't necessarily mean that a new line will be read.

Program 4-5

```
main ()
{
    int i;
    float f;
    double d;

    scanf ("%d %f", &i, &f);
    scanf ("%lf", &d);

    printf ("%d %.3f %.3f\n", i, f, d);
}
```

```
$ a.out
100        123.456       -158.77
100 123.456 -158.770
$ a.out
-156
          -557.34
100.22e+7
-156 -557.340 1002200000.000
```

Note that the first time the program is executed, one line of input data satisfies both scanf calls, whereas the second time three lines of input are read before the two calls are satisfied. Remember that when reading numbers or strings, scanf skips over any leading whitespace characters, where a whitespace character is a space, tab, or newline character.

The next example illustrates the importance of considering whitespace characters in the input when reading characters.

Program 4-6

```
main ()
{
    char c1, c2, c3;

    scanf ("%c%c%c", &c1, &c2, &c3);
    printf (":%c%c%c:\n", c1, c2, c3);
}

$ a.out
x y
:x y:
$ a.out
x
y
:x
y:
$ a.out
 x y
: x :
```

This program was executed three times. The scanf call

```
scanf ("%c%c%c", &c1, &c2, &c3);
```

says to read three characters from standard input and to store them into the variables c1, c2, and c3.

The first line of input typed is the character x, followed by a space, followed by the character y, followed by the pressing of the *RETURN* key. Note that even though you're reading single characters, the characters are not sent to the program until the *RETURN* key is pressed.[†] So the characters assigned to the three variables, as verified by the output, are x, space, and y.

The next time the program is run, an x is typed, followed by the *RETURN* key. This causes these two characters to be read by the program and stored in the variables c1 and c2, respectively. Since scanf still wants to read another character, it will wait for you to type more input. Typing the character y and pressing the *RETURN* key causes the y to be sent to the program and stored into the variable c3. It's important to stress that any whitespace characters—spaces, tabs, or newlines—are read and assigned by scanf when reading single characters with %c (also when reading strings with %[...] or %[^...])

The next program example is similar to the previous one, except the scanf call was slightly modified to show the effect of spaces in the format string.

Program 4-7

```
main ()
{
    char c1, c2, c3;

    scanf (" %c %c %c", &c1, &c2, &c3);
    printf (":%c%c%c:\n", c1, c2, c3);
}

$ a.out
    x       y
z
:xyz:
```

An important fact when using scanf is that one or more spaces in a scanf format string causes scanf to automatically skip over any whitespace characters in the input. So the format string

```
" %c %c %c"
```

says to skip over any leading whitespace characters, read a single character, skip any whitespace characters that follow, read a second character, skip any whitespace characters after that, and then read a third character. The net effect is that this format string causes the next three nonwhitespace characters to be read from standard input. This is certainly very different from the previous program, which read the next three characters from standard input—whether they were whitespace or not.

---

† This is because terminal input is *line* buffered under the UNIX system. In the next chapter, you'll see how you to place a terminal into "raw" mode so that characters can be seen by the program as they are typed.

The program that follows shows the same considerations for whitespace characters that must be made when reading strings with the [...] conversion characters.

Program 4-8

```
main ()
{
    char s1[100], s2[100];

    scanf ("%s%s", s1, s2);
    printf ("%s:%s\n", s1, s2);

    scanf (" %[a-z]", s1);
    scanf ("%s", s2);
    printf ("%s:%s\n", s1, s2);

    scanf (" %[^\n]", s1);
    printf ("%s\n", s1);
}
```

```
$ cat test
scanf
            test
nonlowercaseistheDelimiter
here is an entire line for scanf
$ a.out < test
scanf:test
nonlowercaseisthe:Delimiter
here is an entire line for scanf
```

The input from this program was first typed into a file called test and then supplied to the program by using input redirection on the command line.
The first scanf call

```
scanf ("%s%s", s1, s2);
```

says to read two whitespace-delimited character strings and to store them into s1 and s2. This causes scanf to read the first line of test and to store the string scanf into s1. As noted, scanf skips over leading whitespace characters when reading strings. So scanf will then read past the newline character at the end of the first line and the spaces at the beginning of the second line until it encounters the string test, which will be read and stored into s2.

When `scanf` returns from its first call, the input pointer is left at the newline character at the end of the second line of the file `test`. So the next call to `scanf` causes it to start reading from that character. This call,

```
scanf (" %[a-z]", s1);
```

says to skip over any whitespace characters (as indicated by the space) and then to read in all of the successive lowercase letters on input. This causes the characters `nonlowercaseisthe` to be read and stored into `s1`. The capital letter `D` terminates the scan here. Note that the leading space character in the `scanf` format string is critical to proper operation here. If the `scanf` call looked like this instead:

```
scanf ("%[a-z]", s1);
```

then the leading whitespace characters would not have been skipped. Recalling that `scanf` stopped at the newline character at the end of line two the last time it was called, this `scanf` call would have caused that newline character to be read. Since a newline isn't a lowercase letter, the net effect is that *nothing would have been read and assigned to* `s1`, and `scanf` would have left its input pointer at that same newline character at the end of line two. Review this discussion if you have to. Understanding this is key to your understanding the way `scanf` works when reading characters with `%c` and `%[...]`.

The next call

```
scanf ("%s", s2);
```

says to read the next series of characters up to a whitespace. Since `scanf` stopped at the `D` last time, it starts reading from that character. The newline at the end of line three is the terminating character for this read, thus causing the characters `Delimiter` to be read and stored inside `s2`.

The last call to `scanf`:

```
scanf (" %[^\n]", s1);
```

says to skip leading whitespace characters and to read and store all of the characters up to a newline inside `s1`. Once again, the leading space in the format string is key here, as it causes `scanf` to skip the newline character at the end of line three and start reading with the first nonwhitespace character from line four. That causes the entire line to be read and assigned.

Any characters in `scanf`'s format string, other than conversion characters and spaces, must be literally matched on input. So to read a date typed in the format *mm/dd/yy*, the following `scanf` call could be used:

```
scanf ("%d/%d/%d", &month, &day, &year);
```

Here scanf must see three integers separated by slashes in order to succeed. If the input looks like this

```
8/8/86
10 / 28 / 87
7/16x55
```

then the first date will be read correctly but the last two will not.

Getting familiar with scanf's idiosyncracies takes some time. Study Table 4-5, which shows for different format strings and input data what will be assigned by scanf, what value will be returned, and what character will be read the next time scanf is called. In the table, i and j are ints, l and s are long and short ints, respectively, f is a float, c1 and c2 are chars, and s1 and s2 are pointers to character arrays.

TABLE 4-5. scanf examples

scanf arguments	Input	Values assigned	Return value	Next char
"%d", &i	1234	i=1234	1	'\n'
"%2d", &i	1234	i=12	1	'3'
"%d", &i	1234xyz	i=1234	1	'x'
"%d", &i	xyz	–	0	'x'
"%d:%d", &i, &j	100:200	i=100, j=200	2	'\n'
"%d:%d", &i, &j	100 200	i=100	1	':'
"%ld %hd", &l, &s	100 200	l=100, s=200	2	'\n'
"%x %f", &i, &f	a5b0 1.2e+5	i=0xa5b0, f=1.2e+5	2	'\n'
"%c%c", &c1, &c2	ab	c1='a', c2='b'	2	'\n'
"%c%c", &c1, &c2	a b	c1='a', c2=' '	2	'b'
"%c %c", &c1, &c2	a b	c1='a', c2='b'	2	'\n'
"%c%*c%c", &c1, &c2	a b	c1='a', c2='b'	2	'\n'
"%s %s", s1, s2	try this out	s1="try", s2="this"	2	' '
"%[a-z]%[A-Z]", s1, s2	down UPs	s1="down"	1	' '
"%[a-z] %[A-Z]", s1, s2	down UPs	s1="down", s2="UP"	2	's'
"%[^:]%[^:]", s1, s2	one:two	s1="one"	1	':'
"%[^:]:%[^:]", s1, s2	one:two	s1="one", s2="two"	2	'\n'
"%[^\n]", s1	a whole line	s1="a whole line"	1	'\n'
"%[^\n]\n", s1	a whole line	s1="a whole line"	1	–

Since scanf returns the number of values successfully assigned, it can be used in a loop to process all of the data from standard input. This program reads a file of data and adds the first and third integers from each line.

Program 4-9

```
/*
    program to sum first and third integers on a line
*/

main ()
{
        int i1, i3;

        while ( scanf ("%d %*d %d", &i1, &i3) == 2 )
                printf ("%d\n", i1 + i3);
}
```

```
$ cat data
-120    12      585
12      99      780
7       16      55
84      32      103
$ a.out < data
465
792
62
187
```

Since the second integer is not needed by the program, it is not assigned. As long as scanf successfully reads two integers, it returns the value 2. In that case, the printf is executed to display the sum of the two integers. When the last line has been read from standard input, scanf returns 0, since it can't read any more integers. This causes the while to terminate.

Be aware that a slight mistake in the input data will alter the program's results dramatically:

```
$ cat data
-120    12      585
12      x9      780
7       16      55
84      32      103
$ a.out < data
465
```

The first three integers, -120, 12, and 585 were correctly read and the first and third stored into `i1` and `i3`, respectively. The sum of `i1` and `i3` was then calculated and displayed.

The second time `scanf` is called, the first integer on the second line, 12, is read and assigned to `i1`. `scanf` then tries to read another integer on the line and encounters the character 'x'. This causes it to terminate its scan early, since x is not a valid integer character. So `scanf` leaves the value of `i3` unchanged and returns 1, since that's how many values were read and assigned.

Consider what happens if a number is missing from the file:

```
$ cat data
-120        585
12    99    780
7     16    55
84    32    103
$ a.out < data
-108
106
100
```

Here `scanf` is thrown out of sync. It reads the first integer (-120), skips the second (585), reads the third (12), adds them together (-108), and displays the result. This continues for the remainder of the data (verify the output on your own).

The moral of this last example is that `scanf` is not suited to processing data line by line; it's very easy to get it (and you) confused. There is a better approach that we'll show shortly. It allows you to ensure that you are processing the data from your file line by line.

sscanf

Like `sprintf`, `sscanf` has nothing whatsoever to do with actual input of data. Instead, it "reads" data from a character array given as its first argument according to the format given as its second argument. It stores the values "read" into the variables pointed to by the subsequent arguments.

`sscanf` is useful for converting character data into integers, floating point numbers, and smaller strings. It's often used to take a previously read line of data and to "pick apart" its fields. For example, let's say you have the following characters sitting inside a character array called `buf`:

```
123.456 + 595.36
```

Then the declarations

```
float val1, val2;
char  oper;
```

and subsequent `sscanf` call

```
sscanf (buf, "%f %c %f", &val1, &oper, &val2);
```

will "read" from `buf` the number 123.456 and store it into `val1`, the character + and store it in `oper`, and the number 595.36 and store it into `val2`.

We'll show another example with `sscanf` shortly.

getchar and putchar

`getchar` reads a single character from standard input, while `putchar` writes a single character to standard output. On UNIX systems, these two routines are actually defined both as macros inside `stdio.h` and as functions in the Standard C Library.

The following program simply copies standard input to standard output a single character at a time.

Program 4-10

```
/* Copy standard input to standard output */

#include <stdio.h>

main ()
{
    int c;

    while ( (c = getchar()) != EOF )
        putchar (c);
}
```

```
$ a.out
isn't this
isn't this
fun?
fun?
CTRL-d
$ a.out < text
Here are some
sample lines of text to
see how the various I/O
```

```
routines work
$ a.out < text > text2
$ cat text2
Here are some
sample lines of text to
see how the various I/O
routines work
```

Notice that c is declared as an int and not a char, even though you're using getchar to read characters. The reason for this is as follows: getchar is defined to return all possible character values, not just those in the normal character set. On most systems, this means that getchar can read and return any possible eight-bit value. In order to signal to the programmer that no more characters are left to be read from standard input, getchar returns the special defined value EOF (defined as -1 in stdio.h). Since this return value has to be distinguishable from any valid character that getchar can otherwise return, getchar is therefore defined to return an int. If c is wrongly declared to be a char, then on some systems the program shown will work and on others it won't. It all depends on whether or not the system does sign extension when characters are converted to ints. If c is a char, then the value of -1 that is returned on end of file will be truncated and stored inside c. On most systems, this will be the value 255 (eight bits of all ones). When the value in c is then compared to the defined value EOF, on systems that do sign extension 255 will be converted back to -1, and the comparison will succeed. On systems that don't do sign extension, 255 will be compared against -1 and the while will theoretically execute forever.

Getting back to the program, the characters read by getchar are written to standard output with putchar. Note that putchar can be given an int to write, since characters are converted to ints anyway when they're passed to functions. Eventually, getchar will return EOF after the last character has been read, causing the loop to terminate.

Even though this is such a simplistic program, it is actually quite powerful. The first time the program is executed, two lines are typed at the terminal. The program reads the lines one character at a time and then prints them back out. Remember that the line that is typed is not made available to the program until the *RETURN* key is pressed, even though you're reading in single characters. Typing *CTRL-d* sends an end-of-file condition to the program, causing it to terminate.

The second time the program is run, standard input is redirected from the file text. When getchar is called to read a character from standard input, it will actually be reading characters from the file text. putchar still writes to standard output, so the net result is that this form of execution of the program allows you to view the contents of a file (as in the cat command).

The last time the program is run, standard input is redirected from text and standard output is redirected to text2. This results in getchar reading its characters from text and putchar writing its characters to text2. This form of execution allows you to copy one file to another (as in the cp command).

Program 4-11 is a simple filter program. It allows you to view the contents of files at your terminal with the "invisible" characters displayed in a readable form. Characters like tabs and formfeeds are displayed using conventional C escape character notation (e.g., as \t and \f), control characters are displayed with a leading ^, followed by the corresponding letter (e.g., ^X means *CTRL-x*), and anything else is displayed as a three digit octal number preceded by a backslash (e.g. \177).

Notice how putchar and printf are both used for output. In general, all of the routines in the Standard I/O Library work quite well together.

After each character is read, a switch is entered to test the character. If it's a newline (\n), then a newline character is literally printed. If it's any other special C escape character (\t, \f, \r, \b, \v), then printf is called to display the corresponding two-character sequence (remember that to represent a backslash in a character string in C, you have to use two). Two separate calls to putchar could have worked as well.

The default case checks to see if the character is printable and, if it is, simply prints it by passing it to putchar. Otherwise, if it's a control character, then it is displayed as a ^ followed by the corresponding letter. If it's not printable and isn't a control A-Z, then the three-digit octal value of the character is written to standard output.

The sample output shows a file that contained some tab characters, the ASCII bell character (007), an ESC (ASCII 033), and a delete character (ASCII 0177).

Program 4-11

```
/* filter standard input */

#include <stdio.h>
#include <ctype.h>

main ()
{
    int  c;

    while ( (c = getchar ()) != EOF )
        switch ( c ) {
                case '\n':  /* newline */
                    putchar ('\n');
                    break;
                case '\t':  /* tab */
                    printf ("\\t");
                    break;
                case '\f':  /* formfeed */
                    printf ("\\f");
                    break;
                case '\r':  /* return */
                    printf ("\\r");
                    break;
                case '\b':  /* backspace */
                    printf ("\\b");
                    break;
                case '\v':  /* vertical tab */
                    printf ("\\v");
                    break;
                default:
                    if ( isprint (c) )
                        putchar (c);
                    else if ( c >= 1 && c <= 26 ) {
                        putchar ('^');
                        putchar (c + 'A' - 1);
                    }
                    else
                        printf ("\\%.3o", c);
                    break;
        }
}
```

```
$ cat data
        Some sample data
Here is a bell character (CTRL-g):
        Tab     chars in      the     file
Other nonprintables:

$ a.out < data
\tSome sample data
Here is a bell character (CTRL-g): ^G
\tTab\tchars\tin\tthe\tfile
Other nonprintables: \033 \177
```

gets and puts

You saw how scanf could be used to read in an entire line from standard input. A much more elegant method is to use the function gets. This function takes a single argument which is a pointer to a character array. gets reads characters from standard input until it encounters a newline. All such characters read—*excluding the newline*—are stored inside the array, which gets automatically terminates with a null character. As long as gets successfully reads at least one character from standard input, it returns the pointer that is passed as its argument; otherwise it returns a null pointer to signal that the end of file was reached and no characters read.

puts writes the null terminated string passed as its argument to standard output, *automatically writing a newline character at the end.*

The following program copies standard input to standard output, as before. This time, the copying is done a line at a time with gets and puts.

Program 4-12

```
/* Copy standard input to standard output */

#include <stdio.h>

main ()
{
    char buf[500];

    while ( gets (buf) != (char *) NULL )
        puts (buf);
}
```

```
$ a.out < text
Here are some
sample lines of text to
see how the various I/O
routines work
```

As long as `gets` doesn't return the value `NULL`, the line that is read from standard input is copied to standard output by calling `puts`. Note that it's up to you to ensure that your character array is large enough to store the longest possible line; `gets` simply reads characters until it reads a newline, however many that may be. The `fgets` function, which we'll describe shortly, does allow you to place a maximum size on the line that is read to prevent accidental overflow of your array.

In case you're curious, the following function called `readline` mimics the operation of `gets` using `getchar`. Study the logic of this function to see when it returns `NULL` and also to verify that the newline character is not stored in the array.

```
#include <stdio.h>

/*
    Function to read a line from standard input
    (like the gets function)
*/

char *readline (buf)
char *buf;
{
        int c;
        char *savebuf = buf;

        while ( (c = getchar()) != EOF  &&  c != '\n' )
                *buf++ = c;

        *buf = '\0';

        if ( c == EOF  &&  buf == savebuf )
                return ( (char *) NULL );
        else
                return (savebuf);
}
```

`gets` and `sscanf` are particulary useful together for processing data line by line. Suppose you have some input data that contains two integers on each line. The following code fragment allows you to process the data a line at a time and to identify any line that is in error:

```
char  buf[81];
int   i1, i2;

while ( gets (buf) != (char *) NULL )
    if ( sscanf (buf, "%d %d", &i1, &i2) != 2 )
        printf ("Bad input line: %s\n", buf);
    else
        process (i1, i2);
```

A line is read into buf and then sscanf is used to "read" two integers from buf. If the format of the data in buf is no good, then sscanf returns a value less than 2. In that case, an error message is written and the ill-formed input line is printed out in its entirety. If the line is correct, then the two integers are passed to a function called process, presumably to be processed.

Note that this technique gives you complete control over your input data. Recall that scanf reads ahead in your data if it has to, or can get stuck on a line if it contains extraneous or invalid data. This approach ensures that you have not read ahead in your input and that you're not stuck on a previous line. And as noted, it also gives you access to the entire line for error processing.

· I/O with Files ·

fopen	opens a file with a specified mode
fdopen	associates a stream with a specified file descriptor
freopen	closes a file and opens another in its place
fclose	closes a file
fprintf	writes formatted output to a file
fscanf	reads formatted data from a file
fgetc	reads a character from a file
getc	reads a character from a file (macro)
fputc	writes a character to a file
putc	writes a character to a file (macro)
ungetc	"unreads" a character from a file
getw	reads a word from a file
putw	writes a word to a file

fgets   reads a line from a file

fputs   writes a line to a file

fread   reads data from a file

fwrite   writes data to a file

These functions allow you to do operations on specific files. Sometimes you want to open a file in your program to read some data from it, or you may want to write some results to a specific file. The UNIX system permits 20 files to be open at once. Three of these are opened by default—standard input, standard output, and standard error—leaving room for 17 additional files.

Working with files always proceeds the same way: you first *open* the file, do your operations on the file, and then *close* the file when you're done with it.

The FILE Define

As noted, the first step in working with a file is opening it. Since many files can be open at once, the Standard I/O Library needs a unique way of identifying open files. Rather than using the file name, a special pointer of type FILE is used. In fact, the file name comes into play only once—when the file is opened. Thereafter, the FILE pointer is used to identify the particular file that is the target of an I/O operation.

The following fragment is from the include file stdio.h:

```
#define   _NFILE    20
#define   FILE      struct _iobuf

extern   struct _iobuf {
    char   *_ptr;
    int    _cnt;
    char   *_base;
    char   _flag;
    char   _file;
} _iob[_NFILE];
```

As you can see, FILE is defined as a structure of type _iobuf. The Standard I/O Library keeps all necessary information about open files (e.g., where the associated buffer is, where the pointer in the buffer is, and so forth) inside these structures. In fact, the array _iob is used to keep all the information about open files together in one place. _iob[0] stores the information about standard input; _iob[1], standard output; and _iob[2], standard error. You never need to deal directly with the _iobuf structure or the _iob array; the routines in the Standard I/O Library do that for you.

fopen

In order to perform any I/O operation on a file, it first must be opened. `fopen` is most often used to open a file. It takes two arguments: the name of the file to be opened and the *mode*. Both arguments are of type `char *`. The mode specifies the type of operation you want to perform on the file: read from it, write to it, add data to the end of it, or update it (do both reading and writing). The various modes recognized by `fopen` are summarized in Table 4-6.

TABLE 4-6. fopen access modes

Access Mode	Allows you to
r	Read from the file
w	Write to the file; if file already exists, its previous contents are lost; if file doesn't exist, it's created
a	Write to the end of the file; if file doesn't exist, it's created
r+	Read and write to the file (like r, but data can also be written to the file)
w+	Read and write to the file (works like w, but data can also be read from the file)
a+	Read and write to the file (works like a—writes can only go to the end of the file—but reading also permitted anywhere in the file)

If you want to simply read some data from an existing file, then you open it in `r` mode:

```
fopen ("datafile", "r")
```

If you want to create a new file to write some data to, you open it in `w` mode, being careful to remember that if the file already exists, you'll lose its contents forever:

```
fopen ("results", "w")
```

When a file is opened in append mode (a or a+), it's guaranteed that you won't be able to overwrite exisiting data in the file; all write operations will simply automatically append data to the end of the file:

```
fopen ("logfile", "a")
```

The three "update" modes—"r+", "w+", "a+"—should be understood by you before you use them. They all allow both reading from and writing to the same file. With read update, it's assumed that you have an existing data file that you want to read and write. w+ behaves like w except you can also read from the file. It's important to note that if the file already exists, its contents will be erased. So if you have a database that you want to make changes to, the file should be opened r+ and not w+:

```
fopen ("database", "r+")
```

As noted, a+ guarantees that writes will go the end of the file; reads can be performed anywhere on the file.

After fopen opens the indicated file with the specified mode, it returns a FILE pointer that you must use to subsequently identify the file. If the open fails for some reason (e.g., you try to open a nonexistent file in r or r+ mode, or you don't have the proper access permissions on the file), then fopen returns a NULL FILE pointer. You should always check the return value from fopen to make sure it succeeds. Using a NULL pointer for a subsequent I/O operation will frequently cause your program to terminate abnormally with a core dump.

fclose

In order to close an open file, you call fclose. It takes a FILE pointer as its argument, writes any data that may be sitting in the buffer to the file, and then closes the file.

Under the UNIX system, all files are automatically closed whenever your program terminates normally (i.e., not due to a memory violation, floating point exception, or program interrupt). So in many cases, it's not necessary for you to close your files yourself. However, if for some reason you need to work with more than 20 files in a program, then you'll have to close files when you're done with them in order to work within the 20 file maximum.

fprintf and fscanf

These two routines are equivalent to their standard input and standard output counterparts, printf and scanf, except that they take an additional first argument that specifies the file the data is to be written to or read from. For example, if infile is a FILE pointer for a file that has been opened for reading, then the call

```
fscanf (infile, "%d %d", &month, &year)
```

will read two integers from the file. And if outfile points to a file opened for writing, then the call

```
fprintf (outfile, "The answer is %d\n", result)
```

will write the specified line to the file.

The following program creates a file called `names` by opening it in write mode and then writes some data to it.

Program 4-13

```
/* creating a file */

#include <stdio.h>

main ()
{
    FILE   *outfile;

    if ( (outfile = fopen ("names", "w")) ==  (FILE *) NULL ) {
        printf ("Can't write names\n");
        exit (1);
    }

    fprintf (outfile, "Bob\n");
    fprintf (outfile, "Bill\n");
    fprintf (outfile, "Alice\n");

    fclose (outfile);
}

$ a.out
$ cat names
Bob
Bill
Alice
```

The `if` that starts

```
if ( (outfile = fopen ("names", "w")) == (FILE *) NULL ) {
```

calls `fopen` to open the file `names` for writing (remember that *both* arguments to `fopen` must be character pointers). The resulting `FILE` pointer that is returned is assigned to the variable `outfile` and then is tested against `NULL` (typecast to the appropriate pointer type) to see if the `fopen` succeeded. If it failed, then the following `printf` is executed and the program exits.

The `perror` function described in Chapter 3 is useful for reporting errors from Standard I/O Library routines. In the example above, replacing the `printf` with

```
perror ("fopen call");
```

would cause a description of the cause of the error (such as invalid permission, or a bad file name) to be printed, preceded by the string `"fopen call: "`.

Returning to the program, if the `fopen` succeeds, then three `fprintf`s are executed to write three lines to the file (it could have been done with a single `fprintf`, but we chose to use three here).

After the lines have been written, `fclose` is called to close the file. Remember that this is actually not necessary, since the file would have been automatically closed anyway upon program termination.

The following program shows how to use append mode to add data to the end of the `names` file.

Program 4-14

```
/* appending data */

#include <stdio.h>

main ()
{
    FILE   *outfile;

    if ( (outfile = fopen ("names", "a")) == (FILE *) NULL ) {
        printf ("Can't append to names\n");
        exit (1);
    }

    fprintf (outfile, "Ruth\n");
    fprintf (outfile, "Tony\n");
}
```

```
$ cat names
Bob
Bill
Alice
$ a.out
$ cat names
Bob
Bill
Alice
Ruth
Tony
```

Recall that the Standard I/O Library has three predefined streams—stdin, stdout, and stderr—that refer to your standard input, standard output, and standard error streams. These predefined streams can be given as arguments to *any* routine in the Standard I/O Library that takes a FILE pointer as an argument. So, for example, the call

```
fprintf (stderr, "Couldn't open the file for reading\n")
```

writes the indicated message to standard error. The call

```
fprintf (stdout, "hello\n")
```

is equivalent to

```
printf ("hello\n")
```

just as the call

```
fscanf (stdin, "%d", &i)
```

is equivalent to

```
scanf ("%d", &i)
```

getc, fgetc, putc, and fputc

These routines perform character I/O on specified files. getc and fgetc work like getchar and read single characters, returning the integer EOF on end of file. putc and fputc work like putchar and write single characters. The difference between getc and fgetc is that the former is implemented as a macro for speed. You should use the former routine unless you specifically need a function (i.e., if you need to create a pointer to a character input routine, you can't make a pointer to getc but you can to fgetc). The same distinction exists betweem putc and fputc: the former is a macro and the latter a function.

Suppose you have the following stored inside a file called instructions:

```
To use this program, first set the TERM
variable to your terminal with the command
    TERM=type
then export it with the following:
    EXPORT TERM
At that point, type in 'emacs' followed by
the name of the file you want to edit, e.g.,
    emacs memo
```

and you want to write the contents of this file to the terminal (standard output). The following program does just that.

Program 4-15

```
#include <stdio.h>

main ()
{
    FILE   *helpfile;
    int    c;

    if ( (helpfile = fopen ("instructions", "r"))
              == (FILE *) NULL ) {
        fprintf (stderr, "Can't open instructions!\n");
        exit (1);
    }

    while ( (c == getc (helpfile)) != EOF )
        putchar (c);
}
```

```
$ a.out
To use this program, first set the TERM
variable to your terminal with the command
    TERM=type
then export it with the following:
    EXPORT TERM
At that point, type in 'emacs' followed by
the name of the file you want to edit, e.g.,
    emacs memo
```

The program calls `fopen` to open the file `instructions` for reading. The returned `FILE` pointer is assigned to `helpfile` and then is tested against `NULL` to see if the `fopen` succeeded. If it fails, then `fprintf` is called to write an error message to standard error and the program exited.

If the `fopen` succeeds, then a `while` loop is entered to read the characters from the file. `getc` reads a character from the file specified by its argument. The character that is read is stored into the *integer* variable `c`, and then tested against `EOF`. If a character was read, then `putchar` is called to write the character to standard output.

After the last character has been read from `instructions`, `getc` returns `EOF` and the `while` loop terminates.

The following program copies the contents of the file `names` to `names2`.

Program 4-16

```
/* Copy files */

#include <stdio.h>

main ()
{
    FILE *infile, *outfile;
    int  c;

    if ( (infile = fopen ("names", "r")) == (FILE *) NULL ) {
        fprintf (stderr, "Can't read names\n");
        exit (1);
    }

    if ( (outfile = fopen ("names2", "w")) == (FILE *) NULL ) {
        fprintf (stderr, "Can't write names2\n");
        exit(2);
    }

    while ( (c = getc(infile)) != EOF )
        putc (c, outfile);
}
```

```
$ cat names
Bob
Bill
Alice
Ruth
Tony
$ a.out
$ cat names2
Bob
Bill
Alice
Ruth
Tony
```

The input file `names` is opened for reading and the `FILE` pointer returned by `fopen` is assigned to the `FILE` pointer `infile`. If the `fopen` fails, a message is logged and the program exits.

The output file `names2` is then opened for writing and the `FILE` pointer returned by `fopen` is assigned to the pointer variable `outfile`. As before, if the `fopen` fails, a message is displayed and the program exits. Remember that if `names2` already exists and has some data in it, then that data will be lost when the file is opened in write mode.

If both opens succeed, then the input file is copied to the output file one character at a time by corresponding calls to `getc` and `putc`.

The sample output shows that the copy was successful.

Rather than hard coding the two files `names` and `names2` into the program, a more flexible approach would be to allow for the file names to be typed on the command line. The following program does just that.

Program 4-17

```
/* Copy files specified on command line */

#include <stdio.h>

main (argc, argv)
int argc;
char *argv[];
{
    FILE *infile, *outfile;
    int  c;

    if ( argc != 3 ) {
        fprintf (stderr, "Bad arg count\n");
        exit (1);
    }

    if ( (infile = fopen (argv[1], "r")) == (FILE *) NULL ) {
        fprintf (stderr, "Can't read %s\n", argv[1]);
        exit(2);
    }

    if ( (outfile = fopen (argv[2], "w")) == (FILE *) NULL ) {
        fprintf (stderr, "Can't write %s\n", argv[2]);
        exit(3);
    }

    while ( (c = getc (infile)) != EOF )
        putc (c, outfile);
}
```

```
$ a.out numes names3
Can't read numes
$ a.out names names3
$ cat names3
Bob
Bill
Alice
Ruth
Tony
```

The name of the file to be copied is passed to the program through `argv[1]`, and the name of the output file through `argv[2]`. The two files are then opened as before and the contents copied.

ungetc

Sometimes you may discover that you read one character too many from a file. For example, if you're writing a parser and you read a delimiter character, you may want to "put back" the delimiter character so that it will be "read" again the next time you call an input routine like `getc` or `fgetc`.

The call

```
ungetc (c, infile)
```

will put back the character `c` to the stream designated by the `FILE` pointer `infile`. The next time `getc` (`fgetc`) is called, `c` will be returned.

You should note that the character is really not re-inserted into the file, but into the buffer associated with that file. Obviously, in order to put back a character, something must have been previously read from the stream (although you are allowed to put back a character to standard input without having previously read from it). Finally, note that the system only guarantees that one character will be pushed back at a time (i.e., without an intervening read operation), so that in

```
ungetc (c, infile);
ungetc (c2, infile);
```

it's not guaranteed that both `c` and `c2` will be put back.

`ungetc` returns `EOF` if for some reason it can't put back the character.

freopen

Sometimes you'd like to close a file and open another file in its place. This is most commonly done with standard input and standard output. For example, suppose you want to read from a specific file in your program. If you don't need to read from the terminal, then you can close standard input and open the specified file in its place. That way, you can then read from the file like you were reading from the terminal, using your standard input routines like `scanf`, `getchar,` and `gets`.

The same discussion applies to standard output: if you only need to write data to one file and don't need to write to the terminal, then you can call `freopen` to close standard output and open the specified file in its place. In that way, you can then use your standard routines like `printf`, `putchar,` and `puts` to write data to the file.

`freopen` takes three arguments: the first is the name of the file to open, the second its desired access mode, and the third is a `FILE` pointer indicating the file that is to be closed. `freopen` returns a `FILE` pointer just like `fopen`.

The next program shows how our copy program can be rewritten to use `freopen`.

Program 4-18

```
/* Copy files typed on command line */

#include <stdio.h>

main (argc, argv)
int argc;
char *argv[];
{
    int c;

    if ( argc != 3 ) {
        fprintf (stderr, "Bad arg count\n");
        exit (1);
    }

    if ( freopen (argv[1], "r", stdin) == (FILE *) NULL ) {
        fprintf (stderr, "Can't read %s\n", argv[1]);
        exit (2);
    }

    if ( freopen (argv[2], "w", stdout) == (FILE *) NULL ) {
        fprintf (stderr, "Can't write %s\n", argv[2]);
        exit (3);
    }

    while ( (c = getchar()) != EOF )
        putchar (c);
}
```

```
$ a.out names names4
$ cat names4
Bob
Bill
Alice
Ruth
Tony
```

Notice that no variables of type `FILE *` need to be declared; that's because this program deals strictly with standard input and output. The call

```
freopen (argv[1], "r", stdin)
```

says to close standard input and to open in its place the file specified by `argv[1]`. The specified file is opened for reading. Similarly, the call

```
freopen (argv[2], "w", stdout)
```

says to close standard output and to open in its place the file specified by `argv[2]`. This file is opened for writing. If both `freopen`s are successful, then the file is copied, using the standard input and output routines `getchar` and `putchar`.

fdopen

This function is used to create a `FILE` pointer for a file that has been opened by a function other than `fopen` or `freopen`. These routines—open, `dup`, `pipe`, `fcntl`, and `creat`—are part of the UNIX System Interface, described in the next chapter. As you'll see there, files opened by these routines are identified differently, by an *integer* called a *file descriptor*.

fdopen takes two arguments: the first is an integer file descriptor and the second is a character pointer specifying the access mode for the stream (as in `fopen`). The `FILE` pointer that is returned by `fdopen` can now be used with all of the Standard I/O Library routines to perform I/O operations on the file. As with `fopen`, `fdopen` returns the `NULL FILE` pointer if it fails.

getw and putw

These two functions are used for reading and writing words, where the size of a word is defined to be the size of an integer. The call

```
getw (infile)
```

will read an integer from the stream `infile`, returning the result.

Since `getw` returns an integer, the function `feof` (described later) should be called to determine when end of file has been reached.

`putw` takes two arguments, the first a word (integer), and the second a `FILE` pointer specifying the stream that integer is to be written to.

Note that machines may store bytes inside words in different orders. Therefore, if you create a data file using `putw`, you may not be able to read that file back on a different machine using `getw`.

fgets and fputs

These are routines analagous to `gets` and `puts` for reading and writing lines from and to files. There are, however, some important differences. `fgets` takes three arguments: a pointer to the buffer to store the read-in line, the maximum number of characters to read from the file *minus one*, and a `FILE` pointer. So the call

```
fgets (buf, 81, infile)
```

says to read up to 80 characters from `infile` and store it into `buf`. `fgets` will read less than 80 characters if it reaches the end of the file or if it reads a newline character first. In any case, `fgets` stores a null character at the end of the array. Remember that the count given to `fgets` is one greater than the maximum number of characters it will read. Typically, this number will be the actual size of your array.

An important distinction between `fgets` and `gets` is that the former *will* store the newline character into the array if it reads it, whereas the latter will not. Also, since `fgets` takes an upper bound on the number of characters to read, it's better to use `fgets` than `gets` if you're not sure how long the lines you're reading are. In such a case, simply give `stdin` as the third argument to `fgets`:

```
fgets (buf, 81, stdin)
```

This will read up to 80 characters from standard input. Like `gets`, `fgets` returns a `NULL` pointer when it reaches the end of the file without reading any characters.

`fputs` writes a line to a specified stream, so

```
fputs (buf, outfile)
```

writes the contents of `buf` to `outfile`. Unlike `puts`, `fputs` *does not* append a newline character to the file. Only if a newline is stored inside `buf` will one be written to the file. So, while the call

```
puts (buf)
```

is equivalent to

```
printf ("%s\n", buf)
```

The call

```
fputs (buf, stdout)
```

is equivalent to

```
printf ("%s", buf)
```

Be careful not to mix fgets and fputs calls with gets and puts calls; they were designed to work in pairs. For example, if you read a line from standard input with gets and then write it to a file with fputs, no newline character would be written to the file. On the other hand, if you read a line from a file with fgets and then write it to standard output with puts, you'll get an extra newline inserted after each line (because fgets stores the newline and puts displays one on its own).

The following program displays the contents of the file instructions at the terminal.

Program 4-19

```
#include <stdio.h>

main ()
{
    FILE   *helpfile;
    int    c;
    char   buf[81];

    if ( (helpfile = fopen ("instructions", "r"))
           == (FILE *) NULL ) {
        fprintf (stderr, "Can't open instructions!\n");
        exit (1);
    }

    while ( fgets (buf, 81, helpfile) != (char *) NULL )
        fputs (buf, stdout);
}


$ a.out
To use this program, first set the TERM
```

```
variable to your terminal with the command
    TERM=type
then export it with the following:
    EXPORT TERM
At that point, type in 'emacs' followed by
the name of the file you want to edit, e.g.,
    emacs memo
```

fread and fwrite

These two routines are used for performing binary (i.e., unformatted) read/write operations. The call to fread is

```
fread (buf, size, n, stream)
```

which says to read n items from *stream*, where the size of each item to read is *size* bytes long. The data that is read is stored into the area of memory pointed to by the character pointer *buf*. fread returns the number of items that were successfully read from the stream. This will be equal to n if all items were read and less than n if the end of the file was encountered during the read. A return value of zero means that no items were read (i.e., the end of the file was reached before a single item could be read).

So if you want to read 80 characters from the stream infile into the character array line, the call would look like this:

```
fread (line, sizeof (char), 80, infile);
```

Realize here that fread does *not* insert a null character at the end of the array.

With the help of the typecast operator, any type of binary data can be read. If you have 100 integers stored in a data file in binary format and you want to read them into an array of 100 integers called values, the call would look like this:

```
fread ((char *) values, sizeof (int), 100, datafile);
```

Here we coerce the integer pointer given by the expression values into a character pointer, since that's the type of pointer expected by the first argument to fread.[†]

The call to fwrite is similar to fread's call:

```
fwrite (buf, size, n, stream)
```

In this case, n items, each *size* bytes long, are written from the character array pointed to by *buf* to the stream specified by *stream*. Like fread, fwrite

---

† Note that on most machines this is really unnecesary; it's only an issue when pointers to varying data types are of different sizes on a machine. Anyway, as the adage goes, "Better safe than sorry."

returns the number of items successfully written (which should be equal to *n*, unless an error has occurred).

The `stdio.h` header contains a define for `BUFSIZ`, which is the size of a buffer on your system. For most System V machines, this will be equal to 1,024 (on Amdahl UTS machines, it will be equal to 4,096). You can use this definition to read and write data by the buffer-full.

```c
/* Copy files typed on command line */

#include <stdio.h>

main (argc, argv)
int argc;
char *argv[];
{
    char buf[BUFSIZ];
    int  n;

    if ( argc != 3 ) {
        fprintf (stderr, "Bad arg count\n");
        exit (1);
    }

    if ( freopen (argv[1], "r", stdin) == (FILE *) NULL ) {
        fprintf (stderr, "Can't read %s\n", argv[1]);
        exit(2);
    }

    if ( freopen (argv[2], "w", stdout) == (FILE *) NULL ) {
        fprintf (stderr, "Can't write %s\n", argv[2]);
        exit(3);
    }

    do  {
        n = fread (buf, sizeof (char), BUFSIZ, stdin);
        fwrite (buf, sizeof (char), n, stdout);
    }
    while ( n == BUFSIZ );
}
```

```
$ a.out names names5
$ cat names5
Bob
Bill
Alice
Ruth
Tony
```

The input and output files are opened on standard input and standard output as before using `freopen`. Then a `do` loop is entered to copy the file. The loop copies buffer-fulls from standard input to standard output until less than a buffer-full is read and written. At that point, no more data remains on standard input and the `do` is exited. Remember that the value of `n` should be equal to `BUFSIZ` for all but the last read. On the last read, its value will be between 0 and `BUFSIZ` - 1, inclusive.

Later in this chapter we'll take another look at `fread` and `fwrite`, and you'll see them used to read and write structures.

· Random I/O ·

`fseek`	sets file offset to specified value
`rewind`	resets file offset to the beginning
`ftell`	returns current offset from start of file

Normally, I/O operations on a file are sequential in nature. So when you open a file and call `getc` to read a character from it, it's the first character from the file that you read. Calling `getc` again wll return the second character from the file, and so on. Writing to a file works in a similar sequential fashion.

Actually, there is a special number called a *file offset* that is associated with every open file. All reading and writing to a file is based upon the value of this offset. Initially when a file is opened for reading, this offset is automatically set to zero. Reading a character with a function like `getc` causes the character specified by the current file offset to be read (where an offset of zero means the first character) and the file offset to be incremented by one. Reading five characters at once would cause a similar action to occur: the next five characters specified by the current file offset would be read and the offset incremented by five.

Writing to a file is also influenced by the file offset: the writing takes place at the location in the file specified by the file offset, and then the offset is appropriately incremented in anticipation for the next read/write operation. When a file is initially opened for writing, the file offset is set to zero; when it's opened for appending, the file offset is set to one past the last character in the file.

When performing sequential I/O operations, this file offset is of no concern to you. However, you don't always want your I/O operations to be sequential. For instance, you may want to read a record from the middle of a file and write a new record to the end of the file. Or you might want to read the fifth record of a file, followed by the second, followed by the first, and so forth.

When I/O operations are not performed sequentially, then the process is termed *random I/O*, where random means the ability to read from or write to any (random) place in a file. Random I/O is accomplished quite easily under the UNIX system with the three functions `fseek`, `rewind`, and `ftell`. The first two functions simply set the file offset to a desired location in the file prior to performing a read or write operation on the file. The last function tells you what the current file offset is (in case you want to get back to that spot later).

The `fseek` function takes three arguments: a `FILE` pointer, an offset, and a control value. The pointer specifies the file whose offset you want to change. The offset is a *long* integer whose meaning is determined by the third argument to `fseek`. If the third argument is zero, then the second argument is taken as an absolute offset from the start of the file. If the third argument is one, then the second argument (which may be positive or negative) is taken as a relative offset from the *current* file offset. Finally, if the third argument is two, then the second argument is treated as an offset from the end of the file.

A program example will help to show how `fseek` works.

Program 4-20

```
#include <stdio.h>

main ()
{
    FILE *infile;
    int   c;

    if ( (infile = fopen ("test", "r"))  ==   (FILE *) NULL ) {
        fprintf (stderr, "open failed\n");
        exit (1);
    }

    c = fgetc(infile);
    printf ("%c\n", c);

    /* seek from beginning */
    fseek (infile, 4L, 0);
    c = fgetc(infile);
    printf ("%c\n", c);

    /* seek  relative */
    fseek (infile, -2L, 1);
    c = fgetc(infile);
    printf ("%c\n", c);
```

```
        /* seek  from end */
        fseek (infile, -5L, 2);
        c = fgetc(infile);
        printf ("%c\n", c);

        /* rewind */
        rewind (infile);
        c = fgetc(infile);
        printf ("%c\n", c);
}
```

```
S cat test
abcdefghij
$ a.out
a

e

d

g

a
```

The file test contains 10 letters *plus the trailing newline character.* When the file is initially opened, the offset is set to zero; i.e., it "points" to the first character in the file:

```
abcdefghij
↑
```

Calling getc has the effect of reading the character specified by the current file offset. Therefore, the first character, a, is read and then printed. As you'll recall, after the character is read, the file offset points to the next character in the file, the character b:

```
abcdefghij
 ↑
```

The first call to fseek gives a second argument of four (remember the second argument must be a *long* integer, hence the *long* constant 4L), and a third argument of zero. This indicates a seek to relative to the start of the file. Therefore, counting four characters from the start of the file positions the file offset as shown:

```
abcdefghij
    ↑
```

or to the *fifth* character in the file. This is verified by the subsequent getc and `printf` calls: the character `e` is read and printed. The file offset is advanced after the `getc` call as shown:

```
abcdefghij
    ↑
```

The second call to `fseek` gives a third argument of one, meaning that the offset argument should be interpreted relative to the current offset. Counting back two characters from the current offset leaves the file offset like this:

```
abcdefghij
 ↑
```

The third line of output verifies that the character `d` is what then gets read and displayed.

The last call to `fseek` says to move the offset back five characters from the end of the file. Recalling the there is a newline character in the file, the end of the file is interpreted this way by `fseek`:

```
abcdefghij\n
          ↑
```

So the end of the file actually means one character after the last character in the file. Moving it back by five brings it to the character `g` in the file, which is then read and printed.

The `rewind` function is then called to set the offset back to zero, and is equivalent to calling `fseek` this way:

```
fseek (infile, 0L, 0);
```

The last line of output verifies that after a rewind the file offset is set pointing to the start of the file.

Seeking past the end of a file opened for read access will leave the offset at the end of the file. Seeking past the end of a file opened for write access will extend the length of the file by the appropriate amount. In that case, the characters between the old and the new end of the file are meaningless (they're nulls) and you have to fill them in yourself.

Now is a good time to tie together much of the material presented in this chapter. The next example creates a small database of employee information. It uses the `emprec` structure introduced in Chapter 2. The program takes an array of `emprec` structures and writes it to a file called, appropriately enough, `data-base`:

Program 4-21

```
#include <stdio.h>

struct date {
    int         month;
    int         day;
    int         year;
};

struct emprec {
    char        name[25];
    char        room[10];
    int         joblevel;
    long int    salary;
    struct date startdate;
};

main ()
{
    FILE *data;

    static struct emprec employees[1000] = {
        { "Pat Ippolito", "4B-208", 10, 35400, {6, 1, 1984} },
        { "John Musa",    "3G-711", 5,  25000, {1, 9, 1966} },
        { "Steven Levy",  "2D-928", 12, 65500, {9, 15, 1977} },
        { "Ruth Salmon",  "3H-113", 5,  27500, {8, 7, 1964} },
        { "Sue Goldberg", "5D-206", 11, 62000, {7, 1, 1983} },
        { "Leslie Wood",  "4E-313", 10, 32000, {3, 13, 1984} },
    };

    int  entries = 6;

    if ( (data = fopen ("database", "w")) == (FILE *) NULL ) {
        fprintf (stderr, "Can't create database\n");
        exit (1);
    }

    if ( fwrite ( (char *) employees, sizeof (struct emprec),
                        entries, data) != entries ) {
        fprintf (stderr, "error in write\n");
        exit (2);
    }

    printf ("Created database file.\n");
}

$ a.out
Created database file.
```

The program reserves enough space for 1,000 employees but only fills in the first six entries for this example. More realistically, the initial data for such a table would be keyed in from the terminal or come from some other file.

The integer variable `entries` is set to the number of entries in the `employees` table: 6. The file `database` is then opened for writing, and the resulting `FILE` pointer assigned to `data`.

After the file has been opened, the `employees` table is written with a single call to `fwrite`. The first argument says where to start writng from; the second is the size of each entry; the third is the number of such entries, and the last is the file to write the data to. Here you can see how easy it is to transfer large amounts of data to a file with a single call to `fwrite`.

If the `fwrite` call succeeds, then it should return the value `entries`, since that's how many items we asked it to write.

When execution is complete, the file `database` now contains the data stored inside our `employees` table. This data is stored in the file in *binary* form (i.e., the numbers have not been converted to ASCII as a function like `printf` does), and is therefore not suitable for `cat`ing or editing with a text editor like `vi`.

With the `database` file in place, we can now proceed to the next step in this example: to write a program to search through the database for a particular employee's record, and to update the information stored in that record.

Program 4-22

```
/* read in and update employee record */

#include <stdio.h>

struct date {
        int        month;
        int        day;
        int        year;
};

struct emprec {
        char        name[25];
        char        room[10];
        int         joblevel;
        long int    salary;
        struct date startdate;
};
```

```
main ()
{
    FILE            *data;
    struct emprec   emp_entry;
    long            ftell (), spot;
    int             n;

    /* here's the employee to search for */

    char  *search = "John Musa";

    /* open data base for read update */

    if ( (data = fopen ("database", "r+")) == (FILE *) NULL ) {
        fprintf (stderr, "Can't open database\n");
        exit (1);
    }

    /* find particular employee in data base */

    do {
        spot = ftell (data);
        n = fread ( (char *) &emp_entry,
                        sizeof(struct emprec), 1, data );
    }
    while ( n == 1 && strcmp (emp_entry.name, search) != 0 );

    if ( n != 1 ) {
        fprintf (stderr, "%s not found!\n", search);
        exit (2);
    }

    /* now make update and write result back */

    emp_entry.salary = 28000;

    /* position file offset at record to be updated */

    fseek (data, spot, 0);

    fwrite ( (char *) &emp_entry,
                    sizeof (struct emprec), 1, data );
}
```

In this example, we assume that we want to update the information for an employee named John Musa. In particular, we'll assume John has been given a raise from $25,000 to $28,000.

Rather than reading the entire database into memory, the program will sequentially read through the database a single record at a time. This is a more appropriate technique for a very large database. As each record is read, it is stored in the `emprec` structure variable `emp_entry`.

The `database` file is opened in update mode, since we need to do both reading (to find the record we're looking for) and writing (to change it). Care is taken to open the file in read update and not write update, since the latter would destroy the previous contents of the file.

After opening the file, the `do` loop reads a single record from the file into the variable `emp_entry`. Before doing so, `ftell` is called to record the current file offset into the variable `spot`. (Note that `ftell` returns a `long` and must therefore be declared as such.) This will be used later to reposition the file offset back to the start of the matching record.

The loop continues reading records from the file until either the end of file is reached (in which case the returned value from `fread` will not be equal to one—the number of items we requested) or until we find the employee that we're looking for. This latter decision is made by comparing the name of the employee just read into our `emp_entry` structure against the employee's name pointed to by the variable `search`.

After the loop exits, a test is made to determine the cause of its termination. If the value of `n` is not one, then the loop exited due to end of file, in which case a message is logged noting that the employee could not be found in the database.

If the value of `n` is one, then the information for the employee in question now sits inside the `emp_entry` structure variable. The `salary` member is then changed to reflect the raise.

All that now remains is to write the updated record to the file, replacing the old one. To do this, `fseek` is used to reposition the file offset to the start of the employee's record (that's the value returned by the last call to `ftell`) and then `fwrite` is used to write the updated record out to the file.

While this example shows an update operation on a tiny database file, the same techniques would apply to a database containing information for, say, thousands of employees. The only recommended change would be in the search strategy. Locating the employee by a sequential search would be slow. If the database were alphabetically sorted by employee name, for instance, then a binary search could be done on the file (using the random I/O routines you've just learned about) to quickly locate the employee's record.

• Temporary Files •

`tmpfile`	creates and opens a temporary file
`tmpnam`	creates a name for a temporary file
`tempnam`	creates a name for a temporary file in a specified directory

Sometimes during program execution you may need to write some data to a file temporarily. Perhaps you're creating a temporary copy of a file for updating, or you need to store some data someplace during program execution and the data won't all fit into memory. Whatever the reason for needing the temporary file, the three functions listed above provide mechanisms to allow you to easily create and manage these files.

The UNIX system maintains two directories just for working with temporary files: `/tmp` and `/usr/tmp`. These directories are readable and writable by anyone on the system, meaning anyone can create and remove files in these directories.[†] One of the nicest features of these two special directories is that their contents are automatically wiped on system reboot. So lazy programmers who tend to leave temporary files lying around (a bad practice) are assured that they'll be removed the next time the system is restarted.

tmpfile

This function does all of the work for you. It creates a temporary file (in `/usr/tmp` on most UNIX systems) with a unique name, opens the file for write update (`"w+"`), and returns a `FILE` pointer for the opened file. If the file can't be opened, `tmpfile` prints an error message to standard error and returns a `NULL` pointer.

You can now go ahead and do I/O operations on the file. When the process terminates, the file is automatically removed.

This short program simply creates a temporary file, writes a line to it, reads it back, and then displays it at the terminal:

---

† Because these directories are writable by anyone, there are security risks involved when working with files in these directories. For more information, consult [1].

Program 4-23

```
#include <stdio.h>

main ()
{
    FILE    *temp, *tmpfile ();
    char    buf[100];

    if ( (temp = tmpfile ()) == (FILE *) NULL )
        exit (1);

    fputs ("Some data written to a temporary file.\n", temp);
    rewind (temp);
    fgets (buf, 100, temp);
    fputs (buf, stdout);
}
```

```
$ a.out
Some data written to a temporary file.
```

Note that if the call to `tmpfile` fails, no error message is displayed by the program, since `tmpfile` takes care of it.

tmpnam

This function doesn't do quite as much work as `tmpfile`. It simply creates a unique temporary file name. You have to open the file yourself and remove the file when you're through with it. The argument to `tmpnam` is a pointer to a character array. The function places the temporary file name into that array and returns the character pointer as its result. The array should be made large enough to accommodate the temporary file name. The best way to do this is to declare the array to be `L_tmpnam` characters long, where `L_tmpnam` is defined in `stdio.h`.

The argument to `tmpnam` can be a null pointer, in which case `tmpnam` places the temporary file name in a statically allocated array and returns a pointer to it. Subsequent calls to `tmpnam` by the program will overwrite this internal storage area.

Here's the previous program changed to use `tmpnam` to first generate the file name and then `fopen` to open the file.

Program 4-24

```
#include <stdio.h>

main ()
{
        FILE   *temp;
        char   filename [L_tmpnam], buf[100];

        tmpnam (filename);
        if ( (temp = fopen (filename, "w+")) == (FILE *) NULL ) {
                fprintf (stderr, "Couldn't open temp file\n");
                exit (1);
        }

        fputs ("Some data written to a temporary file.\n", temp);
        rewind (temp);
        fgets (buf, 100, temp);
        fputs (buf, stdout);
}
```

```
$ a.out
Some data written to a temporary file.
```

Remember that the temporary file created by this program is not automatically removed when the program terminates. The `unlink` system call, described in the next chapter, can be used to remove the file from inside the program, if desired.

tempnam

This function provides the most control over temporary files. It allows you to specify the directory to be used for creating the temporary file, as well as the prefix characters to be used for the file name.

`tempnam` takes two character pointers as arguments: the first is the name of the directory that the temporary file name is to be created for, and the second is the prefix letters to be used for the file name. If the first argument is null, then the directory specified by `P_tmpdir`, which is defined inside `stdio.h`, is used. Up to five characters can be specified for the prefix. A null second argument specifies no prefix characters are to be used.

`tempnam` returns a pointer to the new file name, which you can then open and use. As with `tmpnam`, the file is not removed automatically when the process terminates.

The next program example shows various file names generated by `tempnam`.

Program 4-25

```
#include <stdio.h>

#define NULLPTR    (char *) NULL

main ()
{
        char *tempnam ();

        printf ("%s\n", tempnam ("/tmp", "XYZ"));
        printf ("%s\n", tempnam ("/tmp", "XYZ"));

        printf ("%s\n", tempnam (NULLPTR, "temp"));
        printf ("%s\n", tempnam (NULLPTR, NULLPTR));
}
```

```
$ a.out
/tmp/XYZAAAa19559
/tmp/XYZBAAa19559
/usr/tmp/tempCAAa19559
/usr/tmp/DAAa19559
```

The first two calls create temporary file names in the /tmp directory, with the prefix letters XYZ. The third call gives a null first argument, so tempnam creates the file name in the default directory /usr/tmp with the prefix characters temp. The last call passes null pointers as both arguments, so tempnam creates a temporary file name in the default directory with no prefix characters.

If for some reason tempnam fails, it returns a null pointer, which should be checked by the program.

Remember that no files get created by calls to either tmpnam or tempnam; only temporary file *names*.

Before leaving this discussion on temporary files, you should note that the Standard C Library also has a routine called mktemp that allows for the creation of temporary file names. It takes as its argument a pointer to a character array that mktemp will use to store the file name in. Inside that array you must put six trailing X characters. mktemp will replace those Xs with other characters to make the resulting file name unique.

The following example shows how mktemp can be used to create file names. Here two file names are generated, one in the directory /tmp and the other in /usr/steve.

To see the results of the mktemp calls, the program uses the fact that mktemp returns its argument (the pointer to the character array) and passes that returned pointer directly to printf.

Program 4-26

```
main ()
{
    static char  t1[] = "/tmp/XXXXXX";
    static char  t2[] = "/usr/steve/tmp.XXXXXX";

    printf ("%s\n", mktemp (t1));
    printf ("%s\n", mktemp (t2));
}
```

```
$ a.out
/tmp/a02232
/usr/steve/tmp.a02232
```

Remember, `mktemp` only generates a file name and doesn't open the file or remove it when the process terminates.

· Shell Command Execution ·

system	gives a command line to the shell for execution
popen	gives a command line to the shell for execution, connecting its input or output to the program
pclose	closes stream opened by `popen`

The `system` and `popen` functions both allow you to execute any standard UNIX commands or your own programs. They take as arguments a command line that is handed to the UNIX system's shell for execution.† Since the shell executes the command line, any shell constructs can be used in the command line. That means, for example, that multiple commands can be executed with a single `system` or `popen` call by separating the commands with semicolons; pipes can be used (e.g., `who | wc -1`), and I/O redirection (e.g., `prog > out`), file name substitution (e.g., `memo*`), and variable substitution (e.g., `$HOME`) can all be specified.

In the case of the `system` function, the input to and output from the command goes to the standard places. If the command writes to standard output, then it goes to the terminal by default. If the command reads from standard input, then it comes from the terminal by default.

---

† You should always specify a *full* path to the program you want the shell to execute. The reason for this is described in [1].

system and popen differ in that a second argument to popen allows you either to read the output of the command directly into your program or to write to the input of the command. popen does this by connecting a pipe (more on that in the next chapter) to the command being executed.

Here is a program example that shows how to use the system function. The program prints the date and time at the terminal using the date command. Then it displays the contents of the file plotlist using the cat command. Presumably, this file contains some dates to be plotted by the program. After displaying the file, the program starts up the UNIX editor ed on the file plotlist to allow the user to make changes to it. After the user makes any needed changes and quits the editor, control is given back to the program, which then redisplays the contents of the plotlist file.

As you can see, system takes a single argument: the command line to execute.

Program 4-27

```
main ()
{
     char buf[100];
     char *file="plotlist";

     printf ("\nPlot list:\n");
     system ("/bin/date");
     sprintf (buf, "/bin/cat %s", file);
     system (buf);

     printf ("\nMake changes with ed:\n");

     sprintf (buf, "/bin/ed %s", file);
     system (buf);

     printf ("\nCurrent Plot list:\n");
     sprintf (buf, "/bin/cat %s", file);
     system (buf);
}
```

```
$ a.out
Mon Oct 18 12:03:32 EDT 1987

Plot list:
2/86
5/86
9/86
```

```
Make changes with ed:
15
$a
10/86          Add a new date to the end of the file
w
21
q          Quit the editor

Current Plot list:
2/86
5/86
9/86
10/86
```

When you start up an interactive program, that program gets full control of the terminal. If the standard input and/or standard output to your C program has been redirected, then the program executed with the system call will also have its input and/or output redirected. You can override this by explicitly redirecting input and/or output of the command executed by system. For example, since /dev/tty refers to your terminal, the call

```
system ("/bin/ed plotlist </dev/tty >/dev/tty");
```

causes standard input and output for ed to be taken from the terminal, overriding any redirection that may be in effect for the program initiating the system function call. A program that calls system is suspended until the shell finishes executing the command line given as its argument.

Some things can't be easily done without system. For instance, you can't create a directory from a C program unless your program runs with special privileges. However, the UNIX system's mkdir command can be used to avoid this inconvenience. So

```
system ("mkdir tempdir");
```

will create the directory tempdir, provided of course that you have the appropriate permission to do so in the current directory.

As noted, popen works similarly to system, except that it takes a second argument that indicates whether you want to read ("r") the standard output from the command into your program or write ("w") to the standard input of the command from your program. popen returns a FILE pointer that can be treated just as if the pointer were returned by fopen. So any of the I/O routines discussed in this chapter—with the exception of the random I/O ones—can be used.

fclose is not used to close a stream opened by popen. Instead, pclose must be used. pclose will wait for the command to finish (if it hasn't already), returning its exit status.

The following example shows how easy it is to read the output of any command into your program. Here the program reads the output from the command sequence who | wc -l, which represents the number of users logged on to the system. Once that result has been read by the program, it simply displays the result at the terminal.

Program 4-28

```
/* Display number of users logged on */

#include <stdio.h>

main ()
{
    FILE   *in, *popen ();
    int    numusers;

    in = popen ("/bin/who | /bin/wc -l", "r");

    if ( in == (FILE *) NULL ) {
        fprintf (stderr, "popen failed\n");
        exit (1);
    }

    fscanf (in, "%d", &numusers);

    printf ("There are %d users logged on.\n", numusers);
    pclose (in);
}
```

```
$ a.out
There are 15 users logged on.
```

popen must be declared to return a FILE pointer, since that's not done by most versions of stdio.h.

The FILE pointer that popen returns should be checked to see if it's NULL. If it is, then the popen failed. (Maybe you gave an invalid command name.)

The program calls pclose to close the stream opened by popen. It's really not necessary here, since the output has been read by the program and nothing is left to be done.

The next example shows how to use popen to write data to a command. Here the program executes the mail command to send electronic mail to the user pat. mail reads the message to send to the specified user from standard input. Since we want the program to write that message, popen is called with a second argument of "w". The FILE pointer that popen returns is then used in subsequent fprintf calls to write data to the command. When finished, pclose is called to close the input to mail and to wait for it to finish.

Program 4-29

```
#include <stdio.h>

main ()
{
    FILE   *out, *popen ();

    /* send some mail to pat */

    out = popen ("/bin/mail pat", "w");

    if ( out == (FILE *) NULL ) {
        fprintf (stderr, "popen failed\n");
        exit (1);
    }

    /* now write the message */

    fprintf (out, "Pat:\n");
    fprintf (out, "Here's some mail sent to you\n");
    fprintf (out, "from my C program\n");
    fprintf (out, "---Steve\n");

    pclose (out);
}
```

(Note that the mail command may be stored in /usr/bin on some systems.)

So you can see that system and popen can be quite useful. Not just for executing standard UNIX commands, but for your own programs as well. However, before you go ahead and do everything with system and/or popen, here's some advice: Because the shell is used to execute each command line, there is an enormous amount of overhead associated with each system/popen call.[†] To reduce this overhead somewhat when using system, try to group as many commands together (remember you can do this by separating them with

---

† Technically, what happens is that the program has to *fork* and *exec* the shell, and then the shell has to fork and exec the requested program (unless a shell built-in is being executed).

semicolons) and execute them with a single call to `system`. Better yet, if you're not using any of the shell's features, then the program should be executed directly by using the `fork` and `exec` system calls in the case of `system`, and by using the `pipe`, `fork`, and `exec` system calls in the case of `popen` (see the next chapter).

If your program needs to run with its SUID or SGID permission bit turned on, then `system` and `popen` represent potential security hazards. For more details, consult reference [1], which goes into this topic in detail.

▪ Buffering ▪

`fflush`	forces buffered output to be written to a file
`setbuf`	sets up buffering for a file
`setvbuf`	sets up buffering for a file

As noted at the start of this chapter, data written to a file is kept in memory inside a character array (the *buffer*) and is not actually written to the file until the buffer is filled, the file is closed, or the process terminates normally.

Data read from a file is handled in a similar fashion: when a request is made to read from a file, at least an entire buffer-full is read into a character array (the *buffer*) where it is kept to process subsequent reads. When the buffer is emptied (because all of its data has been read), the next buffer is read from the file. This input buffering scheme is quite effective when doing sequential reads of small amounts of data from a file. If you're doing random I/O on a large file, then a buffering scheme like this can actually hurt the performance of your program instead of improving it.

I/O to a terminal is handled differently. As each character is written to the terminal by the program, it is buffered and not written to the device until a new-line character is written or until input from the terminal is requested.[†] This is known as *line buffering*.

As noted earlier in this chapter, input from a terminal is line buffered. That is, your program won't see any data being typed from a terminal until you press the *RETURN* key.

Output to standard error is handled differently: it isn't buffered at all. So if your program writes some error messages and then abnormally terminates, you still should see those messages, even if standard error has been redirected to a file.

---

† On XENIX III, output to a terminal is unbuffered; each character is sent to the terminal as it's written.

fflush

Sometimes you want to force data to be written to a file. The fflush function allows you to force any output data that may be sitting in a buffer to be written to the file. Its argument is a FILE pointer; it returns zero on success, and EOF on failure, which may be caused by trying to flush output to a file that's already been closed.

So the call

```
fflush (stdout);
```

forces any pending output for standard output to be written.

You can insert in your program as many calls to fflush as desired to force data to be written to a file. Obviously, calls to fflush are only needed in special circumstances. One might be when a program terminates abnormally for some reason (maybe division by zero or an invalid memory reference). Inserting calls to fflush will allow you to see the data that your program wrote to a particular file before terminating.

Another use of fflush might be when writing data to a file that is to be read by another program. fflush will force the data to be written to the file so that it then can be read by that program (there are more elegant ways of passing data between two programs—such as with named pipes—that are beyond the scope of this book).

setbuf

setbuf allows you to supply your own character array to be used as the buffer for I/O operations on a file, in place of the one that is automatically allocated for you. It also allows you to turn off buffering on an open stream.

The first argument is a FILE pointer. This should be for a file from which no data has yet been read or written. The second argument to setbuf is a pointer to a character array to be used as the buffer. This array should be BUF-SIZ characters in length, where BUFSIZ is defined inside stdio.h. If the second argument is a null pointer, then I/O on the specified stream will not be buffered.

setbuf does not return a value.

To make standard output unbuffered, you write:

```
setbuf (stdout, (char *) NULL);
```

To specify that databuf be used as the buffer for a file called data, the following code can appear can appear in the program:

```
#include <stdio.h>

    ...

FILE   *infile;
char   databuf[BUFSIZ];

if ( (infile = fopen ("data", "r")) == (FILE *) NULL ) {
    fprintf (stderr, "fopen failed\n");
    exit (1);
}

setbuf (data, databuf);
```

In this case, you must be careful where databuf is declared. If it's defined as an automatic array inside a function, then make sure you're done with the file before returning from the function, as the stack space reserved for the array will be deallocated when the function returns.

Obviously, this use of setbuf is only for specialized situations where you need access to the actual buffer that is used for performing I/O to a file, or when you require that output to a file be unbuffered (remember, output to standard error is always unbuffered anyway).

setvbuf

This routine gives more control over the buffering strategy than does setbuf. It takes four arguments: a FILE pointer, a pointer to the buffer, an integer specifying the buffering strategy to be employed, and an integer specifying the size of the buffer.

If the second argument (the buffer pointer) is null, then the buffer is allocated by the system, and the last argument is the size of the buffer to allocate.

The third argument, which indicates the type of buffering to be used, is specified as values defined inside stdio.h:

_IOFBF   means full buffering of input and output (the default for normal files)

_IOLBF   means line buffering of output

_IONBF   means no buffering of input or output

Line buffering of output means that the buffer is not flushed until either a newline is written, the buffer is filled, the file is closed, or data is read from the file.

If _IONBF is specified, the second argument, the buffer pointer, and the last argument, the buffer size, are ignored.

The following opens a file called `data` for reading, specifying that reads from the file are not to be buffered (this may be useful if random reads will be done exclusively on a large file).

```
#include <stdio.h>

    ...

FILE   *infile;

if ( (infile = fopen ("data", "r")) == (FILE *) NULL ) {
             fprintf (stderr, "fopen falied\n");
             exit (1);
       }

setvbuf (infile, (char *) 0, _IONBF, 0);
```

▪ Error Handling ▪

clearerr	clears error condition on specified stream
feof	tests for end of file on specified stream
ferror	tests for I/O error on specified stream

clearerr

There are two indicators associated with every open stream. One indicates whether an error occurred on the last I/O operation to the stream. The other indicates whether the end of the file was reached on the last read from the stream. `clearerr` takes a `FILE` pointer as its argument and resets the error indicator and the end of file indicator on the specified stream.

feof

This function returns nonzero if the stream specified by its argument has its end of file indicator set, zero otherwise. This indicator is set when a *previous* read operation on the stream encountered the end of the file.

As noted earlier in this chapter, if you're using `getw` to read words, you must test for end of file using `feof`. The following program copies standard input to standard output one word at a time:

Program 4-30

```
#include <stdio.h>

main ()
{
   int  word;

   word = getw (stdin);

   while ( ! feof (stdin) ) {
      putw (word, stdout);
      word = getw (stdin);
   }
}
```

Remember, `feof` returns nonzero if the end of file has already been read on the specified stream. It's not testing to see if the next read will result in end of file.

ferror

This function returns nonzero if the stream specified by its argument has the error indicator set, zero otherwise. The error indicator will be set if for some reason a prior I/O operation on the stream failed. Note that reading to the end of the file doesn't set the error indicator; it sets the special end of file indicator that can be tested by `feof`.

· Information Routines ·

`ctermid`	gives the path name to the terminal associated with the process
`cuserid`	gives the name of the owner of the terminal or of the process, if the process is not attached to a terminal
`fileno`	returns integer file descriptor associated with a file

ctermid and cuserid

These routines give information about the process: the path name of the *controlling* terminal and the name of the user associated with the process. The controlling terminal is usually the terminal that the user is logged on to, and the path name returned by `ctermid` is usually `/dev/tty`.[†] `cuserid` is similar to

---

† Technically, the controlling terminal is the first terminal opened by the process' *group leader*. The group leader is usually your login shell, but a process can make itself the leader of a new group with the `setpgrp` system call, discussed in the next chapter.

getlogin (described in the previous chapter), except that it doesn't require that the process be associated with a terminal (getlogin returns a null pointer if neither standard input, standard output, nor standard error is associated with a terminal).[†] If the process is being run from a terminal, then cuserid returns a pointer to the name of the owner of that terminal; otherwise, it returns a pointer to the name of the owner of the process.

Both ctermid and cuserid take arguments—pointers to character arrays—where the result is placed. In the case of ctermid the array should be at least L_ctermid characters in length. For cuserid it should be L_cuserid characters in length. Both L_ctermid and L_cuserid are defined in stdio.h. The argument to either routine can be null, in which case a pointer to an array that is statically allocated by the routine is returned.

cuserid returns a null pointer on failure.

Program 4-31

```
#include <stdio.h>

main ()
{
        char   name [L_cuserid];

        cuserid (name);
        printf ("Your login name is: %s\n", name);

        printf ("Your controlling terminal is %s\n",
                ctermid ((char *) NULL));
}
```

```
$ a.out
Your login name is: steve
Your controlling terminal is /dev/tty
```

cuserid is called here with a pointer to the name array; ctermid is called with a null pointer. This was done simply to illustrate the two ways either routine can be used.

fileno

This function takes a FILE pointer and returns the integer *file descriptor* associated with the stream. Recall that brief mention was made of file descriptors when fdopen was described.

---

† As noted when getlogin was described, you shouldn't use ctermid to reliably get the name of the owner of the current process—it can be fooled. Again, for more details, consult [1].

File descriptors are treated in detail as part of the topic material in the next chapter. Before continuing with that chapter, however, why not try the exercises that follow?

▪ References ▪

[1]   P. H. Wood and S. G. Kochan, *UNIX System Security*, Hayden Books, Indianapolis, IN, 1985.

▪ Function Summary ▪

Table 4-7 summarizes the functions described in detail in this chapter. Each entry in the table lists the function's return value, its arguments, and provides a brief summary of its use. You should assume that all functions from the Standard I/O Library require the header file `stdio.h`.

The following notations are used for depicting argument types in the table:

Argument	Type
a	*any data type*
c	char
f	FILE *
i1, i2	int
l	long int
p	*any pointer data type*
s, s1, s2	char *

TABLE 4-7. Summary of Standard I/O Library Routines

Function	Description
void clearerr (f)	Reset error indicator on f
char *ctermid (s)	Get name of terminal associated with process
char *cuserid (s)	Get name of owner of terminal or of process
int fclose (f)	Close f
FILE *fdopen (i, s)	Associate a stream with open file descriptor i, mode s
int feof (f)	TRUE if end of file previously detected on f
int ferror (f)	TRUE if I/O error occurred on f
int fflush (f)	Force data to be written to file
int fgetc (f)	Read next char from f
char *fgets (s, n, f)	Read up to n–1 bytes from f into s; storing newline if read
int fileno (f)	Return file descriptor number for f
FILE *fopen (s1, s2)	Open file s1, mode s2 ("r"=read, "w"=write, "a"=append, "r+", "w+", "a+", are update modes)
int fprintf (f, s, a, ...)	Write args a, ... to f according to format s
int fputc (c, f)	Write c to f
int fputs (s, f)	Write s to f
int fread (s, i1, i2, f)	Read i1 * i2 bytes from f into s, returning number of bytes read
FILE *freopen (s1, s2, f)	Close f and open s1 in its place, mode s2
int fscanf (f, s, p, ...)	Read data from f according to format s, storing values into variables pointed to by p, ...
int fseek (f, l, i)	Position file offset in f; if i=0, l is offset from start; i=1, l is offset from current position; i=2, l is offset from end
long ftell (f)	Return current offset in f
int fwrite (s, i1, i2, f)	Write i1 * i2 bytes from s to f
int getc (f)	Read next char from f
int getchar ()	Read next char from standard input
char *gets (s)	Read next line from standard input into s (newline not stored)
int getw (f)	Read next word from f
int pclose (f)	Close stream f previously opened by popen
FILE *popen (s1, s2)	Execute shell command line s1; s2 is "r" to read its output, "w" to write to its input
int printf (s, a, ...)	Write args a, ... to standard output according to format s
int putc (c, f)	Write c to f
int putchar (c)	Write c to standard output
int puts (s)	Write s to standard output (newline appended)
int putw (i, f)	Write i to f
void rewind (f)	Reset file offset on f to zero
int scanf (s, p, ...)	Read data from standard input according to format s, storing values into variables pointed to by p, ...
void setbuf (f, s)	Use s as buffer for f (if s is null, f is unbuffered)
int setvbuf (f, s, i1, i2)	Use s as buffer for f; i1 is buffer type, i2 is size
int sprintf (s1, s2, a, ...)	Write args a, ... into s1 according to format s2
int sscanf (s1, s2, p, ...)	Convert data in s1 according to format s2, storing values into variables pointed to by p, ...
int system (s)	Execute shell command line s
char *tempnam (s1, s2)	Create temporary file name for directory s1, prefix chars s2
FILE *tmpfile ()	Create and open temporary file
char *tmpnam (s)	Create temporary file name in s (if s is null, just return name)
int ungetc (c, f)	Insert c into f, as if it weren't read

E X E R C I S E S

1. Write a function called `fopenp` that is modeled after `fopen`. As with `fopen`, have it take two arguments: the file to open and its mode. The function should then pass these arguments along to `fopen` to open the file. If the `fopen` fails, write a message to standard error that identifies the file that couldn't be opened. Then call `perror` to more precisely identify the cause of the error. Have `fopenp` return the `FILE` pointer that `fopen` returns.

    Modify the programs presented in this chapter to use `fopenp` instead of `fopen`. Test them out.

2. Write a program called `mypg` that displays the contents of a file at the terminal one screenful at a time. At the end of each screenful, prompt the user to type a disposition character. If the character is `q`, then exit the program. Anything else should cause the next screenful from the file to be displayed. Assume the terminal is capable of displaying 24 lines.

    Take the name of the file to be displayed from the command line.

3. Modify `mypg` so that if the variable `LINES` is set in the environment, its value is used as the number of lines the terminal can display. Use the `getenv` function described in Chapter 3 to get the variable from the environment.

4. Modify `mypg` to allow the user to type a `p` to view the previous screenful from the file. Allow the user to type multiple `p`'s in succession. Think about how to handle this efficiently.

5. Implement the UNIX system's `cat` command. Be sure to handle all of its options (consult your Reference manual for a list of available options).

6. Modify Program 4-22 so that it interactively allows the user to change one or more fields in the database file.

7. Assume that the database created by Program 4-21 is sorted alphabetically by the employee's first name. Modify Program 4-22 to do a binary search on the database file to quickly locate an employee by name. Test the program with a larger data base.

    (Hint: You need to determine the size of the file for the binary search. Use `fseek` and `ftell` for this.)

5

THE UNIX SYSTEM INTERFACE

T his chapter deals with the routines described in Section 2 of the *UNIX Programmer Reference Manual*. These routines are often referred to as *system calls*, *kernel calls*, *kernel entry points*, and *system routines*; they are the UNIX programmer's interface into the operating system and are the foundation of the C subroutines described in previous chapters.

The Standard I/O and Standard C routines are exactly what they're called: standard. They exist in most versions of the C language regardless of the operating system being used. Programs that use these routines exclusively are fairly portable, requiring little or no change to move from one environment to another. The routines described in this chapter are altogether different. They are implemented only on UNIX or UNIX-like systems; although some non-UNIX C compilers come with libraries that approximate these routines, few come close to implementing all of them, as the UNIX interface routines are closely tied to the UNIX system itself. The interface routines on different versions of UNIX tend to differ, with the greatest divergence occuring in the routines that perform I/O. One of the best features of the Standard I/O Library is that it insulates the programmer from these incompatibilities. You may wonder why anyone would want to use the UNIX interface routines at all, considering these incompatibilities; however, as you'll see, there are a great many things you can do with the UNIX interface routines that you can't do with the Standard I/O or Standard C Libraries. You'll also see that sometimes the UNIX interface routines are more efficient.

The Standard I/O and Standard C (as well as other) libraries make use of the UNIX interface routines to perform functions such as creating, opening, reading, and writing files, devices, and pipes; creating processes; executing programs; and allocating memory. These libraries can be thought of as a layer of insulation between the programmer and the system routines, providing a uniform, "standard" appearance. For example, `fopen` doesn't actually open the specified file; instead, it calls the system routine `open` to open the file. `fopen` makes use of the value returned by `open` to create a file pointer for later use by routines such as `fread`, `fwrite`, `fscanf,` and `fprintf`. These routines, in turn, make use of other system routines to perform reading and writing on the previously opened file.

The routines described in this chapter are a subset of the ones available on UNIX System V Release 2.0. There are several reasons for covering a subset instead of all the system routines: many routines are available on only one version of UNIX or machine type (vlimit, sys3b); others are implemented differently on different versions (interprocess communication, and file locking[†]); and some are only used for system maintenance and administration (mount, acct). Except as noted, the routines covered in this chapter are the same on System V, System III, Version 7, XENIX III, UTS, and BSD 4.1 and 4.2.

The system routines can be divided into five general categories:

1. I/O Routines: opening and closing files, reading and writing, performing random I/O, creating and using pipes, and controlling terminal I/O.

2. File Manipulation Routines: creating, removing, and linking files; changing file mode and ownership; and getting file status.

3. Process Control Routines: creating new processes, executing programs, communicating between processes with pipes, getting and setting process information.

4. Signal Handling Routines: sending, waiting for, and receiving signals.

5. System Information Routines: accessing the time of day and system name.

· I/O Routines ·

open	opens file for reading and/or writing
close	closes file descriptor
dup	duplicates file descriptor
fcntl	controls open file
read	reads data from open file
write	writes data to open file
lseek	moves read/write file position
pipe	creates a FIFO I/O channel

These routines are used to perform I/O on files and pipes on the UNIX system. They should not be confused with the Standard I/O Library routines.

---

† For in-depth coverage of IPC and file locking, see [1].

Considering that the Standard I/O routines are flexible enough to perform almost all of the functions that the above routines perform, you may be wondering why you should learn about them at all. Actually, the Standard I/O routines are more efficient in most cases; however, in some cases, considerable speed can be gained in bypassing Standard I/O and performing I/O directly with the UNIX interface routines.

As we noted in Chapter 4, the Standard I/O routines buffer their data, performing input and output when the buffers are empty and full, respectively. This buffering makes I/O that is performed on small amounts of data (e.g., single character I/O) more efficient. Since many of the Standard I/O routines are not actually implemented as subroutines, but as macros, performance is improved by removing the overhead of a subroutine call. Also, calls to the UNIX interface routines have their own overhead, varying in degree depending upon both the hardware UNIX is running on and the specific implementation of UNIX for that system. Because of this, you don't want to call `read` or `write` repeatedly to read or write single characters.

On the other hand, the buffering performed by the Standard I/O routines is inefficient when I/O can be performed in large chunks, as when copying large files. In this case, the buffering performed by the Standard I/O routines simply forces the system to copy the data an extra time. Turning off buffering (with `setbuf`) brings `fread` and `fwrite` close to the speed of `read` and `write`; however, since the Standard I/O routines call `read` and `write` to perform the actual I/O, there's still the overhead of an extra subroutine call in each case.

In general, when performing I/O in amounts larger than the block size on the system, it's faster to use the UNIX interface routines directly. The block size on System V and later releases of AT&T's UNIX is specified by the `BSIZE` preprocessor constant in `<sys/param.h>`, which is usually the same as the `BUFSIZ` in `<stdio.h>` (however, there's no *guarantee* they are the same). When performing block I/O in this chapter, we'll assume the block size is 1024 bytes.[†]

Another advantage of not using the Standard I/O routines is that your programs will be smaller without the extra code and data structures. Also, as you'll see later on, when you need complete control over terminal I/O, the Standard I/O routines don't suffice—you have to resort to using the following routines.

open

The `open` routine is called to open a file. It's called with the name of the file to open, along with some status flags that specify (among other things) whether the file is to be opened for reading, writing, or both reading and writing. These flags are defined in the include file `fcntl.h`. If the file being opened is also being created, a third argument must be given specifying the mode or permissions that the new file will have.[‡]

---

† Block sizes can vary widely between systems, and even the same system can have different sized blocks. On System V micro- and minicomputer systems, the block size is usually 512 or 1024 bytes; on IBM mainframes, it's usually 4096 or 8192 bytes; and on BSD UNIX systems it can vary from 512 to 8192 bytes. Since `param.h` doesn't exist on all UNIX systems, using 1024 for the block size as a rule of thumb is as good as any.

‡ On Seventh Edition and Berkeley 4.1 UNIX systems, `open` cannot be used to create files. The only flags available are `0` (read), `1` (write), and `2` (read and write).

If open is successful in opening the file, it returns an integer number between 0 and 19 called the *file descriptor*; otherwise, it returns −1. The file descriptor is similar to the FILE pointer returned by fopen, in that it is used by other interface routines for reading and/or writing to the file. Note that all I/O on UNIX is performed on file descriptors, *not the files themselves*, and you cannot perform I/O on a file descriptor unless it has been opened via a previous call to open. The Standard I/O routine fopen uses open to open files for I/O and maps the returned file descriptors onto FILE pointers.

File descriptors are allocated starting with the lowest unused one; usually, the first three file descriptors are already in use: zero is standard input, one is standard output, and two is standard error. So usually the first file you open is put on file descriptor three, the next on descriptor four, and so on.

The following call to open opens the file foo in the current directory for reading, assigning the file descriptor to the integer variable fdesc:

```
fdesc = open ("foo", O_RDONLY);
```

The flag O_RDONLY is defined in fcntl.h; it means that the file should be opened for reading only, and any output attempted on the returned file descriptor is illegal.

A similar flag, O_WRONLY, is used to open a file for writing only:

```
fdesc = open ("fool", O_WRONLY);
```

The following are the flags that may be used in a call to open:

O_RDONLY	Open the file for reading only.
O_WRONLY	Open the file for writing only.
O_RDWR	Open the file for both reading and writing.
O_NDELAY	Open immediately. This is covered in detail in the sections on communication lines and pipes.
O_APPEND	Open the file for appending. If the file is also opened for writing, all output to the file will be appended to the data already in the file, i.e., once data is in the file, it won't be overwritten.
O_TRUNC	If the file exists and is being opened for writing, its size is set to zero (its contents are clobbered).
O_CREAT	If the file is opened for writing and it doesn't exist, it is to be created. A mode must be specified as the third argument.
O_EXCL	If the file already exists and is being opened for writing and creation (O_CREAT), open will fail.

The first three flags are mutually exclusive, and the others are ignored if used in combinations that don't make sense (e.g., O_RDONLY and O_APPEND). Flags are combined with the OR (|) operator:

```
fdesc = open ("foo", O_WRONLY | O_CREAT, 0666);
```

Open the file foo for writing; if it doesn't exist, create it with mode 0666 (readable and writable by everyone).[†]

Several examples showing the use of open and these flags will be given at the end of the next section.

fopen calls open with different combinations of the above flags to satisfy its various access modes. Table 5-1 shows the relationship between fopen and open modes.

TABLE 5-1. fopen vs. open Modes

fopen *Mode*	open () *Flags*			*Meaning*
"r"	O_RDONLY			Open for reading only
"w"	O_WRONLY	O_TRUNC	O_CREAT	Open for writing only, truncate existing file or create new file
"a"	O_WRONLY	O_APPEND	O_CREAT	Open for writing at end of file, create if file doesn't exist
"r+"	O_RDWR			Like "r" but allow writing
"w+"	O_RDWR	O_TRUNC	O_CREAT	Like "w" but allow reading
"a+"	O_RDWR	O_APPEND	O_CREAT	Like "a" but allow reading

close

A file descriptor may be closed with the close routine. It closes the specified file descriptor and makes it available for use by a subsequent call to open:

```
fdesc = open ("foo", O_RDONLY);
    . . .
close (fdesc);
```

As noted, since valid file descriptors range from 0 to 19, a program may only have 20 files open at any given time. If, after opening 20 files, a program needs to open another file, one of the open file descriptors must first be closed with a call to close.

---

† The mode is actually masked with the file creation mask, or *umask*. See the discussion of umask later in this chapter.

dup

A file descriptor may be duplicated onto another file descriptor with the dup system routine. dup takes an open file descriptor as its only argument, and returns a duplicate of it on the lowest unused file descriptor. So after a call to dup, you have two file descriptors referring to the same file. Although right now this may seem rather strange, later on in this chapter you'll see how useful dup is with pipes.

fcntl

The fcntl routine provides control over open file descriptors. It can be used to duplicate a file descriptor (similar to dup), get or set the *close-on-exec* flag, and get and set flags that are used by open. fcntl takes three arguments: a file descriptor, a command, and an optional argument. The commands, as defined in fcntl.h are:

F_DUPFD Duplicates the file descriptor (like dup) onto the lowest available file descriptor *greater than or equal to the argument*. Returns the new file descriptor.

F_GETFD Returns the close-on-exec flag associated with the specified file descriptor. If the returned value is one, the flag is on and if zero, the flag is off. See the section on exec for more information on this flag.

F_SETFD Sets the close-on-exec flag associated with the specified file descriptor to the low-order bit of the argument; so if the argument is odd, the flag is turned on, and if the argument is even, the flag is turned off.

F_GETFL Returns the file status flags set when opening a file or by a previous call to fcntl: O_RDONLY, O_WRONLY, O_RDWR, O_NDELAY, and O_APPEND.

F_SETFL Sets the file status flags to those specified in the argument. Only O_NDELAY and O_APPEND may be set from fcntl.

If successful, fcntl returns the specified value (if any), and if unsuccessful, it returns -1.

We'll discuss fcntl's most useful feature, the ability to set the O_NDELAY flag, when we get into terminal I/O.

read

The read routine is used to input data from a file descriptor opened for reading. It uses the first argument as the file descriptor to read from and places the data into the area of memory pointed to by the second argument. Its third argument specifies the number of bytes to input. read returns the number of bytes actually read, which should match the number of bytes requested, unless the end of the file has been reached or the read is being performed on a terminal (we'll talk about terminal I/O later).   read returns zero if it's already at the end of the file, and –1 if an error occurs (e.g., invalid file descriptor).

The following program reads ten bytes from the file foo and outputs them followed by a newline; it then repeats these actions.

Program 5-1

```
#include <fcntl.h>

main ()
{
    int  fdesc;
    char input[11];

    /* open foo for reading */
    fdesc = open ("foo", O_RDONLY);

    /* make sure it was really opened */
    if ( fdesc == -1 ) {
        printf ("cannot open foo for reading\n");
        exit (1);
    }

    /* read 10 bytes from fdesc (foo) */
    read (fdesc, input, 10);

    /* make sure there's a zero byte at the end */
    input[10] = '\0';

    /* output the data */
    printf ("%s\n", input);

    /* one more time */
    read (fdesc, input, 10);

    /* output the data */
    printf ("%s\n", input);
}
```

```
$ cat foo
this is the first test line
this is another test line
$ a.out
this is th
e first te
```

The `read` routine isn't line oriented—it just reads in the number of bytes it's told to.

Remember that `open` doesn't return a `FILE` pointer, it returns a *file descriptor*, which cannot be used by `fread`, `fscanf`, and other Standard I/O routines. As was mentioned in the previous chapter, the `fdopen` routine in the Standard I/O Library may be used to create a `FILE` pointer from a file descriptor, and the `fileno` routine may be used to access the file descriptor associated with a `FILE` pointer.

write

The `write` routine is used to output data to a file descriptor opened for writing. It uses the first argument as the file descriptor to write to and takes the data from the area of memory pointed to by the second argument. Its third argument specifies the number of bytes to output. `write` returns the number of bytes written, which normally will be the same as the number of bytes requested; if there is an error (e.g., invalid file descriptor), it returns –1.

Program 5-2

```c
#include <fcntl.h>

main ()
{
    int fdesc;

    /* open foo for writing */
    fdesc = open ("foo", O_WRONLY);

    /* make sure it was really opened */
    if ( fdesc == -1 ) {
        printf ("cannot open foo for writing\n");
        exit (1);
    }

    /* write some data to fdesc (foo) */
    write (fdesc, "1234567890", 10);
}
```

```
$ cat foo
this is the first test line
this is another test line
$ a.out
$ cat foo
1234567890e first test line
this is another test line
```

Since foo was opened for writing, but wasn't truncated, the write merely replaced the first ten bytes of foo with 1234567890. If we replace the above open with

```
fdesc = open ("foo", O_WRONLY | O_TRUNC);
```

the O_TRUNC flag throws away the contents of the file being opened, so now things will be different when we run writefoo:

```
$ cat foo
1234567890e first test line
this is another test line
$ a.out
$ cat foo
1234567890$
```

write doesn't append a newline (\n) to the end of the bytes that it writes out, so the shell's prompt ($) comes out on the same line as the output of write. A simple way to fix that is to replace the above call to write with

```
write (fdesc, "1234567890\n", 11);
```

Program 5-3 uses read and write to copy the file foo to the file foo1.

Program 5-3

```c
#include <fcntl.h>

#define BUFLEN    1024

main ()
{
    char  buf[BUFLEN];
    int   nread, ifdesc, ofdesc;

    /*
    ** open input file "foo"
    ** print error message if can't open
    */

    if ( (ifdesc = open ("foo", O_RDONLY)) == -1 ) {
        printf ("cannot open foo for reading\n");
        exit (1);
    }

    /*
    ** open output file "foo1"
    ** print error message if can't create/open
    */

    if ( (ofdesc = open ("foo1", O_WRONLY | O_CREAT | O_TRUNC, 0666))
            == -1 ) {
        printf ("cannot open foo1 for writing\n");
        exit (2);
    }

    /*
    ** keep copying until empty; nread should equal BUFLEN
    ** except on last read
    */

    while ( (nread = read (ifdesc, buf, BUFLEN)) > 0 )
        write (ofdesc, buf, nread);
}
```

```
$ cat foo
this is a simple test for copying
line 2: this is a simple test for copying
line 3: this is a simple test for copying
line 4: this is a simple test for copying
$ a.out
$ cat foo1
this is a simple test for copying
line 2: this is a simple test for copying
line 3: this is a simple test for copying
line 4: this is a simple test for copying
```

Notice that we use O_CREAT and O_TRUNC when opening the output file. If we don't use O_CREAT, open will fail if foo1 doesn't already exist. Similarly, if we don't use O_TRUNC and foo1 exists, we may not overwrite all the old data in it.

Program 5-3 can be rewritten slightly to make it a more general copy program that takes its source and destination file names as command line arguments:

Program 5-4

```c
#include <fcntl.h>

#define BUFLEN    1024

main (argc, argv)
int argc;
char *argv[];
{
    char  buf[BUFLEN];
    int   nread, ifdesc, ofdesc;

    /* make sure we have both file names */

    if ( argc != 3 ) {
        printf ("usage:  %s infile outfile\n", argv[0]);
        exit (1);
    }

    /* open input file -- print error if can't open */

    if ( (ifdesc = open (argv[1], O_RDONLY)) == -1 ) {
        printf ("cannot open %s for reading\n", argv[1]);
        exit (2);
    }

    /* open output file -- print error if can't open */

    if ( (ofdesc = open (argv[2], O_WRONLY | O_CREAT | O_TRUNC, 0666))
            == -1 ) {
        printf ("cannot open %s for writing\n", argv[2]);
        exit (3);
    }

    /*
    ** keep copying until empty; nread should equal BUFLEN
    ** except on last read
    */

    while ( (nread = read (ifdesc, buf, BUFLEN)) > 0 )
        write (ofdesc, buf, nread);
}
```

```
$ cat foo1
this is a simple test for copying
line 2: this is a simple test for copying
line 3: this is a simple test for copying
line 4: this is a simple test for copying
$ a.out foo1 foo2
$ cat foo2
this is a simple test for copying
line 2: this is a simple test for copying
line 3: this is a simple test for copying
line 4: this is a simple test for copying
$ a.out /usr/include/fcntl.h test1
$ cat test1
/*
 *  @(#) /usr/include/fcntl.h 1.1
 *  fcntl.h
 */

/* Flag values accessible to open(2) and fcntl(2) */
/*  (The first three can only be set by open) */
#define   O_RDONLY  0000
    .  .  .
```

One aspect of the UNIX system that some programmers find odd is that it allows more than one program to open a file for writing at the same time. This means that if two programs write data to a file at the same time, the data from one `write` will overwrite the data from the other. Also, if a file opened for reading is later truncated via an `open` or a `creat`, then the next read will return an end of file condition. The system simply doesn't check to see if a file is already opened when someone else opens it for writing or truncates it.[†]

lseek

Each file descriptor has a *current position* in the file associated with it. `read` and `write` maintain this; when either routine performs I/O, it is done at the current position, and the current position is incremented by the number of bytes read or written. When a file is first opened, the file descriptor's current position is at the beginning of the file, i.e., before the first byte of the file. When a `read` causes the current position to be incremented past the last byte in a file, or when a `write` is performed at the end of a file, subsequent `reads` return zero—end of file.

Normally, I/O is performed *sequentially* on a file descriptor, meaning that `read` and `write` cause the current position to be incremented so that each byte in a file is accessed in turn. It is possible to change the current position and either skip bytes or go back to ones previously read or written. This capability is

---

† Some UNIX systems (including XENIX and System V Release 3) implement *file locking*, so that only one process may have a file open for writing at a time.

referred to as *random I/O*, as it allows you to move to arbitrary positions in a file. Random I/O is performed on UNIX by calling `lseek` to change a file descriptor's current position, or *seek* to a particular place in a file.   `lseek` is the same as `fseek` in the Standard I/O Library, except that it takes a file descriptor as its first argument instead of a file pointer.

`lseek` takes three arguments: a file descriptor, an offset (`long int`), and a flag that describes how the offset is to be applied to the current position. If the flag is zero, the offset becomes the current position; If the flag is one, the offset is added to the current position; and if the flag is two, the offset is added to the end of the file. If the flag is one or two, the offset may be negative. For example,

```
lseek (infile, 0L, 0);
```

"rewinds" `infile`'s current position to the beginning of the file (zero bytes from the beginning),

```
lseek (infile, 0L, 2);
```

moves the current position to the end of the file,

```
lseek (infile, -10L, 1);
```

moves the current position back ten bytes, and

```
offset = lseek (infile, 0L, 1);
```

assigns the current file position to `offset`.

`lseek` cannot seek on a pipe or a character device (e.g., a terminal). `lseek` will not allow you to seek past the end of a file if the file descriptor was opened for reading only (`O_RDONLY`); however, if the file descriptor was opened for writing (`O_WRONLY` or `O_RDWR`), seeking past the end increases the file size to reflect the new current position, and the new area of the file is filled with zero (null) bytes. Also, `lseek` will not allow you to use an offset and flag combination that results in a negative current position.

`lseek` returns the current position when successful and –1 when unsuccessful.

The following program performs the same database update function as Program 4-22 shown in the Random I/O section of the previous chapter. The only differences are that the standard I/O stream for the database has been replaced by a file descriptor and system routines are used to perform I/O on the database:

Program 5-5

```
/* read in and update employee record */

#include <stdio.h>
#include <fcntl.h>

struct date {
    int         month;
    int         day;
    int         year;
};

struct emprec {
    char        name[25];
    char        room[10];
    int         joblevel;
    long int    salary;
    struct date startdate;
};

main ()
{
    int    datafile;
    struct emprec emp_entry;
    long   lseek (), spot;
    int    n;

    /* here's the employee to search for */
    char  *search = "John Musa";

    /* open data base for read update */

    if ( (datafile = open ("database", O_RDWR)) == -1 ) {
        fprintf (stderr, "Can't open database\n");
        exit (1);
    }

    /* find particular employee in data base */

    do  {
        spot = lseek (datafile, 0L, 1);
        n = read (datafile, (char *) &emp_entry,
                        sizeof(struct emprec));
    }
    while ( n > 0 && strcmp (emp_entry.name, search) != 0 );
```

```
    if ( n <= 0 ) {
        fprintf (stderr, "%s not found!\n", search);
        exit (2);
    }

    /* now make update and write result back */

    emp_entry.salary = 28000;

    /* position file offset at employee's record to be updated */

    lseek (datafile, spot, 0);

    write (datafile, (char *) &emp_entry, sizeof (struct emprec));
}
```

pipe

A *pipe* is a buffer that is accessed with file descriptors. The data that is written into a pipe is read on a first-in first-out (FIFO) basis, meaning that once read, data in a pipe is lost. A pipe has two ends, a read end and a write end; both are file descriptors. Data is written to the write end file descriptor, and read from the read end (see Fig. 5-1); read and write are used on pipes in the same manner as they are used on files.

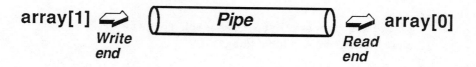

Fig. 5-1. Read and write ends of a pipe

Pipes may be created in one of two ways: by calling the pipe system routine or by opening a *FIFO file*† (sometimes called a *named pipe*) twice, once for reading and once for writing. (FIFO files can be distinguished by a "p" in the first column of output from ls -l.) Once created, pipes from the pipe system call and pipes from FIFO files behave the same.

---

† FIFO files are available on System III and later versions of UNIX.

pipe is called with a two-element integer array; it fills the array with the read and write file descriptors:

```
int array[2];
    . . .
pipe (array);
```

Now `array[0]` contains the read end file descriptor, and `array[1]` contains the write end file descriptor.

pipe returns zero when successful, and –1 when unsuccessful.

The following program shows a simple use of the pipe system call.

Program 5-6

```
#include <stdio.h>

main ()
{
    int  fifo[2];
    char line[81];

    if ( pipe (fifo) == -1 ) {
        fprintf (stderr, "cannot create pipe\n");
        exit (1);
    }

    /* write "this is a test" (and trailing null) to pipe */

    write (fifo[1], "this is a test", 15);
    read (fifo[0], line, 15);
    printf ("%s\n", line);
}

$ a.out
this is a test
```

The string this is a test is written to the pipe, and then 15 bytes are read from the pipe and placed in the array line. As you can see, the characters read are the same as those that were written.

The advantages of pipes are realized when they are used as interprocess communications channels and when they are used to connect the standard output of one process to the standard input of another (à la the shell). We'll show you how this is done later in this chapter in the **Process Control** section.

▪ Controlling Terminal I/O ▪

ioctl

Most programs on UNIX systems interact with your terminal. The shell, editors, and other interactive programs perform a great deal of I/O on terminals. Even programs that don't take user-specified input, like who, interact with your terminal when writing their output to standard output. A program run from the shell has three file descriptors already opened for it: 0—standard input, 1—standard output, and 2—standard error. Unless they are redirected (using <, >, <<, >>, or |), these file descriptors refer to your terminal.

On UNIX systems, I/O is performed on terminals with the same routines as files: read inputs bytes, and write outputs bytes. For example, this program copies standard input to standard output:

Program 5-7

```
#define BUFLEN    1024

main ()
{
    char buf[BUFLEN];
    int nread;

    /* keep copying til empty */

    while ( (nread = read (0, buf, BUFLEN)) > 0 )
        write (1, buf, nread);
}
```

Most UNIX programs don't have to worry about whether they will be doing I/O on files or terminals; they just use read and write and let UNIX worry about the dirty details. This feature is referred to as *device independent I/O*. read and write provide common interfaces to dozens of devices, such as disks, tapes, terminals, and printers, allowing programs to be written without knowledge of the input and output devices and allowing them to work with new devices without having to be rewritten or recompiled.

Sometimes, however, a program must do something that is terminal-specific. For example, networking programs such as those used by uucp must worry about certain communication features that simply have no corresponding file attributes (e.g., baud rate and parity). The ioctl system routine is used to control terminal-specific features. It is called with a file descriptor that *must correspond to a terminal*, a command, and an argument that is interpreted either as a pointer to a structure of type termio (defined in <termio.h>) or an integer, depending upon the command.[†] For example,

```
ioctl (0, TCGETA, &term);
```

populates the `termio` structure `term` with information about the communication line that standard input (file descriptor zero) is attached to, and

```
ioctl (0, TCSETA, &term);
```

uses `term` to set the current state of the communication line that standard input is attached to.

The following commands are defined in `<termio.h>`:

TCGETA	Copy the specified terminal's state into the structure pointed to by the third argument.
TCSETA	Set the specified terminal's state using the contents of the structure pointed to by the third argument. Any changes are immediate.
TCSETAW	Set the specified terminal's state using the contents of the structure pointed to by the third argument. `ioctl` waits for any pending output to be completed before setting the state and returning.
TCSETAF	Set the specified terminal's state using the contents of the structure pointed to by the third argument. `ioctl` waits for any pending output to be completed before setting the state and returning and throws away (*flushes*) any pending input (i.e., typed in by the user but not yet read via `read`).
TCSBRK	Wait for any pending output to finish. If the third argument is zero, send a *BREAK* on the line.
TCXONC	If the third argument is zero, suspend output; if one, restart suspended output.
TCFLSH	If the third argument is zero, flush any pending input; if one, flush any pending output; if two, flush input and output.

The `termio` structure in `/usr/include/termio.h` looks like this:

[†] Seventh Edition UNIX systems have different `ioctl` commands and use the header file `<sgtty.h>`.

```
struct termio {
    unsigned short   c_iflag;       /* input modes */
    unsigned short   c_oflag;       /* output modes */
    unsigned short   c_cflag;       /* control modes */
    unsigned short   c_lflag;       /* local modes */
    char             c_line;        /* line discipline */
    unsigned char    c_cc[NCC];     /* control chars */
};
```

`c_iflag` contains information about various input modes, including XON and XOFF (*CTRL-s* and *CTRL-q*) handling, upper- to lowercase mapping, *NEW-LINE* mapping, and *BREAK* handling.

`c_oflag` contains information about various output modes, including *RETURN* delays, tab expansion, *NEWLINE* mapping, and lower- to uppercase mapping on output.

`c_cflag` contains information about terminal hardware modes, including baud rate, number of bits/character, and parity checking.

`c_lflag` contains information that is interpreted differently for various line disciplines, determined by the value of `c_line`. Line discipline zero (the only discipline implemented on many systems) defines `c_lflag` to contain information about terminal-generated signal handling (*DELETE* and *QUIT*), erase and line kill processing, upper- to lowercase mapping, character echoing, erase echoing, *NEWLINE* echoing, and I/O flushing on interrupt.

The above information is stored in one or more bits of the relevant structure member; various preprocessor constants are defined to the bit or bits for each different field. For example, `B300` (300 baud) is set to octal 7, `B1200` (1200 baud) is set to octal 11, and `CBAUD` (the four-bit portion of `c_cflag` that is used to determine baud rates) is set to octal 17.

The last member of a `termio` structure is the `c_cc` array. `c_cc` contains up to eight characters that have special meaning to the system. On System V Release 2, seven of the eight have been defined: the interrupt character (*DELETE*), the *QUIT* character (*CTRL-*), the erase character (#), the line kill character (@), the end of file character (*CTRL-d*), the end of line character (*CTRL-@*), and the process switch character (for *shell layers*, no default). Several preprocessor constants such as `VERASE`, `VINTR`, and `VEOF` are defined to index into this array.

All of the above modes are described in the manual pages for `termio` in Section 7 of the *UNIX Administrator's Manual*. We'll discuss the most commonly used ones here. Appendix A gives a short description of all the modes.

`ioctl` returns zero when successful and –1 when unsuccessful.

Usually, a program will have to change only one or two modes of a terminal—for example, the baud rate or erase character. This is easily performed by first getting the current terminal state with `TCGETA`, changing a value or two in the `termio` structure, and setting the terminal state with `TCSETA`, `TCSETAF`, or `TCSETAW`:

Program 5-8

```
#include <stdio.h>
#include <termio.h>

main ()
{
    struct termio term;

    /*
    ** put current state in term;
    ** make sure file descriptor 0 is a terminal
    */

    if ( ioctl (0, TCGETA, &term) == -1 ) {
        fprintf (stderr, "standard input not a tty\n");
        exit (1);
    }

    /* zero out baud rate portion of c_cflag */

    term.c_cflag &= ~CBAUD;

    /* set new baud rate to 4800 */

    term.c_cflag |= B4800;

    /*
    ** wait for current output to finish then change
    ** terminal state; note that since only the baud
    ** rate has been changed, everything else is untouched
    */

    ioctl (0, TCSETAW, &term);
}
```

Program 5-8 changes the baud rate to 4800. It uses TCSETAW so that any output that is pending is finished at the old baud rate.

The following program changes the erase character to an octal 10, or *CTRL-h*. Note that its structure is the same as the previous program, except that c_cc is being changed instead of c_cflag:

Program 5-9

```
#include <stdio.h>
#include <termio.h>

main ()
{
    struct termio  term;

    if ( ioctl (0, TCGETA, &term) == -1 ) {
        fprintf (stderr, "standard input not a tty\n");
        exit (1);
    }

    /* set erase character to CTRL-h */

    term.c_cc[VERASE] = '\010';

    /* set terminal state to reflect change */

    ioctl (0, TCSETA, &term);
}
```

The following program uses ioctl to turn off character echo:

Program 5-10

```
#include <stdio.h>
#include <termio.h>

main ()
{
    struct termio term;

    /* put current state in term; make sure fd 0 is a terminal */

    if ( ioctl (0, TCGETA, &term ) == -1) {
        fprintf (stderr, "standard input not a tty\n");
        exit (1);
    }

    /* zero out echo bit of c_lflag */

    term.c_lflag &= ~ECHO;

    ioctl (0, TCSETA, &term);
}
```

After Program 5-10 is run, input typed by the user is no longer echoed.

One of the most commonly used modes is *raw* mode; raw mode is entered by turning off *canonical mode*. Canonical mode is the default I/O mode on the UNIX system. It specifies that lines are processed when a *RETURN* or *NEWLINE* is entered, and at that time, the erase and line kill characters are interpreted, editing the user's input (often referred to as the *raw queue*). The edited line (the *canon queue*) is passed to the program that is performing a `read` on that terminal. This means that in canonical mode, individual characters are not available as they are typed in, but are queued up until a *RETURN* or *NEWLINE* is entered.

In raw mode, characters are available as they are typed in, and they are given to the program directly from the raw queue, without any erase or kill processing. Good examples of programs that must run in raw mode are screen editors like `vi` and `emacs`, which read in single character commands from the terminal without waiting for a *RETURN*. The `c_cc` elements corresponding to the end of file and end of line characters are redefined in raw mode. The end of file character (called MIN in raw mode) specifies the number of characters that must be typed in to cause `read` to return, and the end of line character (called TIME in raw mode) specifies the amount of time (in tenths of a second) that a `read` will wait between characters typed before returning. By turning on the timeout feature, `read` will return *even if no characters have been typed*, and by turning on the minimum character feature, `read` will return after that many characters have been typed in. If both features are turned on, then `read` will return, either after the specified number of characters has been typed *or* after the specified amount of time has expired and at least one character has been typed. If TIME or MIN is set to zero, the timeout or minimum character feature, respectively, is disabled.

Program 5-11 illustrates raw mode where a character is read as soon as it is typed. It turns off `ICANON`, sets MIN to one, and sets TIME to zero. It then reads in characters, one at a time, and prints the character it read in with the message `got a 'x'`. Note that the program doesn't wait for a *RETURN* to print out its message about what character was typed in; also note that the old `termio` structure is saved in the structure `save` and later used to reset the terminal's state to its original settings. This is a good habit to get into—it keeps programs from making changes to the terminal's state that persist after the program finishes. Also note that we use `write` here instead of `printf` to print the prompt and the message; we can't use the Standard I/O routines here due to the buffering they perform. (Well, we could, but we'd have to turn off the buffering.)

Program 5-11

```c
#include <termio.h>
#include <stdio.h>

main ()
{
    struct termio  save, term;
    char           in, outbuf[20];
    int            nchar;

    if ( ioctl (0, TCGETA, &term) == -1 ) {
        fprintf (stderr, "standard input not a tty\n");
        exit (1);
    }

    /* save old tty state */

    save = term;

    /* turn off canonical processing */

    term.c_lflag &= ~ICANON;

    /*
    ** set MIN to one and TIME to zero
    ** can read each character as it is typed
    */

    term.c_cc[VMIN] = 1;
    term.c_cc[VTIME] = 0;

    /* set new terminal state */

    ioctl (0, TCSETA, &term);

    /* input characters until q is typed */

    do {
        write (1, ": ", 2);
        read (0, &in, 1);
        sprintf (outbuf, " got a '%c'\n", in);
        write (1, outbuf, strlen (outbuf));
    } while ( in != 'q' );

    /* reset old tty state */

    ioctl (0, TCSETA, &save);
}
```

```
$ a.out
: x got a 'x'
: y got a 'y'
: z got a 'z'
: q got a 'q'
$
```

The next program sets TIME to 10, causing read to wait up to a second for terminal input (recall that the time is set in tenths of a second). MIN is set to zero so that read returns if nothing is typed in; if MIN is set to a nonzero value, read will wait for at least one character to be typed in before timing out and returning, no matter what TIME is set to.

Program 5-12

```c
#include <termio.h>
#include <stdio.h>

main ()
{
    struct termio  save, term;
    char           in, outbuf[20];
    int            nchar;

    if ( ioctl (0, TCGETA, &term) == -1 ) {
        fprintf (stderr, "standard input not a tty\n");
        exit (1);
    }

    /* save old tty state */

    save = term;

    /* turn off canonical processing */

    term.c_lflag &= ~ICANON;

    /*
    ** set MIN to zero, TIME to ten
    ** times out after one second
    */

    term.c_cc[VMIN] = 0;
    term.c_cc[VTIME] = 10;

    /* set new terminal state */

    ioctl (0, TCSETA, &term);
```

```
    /* input characters until q is typed */

do {
    write (1, ": ", 2);
    nchar = read (0, &in, 1);

    if ( nchar != 0 )
        sprintf (outbuf, " got a '%c'\n", in);
    else
        sprintf (outbuf, " timed out!\n");

    write (1, outbuf, strlen (outbuf));
} while ( in != 'q' );

/* reset old tty state */

ioctl (0, TCSETA, &save);
}
```

```
$ a.out
: x got a 'x'                          x typed within one second
:  timed out!                          Nothing typed for two seconds
:  timed out!
: y got a 'y'                          y typed within one second
: q got a 'q'                          q typed within one second
$
```

By changing MIN to 8 in Program 5-12:

```
term.c_cc[VMIN] = 8;
```

we can alter its behavior—instead of returning after one second, read waits for at least one character to be typed in, and doesn't return until one second expires *between characters being typed in* or eight characters have been typed.

```
$ a.out
: 1234 got a '1'                       One second after typing 4
got a '2'
got a '3'
got a '4'
: abcdefgh got a 'a'                    Type in eight characters quickly
got a 'b'
got a 'c'
got a 'd'
got a 'e'
```

```
got a 'f'
got a 'g'
got a 'h'
: q got a 'q'                                    Reads in after one second
$
```

There are many other `ioctl` flags; however, there just isn't enough space here to go into every one. The tables in Appendix A list all `ioctl` flags and their meanings for UNIX System V Release 2.

Using `fcntl` to Control Terminal I/O

`fcntl` can be used to set `O_NDELAY` on a file descriptor associated with a terminal. This allows `read` to return immediately if no data has been typed in on the terminal. This type of input is referred to as *polling* and is often used in programs that must regularly perform some actions regardless of user input. These programs cannot always wait for a user to type something in. Games and other programs that must continually update the screen, even if nothing is typed in, must be able to poll user input. Note that polling can't be done by simply setting MIN and TIME to zero, since zero values disable them.

The following program is similar to the previous one, except that after printing the prompt (`:`) if nothing is typed in, `read` returns zero and the loop continues. The routine `do_things` simply sleeps for a second, although it could be doing anything in between the polling.

Program 5-13

```c
#include <stdio.h>
#include <termio.h>
#include <fcntl.h>

main ()
{
    struct termio   save, term;
    char            in, outbuf[20];
    int             nchar, savefcntl;

    /* turn on O_NDELAY to allow polling */

    savefcntl = fcntl (0, F_GETFL, 0);
    fcntl (0, F_SETFL, savefcntl | O_NDELAY);

    if ( ioctl (0, TCGETA, &term) == -1 ) {
        fprintf (stderr, "standard input not a tty\n");
        exit (1);
    }
```

```
        /* save old tty state */

        save = term;

        /* turn off canonical processing */

        term.c_lflag &= ~ICANON;

        /*
        ** set MIN to one and TIME to zero
        ** can read each character as it is typed
        */

        term.c_cc[VMIN] = 1;
        term.c_cc[VTIME] = 0;

        /* set new terminal state */

        ioctl (0, TCSETA, &term);

        /* input characters until q is typed */

        do {
            write (1, ": ", 2);
            do_things ();
            nchar = read (0, &in, 1);

            if ( nchar != 0 )
                sprintf (outbuf, " got a '%c'\n", in);
        } while ( in != 'q' );

        /* reset old tty state */

        ioctl (0, TCSETA, &save);
        fcntl (0, F_SETFL, savefcntl);
}


do_things ()
{
    sleep (1);
}
```

Note the two calls to `fcntl` at the beginning of the program. The first gets the status flags associated with standard input; the second ORs the current flags with `O_NDELAY`, turning on "no delay" mode on standard input. `ioctl` is then called to allow each character to be read as it's typed in. Now when `read` is called, it will read a single character if something has been typed since the last `read`, and it will return without waiting if nothing has been typed.

```
$ a.out
: : : j got a 'j'
: : k got a 'k'
: : : : : q got a 'q'
$
```

A useful thing to note here is that `O_NDELAY` is independent of MIN and TIME. You can turn on no delay mode and leave canonical processing turned on; however, `read` will return without reading anything until a *RETURN* is entered, then the entire line will be available. If you turn on no delay mode and raw mode, setting MIN or TIME, then `read` will again return without reading anything until either MIN characters have been read or TIME tenths of a second have elapsed.

▪ File Manipulation Routines ▪

`stat`	gets status of a file
`fstat`	gets status of an open file
`access`	determines accessibility of a file
`utime`	sets file access and modification times
`creat`	creates a new file or truncates an existing file
`mknod`	makes a directory, special file, or ordinary file
`umask`	gets and sets file creation mask
`chmod`	changes mode of a file
`chown`	changes owner and group of a file
`link`	creates link to a file or directory
`unlink`	removes directory entry

These routines are used to create, remove, and manipulate UNIX files and directories.

stat and fstat

stat is used to get the status of a file, and fstat is used to get the status of the file associated with a file descriptor. The "status" or **attributes** of a file includes information such as the owner, group, size, type, and mode—in other words, the kind of information that ls -l prints out.   stat takes a file name and a pointer to a structure of type stat (defined in <sys/stat.h>) as arguments;[†] fstat takes a file descriptor and a pointer to a stat structure. The stat structure pointed to by the second argument is filled with the information about the file specified by the first argument. If for some reason the file can't be stated (e.g., it doesn't exist or the file descriptor is invalid), both routines return –1.

The stat structure has eleven members:

```
struct stat {
      ino_t     st_ino;     /* inode number */
      ushort    st_mode;    /* file mode, see mknod */
      dev_t     st_dev;     /* id of device containing this file */
      dev_t     st_rdev;    /* id of device.  Only defined for
                             * character and block special files */
      short     st_nlink;   /* # of links */
      ushort    st_uid;     /* uid of file's owner */
      ushort    st_gid;     /* gid of file's group */
      off_t     st_size;    /* file size in bytes */
      time_t    st_atime;   /* time of last access */
      time_t    st_mtime;   /* time of last data modification */
      time_t    st_ctime;   /* time of last file status 'change' */
};
```

On System V Release 2, ino_t and ushort are unsigned shorts, dev_t is short, and off_t and time_t are longs. These types are defined in the <sys/types.h> include file.

st_ino is the file's inode number. The inode number is used by the system to uniquely identify files; it is used as an index into a table that contains information about all the files on the system.

st_mode contains both the file type and access permissions of this file.[‡]

st_dev and st_rdev specify device (e.g., disk drive) information about this file.

st_nlink is the number of links to this file; we'll talk about links more in the discussion of the link system routine.

st_uid is the owner of the file. This information is stored as an unsigned integer called the UID or user ID number. This number is specified for every user in the /etc/passwd file. When ls -l lists the owner of a file, it maps the st_uid number into a user's login name by looking up the number in the passwd file (by calling getpwuid).

---

† Remember we talked briefly about this stat structure in Chapter 3 when we described the ftw routine.
‡ See page 279 for details on how to interpret the type bits.

st_gid is the file's group. Like st_uid, it is stored as an unsigned integer. It is referred to as the group ID or GID number. The file /etc/group is used to determine the mapping of GIDs to group names.

st_size is the size of the file in bytes.

st_atime is the last time the file was read, st_mtime is the last time the file was modified, and st_ctime is the last time the file's inode information was changed (change of ownership, size, number of links, etc.). All times are stored as long integers and contain the time in number of seconds since January 1, 1970 (and can therefore be processed by ctime).

The following program prints the UID number and name of the specified file's owner:

Program 5-14

```
#include <stdio.h>
#include <sys/types.h>
#include <sys/stat.h>
#include <pwd.h>

main (argc, argv)
int argc;
char *argv[];
{
    struct passwd    *pwentry, *getpwuid();
    struct stat   status;

    if ( argc != 2 ) {
        fprintf (stderr, "Usage: %s file\n", argv[0]);
        exit (1);
    }

    /* get stat structure for specified file */

    if ( stat (argv[1], &status) == -1 ) {
        fprintf (stderr, "Cannot stat %s\n", argv[1]);
        exit (2);
    }

    printf ("%d ", status.st_uid);

    /* look up owner in /etc/passwd */

    if ( (pwentry = getpwuid (status.st_uid))
                        == (struct passwd *) NULL ) {
        printf ("not found\n");
    }
    else
        printf ("%s\n", pwentry->pw_name);
}
```

```
$ a.out tstat.c
201 phw
$ a.out /etc/passwd
0 root
```

The file name typed on the command line is `stated`, and the UID is printed along with the user's name associated with that UID in the `/etc/passwd` file.

The following program uses `fstat` to determine whether or not standard input, output, and error are terminals. It works by checking the upper four bits of the mode field, which specify what type of file is associated with the file descriptor — if these four bits are 020000 then the file is a character special file and therefore a terminal.[†] See the section on `mknod` for more information on the different types of files and their properties.

Program 5-15

```c
#include <stdio.h>
#include <sys/types.h>
#include <sys/stat.h>

#define TYPEMASK     0170000
#define CHARSPECIAL  020000

main ()
{
    struct stat  status;

    if ( fstat (0, &status) == -1 )
        fprintf (stderr, "Cannot fstat stdin\n");
    else if ( (status.st_mode & TYPEMASK) == CHARSPECIAL )
        printf ("stdin is a tty\n");

    if ( fstat (1, &status) == -1 )
        fprintf (stderr, "Cannot fstat stdout\n");
    else if ( (status.st_mode & TYPEMASK) == CHARSPECIAL )
        printf ("stdout is a tty\n");

    if ( fstat (2, &status) == -1 )
        printf ("Cannot fstat stderr\n");
    else if ( (status.st_mode & TYPEMASK) == CHARSPECIAL )
        printf ("stderr is a tty\n");
}
```

---

† This isn't quite true: as you'll see, there are quite a few devices that fall into the category of character special, including printers and memory; however, for the purposes of this example, we can be a little loose with our definitions.

Note that in the last case, the "Cannot fstat" message is written to standard output and not to standard error since the fstat on standard error failed (indicating some problem with standard error).

```
$ a.out
stdin is a tty
stdout is a tty
stderr is a tty
$ a.out 2> x
stdin is a tty
stdout is a tty
$ a.out < x
stdout is a tty
stderr is a tty
```

access

access is used to determine the accessibility of the file specified as its first argument. Its second argument is an integer between zero and seven that specifies what type of access you want to test. The different access types are:

0	check to see if the file exists
1	execute (or search)
2	write
3	write and execute
4	read
5	read and execute
6	read and write
7	read, write, and execute

access returns zero if the file can be accessed in the specified way and –1 if it can't (or doesn't exist).

The following program shows a use of access to display the accessibility of the file specified on the command line:

Program 5-16

```c
#define  EXECUTE    1
#define  WRITE      2
#define  READ       4

main (argc, argv)
int argc;
char *argv[];
{
    char  *file = argv[1];

    if ( argc != 2 ) {
        printf ("%s: requires one argument\n", argv[0]);
        exit (1);
    }

    if ( access (file, 0) == -1 ) {
        printf ("%s: can't be accessed\n", file);
        exit(2);
    }

    if ( access (file, EXECUTE) == 0 )
        printf ("you can execute %s\n", file);

    if ( access (file, WRITE) == 0 )
        printf ("you can write %s\n", file);

    if ( access (file, READ) == 0 )
        printf ("you can read %s\n", file);
}
```

```
$ ls -l rdwr
-rw-r--r--    1 phw       book          3200 May 14 16:24 rdwr
$ who am i
phw        tty03    May 11 10:29
$ a.out rdwr
you can write rdwr
you can read rdwr
```

access uses the *real* UID in determining the accessibility of a file. We'll discuss this shortly in the **Process Control** section.

utime

utime changes the access and modification times of the file specified as its first argument. Its second argument is a pointer to a structure of type utimbuf, defined in <sys/types.h>:

```
struct utimbuf {
    time_t  actime;      /* last access time */
    time_t  modtime;     /* last modification time */
};
```

If the structure pointer is null, the access and modification times of the file are set to the current time; otherwise, the times are set to the times stored in the structure. This allows a file's times to be set to some time in the past.

The owner of a file and any user who has write permission on it may change its times to the current time; however, only the owner may change the times to anything else.   utime returns zero when successful and –1 when unsuccessful.

The following program changes the access and modification times of the specified file to the current time (like the touch command):

Program 5-17

```
#include <stdio.h>
#include <sys/types.h>

main (argc, argv)
int argc;
char *argv[];
{
    struct utimbuf  utim;
    long  time ();

    if ( argc != 2 ) {
        fprintf (stderr, "%s: requires one argument\n", argv[0]);
        exit (1);
    }

    utim.actime = utim.modtime = time ((long *) 0);

    if ( utime (argv[1], &utim) == -1 ) {
        fprintf (stderr, "can't change modification time on %s\n",
            argv[1]);
        exit (2);
    }
}
```

```
$ ls -l rdwr
-rw-r--r--   1 phw      book        3200 May 14 16:24 rdwr
$ date                              Get the current time
Fri May 15 18:06:10 EDT 1987
$ a.out rdwr                        Change time on rdwr
$ ls -l rdwr                        Now see if it changed
-rw-r--r--   1 phw      book        3200 May 15 18:06 rdwr
$ a.out /etc/passwd
can't change modification time on /etc/passwd
```

creat

creat is used to create new files or truncate existing ones. It is functionally the same as using open with the O_WRONLY, O_CREAT, and O_TRUNC flags.

creat takes a file name and a mode as arguments. If the file doesn't exist, then creat attempts to create it and gives the new file the specified mode; if the file exists and is writable, creat truncates it and ignores the mode; in both cases, it returns a file descriptor opened for writing. So the following two lines do *exactly the same thing*:

```
ofile = open ("foo", O_WRONLY | O_CREAT | O_TRUNC, 0666);

ofile = creat ("foo", 0666);
```

Like open, creat returns –1 when unsuccessful.

The reason for creat's existence is that older versions of open only take three flags: read, write, and read/write (0, 1, and 2, respectively) and can only open files that already exist. The ability to create files using open was added in System III and BSD 4.2.

mknod

Another system routine that creates files is mknod. Before getting into mknod in any detail, we have to talk a little about the different files that exist on UNIX systems.

You should already be familiar with regular files (the kind that store data and programs and show up with a – in the first column of ls -l's output), directories, and FIFO special files. UNIX also has special files called *device files*. A UNIX system communicates with the various devices attached to it through these special files. As far as any program is concerned, disks are files, modems are files, even memory is a file. All the devices attached to your system have files associated with them, usually in the directory /dev. When I/O is performed on these files, the actions are translated by the UNIX system into actions on the actual devices.

UNIX supports two types of device files: *block* and *character* special files. Block special files are devices like tapes and disks, which access data in blocks. Character special files are devices such as terminals, printers, modems, or any other device that communicates with the system one character at a time. Every device file is specified by two numbers, the *major* and *minor* device numbers. The major device number specifies a system routine (device driver) that the system will use when I/O is performed on the device, and the minor device number is passed to the device driver when it is called. The minor number usually determines which of several devices the I/O will be performed on, since a single device driver (say, a terminal driver) often has to perform I/O on many separate devices (every terminal on the system). Typically, each type of device (disks, tapes, floppies, terminals, and printers) has its own driver.

Up to now, we've only been discussing creation of regular files.   open and creat cannot be used to make special files.   mknod, however, can create any type of file (including directories and special files), but except for FIFOs, only superusers can use mknod to create files. It takes two or three arguments, depending upon what type of file is being created. The first argument is the name of the file; the second is the mode; and the third is the major and minor device numbers, which is only used when creating character or block-special device files. The upper byte of the third argument is the major number and the lower byte is the minor number. The file mode contains information about what type of file is being created; the upper four bits determine the file's type, the last nine the file's permissions, and the middle three how the file is to be executed (we'll cover these later in this chapter);

The upper four bits of the mode are interpreted as follows:

0000000 0100000	Regular file
0010000	FIFO special file
0020000	Character special file
0040000	Directory
0060000	Block special file

mknod returns zero when successful and –1 when unsuccessful.

The following lines use mknod to create a directory, a FIFO special file, a block special file (major number = 2, minor = 10), and a character special file (major number = 22, minor = 33), respectively:

```
mknod ("directory", 040777);
mknod ("fifo", 010666);
mknod ("block", 060666, (2 << 8) | 10);
mknod ("character", 020666, (22 << 8) | 33);
```

umask

umask is called to change the default file creation mask, or umask. The mask is used to specify what permissions will *not* be left on when a file is created. The only ways on a UNIX system to create a file is through a call to open, creat, or mknod. All these routines take a mode as one of their arguments, and they all combine that mode with the umask to determine the permissions the file is actually given. The computation used is fairly simple: the umask is inverted (bitwise NOT) and then ANDed with the specified mode. For example, if the umask is 022 (octal) and the specified mode is 0666, then the resulting mode of the newly created file is 0644 (0666 & ~022). The corresponding C statements look like this:

```
umask (022);
  . . .
ofile = creat ("foo", 0666);
```

Typical umask values are shown in Table 5-2.

TABLE 5-2. Typical umask values

Mask	Description
002	Create files without write permission to others
022	Create files without write permission to group or others
006	Create files without read or write permission to others
026	Create files without read or write permission to others and without write to group
007	Create files without read, write, or execute to others
027	Create files without read, write, or execute to others and without write to group
077	Create files without read, write, or execute to anyone but the owner

umask returns the old umask value; the following statement prints out the umask:

```
printf ("umask = %d\n", umask (0));
```

Note that there is no way to find out what the umask is without possibly changing its value. So in order to get the umask and have no net effect on it, `umask` has to be called twice:

```
int mask;
. . .
mask = umask (0);
umask (mask);
printf ("umask = %d\n", mask);
```

A change to the umask affects only the calling process and its children.

chmod

`chmod` is used to change the mode of a file. It is called with a file name and a new mode for that file:

```
chmod ("foo", 0600);        /* read/write to owner */
chmod ("/tmp/foo", 0750);   /* read/write/execute to owner,
                               read/execute to group */
```

The umask is *not* used when changing the modes of the file, and only the owner of a file may change its modes. `chmod` returns zero when successful and -1 when unsuccessful.

chown

`chown` is used to change the owner and group of a file. Normally, the owner of a file is the user who created the file, and the group is the group that the user belonged to when the file was created. `chown` is called with three arguments: a file name, a new UID number, and a new GID number. The owner and group of the file are set to the specified UID and GID numbers:

```
chown ("foo", 0, 0);
chown ("/tmp/foo", 200, 110);
```

Only the owner of a file may change its owner or group. Note that after changing the ownership of a file, you may no longer be able to access it. For example, if you have a file that is readable only by you, and you give up ownership of that file, you will no longer be able to read it. `chown` returns zero when successful and -1 when unsuccessful.

The following program works the same as the `chown` *command*. It changes the ownership of files to the user specified on the command line and leaves the group unchanged. It looks up the specified user in `/etc/passwd` with `getpwnam` to get the new owner's UID. It then uses that UID in a call to `chown` to change the owner of each file specified on the command line.

Program 5-18

```
#include <stdio.h>
#include <sys/types.h>
#include <sys/stat.h>
#include <pwd.h>

main (argc, argv)
int argc;
char *argv[];
{
    struct passwd    *pwent, *getpwnam();
    struct stat      status;

    if ( argc < 3 ) {
        fprintf (stderr, "Usage: %s user file(s)\n", argv[0]);
        exit (1);
    }

    /* look up user (argv[1]) in /etc/passwd to get UID */

    if ( (pwent = getpwnam (argv[1])) == (struct passwd *) NULL ) {
        fprintf (stderr, "No such user %s\n", argv[1]);
        exit (2);
    }

    /*
    ** change ownership for all files given on the
    ** command line, leaving the group unchanged
    */

    while ( argc-- > 2 )
        if ( stat (argv[argc], &status) == -1 )
            fprintf (stderr, "Can't stat %s\n", argv[argc]);
        else if ( chown (argv[argc], pwent->pw_uid,
                status.st_gid) == -1 )
            fprintf (stderr, "Can't change %s\n", argv[argc]);
}
```

```
$ ls -l rdwr
-rw-r--r--   1 phw        book        3200 May 15 18:06 rdwr
$ a.out steve rdwr                    Change owner from phw to steve
$ ls -l rdwr
-rw-r--r--   1 steve      book        3200 May 15 18:06 rdwr
```

`argv[1]` is the user's name, and `argv[2]` through `argv[argc-1]` are the files. The user's password entry is looked up using `getpwnam`. Then each file's `stat` structure is retrieved and its ownership changed by calling `chown` with the user's UID and the file's group. Note the use of `status.st_gid` in the call to `chown`:

```
chown (argv[argc], pwentry->pw_uid, status.st_gid)
```

This has the net effect of causing the group to remain unchanged.

link

`link` is used to create a link to a file. In order to understand what a link is, you'll first need to understand what a directory is. A directory is a special type of file that contains two or more 16 byte entries, one for each file or directory in it. When a directory is first created, there are two of these entries in it, . (the directory itself) and .. (the parent directory). As files and directories are created in it, the directory file grows in size. Each 16 byte entry contains two fields: the name of a file (14 bytes) and an inode number (two bytes), as in Fig. 5-2.

File name	Inode number
.	104
..	200
prog1	492
raw.c	400
inonechar.c	21
inonechar	44

Fig. 5-2. Directory file organization

(Note that the entries in a directory aren't in alphabetical order; `ls` sorts the file names before listing them.) When a file is accessed (e.g., opened), the inode number associated with the directory entry is used by the system to look up the inode in a system table. That inode contains all the information needed by the system to open the file (owner, permissions, etc.) and perform I/O on the file's contents (where the file's data resides on the disk). So a directory entry is merely a pointer to the information that actually defines the file. This entry is called a link. The UNIX system allows a file to have more than one link, or more than one directory entry that refers to the same inode and therefore the same attributes and data.

link is called with two arguments, the name of a file that already exists, and the name that file is to be linked to. For example, if we do a `ls -l` on the directory in Fig. 5-2, we'd get something like this (note that by default, `.` and `..` aren't listed):

```
$ ls -l
total 100
-rwxrwxr-x   1 phw      book       7202 May   5 18:46 inonechar
-rw-rw-r--   1 phw      book        746 May   5 11:36 inonechar.c
-rwxrwxr-x   1 phw      book      23414 May   4 11:32 prog1
-rw-rw-r--   1 phw      book        982 May   5 12:17 raw.c
```

Now if we run a program that contains the following statement:

```
link ("raw.c", "abc");
```

The directory contents will be as in Fig. 5-3.

File name	Inode number
.	104
..	200
prog1	492
raw.c	400
inonechar.c	21
inonechar	44
abc	400

Fig. 5-3. Directory after call to link

and the output of `ls -l` will look like this:

```
$ ls -l
total 100
-rw-rw-r--   2 phw      book        982 May   5 19:33 abc
-rwxrwxr-x   1 phw      book       7202 May   5 18:46 inonechar
-rw-rw-r--   1 phw      book        746 May   5 11:36 inonechar.c
-rwxrwxr-x   1 phw      book      23414 May   4 11:32 prog1
-rw-rw-r--   2 phw      book        982 May   5 12:17 raw.c
```

The file names abc and raw.c now refer to the same data—the same contents and attributes. Notice that the number of links (the second field in the output) is 2 for these files instead of 1. Each time a link is made to a file, the number of links gets incremented by one.

Just to make sure that the two names refer to the same thing, let's try a little experiment; we'll put something different in the file:

```
$ echo nothing > abc
$ ls -l
total 100
-rw-rw-r--    2 phw        book          8 May  5 19:35 abc
-rwxrwxr-x    1 phw        book       7202 May  5 18:46 inonechar
-rw-rw-r--    1 phw        book        746 May  5 11:36 inonechar.c
-rwxrwxr-x    1 phw        book      23414 May  4 11:32 prog1
-rw-rw-r--    2 phw        book          8 May  5 19:35 raw.c
$ cat raw.c
nothing
$
```

One thing to keep in mind about links is that there really aren't two files, simply one file with two names.

link returns zero when successful and –1 when unsuccessful. link will fail if the file name being linked to (the second argument) already exists, or if the calling user doesn't have permission to create a file in the directory of the second link. Links cannot be created across files systems on the AT&T versions of UNIX; on BSD 4.2 and later Berkeley versions, links are allowed across file systems. Also, only the superuser may create a link to a directory.

unlink

unlink is used to remove a directory entry. It is called with the name of the entry to unlink. The inode number for the directory entry being unlinked is set to zero to indicate that it is an unused entry. If the entry being unlinked is the last link to a file, the file is also removed, and the associated inode is put into a free pool for subsequent use by a newly created file.

For example, the following statement

```
unlink ("abc");
```

would cause the directory in Fig. 5-3 to look like this:

File name	Inode number
.	104
..	200
prog1	492
raw.c	400
inonechar.c	21
inonechar	44
abc	0

Fig. 5-4. Directory after call to `unlink`

`unlink` returns zero when successful and -1 when unsuccessful. `unlink` will fail if the calling user doesn't have permission to remove a file from the directory the file is in. Also, only the superuser may unlink a directory.

The following program removes files (similar to the `rm` command) by calling `unlink` on each of the files specified on the command line:

Program 5-19

```
#include <stdio.h>

main (argc, argv)
int argc;
char *argv[];
{
    while ( argc-- > 1 )
        if ( unlink (argv[argc]) == -1 )
            fprintf (stderr, "Cannot remove %s\n", argv[argc]);
}

$ ls
a.out
file1
file2
file3
$ a.out file1 file2
$ ls
a.out
file3
$ a.out foo
Cannot remove foo
```

▪ **Process Control** ▪

`fork`	creates a new process
`wait`	waits for child process to stop or terminate
`exit`	terminates calling process
`_exit`	terminates calling process without standard I/O cleanup
`execl`	executes a program with argument list
`execv`	executes a program with argument vector
`execle`	executes a program with argument list and environment vector
`execve`	executes a program with argument vector and environment vector
`execlp`	executes a program with argument list and `PATH` search
`execvp`	executes a program with argument vector and `PATH` search
`getpid`	gets process number
`getppid`	gets parent process number
`getpgrp`	gets process group leader number
`setpgrp`	sets process group leader to current process
`getuid`	gets real UID
`getgid`	gets real GID
`geteuid`	gets effective UID
`getegid`	gets effective GID
`setuid`	sets UID
`setgid`	sets GID
`chdir`	changes working directory
`chroot`	changes root directory
`sbrk`	changes memory allocation
`brk`	changes memory allocation
`ulimit`	gets and sets process limits
`nice`	changes priority of calling process

These routines are used to create and manipulate processes and programs. The difference between a *program* and a *process* is very subtle. A program is a file that resides on the system's disk. It is created by other programs, like the C compiler. A process is a copy of this program in memory that is doing something. A simple definition of a process is that it is an executing program. Actually, a process is the entire environment of an executing program, including all the variables, all the open files, the process's current directory, information about the user running the process and the terminal the process is run from, as well as the object code of the program itself.

Processes are dynamic entities on UNIX systems, since they come and go as programs execute and complete. There are several system calls that are used to manage processes. This section will deal with these, with particular emphasis on creating processes and using pipes to send information between processes.

fork

`fork` is used to create processes. Calling `fork` is, in fact, the only way for a user to create a process on the UNIX system. If we think of a process in terms of the above definition, i.e., that it is a copy of a program that is executing in memory, then we can think of the `fork` routine as an operation that creates a duplicate of the calling process in another area of memory, and this becomes the new process. The process that calls `fork` is called the *parent* and the new process is called the *child*. See Figs. 5-5 and 5-6.

```
main ()
{
    fork ();

    printf ("this is a test\n");
}
```

Fig. 5-5. Process before call to `fork`

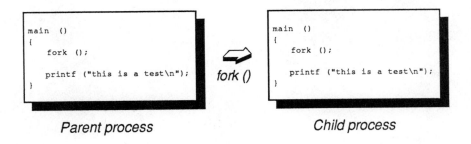

Parent process   Child process

Fig. 5-6. Process after call to `fork`

The child process inherits the environment of the parent, including open files, user information, etc. In fact, the child even inherits the information that keeps track of where a process is executing—the actual statement or instruction. This means that the child doesn't start executing at the beginning of the program (the first executable statement after `main()`), but starts instead at the same place that the parent resumes—right after `fork` returns. So, after calling `fork`, you end up with two processes executing the same code; this may seem redundant, but as we'll see in a bit, it really isn't.

The following program calls `fork` and proceeds to write a line to the terminal. The net effect of this is for a second process to be created before calling `printf`, so that two lines are written to the terminal, one by each process:

Program 5-20

```
main ()
{
    fork ();

    printf ("this is a test\n");
}

$ a.out
this is a test
this is a test
```

It is possible to determine which process is the parent and which is the child: `fork` returns different values to each process. (So the new process isn't an *exact* duplicate of the calling one; we'll go into some of the other differences later on.) In the parent, `fork` returns the *process id* of the child (an integer number between 1 and 30,000, inclusive), and in the child, `fork` returns zero.

See Fig. 5-7. So the above program can be rewritten to produce different output by the parent and the child:

Program 5-21

```
main ()
{
    if ( fork () == 0 )
        printf ("this is the child\n");
    else
        printf ("this is the parent\n");
}

$ a.out
this is the parent
this is the child
```

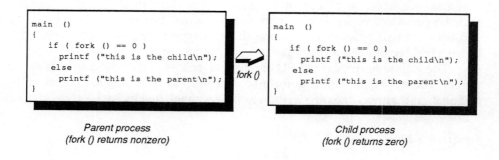

Fig. 5-7. fork returns nonzero to parent, zero to child

Note that even though in this example the output from the parent comes out before the output of the child, *you are not guaranteed that this will be true for every UNIX system.* Which process begins execution after fork is not defined. On most systems, you will find that you can determine which of the two processes will begin first after a fork; however, you should never write a program based on this knowledge, as there is no guarantee that this will continue to be true in later releases of UNIX.

fork will fail and return −1 when it cannot create a new process. There are two conditions on a UNIX system that can cause this:

1. The user calling `fork` has reached the maximum number of processes per user and cannot create a new one until one of the presently running processes finishes.

2. The number of processes on the system has reached a maximum. No new processes can be created by any user until one of the presently running processes finishes.

After a `fork`, the only detectable differences between the parent and the child are the return value, the process number, and the parent process number. We'll show you how to access these in a bit.

wait

You can control the execution of child processes by calling `wait` in the parent. `wait` forces the parent to suspend execution until the child is finished. `wait` returns the process number of a child process that finished. If the child finishes before the parent gets around to calling `wait`, then when `wait` is called by the parent, it will return immediately with the child's process number. (It is possible to have more than one child process by simply calling `fork` more than once.) The following program is similar to the previous one, except that it guarantees that the output of the child will *precede* that of the parent:

Program 5-22

```
main ()
{
    if ( fork () == 0 )
        printf ("this is the child\n");
    else {
        wait ((int *) 0);
        printf ("this is the parent\n");
    }
}

$ a.out
this is the child
this is the parent
```

Note that `wait` takes an integer *pointer* as an argument. The *exit status* of the child is placed in the location the argument points to. If a null pointer is supplied as in the above example, the exit status is not stored.

`wait` returns –1 on failure (e.g., there are no child processes or the argument is an illegal address).

exit

`exit` is used to cause a process to finish. It can be called with an integer between zero and 255. This number is returned to the parent via `wait` as the exit status of the process. By convention, when a process exits with a status of zero that means it didn't encounter any problems; when a process exits with a nonzero status that means it did have problems (e.g., it couldn't open a particular file).

In the following program, the parent waits for the child to exit, and then prints the exit status of the child. Note that `wait` returns the exit status multiplied by 256 (shifted left eight bits). If a process terminates due to a signal (more on these later on), the signal information is put in the lower eight bits.

Program 5-23

```
main ()
{
    unsigned int   status;

    if ( fork () == 0 ) {   /* == 0 in child */
        scanf ("%d", &status);
        exit (status);
    }
    else {                  /* != 0 in parent */
        wait (&status);
        printf ("child exit status = %d \n", status >> 8);
    }
}


$ a.out
0
child exit status = 0
$ a.out
12
child exit status = 12
$
```

The child reads the exit status to be returned from the terminal and then returns that value to the parent through the `exit` call. The parent then prints the child's exit status after shifting it down by eight bits.

`exit` is actually not a system routine; it is a library routine that calls the system routine `_exit`. `exit` cleans up the standard I/O streams before calling `_exit`, so any output that has been buffered but not yet actually written out is flushed. Calling `_exit` instead of `exit` will bypass this cleanup procedure. `exit` does not return.

The exec Routines

The exec routines are called to execute a program. They do this by *replacing the program that is running with the new program specified to* exec. exec doesn't create a new process—only fork can do that; however, exec does change some of the environment of the calling process, namely, the program that it is executing.

The exec routines do not return when they are successful. If unsuccessful, they return –1.

There are six routines that can be called to execute a program (which we collectively refer to as the exec routines):

execl Takes the path name of an executable program (binary machine instructions) as its first argument. The rest of the arguments are a list of the command line arguments to the new program (argv[]). This list is terminated with a null pointer:

```
execl ("/bin/cat", "cat", "f1", "f2", (char *) 0);
execl ("a.out", "a.out", (char *) 0);
```

Note that, by convention, the argument listed after the program is the name of the command being executed (argv[0]).

execle Same as execl, except that the end of the argument list is followed by a pointer to a null-terminated list of character pointers that is passed as the environment of the new program (i.e., the place that getenv searches for exported shell variables):

```
static char *env[] = {
        "TERM=hp2621",
        "PATH=/bin:/usr/bin",
        (char *) 0
};
        . . .
execle ("/bin/cat", "cat", "f1", "f2", (char *) 0, env);
```

execv Takes the path name of an executable program (binary machine instructions) as its first argument. The second argument is a pointer to a list of character pointers (like argv[]) that is passed as command line arguments to the new program:

```
static char *args[] = {
        "cat",
        "f1",
        "f2",
        (char *) 0
};
        . . .
execv ("/bin/cat", args);
```

execve Same as `execv`, except that a third argument is given as a pointer to a list of character pointers (like `argv[]`) that is passed as the environment of the new program:

```
static char *env[] = {
        "TERM=hp2621",
        "PATH=/bin:/usr/bin",
        (char *) 0
};

static char *args[] = {
        "cat",
        "f1",
        "f2",
        (char *) 0
};
        . . .
execve ("/bin/cat", args, env);
```

execlp Same as `execl`, except that the program name doesn't have to be a full path name, and it can be a shell program instead of an executable module:

```
execlp ("ls", "ls", "-l", "/usr", (char *) 0);
```

`execlp` searches the `PATH` environment variable to find the specified program.

execvp Same as `execv`, except that the program name doesn't have to be a full path name, and it can be a shell program instead of an executable module:

```
static char *args[] = {
        "cat",
        "f1",
        "f2"
        (char *) 0
};
        . . .
execvp ("cat", args);
```

`execvp` searches the `PATH` environment variable to find the specified program.

As you can see, the letters added to the end of exec indicate the type of arguments:

l   argv is specified as a list of arguments.

v   argv is specified as a vector (array of character pointers).

e   Environment is specified as an array of character pointers.

p   User's PATH is searched for command, and command can be a shell program.

    execlp and execvp were added to UNIX as of System III, so they aren't available on all versions. Also, only one of the six exec routines is actually a system call—execve; the other five are simply library routines that convert their argument list and environment into a call to execve.

    execl, execv, execlp, and execvp pass the current environment to the specified program; execle and execve pass only what you explicitly provide.

    The following program illustrates how the exec routines don't return when called successfully, but simply run a different program:

Program 5-24

```
#include <stdio.h>

main ()
{
    printf ("this is the first printf\n");
    fflush (stdout);

    execl ("/bin/pwd", "pwd", (char *) 0);

    printf ("this is the second printf\n");
}
```

```
$ a.out
this is the first printf
/usr/phw/topics/ch6
```

The second printf is never called as long as /bin/pwd exists and can be executed by execl. Also, note that we had to call fflush to cause the output of the first printf to be printed. Since the Standard I/O routines buffer up data before printing it, the string "this is the first printf\n" is stored away somewhere and may not be printed without the fflush once execl is called.

exec routines are usually called after a call to `fork`. This combination, known as a `fork/exec`, allows a process to create a child to execute a command, so that the parent doesn't destroy itself through an `exec`. Most command interpreters (e.g., the shell) on UNIX use `fork` and `exec`.

Program 5-25 shows a practical use of `fork` and `exec` to create a directory (recall that only a superuser can create a directory with `mknod`). The program first forks a child process and then waits for the child to finish. The child process calls `execl` to execute the UNIX system's `mkdir` command to create a directory called `newdir`. When the child finishes, the parent opens a file in the newly created `newdir` directory and writes a line of data to it. The output verifies that everything worked as described. Figs. 5-8 and 5-9 illustrate the `fork` and `exec` calls executed by the program. The code that isn't shaded in the figures indicates what gets executed by the parent and the child.

Program 5-25

```
#include <stdio.h>

main ()
{
    FILE   *fp;

    if ( fork () != 0 )
        wait ( (int *) 0 );
    else {
        execl ("/bin/mkdir", "mkdir", "newdir", (char *) 0);
        fprintf (stderr, "exec failed\n");
        exit (1);
    }

    /* now use newdir */
    if ( (fp = fopen ("newdir/foo", "w")) == (FILE *) NULL ) {
        fprintf (stderr, "fopen failed\n");
        exit (2);
    }

    fprintf (fp, "testing\n");
}


$ a.out
$ cat newdir/foo
testing
```

```
#include <stdio.h>

main ()
{
    FILE *fp;

    if ( fork () != 0 )
        wait ((int *) 0);
    else {
        execl ("/bin/mkdir", "mkdir",
            "newdir", (char *) 0);
        fprintf (stderr, "exec failed\n");
        exit (1);
    }

    /* now use newdir */
    if ( (fp - fopen ("newdir/foo", "w"))
        -- (FILE *) NULL ) {
        fprintf (stderr, "fopen failed\n");
        exit (1);
    }

    fprintf (fp, "testing\n");
}
```

Parent process
(fork () returns nonzero)

fork ()

```
#include <stdio.h>

main ()
{
    FILE *fp;

    if ( fork () != 0 )
        wait ((int *) 0);
    else {
        execl ("/bin/mkdir", "mkdir",
            "newdir", (char *) 0);
        fprintf (stderr, "exec failed\n");
        exit (1);
    }

    /* now use newdir */
    if ( (fp - fopen ("newdir/foo", "w"))
        -- (FILE *) NULL ) {
        fprintf (stderr, "fopen failed\n");
        exit (1);
    }

    fprintf (fp, "testing\n");
}
```

Child process
(fork () returns zero)

Fig. 5-8. Program executes a fork

```
#include <stdio.h>

main ()
{
    FILE *fp;

    if ( fork () != 0 )
        wait ((int *) 0);
    else {
        execl ("/bin/mkdir", "mkdir",
            "newdir", (char *) 0);
        fprintf (stderr, "exec failed\n");
        exit (1);
    }

    /* now use newdir */
    if ( (fp - fopen ("newdir/foo", "w"))
        -- (FILE *) NULL ) {
        fprintf (stderr, "fopen failed\n");
        exit (1);
    }

    fprintf (fp, "testing\n");
}
```

Parent process

```
#include <stdio.h>

main ()
{
    FILE *fp;

    if ( fork () != 0 )
        wait ((int *) 0);
    else {
        execl ("/bin/mkdir", "mkdir",
            "newdir", (char *) 0);
        fprintf (stderr, "exec failed\n");
        exit (1);
    }

    /* now use newdir */
    if ( (fp - fopen ("newdir/foo", "w"))
        -- (FILE *) NULL ) {
        fprintf (stderr, "fopen failed\n");
        exit (1);
    }

    fprintf (fp, "testing\n");
}
```

mkdir

Child process

Fig. 5-9. Child execs mkdir

The following program is a simple command interpreter that uses `execlp` to execute commands typed in by the user:

Program 5-26

```c
#include <stdio.h>

main ()
{
    int    process;
    char   line[81];

    for (;;) {
        fprintf (stderr, "cmd: ");
        if ( gets (line) == (char *) NULL )
            exit (0);

        /* create new process */

        process = fork ();

        if ( process > 0 )              /* parent */
            wait ((int *) 0);
        else if ( process == 0 ) {    /* child */
            /* execute program */
            execlp (line, line, (char *) 0);

            /* some problem if exec returns */
            fprintf (stderr, "Can't execute %s\n", line);
            exit (1);
        }
        else if ( process == -1 ) {  /* can't create proc */
            fprintf (stderr, "Can't fork\n");
            exit (2);
        }
    }
}
```

```
$ a.out
cmd: pwd
/usr/phw/topics/ch6
cmd: whom
Can't execute whom
cmd: ls -l
Can't execute ls -l
cmd: CTRL-d
$
```

Since it uses `execlp` to look up the command in the PATH, the full path name of the command need not be typed; also, arguments are not handled at all—the entire line is given to `execlp` to execute, and blanks aren't interpreted as argument separators. So when `ls -l` is typed, a command by that name (i.e., 'l', 's', ' ', '−', 'l') is sought. In the next section, you'll see another version of Program 5-26 that does perform argument processing.

You should notice that there's a similarity between the `system` routine in the Standard C Library and the `fork/exec` combination. That's because `system` calls `fork` and `exec` to execute the specified command. There are several differences between them:

1. The `system` function runs the shell on the specified command, so argument processing, redirection, etc., are handled by the shell; whereas with `exec` you have to do this yourself.

2. Because `system` runs the shell, `fork/exec` is faster.

3. `system` waits for the command to finish execution before returning; `fork` returns immediately, so the child executes in parallel.

I/O, Pipes, and Processes

The only thing changed in a process by an `exec` is the program and its associated data structures (local and global variables), not the environment it runs in. So, one of the byproducts of the `exec` routines is that open files are passed to the program being executed. You can disable this, but you must do so explicitly for each file descriptor that you want closed when `exec` is called by using `fcntl` to set the close-on-exec flag for these file descriptors. Since all open file descriptors are copied to the child process from the parent by `fork` and are not closed by default during an `exec`, any files or pipes opened by the parent are inherited by the child and passed on to the program that is `exec`ed.

A simple example of open files copied by `fork` can be shown by opening a file in the parent, calling `fork`, and letting the child read the file:

Program 5-27

```
#include <fcntl.h>
#include <stdio.h>

main ()
{
    int    input, nchars;
    char   buf[1024];

    if ( (input = open ("foo", O_RDONLY)) == -1 ) {
        fprintf (stderr, "cannot open foo\n");
        exit (1);
    }

    if ( fork () == 0 ) {     /* child reads */
        nchars = read (input, buf, 1024);
        write (1, buf, nchars);
    }
    else                      /* parent waits */
        wait ((int *) 0);
}
```

```
$ cat foo
this is a line in the file foo
$ a.out
this is a line in the file foo
```

Similarly, we can show that file descriptors are passed through an exec by opening a file and calling exec on a program that reads from a specified file descriptor:

Program 5-28

```
$ cat passfd.c
#include <fcntl.h>
#include <stdio.h>

main ()
{
    int    input;
    char   arg[3];

    if ( (input = open ("foo", O_RDONLY)) == -1 ) {
        fprintf (stderr, "cannot open foo\n");
        exit (1);
    }
```

```
    /* convert the file descriptor number to string */

    sprintf (arg, "%d", input);

    /* run "readit" with file descriptor as arg */

    execl ("readit", "readit", arg, (char *) 0);
}
```

```
$ cat readit.c
/* read from file descriptor given as argument */

#include <stdio.h>

main (argc, argv)
int argc;
char *argv[];
{
    int    input, nchars;
    char   buf[1024];

    if ( argc != 2 ) {
        fprintf (stderr, "readit: needs an arg\n");
        exit (1);
    }

    /* argv[1] specifies file descriptor to read from */

    input = atoi (argv[1]);

    nchars = read (input, buf, 1024);
    write (1, buf, nchars);
}
```

```
$ passfd
this is a line in the file foo
```

passfd opens the file foo and then executes readit, passing the file descriptor returned by open as a command line argument.   readit then reads up to 1024 bytes from the opened file.

Since a pipe is simply a collection of two file descriptors, it too is copied by fork and passed through by exec. The following program opens a pipe and then forks; the child writes to the pipe and the parent reads from it:

Program 5-29

```
#include <stdio.h>

main ()
{
    int    fifo[2];
    char   line[81];
    char   *message = "This message comes from the child";

    if ( pipe (fifo) == -1 ) {
        fprintf (stderr, "cannot create pipe\n");
        exit (1);
    }

    if ( fork () == 0 ) {     /* child */
        /* write message (and trailing null) to pipe */
        write (fifo[1], message, strlen (message) + 1);
    }
    else {                       /* parent */
        read (fifo[0], line, 81);
        printf ("Message = %s\n", line);
    }
}


$ a.out
Message = This message comes from the child
```

(Remember that after the call to pipe, fifo[0] contains the read file descriptor for the pipe, and fifo[1] the write file descriptor.)

One trick that takes advantage of all of this is used extensively on the UNIX system: close standard input (or output, etc.) and open a file. open returns the lowest unused file descriptor, so if you handle everything just right, the new file descriptor will be the same as the one just closed:

```
close (0);
open ("foo", O_RDONLY);
```

This has the effect of *redirecting* standard input from the terminal (or whatever it's presently attached to) to the file foo.[†]

---

† Recall that something similar was done using freopen in the previous chapter. In that case, standard input was closed and a new file opened in its place. This works similarly.

Keep in mind that if the file descriptor you're attempting to redirect isn't the lowest available one (what if standard input is closed before your program is run?), then the redirection will occur on the wrong file descriptor.

The following program performs a simple redirection of standard output. It closes file descriptor 1, opens the file `dir` for writing, and then runs `execl` on the `pwd` command. The result of all this is that `pwd`'s output is redirected to the file `dir`:

Program 5-30

```
#include <fcntl.h>
#include <stdio.h>

main ()
{
    /* close standard output and redirect to file dir */

    close (1);
    if ( open ("dir", O_WRONLY | O_CREAT | O_TRUNC, 0644) == -1 ) {
        fprintf (stderr, "cannot open dir\n");
        exit (1);
    }

    /* run pwd with standard output to file dir */

    execl ("/bin/pwd", "pwd", (char *) 0);
}

$ a.out
$ cat dir
/usr/phw/topics/ch6
```

The following program is based on the command interpreter from the previous section; however, command line arguments and redirection have been added:

Program 5-31

```
/*
** simple command interpreter
** supports < and > redirection and command line arguments
*/

#include <fcntl.h>
#include <stdio.h>
#include <string.h>

main ()
{
    int   process, nargs;
    char  line[81], *args[15];

    for (;;) {
        fprintf (stderr, "cmd: ");

        if ( gets (line) == (char *) NULL )
            exit (0);

        process = fork ();

        if ( process > 0 )            /* parent */
            wait ((int *) 0);
        else if ( process == 0 ) {  /* child */
            /* parse command line */
            nargs = breakup (line, args);

            /* make sure there's something to exec */
            if ( nargs == 0 )
                exit (0);

            /* execute program */
            execvp (args[0], args);

            /* some problem if exec returns */
            fprintf (stderr, "Cannot execute %s\n", line);
            exit (1);
        }
        else if ( process == -1 ) { /* can't create proc */
            fprintf (stderr, "Can't fork\n");
            exit (2);
        }
    }
}
```

```
/*
** break up command line and return in ``args''
** recognize < file and > file constructs and redirect
** standard input/output as appropriate
*/

int breakup (line, args)
char *line;
char *args[];
{
    int     nargs = 0;
    char    *strptr = line, *file;

    while ( (args[nargs] = strtok (strptr, " \t"))
                     != (char *) NULL ) {
        strptr = (char *) NULL;

        if ( args[nargs][0] == '>' ) {
            /* output redirection */

            if ( args[nargs][1] != '\0' )
                file = &args[nargs][1];
            else {
                file = strtok (strptr, " \t");

                if ( file == (char *) NULL ) {
                    fprintf (stderr, "No file after >\n");
                    return (0);
                }
            }

            close (1);

            if ( open (file, O_WRONLY | O_TRUNC | O_CREAT,
                             0666) == -1 ) {
                fprintf (stderr, "can't open %s for output\n",
                              file);
                return (0);
            }

            --nargs;
        }
```

```
            else if ( args[nargs][0] == '<' ) {
                /* input redirection */

                if ( args[nargs][1] != '\0' )
                    file = &args[nargs][1];
                else {
                    file = strtok (strptr, " \t");

                    if ( file == (char *) NULL ) {
                        fprintf (stderr, "No file after <\n");
                        return (0);
                    }
                }

                close (0);

                if (open (file, O_RDONLY) == -1) {
                    fprintf (stderr, "can't open %s for input\n",
                                            file);
                    return (0);
                }

                --nargs;
            }

            ++nargs;
        }

        args[nargs] = (char *) NULL;

        return (nargs);
    }



    $ a.out
    cmd: pwd
    /usr/phw/topics/ch6
    cmd: who am i >tmp
    cmd: cat tmp
    phw        tty04   May 12 15:41
    cmd: wc < tmp
          1      5      30
    cmd: wc < tmp > out
    cmd: cat out
          1      5      30
    cmd: who >
    No file after >
    cmd:
```

The routine breakup is called by the child to scan the command line. It uses strtok to break the line into arguments and places pointers to each argument in successive elements of args. It also looks for > or < followed by a file name. This causes it to redirect standard output or input to that file. Note that the > and < must be preceded by whitespace due to the way we're using strtok. However, the program does allow you to type the file name right after the > or <, as in >output and <data. You should study the code that does this inside breakup to see how its handled.

The preceding discussion of redirection can be applied to pipes as well. For example, we can create a pipe and then use dup to copy the pipe's read or write file descriptor to standard input or output by closing standard input or output and calling dup to copy the pipe's file descriptor. The difference with pipes is that instead of having the I/O redirected to a file, it will go to the pipe, where it can be read by another process.

Consider the following actions that allow a program to read from the standard output of another program (like popen (cmd, "r")):

1. Create a pipe by calling pipe.

2. Call fork. Now both the parent and the child have access to the pipe.

3. Close standard output in the child.

4. Duplicate the write side of the pipe by calling dup. It is duplicated on the lowest unused file descriptor (standard output).

5. The child process execs a program that writes to standard output.

6. The parent process reads from the pipe.

(See Fig. 5-10.) Note that a similar procedure can be followed to write to the standard input of a program (like popen (cmd, "w")) by closing standard input and then doing the dup.

Program 5-32

```c
#include <stdio.h>

main ()
{
    int    fifo[2], proc, n;
    char   line[81];

    pipe (fifo);

    if ( (proc = fork ()) == -1 ) {
        fprintf (stderr, "can't fork\n");
        exit (1);
    }

    if ( proc == 0 ) {                  /* child */
        /*
        ** close standard output and
        ** dup write end of pipe onto it
        */

        close (1);
        dup (fifo[1]);

        /* run pwd with standard output attached to pipe */

        execl ("/bin/pwd", "pwd", (char *) 0);

        /* execl shouldn't return */

        fprintf (stderr, "cannot execl pwd\n");
        exit (2);
    }

    /* parent--read from pipe */

    n = read (fifo[0], line, 80);
    line[n] = '\0';
    printf ("current directory = %s\n", line);
}

$ a.out
current directory = /usr/phw/topics/ch6
```

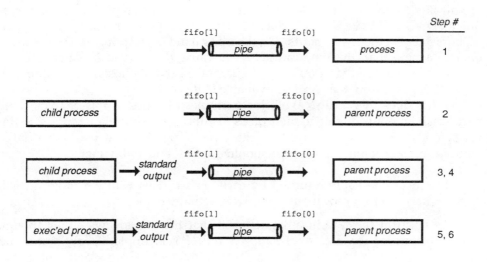

Fig. 5-10. Setting up a pipe between processes

The statements in the program that read

```
close (1);
dup (fifo[1]);
```

close standard output and then duplicate the write end of the pipe (fifo[1]) to the first available file descriptor, standard output. Anything that subsequently writes to standard output will therefore write into the pipe instead. The exec that follows executes the pwd command, a command that writes to its standard output. As noted, this output goes to the pipe, where it is read by the parent process and then printed.

Pipes are maintained by the system, and any process that reads from a pipe or writes to one is subject to the way UNIX handles pipe synchronization. When a process reads from a pipe that has no data in it, it is suspended until data becomes available; i.e., some other process must write data to the pipe. Also, when a process writes to a pipe that is full (ten blocks of data) it is suspended until data is read from the pipe. Setting the O_NDELAY on the read end of a pipe allows read to return with a zero count if no data is in the pipe; similarly, setting the O_NDELAY on the write end allows write to return with a zero count if the pipe is full.

`writes` to pipes are *atomic*, meaning that the `write` operation up to the size of the pipe will finish before any of the processes waiting to read the pipe are awakened. If you `write` up to ten blocks into an empty pipe, the subsequent `read` will have *all* of the data available to it. In other words, the `write` will finish *before* the `read` starts. On the other hand, attempting to `write` more data to a pipe than the pipe can hold will cause the pipe to be filled and the `write` to be suspended. You are *not* guaranteed that a subsequent `read` will have all the data from that `write` available to it.

What does this mean? Well, the examples of pipes in this chapter write such small amounts of data to their pipes that the `writes` are guaranteed to finish before a `read` is performed on the pipe. Programs that work with large amounts of data coming into a pipe should do one of the following:

1. Check the value returned by each `read`. This way the program will know *exactly* how many bytes were actually read.

2. Perform the I/O in amounts such that there is always either enough room for the data or the pipe is full. For example, if you `read` and `write` to a pipe in 512-byte chunks, there will always be a multiple of 512 bytes in the pipe (up to the size of the pipe, ten blocks). When a `write` occurs, either there will be room for the data, or the pipe will be full and the `write` will be suspended until a `read` empties out the pipe (which will leave exactly 512 bytes). This method works as long as the `reads` and `writes` always work on the same amount of data, and that amount is less than or equal to one block.

3. Use the Standard I/O routines when reading data from pipes (use `fdopen` to get a `FILE` pointer for the pipe or use `popen`). The Standard I/O routines automatically buffer the data, so you don't have to worry about counting characters read by `read`.

A `write` to a pipe that has had the read end closed is not allowed (since there can be no more data read from the pipe) and generates a signal that normally terminates the process; a `read` from a pipe that has had the write end closed will return an end-of-file condition. Note that if the pipe is `duped` or if `fork` is called, all read file descriptors on the pipe must be closed to cause a `write` to fail, and all write file descriptors must be closed to cause an end-of-file condition on the pipe. Remember that a process' file descriptors are automatically closed when it finishes.

Pipes created from FIFO special files operate in a manner similar to those created by `pipe`. The only difference between them is that pipes from FIFO files are created by opening the FIFO file twice, once for reading and once for writing. The `open` will not return until both reading and writing ends are established for the FIFO; i.e., an `open` for reading will block until an `open` for writing is performed, and vice versa. The `O_NDELAY` flag to `open` may be used to override this. Setting `O_NDELAY` when opening a FIFO for reading will allow the `open` to return immediately, and setting it when opening for writing will force `open` to return with an error if the FIFO hasn't already been opened for reading.

As you can infer from the method of setting up pipes for interprocess communication, only processes that are related—i.e., connected via `fork`—can use a pipe returned by `pipe`, since the file descriptors for the pipe are passed only via `fork` and `exec`. FIFOs may be used to create pipes between unrelated processes. Any set of processes that have the proper permissions to open a FIFO for reading and writing can communicate through it, making use of the file descriptors as if they were created by a call to `pipe`.

`getpid`, `getppid`, `getpgrp`, and `setpgrp`

`getpid` returns the process number of the calling process. This number is unique for every running process. The process number can be used to create temporary files that have a unique name:

```
char filename[15];
    . . .
sprintf (filename, "/tmp/x.%d", getpid ());
```

In fact, the Standard C routines `tmpfile`, `tmpnam`, and `tempnam` use the process number when constructing a temporary file name.

`getppid` returns the process number of the parent of the calling process.

`getpgrp` returns the process number of the *process group leader* of the calling process. The group leader is usually the program that is started up when a user logs in (the *login shell*); however, any process can make itself a process group leader by calling `setpgrp`. After calling `setpgrp`, all descendent processes (related by `fork`) are considered to be in this process group. Also, the first terminal opened by the process group leader becomes the *controlling terminal* of the process group. The controlling terminal is mapped to the file `/dev/tty` for all processes in a process group. This is how the system can take processes and group them together under a particular terminal (by calling `setpgrp` at login time). Even though a process may not have any file descriptors associated with a terminal (perhaps they were redirected), it still can be related to the terminal it was run from. We'll see how important this is when we cover signals.

`getuid`, `geteuid`, `getgid`, and `getegid`

When a process runs, it is assigned four numbers that indicate who that process belongs to. These are the *real* and *effective* user id (UID) and group id (GID) numbers. Normally, the effective UID and GID are the same as the real and are set to the UID and GID of the user running the process. The effective UID and GID are used by the system to determine a process's access permissions with respect to files. The UID zero has special meaning to the system; any process running with a UID of zero is considered a *super-user* process and has special privileges that normal process don't have (e.g., the ability to open any file for reading or writing, or to call special routines).

If the effective UID of a process is the same as the UID of the owner of a file, then that process has the owner's access permissions to the file; otherwise, if the effective GID of a process matches the GID of the group associated with a file, then that process has the group's access permissions; otherwise, the process is granted the access permissions of others.

When `fork` is called, the child process inherits the effective and real UID and GID from the parent. So a child process has the same permissions with respect to files as the parent. As we said before, the effective UID and GID of a process are usually the same as the real; however, this condition is changed when `exec` is called on a program that has its set UID (SUID) or set GID (SGID) permission turned on. The permission is turned on by a call to `chmod` (or by using the `chmod` command, which calls the `chmod` routine) where bits 11 and 12 of the new mode specify the SGID and SUID permissions, respectively:

```
chmod ("foo", 02555);          Turn on SGID permission
chmod ("foo", 04555);          Turn on SUID permission
chmod ("foo", 06555);          Turn on both SUID and SGID permissions
```

When a program that has its SUID (SGID) permission turned on is `exec`ed, the effective UID (GID) is set to the UID (GID) of the owner (group owner) of the file. Since it is the effective, not the real UID (GID), that is used to determine access permissions, when a program that has its SUID (SGID) permission turned on is run, the process created from that program runs with the access permissions of the file's owner, *no matter who executes the program.*

This mechanism allows programs like `passwd` to work. Since `passwd` must be able to change your password, it needs to have super-user privileges to be able to modify the `/etc/passwd` file. This is done by making the `passwd` program SUID to `root`, the super-user. When `passwd` runs, it runs with `root`'s permissions.

This mechanism also brings up some security concerns, since any program that is SUID runs with special permissions (i.e., those of the owner) and is therefore a potential security hazard. For example, consider the command interpreter from the previous section: if it were made SUID, every command that it ran would be executed with the effective UID of the interpreter's owner (except for commands that are themselves SUID), giving any user the effective privileges of the interpreter's owner—not a pretty sight! The SUID and SGID capabilities should be used sparingly, as it's not easy to write complex programs that are free of security holes. For more information on all of this, including methods of writing secure programs, refer to [2].

`getuid` returns the real UID of the calling process, `geteuid` returns the effective UID of the calling process, `getgid` returns the real GID of the calling process, and `getegid` returns the effective GID of the calling process.

setuid and setgid

setuid is used to change the effective UID of the calling process. It is called with an unsigned integer value. For processes whose effective UID is nonzero (i.e., not a super-user process), setuid's actions are strictly limited: if a process is running SUID, setuid can be used to change the effective UID back to the real UID. After doing this, the process can change its effective UID back to what it previously was by calling setuid with the old effective UID as the argument.† If a non-root process is not running SUID, then calling setuid has no effect.

For processes whose effective UID is zero, setuid changes the effective *and real* UIDs to any integer number specified.

So unless the program being run has the SUID permission turned on or the program is run by the super-user, setuid has no effect.

setgid behaves in a manner similar to setuid. It has an effect only if the effective GID is different from the real GID or if the process has an effective *UID* of zero. Both routines return zero when successful and –1 when unsuccessful.

The following line changes the effective UID to the real UID (assuming they're different to begin with):

```
setuid (getuid ());
```

This is often used within a SUID program after it performs whatever privileged actions required the SUID capability. Once this is done, the program is no longer a security risk, as the effective UID is set back to the real UID, which is that of the user running the program. For more information on setuid and setgid, see [2].

chdir and chroot

Every process has a current directory associated with it. chdir is used to change the current directory. It is called with a new directory name:

```
chdir ("/usr/tmp");
```

All files and directories specified without a leading / (e.g., foo and ../bin) are considered to be relative to the current directory.

chdir returns zero when successful and –1 when unsuccessful.

chroot is used to change a process's idea of what the root or / directory is. After chroot is called, the process cannot change its current directory above the new root, and all file names beginning with / begin at this new root directory. For example, calling

```
chdir ("/usr/phw/chrootdir");
chroot ("/usr/phw/chrootdir");
```

---

† Toggling the effective from the real back to what it was can only be done on System V and later releases.

will cause the calling process to execute in its own subset of the overall file system, beginning at `/usr/phw/chrootdir`.

The actions of both `chroot` and `chdir` are propagated down to child processes. `chroot` is usually used to test commands or set up restricted environments, since child processes also execute in the subset of the file system. For more information on `chroot`, see [2].

`chroot` may only be called by a process whose effective UID is zero (i.e., only the super-user can call it). It returns zero when successful and –1 when unsuccessful.

sbrk and brk

`sbrk` and `brk` are used to change the memory allocation (or *break value*) of the calling process, in effect changing the size of the process. They are called by `malloc`, `calloc`, and `realloc` when more memory is needed. `sbrk` is called with a signed integer that specifies the number of bytes to increase or decrease the break value, and `brk` is called with a pointer that specifies the new break value. `sbrk` returns the old break value when successful, and `brk` returns zero when successful. Both return –1 when unsuccessful.

Note that for most applications, the `malloc` routines are much more flexible than `brk` and `sbrk`; unless you intend to allocate just one big chunk of memory, we suggest that you use the `malloc` routines instead.

ulimit

`ulimit` is used to get a process's maximum break value, and is used to get and set a process's maximum file size limit. The maximum file size limit is the maximum size that a file the process is writing to may attain. It is specified to `ulimit` in units of 512-byte blocks. Only a super-user process may increase this value.

The first argument to `ulimit` is an integer between 1 and 3, where 1 means return the process's file size limit, 2 means set the process's file size limit, and 3 means return the maximum possible break value. The second argument is the new file size limit (only used when the first argument is 2).

When successful, `ulimit` returns a non-negative integer (e.g., the process's file size limit), and when unsuccessful, it returns –1.

For example, the call

```
printf ("%d\n", ulimit (1));
```

will print the maximum file size in blocks, and the call

```
ulimit (2, 100);
```

will set the maximum file size to 100 blocks.

nice

`nice` is used to change the *nice* value associated with the calling process. The nice value is used in calculating a process's priority, and it ranges from zero to 39. If not changed by the parent (or grandparent, etc.), the nice value is 20. A positive argument to `nice` decreases the calling process's priority (meaning it will run slower and is being "nice" to other processes on the system), as in

```
nice (10);
```

A negative argument to `nice` increases the calling process's priority, as in

```
nice (-15);
```

Note that only processes whose effective UID is zero may increase their priority.

An argument that would result in a nice value outside the allowed range sets the nice value to the upper or lower limit, depending upon whether the argument was positive or negative, respectively.

When successful, `nice` returns the new nice value minus 20, and when unsuccessful, it returns –1. This means that if the new nice value is 19, the return value will be –1, which is not distinguishable from an error.

▪ Signal Handling Routines ▪

`signal`	specifies what to do upon receipt of a signal
`kill`	sends a signal to a process or a group of processes
`alarm`	sets alarm clock signal
`pause`	suspends a process until a signal is received

A *signal* is a condition that the UNIX system is attempting to tell a process about. There are many different types of signals, since there are many different conditions that the system may want to indicate. Signals are the result of one of five conditions:

1. An odd program condition of some kind occurred (e.g., an attempt to access memory outside the process's memory area, an attempt to execute an illegal machine instruction, division by zero).

2. The user at the controlling terminal of a process hit the *DELETE*, *BREAK*, or *QUIT* key.

3. `alarm` or `kill` was called to cause a signal to be sent to this process.

4. A child process has finished.

5. The system hardware has detected an impending power failure.

A process can elect to ignore certain signals or to execute various routines when certain signals are received.

Signal numbers range from 1 to 19, and they are given mnemonics in `<signal.h>`:

TABLE 5-3. Signals

Number	Name	Meaning
1	SIGHUP	Hangup on controlling terminal
2	SIGINT	Interrupt from controlling terminal (*DELETE* or *BREAK*)
3	SIGQUIT[†]	*QUIT* from controlling terminal (*CTRL-*)
4	SIGILL[†]	Illegal instruction
5	SIGTRAP[†]	Trace trap
6	SIGIOT[†]	I/O trap
7	SIGEMT[†]	Emulator trap
8	SIGFPE[†]	Floating point exception
9	SIGKILL	Kill
10	SIGBUS[†]	Bus error
11	SIGSEGV[†]	Segmentation violation (memory fault)
12	SIGSYS[†]	Bad argument to system call
13	SIGPIPE	Write on a pipe with no one to read it
14	SIGALRM	Alarm clock (from `alarm` system routine)
15	SIGTERM	Software termination signal
16	SIGUSR1	User defined signal 1
17	SIGUSR2	User defined signal 2
18	SIGCLD	Death of a child
19	SIGPWR	Power-failure

By default, with the exception of SIGCLD and SIGPWR, receipt of any of the above signals will cause a process to exit.

Many of the above signals occur infrequently, are implementation and hardware specific, or are implemented to support a few specific commands. The ones we'll concentrate on are SIGHUP, SIGINT, SIGQUIT, SIGKILL, SIGALRM, and SIGTERM. The first three are usually due to a condition on the controlling terminal of a process, and the last three are usually due to a specific request to send the signal.

---

† The default action for these signals includes producing a *core dump*, or a copy of the process's memory.

signal

Note that by the very nature of signals, a process does not know when one will arrive. Normally, when one arrives, the process exits; however, it is possible to alter this behavior. `signal` is used to change the action a process takes when a signal is received. It takes two arguments: a signal type (one of the above) and an action. The actions are defined in `<signal.h>`:

`SIG_DFL`	Terminate the process upon receipt of the signal (except for `SIGCLD` and `SIGPWR`).
`SIG_IGN`	Ignore the signal. `SIGKILL` cannot be ignored.
function pointer	*Catch* the signal by calling the function pointed to by *function pointer* with an argument of the signal number that was received. When the signal handling routine returns, it returns execution to the same place before the signal arrived. If a signal is caught while waiting for I/O on a terminal (`open`, `read`, `write`, or `ioctl`) or during the execution of a `pause` or `wait`, the system routine will return with a failure value (–1) when the signal handling routine returns. `SIGKILL` cannot be caught.

One of the simplest actions to take on a signal is to ignore it. The following ignores the `SIGHUP` signal (à la `nohup`) which is sent when a process's controlling terminal hangs up or when the process's group leader exits:

```
#include <signal.h>

main ()
{
    signal (SIGHUP, SIG_IGN);

    /* anything */

}
```

Another signal sometimes worth ignoring is the `SIGINT` signal, which is sent when the user at the process's controlling terminal presses *BREAK* or *DELETE*:[†]

---

† *DELETE* is the default interrupt character; `ioctl` can be called to change it to anything.

```
#include <signal.h>

main ()
{
    signal (SIGINT, SIG_IGN);

    /* anything */

    signal (SIGINT, SIG_DFL);

    /* anything else */
}
```

In the above example, SIGINT is ignored for a bit (while anything is executed), and is then set back to the default action (so that anything else *can* be
interrupted). This is often the case with some programs: they turn certain signals off while executing some critical code, and then turn them back on.

Sometimes a program will need to know when a signal has been received;
for example, an editor may want to save the file being edited if a SIGHUP comes
along (usually due to a glitch in the communications between the terminal and
the system). Instead of simply exiting, the program can be set up to save the file
(vi does this):

```
#include <signal.h>

main ()
{
    int hangup ();

    /* call hangup if line is dropped */
    signal (SIGHUP, hangup);

    /* anything */
}

hangup ()
{
    /* save the file */
    exit (1);
}
```

Note that the routine hangup simply exits after saving the file. Since the user
has been hung up, there is no reason to continue after the file is saved.

Usually, when a signal is caught, it's not a good idea to simply resume execution where the program left off when the signal was received. This is because
a signal may interrupt a system routine (like read), and the program would

have to be written with this in mind, perhaps rerunning the system routine. Since signals can occur at any time, all system routine calls that may perform I/O on a terminal would have to be coded to handle the possibility of a signal's arrival.

An example of a program that continues execution after the receipt of a signal is the UNIX shell. When a SIGINT signal (*DELETE*) is received, it simply prints out another prompt ($). The easiest way to do something like this is to use setjmp and longjmp from the Standard C Library:

Program 5-33

```
#include <signal.h>
#include <setjmp.h>

jmp_buf env;

main ()
{
    int    catch_int ();
    char   line[81];

    signal (SIGINT, catch_int);

    setjmp (env);
    printf ("READY\n");

    gets (line);
}

catch_int ()
{
    longjmp (env);
}

$ a.out
READY
DELETE
READY
DELETE
$
```

Oops! What happened here? The first time we hit *DELETE*, the longjmp caused execution to continue after the call to setjmp, but the second *DELETE* killed the process. The problem here is that most signals (SIGILL, SIGTRAP, SIGCLD, and SIGPWR are the exceptions) are reset to their default action before calling the signal handling function, so the first time we sent an interrupt to the program it was caught, but then the catching was also disabled! So the second interrupt caused the program to take the default action—exit. We can fix this by putting a call to `signal` inside `catch_int` to reset the signal handling action:

Program 5-34

```
#include <signal.h>
#include <setjmp.h>

jmp_buf env;

main ()
{
    int    catch_int ();
    char   line[81];

    signal (SIGINT, catch_int);

    setjmp (env);
    printf ("READY\n");

    gets (line);
}

catch_int ()
{
    signal (SIGINT, catch_int);
    longjmp (env);
}
```

```
$ a.out
READY
DELETE
READY
DELETE
READY
DELETE
READY
RETURN
$
```

Now that's better.

The SIGQUIT signal is similar to the SIGINT signal; it is generated by the user by typing the *QUIT* character (default is *CTRL-*). Its default action is to produce a core dump before exiting.

Interactive programs that perform "critical" operations that shouldn't be interrupted by the user have to disable signals before performing those operations. For example, a database manager that must update records shouldn't be interrupted in the middle of writing things out, as the database could be corrupted. There are three types of signals a user can produce from a terminal without using the kill command:

SIGINT   A user can hit *DELETE* or *BREAK*.

SIGQUIT A user can hit *CTRL-*.

SIGHUP   A user can hang up!

At the very least, our database manager should disable these signals:

```
signal (SIGINT, SIG_IGN);
signal (SIGQUIT, SIG_IGN);
signal (SIGHUP, SIG_IGN);
   . . .                              Sensitive code
signal (SIGINT, SIG_DFL);
signal (SIGQUIT, SIG_DFL);
signal (SIGHUP, SIG_DFL);
```

A user can also produce signals by running the kill command or any other program that calls the kill *routine*. Although we can add calls to signal ignoring all of the possible signals, there will always be one that we can't ignore: SIGKILL. So there's little incentive in ignoring any more signals than the above three. On the other hand, it might not be such a bad idea to set up a call to an emergency clean up routine if a SIGPWR is received, as this may indicate an impending power outage. We may want to do the same if SIGTERM is received, since this is the default signal sent by the kill command, and it may indicate that someone is attempting to kill the program and that a SIGKILL may not be far behind. In fact, this is exactly the sequence of events during a system shutdown: first send SIGTERM to all running processes, wait a few seconds, then send SIGKILL.

A child process inherits all signal actions from its parent. A program that is execed receives all default and ignored actions from the previous program; however, signals that were to be caught by a routine are set back to the default, since the routine that was to be called ceases to exist when exec is called. It's good practice to write programs that don't rely on others to set up their signal environment; in other words, programs should be as self-contained as possible when it comes to handling signals.

When a process group leader dies, the system sends a SIGHUP to all processes in the process group. Also, when a signal is generated from the controlling terminal of a process group (either a SIGINT or a SIGQUIT), the signal is sent to *all* processes in the process group; if the terminal is a controlling terminal for more than one process group, the signal is sent to all processes in all process groups attached to that terminal. Also, if a child ignores a signal that the parent doesn't, it may become "orphaned" if the parent dies. (This can actually happen regardless of signals: the parent can simply call exit.) Such a process is "inherited" by process number one (i.e., process one becomes its parent).

kill

kill is used to send a signal to a process or a group of processes. It takes two arguments: a process number and a signal type.

The SIGKILL and SIGTERM signals are generated only when a process calls the kill system routine. The kill *command* sends a SIGTERM by default. A well-coded program will catch this signal, perform any necessary cleanup, and call exit. The SIGKILL signal is often referred to as a *sure kill*, since this signal cannot be ignored or caught by a routine.

Note that for security reasons, the effective or real UID of the process sending a signal via kill must be the same as the effective or real UID of the process receiving the signal.

There are a few special cases of kill:

1. If the specified process number is zero, the signal is sent to all processes in the process group of the caller.

2. If the specified process number is –1, the signal is sent to all processes whose real UID is the same as the effective UID of the caller.

3. If the specified process number is negative (but not –1), the signal is sent to all processes in the process group whose group leader number is the absolute value of the specified number.

The following program will log off the user that runs it by sending a SIGKILL to all processes on that terminal:

Program 5-35

```
#include <signal.h>

main ()
{
    kill (0, SIGKILL);
}
```

and the next program will log off the user that runs it *from all the terminals the user is logged into* by sending `SIGKILL` to all processes run by that user:

Program 5-36

```
#include <signal.h>

main ()
{
    kill (-1, SIGKILL);
}
```

alarm and pause

`alarm` is used to set up receipt of a `SIGALRM` signal *after the specified number of seconds have expired*. It is often called the *alarm clock* routine.

    `pause` is used to put a process to sleep (suspends execution). `pause` can be interrupted only by a signal, and if the signal is caught by a function, `pause` returns –1. `pause` and `alarm` can be combined to put a process to sleep for a certain number of seconds (like the `sleep` function):

Program 5-37

```
#include <signal.h>

main ()
{
    int alrm_catch ();

    printf ("one\n");

    /* call alrm_catch when alarm goes off */
    signal (SIGALRM, alrm_catch);

    /* schedule alarm for ten seconds from now and pause */
    alarm (10);
    pause ();

    printf ("two\n");
}

alrm_catch ()
{
    return;
}
```

```
$ a.out
one                                        Ten seconds elapse
two
```

Note that in order to catch the signal and continue processing, you don't want to take the default action (SIG_DFL) because the process would die when the signal arrived, and you don't want to ignore the signal (SIG_IGN) because the pause wouldn't return when the signal arrived (it too would ignore it).

The following shows how to write a function that emulates sleep:

```
#include <signal.h>

sleep (secs)
int secs;
{
    int alrm_catch ();

    /* call alrm_catch when alarm goes off */
    signal (SIGALRM, alrm_catch);

    /* schedule alarm for specified time and pause */
    alarm (secs);
    pause ();
}

alrm_catch ()
{
    return;
}
```

Calling alarm when an alarm is already in effect overrides the previous value; therefore, only one alarm can be in effect at any time. If the argument is zero, any previous alarm is disabled. alarm returns the number of seconds remaining on the previous alarm, so you can write a routine to "stack" alarms if you want to have several active at the same time.

• System Information Routines •

time

time returns the current time as a long integer. The time is kept as the number of seconds since midnight, January 1, 1970. The ctime routines in the Standard C Library are usually used to convert this to calendar and clock information.

uname

uname returns system specific information, such as the system name, UNIX version, and machine type. uname is called with a pointer to a utsname structure (defined in <sys/utsname.h>):

```
struct utsname {
    char    sysname[9];  /* system name */
    char    nodename[9]; /* system name (for network) */
    char    release[9];  /* UNIX release */
    char    version[9];  /* UNIX version */
    char    machine[9];  /* machine type */
};
```

Since the administrator of a system can put almost any information in the internal structure that this information comes from, there is no standardization of the information stored in it. So, except for the system's name, this information is of very little use. Programs that intend to be portable should not assume a specific format for the release, version, and machine fields.

• Error Handling •

Most of the system routines return –1 when unsuccessful, meaning that it's impossible to determine what went wrong without some other source of information. The external variable errno is set upon failure by all system routines to a value between one and 36. The meaning of these error numbers is given in the *intro(2)* section of the *UNIX Programmer's Reference Manual*.

The perror library routine, described in Chapter 3, is useful for printing out the error that occurred.

Program 5-38

```
#include <fcntl.h>

main ()
{
    /* open a directory for writing (will always fail) */

    if ( open ("/", O_WRONLY) == -1 ) {
        perror ("open / for writing");
        exit (1);
    }

    /* . . . */
}

$ a.out
open / for writing: Is a directory
```

▪ References ▪

[1]   M. Rochkind, *Advanced UNIX Programming*, Prentice-Hall, Englewood Cliffs, NJ, 1985.

[2]   P. H. Wood and S. G. Kochan, *UNIX System Security*, Howard W. Sams & Company, Indianapolis, IN, 1985.

▪ UNIX Interface Summary ▪

The table that follows summarizes the routines described in detail in this chapter. Each entry in the table describes the routine's return value, its arguments, and any required include files.

The following notations are used for depicting argument types in the table:

Argument	Type
c	char
fd	int
fp	int (*()) (pointer to function returning int)
i, i1, i2	int
*i	int *
l	long int
*l	long int *
s, s1, s2	char *
*s, *s1, *s2	char **
*stat	struct stat *
*termio	struct termio *
u	unsigned int
*utimbuf	struct utimbuf *
*utsname	struct utsname *

TABLE 5-4. Summary of UNIX System Routines

Routine	Description (Include File)
int access (s, i)	Determine accessibility of file s (i is bit pattern: 0=file exists, 1=execute, 2=write, 4=read)
unsigned int alarm (u)	Set alarm clock signal to occur in u seconds; returns time remaining on previous alarm
int brk (s)	Change memory allocation to s
int chdir (s)	Change working directory to s
int chmod (s, i)	Change mode of file s to i
int chown (s, i1, i2)	Change owner and group of file s to UID i1 and GID i2
int chroot (s)	Change root directory to s
int close (fd)	Close file descriptor fd
int creat (s, i)	Create file s with modes i, or truncate s if it already exists
int dup (fd)	Return duplicate of file descriptor fd on lowest unused file descriptor
int execl (s1, s2, ..., (char *) 0)	Execute program s1 with list of strings s2, ... as arguments
int execle (s1, s2, ..., (char *) 0, *s)	Execute program s1 with list of strings s2, ... as arguments and *s as environment
int execlp (s1, s2, ..., (char *) 0)	Search PATH for (shell or binary) program s1 and execute with list of strings s2, ... as arguments
int execv (s, *s)	Execute program s with *s as arguments
int execve (s, *s1, *s2)	Execute program s with *s1 as arguments and *s2 as environment
int execvp (s, *s1)	Search PATH for (shell or binary) program s and execute with *s1 as arguments
void exit (i)	Terminate calling process with exit status of i
void _exit (i)	Same as exit without standard I/O cleanup
int fcntl (fd, i1, i2)	Control file associated with file descriptor fd; i1 is a command, and i2 an argument used by some of the commands (fcntl.h)
int fork ()	Create a new process, returning the pid of the new process to the parent and zero to the child
int fstat (fd, *stat)	Place status of file associated with file descriptor fd in structure *stat (sys/types.h, sys/stat.h)
int getegid ()	Get effective GID of process
int geteuid ()	Get effective UID of process
int getgid ()	Get real GID of process
int getpgrp ()	Get process group leader number
int getpid ()	Get process number
int getppid ()	Get parent process number
int getuid ()	Get real UID of process
int ioctl (fd, i1, *termio) int ioctl (fd, i1, i2)	Set modes on terminal associated with fd; i1 is command, *termio is used by some commands, and i2 is by others (termio.h)

`int kill (i1, i2)`	Send signal `i2` to process or processes specified by `i1`
`int link (s1, s2)`	Create link `s2` to file `s1`
`long lseek (fd, l, i)`	Move read/write file position of file `fd` to `l` bytes from beginning of file, current position, or end of file, if `i=0, 1 or 2`, resp.
`int mknod (s, i1, i2)`	Make directory, special file, FIFO file, or ordinary file `s` with mode `i1`; if `s` is a device file, `i2` specifies the major and minor device numbers
`int nice (i)`	Add `i` to calling process' priority
`int open (s, i1, i2)`	Open file `s` for reading and/or writing, returning file descriptor; file status is set to `i1`, and mode is set to `i2` if file is being created (`fcntl.h`)
`int pause ()`	Suspend calling process until signal is received
`int pipe (*i)`	Create a FIFO I/O channel; `i[0]` is set to read end of pipe and `i[1]` is set to write end
`int read (fd, s, u)`	Read `u` bytes from file associated with `fd` into `s`, returning number of bytes successfully read
`char *sbrk (i)`	Add `i` to memory allocation, returning new allocation
`int setgid (i)`	Set effective GID to `i` (superuser sets real as well)
`int setpgrp ()`	Set process group leader to current process
`int setuid (i)`	Set effective UID to `i` (superuser sets real as well)
`int (*()) signal(i1, i2)`	
`int (*()) signal(i1, fp)`	Specify what to do upon receipt of signal `i1`; `i2` specifies either ignore (`SIG_IGN`) or take default action (`SIG_DFL`); `fp` specifies a function to call (`signal.h`)
`int stat (s, *stat)`	Place status of file `s` in structure `*stat` (`sys/types.h`, `sys/stat.h`)
`long time (*l)`	Place time in `*l`, returning same; null arg means just to return value
`long ulimit (i, l)`	Get and set process limits; `i` is a command that specifies getting or setting the file size limit or getting the maximum memory allocation; `l` specifies new file size limit in blocks
`int umask (i)`	Set file creation mask to `i`, returning old mask
`int uname (*utsname)`	Place system name and information in structure `*utsname` (`sys/utsname.h`)
`int unlink (s)`	Remove directory entry `s`
`int utime (s, *utimbuf)`	Set access and modification times of file `s` to those in structure `*utimbuf` (`sys/types.h`)
`int wait (*i)`	Wait for child process to stop or terminate, returning pid of child that stopped or terminated; `i` is set to exit status of child if child terminates or signal if child stops.
`int write (fd, s, u)`	Write `u` bytes of data from `s` to file associated with `fd`, returning number of bytes written

E X E R C I S E S

1. Implement `dup` using `fcntl`.

2. Implement the `echo`, `noecho`, `raw`, `noraw`, `cbreak`, and `nocbreak` functions from the `curses` library. (Read Chapter 6 for more information on the operation of these functions.)

3. Write a `setbaud` program that sets the terminal's baud rate to the value specified on the command line:

        $ setbaud 4800   Set baud rate to 4800

4. Write a function called `isdir` that takes a file name as its argument and returns one if the file is a directory and zero if it is not.

5. Implement the `access` system call using `stat`, `getuid`, and `getgid`. Remember that `access` makes it tests using the process's *real*, and not its effective, UID and GID.

6. Implement the UNIX system's `cp` command. Be sure to recognize the general format that allows one or mores file to be copied into a directory.

7. Implement the UNIX system's `rm` command. Use the `ftw` function described in Chapter 3 to implement the `-r` option.

8. Implement the UNIX systems's `mv` command. Use the `link` and `unlink` system calls where feasible to avoid unecessary file copying. Don't implement the `mv` command's use to rename directories.

9. Write a program called `lsl` that takes one or more file name arguments and produces the same output as `ls -l`. If `lsl` is given a directory name as an argument, you'll have to read the directory to see what files are in it. Use the include file `<sys/dir.h>`, which contains the definition for a structure called `direct` that describes the format of a directory entry. (Note that 14 character file names aren't null terminated.) The program will also need to use `getpwuid`, `getgrgid`, and `ctime`.

10. Write a function called `mypopen` to mimic the action of `popen` from the Standard I/O Library. Hint—you'll have to use `pipe`, `fdopen`, `fork`, and `exec`.

11. Modify Program 5-31 (the command interpreter):

     a. Don't require that whitespace characters appear before the < or > redirection characters, e.g.,

         cmd: **wc<data>count**

         should work okay.

     b. Support the output append redirection characters >>.

     c. Accept a pipe on the command line, e.g.,

         cmd: **ls | wc**

     d. Add the ability to accept an arbitrary number of pipes, e.g.,

         cmd: **who | sort | pr | lp**

     e. Handle the SIGINT and SIGQUIT signals so that the interpreter doesn't exit if they're received. The program that your interpreter is executing *should* receive them, however, so don't simply ignore them.

12. Implement the UNIX system's id command.

13. Implement the UNIX sleep routine. Note that sleep doesn't interfere with any pending alarm signal. Don't forget to take into account a pending alarm that is set to occur **before** sleep is supposed to return!

14. Add error handling to all of the above programs using perror.

6

WRITING TERMINAL INDEPENDENT
PROGRAMS WITH curses

T he curses library is a collection of routines that allows you to write "window-based" programs (like a screen editor or spreadsheet) that are independent of the terminal you or any other user will use when running the program. curses gets its name from what it does: *cursor manipulation*, or moving the cursor around the screen, so that characters can be placed anywhere on the screen.

The original version of curses was developed by Bill Joy and Ken Arnold at the University of California, Berkeley. It incorporated a database known as termcap, or the *terminal capabilities* database. In System V Release 2, the termcap database was replaced by the terminfo database, and curses was rewritten to incorporate it. Both of these versions of curses can be used with more than one hundred terminals. The information in the terminfo or termcap database is used by the curses routines to determine what sequence of special characters must be sent to a particular terminal to cause it to clear the screen, move the cursor up one line, delete a line, etc.

It is these databases that make curses truly terminal independent, since any terminal not already in the database can be added by a system administrator, and since the structure of both databases allows users to add their own local additions or modifications for a particular terminal. We'll cover the structure of these databases at the end of this chapter, along with a brief introduction to creating new entries in them.

In this chapter, we'll cover many of the curses routines; however, there are over 120 routines in the System V Release 2 version of curses, so it's impossible for us to cover every routine and every interaction between them. If you're interested in obtaining more information about curses, please refer to [1], [2], and [3] in the **References** section at the end of the chapter.

· Introduction to curses ·

The Basics

There are a couple of things you have to know before you can start using the curses library. First, when you compile a C program that calls curses routines, you must specify to the cc command that the library is to be linked in with the program. This is done with the -lcurses option, which must be specified *after* all the C program files:[†]

```
cc prog(s) -lcurses
```

Second, all program files that reference the curses routines must include the header file <curses.h>. Lastly, before you run a program that uses curses, you must inform curses what type of terminal you have. You do this by setting the shell variable TERM to the type of terminal you are using (e.g., a Hewlett Packard 2621, a Teletype 5420, or a Lear-Siegler ADM-3a) and exporting the TERM variable into the environment. This is done in the following manner:

```
$ TERM=2621                           Set terminal type to HP 2621
$ export TERM                         Put TERM in environment
```

If this is done for you by your .profile when you log in, you needn't worry about doing it. Once you've typed in these lines, you don't have to repeat them until you log in again.

    If your system has termcap, to find out what terminals are supported you can look at the file /etc/termcap, which contains an entry for each terminal. The lines that do not begin with whitespace or a # list the names of the various terminals, separated by | characters; for example,

```
h2|2621|hp2621|hp2621a|hp2621p|2621|2621a|2621p|hp 2621
```

lists the various valid settings of the TERM variable for the Hewlett-Packard 2621 terminal.

    If your system has terminfo, you can look at all the files in the directories under /usr/lib/terminfo/:

```
$ ls /usr/lib/terminfo/*
/usr/lib/terminfo/2:
2621
2621a
2621p
2623

   . . .
```

[†] Berkeley and pre-System V Release 2 UNIX systems require the termlib library to be linked in as well:
```
cc prog(s) -lcurses -ltermlib
```

If you do not see your terminal in the termcap or terminfo database, you can talk to your system administrator to see if a description is available for it. If one isn't available, you may want to refer to [4]; writing entries for these databases is described there.

The curses.h header file contains declarations for two integer variables that prove to be very useful: LINES and COLS. LINES is automatically set to the number of lines on your terminal; COLS is set to the number of columns. As we talk about various curses routines, you'll see that some of them **address** the terminal's screen, in that they move the cursor to a specific place, or address. This address is specified as a particular row and column (specified as arguments to the routine), where the address of the upper left-hand corner is row zero and column zero (0,0), and the address of the lower right-hand corner is row LINES-1 and column COLS-1 (LINES-1,COLS-1). Fig. 6-1 shows the layout of a terminal screen:

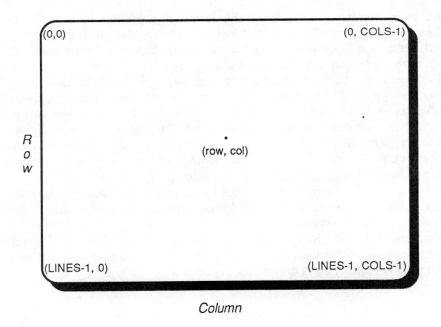

Fig. 6-1. Screen layout for curses

The organization of a curses program is, of course, up to the programmer and the needs of the application; however, there are two basic routines that are called by all programs that use curses: initscr and endwin. initscr initializes the various data elements that curses uses (e.g., LINES and COLS). endwin performs any cleanup needed by the program to restore the terminal to a usable state: some `curses` routines change the terminal's characteristics (e.g., go into raw mode and turn off echoing) and must be undone before the program exits; otherwise, the terminal is left in this odd state, and the user may not know how to change it back.

A Few Simple Examples

The `move` routine moves the cursor to the specified line and column. By combining this routine with an output routine, you can place characters anywhere on the screen. Note that if you specify an address that's not on the screen, `move` ignores the request, leaving the cursor's position unchanged.

In the following example we'll use the output routine `addch`, which places a character at the current cursor position. Note the use of the `refresh` routine. `curses` buffers all output to the terminal until `refresh` is called, at which time the screen is modified to look like `curses`' own internal representation. `refresh` is placed *outside* the `while` loop; the effect of this is to prevent `curses` from sending anything to the terminal until the loop is finished. `refresh` can just as easily be placed inside the loop, but placing it outside is more efficient. You'll see why this is true when we discuss the optimization that `curses` performs when `refresh` is called.

In the next program example and others throughout this chapter, we'll be showing the output in "screens." The programs that take user input will be shown in "before and after" screens: we'll show you the screen, tell you what command has been entered, and then show you another screen that illustrates what the program did with that command. Since the sample screens in this book can only give you a flavor of what's happening, we urge you to try these programs for yourself to see exactly how they work.

As you can see, Program 6-1 places its output in increasing row/column positions. Also, as part of its cleanup duties, `endwin` moves the cursor to the lower left corner of the screen.[†]

Remember that the file `<curses.h>` must be included in every program that uses `curses`. The variables `LINES` and `COLS` are declared in this file, obviating the need for you to declare them yourself.

---

† Note that in older version of `curses`, `endwin` doesn't do this.

Program 6-1

```c
#include <curses.h>

main ()
{
    int    line = 0;
    int    col = 0;
    char   c;

    initscr ();

    /* first call to refresh will clear screen */
    refresh ();

    /* output number at particular column/row */

    while ( line < LINES ) {

        /* move to new position */
        move (line, col);

        /* convert line to single digit char */
        c = line % 10 + '0';

        /* output last digit of line */
        addch (c);

        /* output appears diagonally across screen */
        ++col;
        ++line;
    }
    refresh ();
    endwin ();
}
```

```
0
 1
  2
   3
    4
     5
      6
       7
        8
         9
          0
           1
            2
             3
              4
               5
                6
                 7
                  8
$                  9
```

Here's another version of the previous program. We've replaced the `move` and `addch` with one routine, `mvaddch`. It takes three arguments—a row and column position and a character to put there. Most `curses` output routines come in a *mvroutine* form that simply takes two more arguments (a row and column) up front.

Program 6-2

```
#include <curses.h>

main ()
{
    int    line = 0;
    int    col = 0;
    char   c;

    initscr ();

    /* first call to refresh will clear screen */
    refresh ();
```

```
        /* output number at particular column/row */

    while ( line < LINES ) {

        /* convert line to single digit char */
        c = line % 10 + '0';

        /* move and output last digit of line */
        mvaddch (line, col, c);

        /* output appears diagonally across screen */
        col += 3;
        ++line;
    }
    refresh ();
    endwin ();
}
```

```
0
  1
    2
      3
        4
          5
            6
              7
                8
                  9
                    0
                      1
                        2
                          3
                            4
                              5
                                6
                                  7
                                    8
$                                     9
```

As you can see, we also flattened out the slope of the output characters by incrementing col by 3 instead of 1.

Using the LINES variable instead of hardcoding a number into the program (like 24) makes these two simple programs independent of the actual number of lines on the terminal on which they are run.

The following program displays the time and refreshes the screen once every second, so that the screen resembles a digital clock. The `mvaddstr` routine is used to output a string (the time) at the specified screen coordinates. Of course, there is also an `addstr` routine that just outputs a string at the current cursor position. `mvaddstr` and `addstr` simply call `addch` repeatedly to display successive characters from the string. Note that `refresh` is inside the timer loop; without this, the screen would never be updated.

Program 6-3

```c
#include <curses.h>
#include <time.h>
#include <signal.h>

main ()
{
    void   sig_catch();
    long   seconds;
    char   *title = "The current time is", *convtime, *ctime ();

    /* call sig_catch() if user hits DELETE/BREAK */
    signal (SIGINT, sig_catch);

    /* initial setup of curses */
    initscr ();

    /* output title, centered */
    mvaddstr (LINES / 2 - 1, (COLS - strlen (title)) / 2, title);

    for (;;) {
        /* get time and convert to ascii */
        time (&seconds);
        convtime = ctime (&seconds);

        /* display time, centered under title */
        mvaddstr (LINES / 2, (COLS - strlen (convtime)) / 2,
                            convtime);
        refresh ();
        sleep (1);
    }
}

/* signal handling routine:  call endwin and exit */

void sig_catch ()
{
    endwin ();
    exit (1);
}
```

The title and time are centered vertically by simply dividing LINES by 2. The strings are centered horizontally by subtracting their length from COLS and dividing the result by 2.

Note that the only way to stop this program is to hit *BREAK* or *DELETE*, so `signal` is called to make sure `endwin` is called before exiting. If you write a `curses` program that doesn't call `endwin` before exiting, your terminal will be left in a "funny" state: *NEWLINE* mapping may be off, so *RETURN* will not work; you have to use the `stty` command to set the terminal's state back to a "sane" one. On System III and System V UNIX systems (including XENIX), you can simply type

```
stty saneCTRL-j
```

to reset the terminal state.[†] (Note that the "sane" state is not necessarily the same as the state you're accustomed to; for example, the backspace may be set to # instead of *CTRL-h*.) On Berkeley UNIX systems, you have to turn off (or on) the various states that `curses` affected. The simplest thing to do if you're going to be developing lots of `curses` programs is to write a one-line shell program that contains the following:

```
stty -raw -cbreak -nl echo ek
```

and run it (using *CTRL-j* to end the command line instead of *RETURN*) whenever a `curses` program exits without calling `endwin`.

```
                     The current time is
                 Sun May 18 12:48:35 1987
```

Hit the *BREAK* key:

---

† Note that if character echoing was turned off by your `curses` program (more on this shortly), then you won't see this command echoed at the terminal as you type it. Don't worry, type it anyway.

```
                       The current time is
                    Sun May 18 12:48:37 1987




  $
```

One other important feature of this program is that only those characters on the screen that need to be changed from one second to the next are actually output; in other words, `curses` doesn't repaint the entire screen every second, only a couple of characters on it. This is one of `curses`' best features: optimal screen updating. `curses` keeps track of what's already gone out to the screen, so that when a `refresh` comes along, only those portions of the screen that have been modified by output routines will be updated; the rest remains unchanged. `refresh` must know what the screen looks like at all times; otherwise, it can't perform optimal updating. So all terminal I/O for a program that uses `curses` must be performed using `curses` routines. *Don't use any of the standard I/O routines or read or write to perform terminal I/O in a curses program.*

   `curses` attempts to output as few characters as possible to perform the modifications. It will use tabs instead of blanks where possible, and will attempt to perform output in an orderly fashion. If you were to output characters at random screen coordinates, `refresh` would simply output the characters one line at a time beginning at the top of the screen, since this would require fewer control sequences to move the cursor around.

The `printw` Routine

`printw` outputs a string to the screen using the same formatting and arguments as `printf`:

Program 6-4

```
#include <curses.h>

main ()
{
    int  line = 0;
    int  col = 0;

    initscr ();
```

```
/* first call to refresh will clear screen */
refresh ();

/* output number at particular column/row */

while ( line < LINES ) {

    /* move to new position */
    move (line, col);

    /* output last digit of line */
    printw ("%d", line % 10);

    /* output appears diagonally across screen */
    ++col;
    ++line;
}

refresh ();
endwin ();
}
```

Also, there is a `mv` version of `printw` that takes a row and column coordinate pair as the first two arguments; so the `move` and `printw` can be combined (as we did previously with the `move` and the `addch`):

```
mvprintw (line, col, "%d", line % 10);
```

The following table summarizes the routines covered in this section:

TABLE 6-1. Basic curses Routines

Routine	Description
initscr	Initializes curses package
endwin	Cleans up and exits curses
refresh	Outputs changes to terminal
move	Moves cursor to specified position
addch	Adds a character to current cursor position
mvaddch	Combination of move and addch
addstr	Adds a string to current cursor position
mvaddstr	Combination of move and addstr
printw	Adds a string to current cursor position using printf style formatting
mvprintw	Combination of move and printw

There are a few things you should note about the above routines:

1. When `addch` places a character on the screen, it overwrites any character that might be there. (Note that all of the above routines that produce output use `addch`.)

2. If output goes past the end of a line, it continues on the next line.

3. If an illegal address is given to `curses`, i.e., a row or column less than zero or greater than `LINES - 1` or `COLS - 1`, `curses` simply ignores the address and leaves the cursor's position unchanged.

4. The cursor's position after output is the column immediately to the right of the last character output or the first column on the next line if the last character is placed at `COLS - 1`. So the sequence

```
move (10, 20);
addch ('x');
```

leaves the cursor at (10, 21).

• Handling User Input •

`curses` has its own routines for handling user input. It has to, since any user input when character echoing is on will modify the screen, and `curses` must keep track of what the screen looks like at all times for `refresh`.

Input Routines

There are three basic input routines in `curses`: `getch`, `getstr`, and `scanw`. `getch` reads in a single character from the terminal (like `getchar`); `getstr` reads in a line from the terminal (like `gets`); and `scanw` reads in data from the terminal (like `scanf`). Since most programs that use `curses` perform single character input, we're going to spend most of this section on `getch`.

Here is a program that lists a file one screenful at a time (like the `more` and `pg` commands). It uses `getch` to input a character, which it ignores. Although most programs would use the value returned by `getch`, here it's simply used to suspend the program between pages until the user is ready to view the next screenful. Note that it uses `LINES` to figure out how many lines to output for a screenful. Also note that the `<curses.h>` header file automatically includes `<stdio.h>`, so you don't have to explicitly include it yourself.

Program 6-5

```c
#include <curses.h>
#include <signal.h>

main (argc, argv)
int argc;
char *argv[];
{
    FILE   *pgfile;
    char   buf [512];
    int    line = 0;
    void   finish ();

    if ( argc != 2 ) {
        fprintf (stderr, "Usage: %s file\n", argv[0]);
        exit (1);
    }

    if ( (pgfile = fopen (argv[1], "r")) == (FILE *) NULL ) {
        fprintf (stderr, "Can't open %s\n", argv[1]);
        exit (2);
    }

    initscr ();

    /* cleanup if user hits interrupt */
    signal (SIGINT, finish);

    while ( fgets (buf, sizeof (buf), pgfile) != (char *) NULL ) {
        mvaddstr (line, 0, buf);
        ++line;

        if ( line == LINES - 1 ) {
            /*
            ** bottom of screen:
            ** output prompt and wait for user to hit a key
            */
            mvaddstr (LINES - 1, 0, "more: ");
            refresh ();

            getch ();
            line = 0;
        }
    }

    refresh ();
    finish ();
}
```

```
    /* cleanup routine:  call endwin and exit */

    void finish ()
    {
        endwin ();
        exit (0);
    }
```

$ a.out prog1.c

```
#include <curses.h>

main ()
{
    int line = 0;
    int col = 0;
    char c;

    initscr ();

    /* first call to refresh will clear screen */
    refresh ();

more:
```

Hit *RETURN*:

```
    /* output number at particular location */

    while ( line < LINES ) {

        /* move to new position */
        move (line, col);

        /* convert line to single digit char */
        c = line % 10 + '0';

        /* output last digit of line */
        addch (c);

more:
```

Hit *RETURN*:

```
    /* output appears diagonally across screen */
        ++col;
        ++line;
    }.

    refresh ();
    endwin ();
}
        c = line % 10 + '0';

        /* output last digit of line */
        addch (c);

$ re:
```

Well, now, the last screen looks a little strange. It seems that part of the previous screen was left up there; also, the `re:` part of `more:` was left on the last line. To solve this problem, the program needs to clear the screen before outputting the next one. If we insert a call to the function `clear` right after the `getch`, `curses` will do just that:

```
   . . .
  if ( line == LINES - 1 ) {
      . . .
      getch ();
      clear ();
      line = 0;
  }
   . . .
```

```
#include <curses.h>

main ()
{
    int   line = 0;
    int   col = 0;
    char  c;

    initscr ();

    /* first call to refresh will clear screen */
    refresh ();

more:
```

Hit *RETURN*:

```
        /* output number at particular location */

        while ( line < LINES ) {

            /* move to new position */
            move (line, col);

            /* convert line to single digit char */
            c = line % 10 + '0';

            /* output last digit of line */
            addch (c);

more:
```

Hit *RETURN*:

```
        /* output appears diagonally across screen */
            ++col;
            ++line;
        }

        refresh ();
        endwin ();
}



$
```

That's better!

One problem that could occur here is that lines longer than COLS characters will "wrap around" into the next line and will be subsequently overwritten
when the next line from the file is displayed. Of course, it's not too difficult to
program around this: use strlen to get the length of the input line, incrementing line by strlen (buf) / COLS + 1 instead of by one.

```
        . . .
    mvaddstr (line, 0, buf);
    line += strlen (buf) / COLS + 1;

    if ( line >= LINES - 1 ) {
        . . .
```

This can handle lines of any length up to the size of buf, except when the line wraps around to the next screenful.

Input and Output Modes

One thing to note about the previous program is that you don't have to hit *RETURN* to get it to read the character, that is, canonical processing has been turned off. (See Chapter 5 for more information on canonical vs. raw mode.) By default, if you don't request any change in input modes, all input is done in *cbreak* mode, meaning that canonical processing is turned off, so all characters are available as soon as they are typed in. It isn't truly raw mode, as *CTRL-s*, *CTRL-q*, *CTRL-*, and *DELETE* are still considered special and are not passed to the program when typed in.

curses has several input and output modes that you may use to control terminal attributes. These modes are turned on and off by calling various routines. For example, if you wish to turn off character echoing during input, call noecho. To turn it back on, call echo. The following routines may be called to turn on/off the various input and output modes (they all call ioctl to actually set the modes):

cbreak   Turns on cbreak mode. Cbreak mode turns off canonical processing, allowing characters to be read one at a time. It still allows *CTRL-s*, *CTRL-q*, *CTRL-*, and *DELETE* to be interpreted specially. Note: on many older versions of curses, this mode is often called *crmode* and is set by calling crmode instead of cbreak.

nocbreak   Turns off cbreak mode. (Older versions may use nocrmode.)

raw   Turns on raw mode. Raw mode is like cbreak mode, except that no characters are interpreted specially, and eight-bit characters are passed through without stripping the high-order bit (this has little significance on most terminals).

noraw   Turns off raw mode.

echo   Turns on echo mode. Characters are echoed on the terminal as they are typed in. This mode is on by default.

noecho   Turns off echo mode.

nl   Turns on *NEWLINE* mapping. *RETURN* is mapped into *NEWLINE* (*CTRL-j*, or \n) on input and *NEWLINE* is mapped into *RETURN-NEWLINE* on output. This mode is on by default.

nonl   Turns off *NEWLINE* mapping.

If neither nonl, cbreak, nor raw is called when a curses program runs, *all input routines automatically turn on cbreak mode.*

These modes are very useful, since most of the time your curses programs will not want to have character echo on and will usually need to access characters one at a time (e.g. a screen editor). Turning off *NEWLINE* mapping is also very helpful, as it allows refresh to perform better screen optimization on some terminals (with this mode on, a curses program cannot send just a *NEW-LINE* to the screen, as it is mapped into a *RETURN-NEWLINE* pair). Unless there is some pressing reason not to, we suggest that you call cbreak, noecho, and nonl in all your programs that use curses.

The following program uses getch to get single character commands from the terminal. The program allows the user to move the cursor around the screen and turn individual locations "on" and "off," where an on location has an X in it and an off location has a blank in it. The h, j, k, and l keys are used to move the cursor left, down, up, and right, respectively (like vi); the 1 and 0 keys are used to turn the locations on and off; q is used to exit the program; and any other key is considered an error and is ignored.

Since the characters typed in should not be echoed at the terminal (an h should move the cursor left, not display an h), echoing is turned off by calling the noecho routine. We also call nonl to speed up cursor manipulation; cbreak mode must be explicitly turned on now, since nonl has been set.

Program 6-6

```
#include <curses.h>
#include <signal.h>

main ()
{
    void    finish ();
    int     in, curline = 1, curcol = 0;
    char    *title =
            "h left, j down, k up, l right, 0 off, 1 on, q quit";

    /* call finish() if user hits BREAK or DELETE */
    signal (SIGINT, finish);

    /* initial setup of curses */
    initscr ();
    cbreak ();
    noecho ();
    nonl ();
```

```
/* output title */
mvaddstr (0, (COLS - strlen (title)) / 2, title);

for (;;) {

    /* move to current position and update cursor */
    move (curline, curcol);
    refresh ();

    /* input command and process */
    in = getch ();

    switch (in) {
        case 'j': /* down */
            /* don't move past bottom of screen */
            if ( curline != LINES - 1 )
                ++curline;
            break;
        case 'k': /* up */
            /* don't move into title line */
            if ( curline != 1 )
                --curline;
            break;
        case 'h': /* left */
            /* don't move past left side of screen */
            if ( curcol != 0 )
                --curcol;
            break;
        case 'l': /* right */
            /* don't move past right side of screen */
            if ( curcol != COLS - 1 )
                ++curcol;
            break;
        case '0': /* off */
            addch (' ');
            break;
        case '1': /* on */
            addch ('X');
            break;
        case 'q':
            finish ();
            break;
    }
}
}
```

```
/* cleanup routine:  call endwin and exit */

void finish ()
{
    endwin ();
    exit (0);
}
```

```
h left, j down, k up, l right, 0 off, 1 on, q quit
□



















```

Hit j:

```
h left, j down, k up, l right, 0 off, 1 on, q quit

□


















```

Hit l (letter ell):

```
h left, j down, k up, l right, 0 off, 1 on, q quit

  □



```

Hit 1 (one):

```
h left, j down, k up, l right, 0 off, 1 on, q quit

  ⊠



```

Hit j:

```
h left, j down, k up, l right, 0 off, 1 on, q quit

  X
  □



```

Hit 1 (one):

```
h left, j down, k up, l right, 0 off, 1 on, q quit

  X
 ⊠
```

Hit 0:

```
h left, j down, k up, l right, 0 off, 1 on, q quit

  X
 □
```

Hit q:

```
h left, j down, k up, l right, 0 off, 1 on, q quit

  X













$  □
```

Note that the value returned by getch is an integer and should be assigned to an int. Also keep in mind that addch overwrites the character at the current cursor position; *it doesn't insert a character there.* As you'll see, there is another routine that inserts characters.

The following table summarizes the routines covered in this section.

TABLE 6-2. I/O Routines

Routine	Description
getch	Reads a character from the terminal
mvgetch	Combination of move and getch
getstr	Reads a line from the terminal
mvgetstr	Combination of move and getstr
scanw	Reads a line from the terminal using scanf style formatting
mvscanw	Combination of move and scanw
clear	Clears screen
cbreak	Turns on cbreak mode
nocbreak	Turns off cbreak mode
raw	Turns on raw mode
noraw	Turns off raw mode
echo	Turns on echo mode
noecho	Turns off echo mode
nl	Turns on *NEWLINE* mapping
nonl	Turns off *NEWLINE* mapping

• A Simple Screen Editor •

Now that we've covered some of the basic curses routines, we're going to turn to a realistic application: a screen editor. This program will be developed in stages, starting with the following program, which is simply a souped-up version of Program 6-6.

Program 6-7

```c
#include <curses.h>
#include <signal.h>

/* current line and column */
int curline = 0, curcol = 0;

main ()
{
    void  finish ();
    int  in;

    /* call finish() if user hits BREAK */
    signal (SIGINT, finish);

    /* initial setup of curses */
    initscr ();
    cbreak ();
    noecho ();
    nonl ();

    for (;;) {

        /* refresh screen */
        move (curline, curcol);
        refresh ();

        /* get command and process */
        in = getch ();

        switch (in) {
           case 'j':  /* down */
              if (curline != LINES - 2)
                 ++curline;
              break;
           case 'k':  /* up */
              if (curline != 0)
                 --curline;
              break;
           case 'h':  /* left */
              if (curcol != 0)
                 --curcol;
              break;
           case 'l':  /* right */
              if (curcol != COLS - 1)
                 ++curcol;
              break;
```

```
              case 'd':   /* delete line */
                  deleteln ();
                  break;
              case 'a':   /* add chars */
                  add ();
                  break;
              case 'q':   /* quit */
                  finish ();
                  break;
          }
      }
  }

/*
** character add routine:
** reads characters from terminal and puts on screen
** handles line wraparound and bottom of screen condition
*/

add ()
{
    int in;

    /* read in characters until ESC */
    while ( (in = getch()) != '\033' ) {

        /* output character and get new location */
        addch (in);
        getyx (stdscr, curline, curcol);

        /* if RETURN and not at bottom, go to next line */
        if ( in == '\r' && curline != LINES - 2 )
            ++curline;

        move (curline, curcol);
        refresh ();
    }
}

/* cleanup routine:  call endwin and exit */

void finish ()
{
    endwin ();
    exit (0);
}
```

There are only two additions for the editor. The first is a call to the `deleteln` routine when the user enters the `d` command. `deleteln` simply deletes the line that the cursor is on, moving all lines that follow up by one line, putting a blank line at the bottom of the screen. The cursor's position (relative to the terminal's screen) is not changed.

The second is the input mode routine `add`; when the user enters the `a` command, `add` is called to actually add the characters to the screen. It takes all input up to an *ESC* and puts it on the screen with `addch`. The `getyx` macro is defined in `<curses.h>` and is used to get the current row and column of the cursor; note that since `getyx` is a macro, its second and third arguments are *not* pointers. (We'll get into what `stdscr` means in the next section.) Since `curses` has to keep track of where the cursor is at all times, we don't have to. It's a lot easier for us to get this information from `curses` than to keep track of it ourselves, since certain keys like tabs and backspaces have to be handled specially. `add` must also check to see if the user's input has wrapped around to the last line. The bottom line of the screen is not used by the editor—it will be used in later versions for messages.

One other thing to note about the `add` routine is that `\r` is used instead of `\n` to test for *RETURN*s; when `nonl` is called, *NEWLINE* mapping is turned off, and *RETURN*s are no longer mapped into `\n`s when they are read.

This screen editor is simple, but also not very useful: it doesn't know how to read or save a file (but it's still a good *screen* editor). Shortly, we'll show you how to improve it.

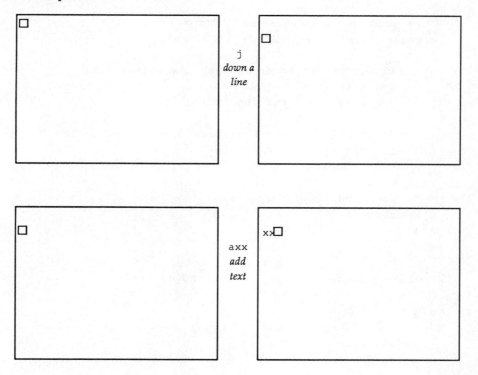

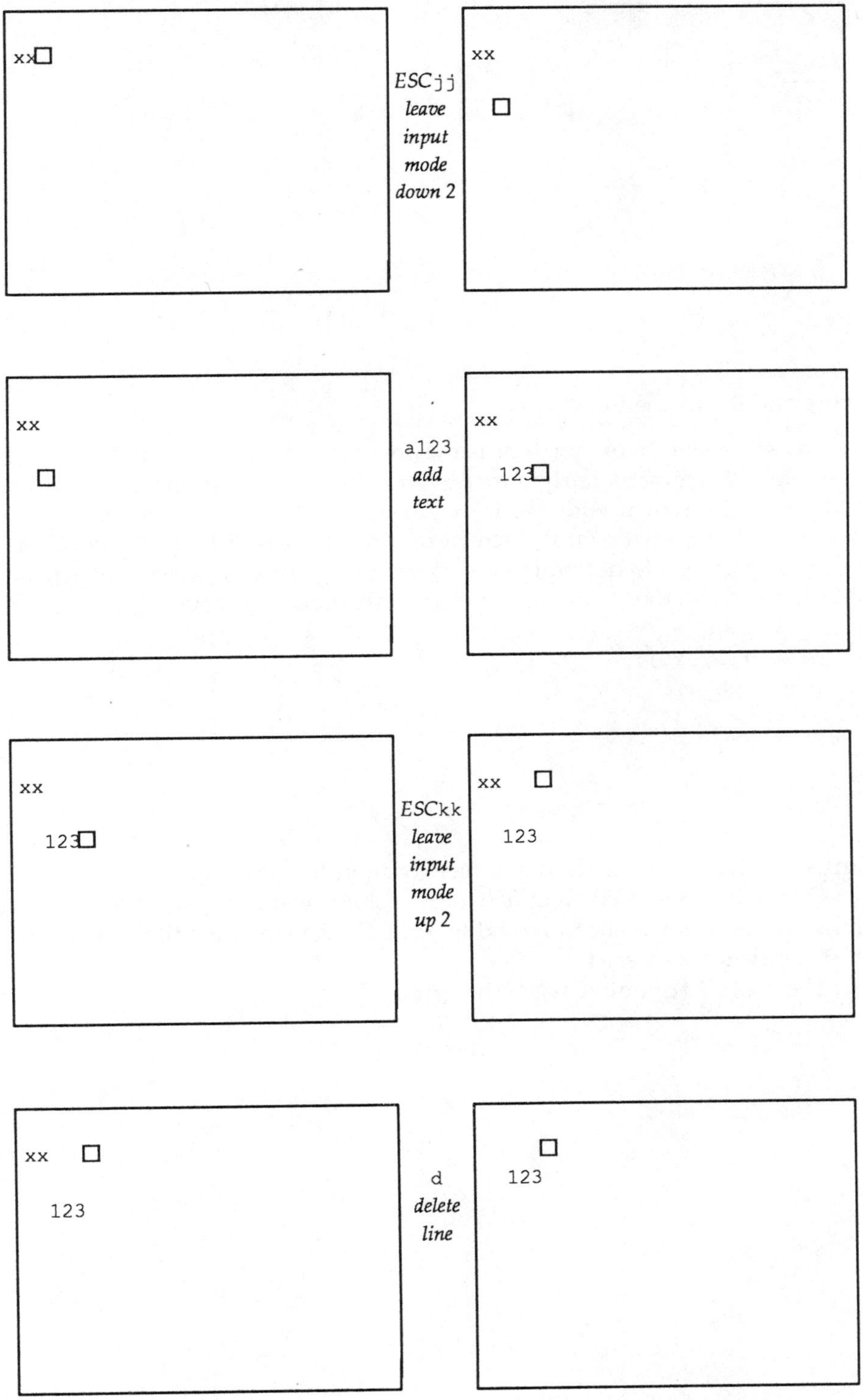

xx▯

*ESC*jj
leave
input
mode
down 2

xx

▯

xx

▯

a123
add
text

xx

123▯

xx

123▯

*ESC*kk
leave
input
mode
up 2

xx ▯

123

xx ▯

123

d
delete
line

▯

123

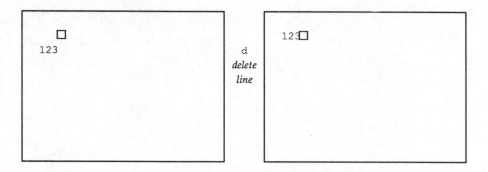

Saving and Restoring Files

One necessary feature of an editor is the ability to save and restore files. Getting a file into our editor is fairly simple: you simply open it and read each line, adding it to the screen with `addstr`. Saving a file is more difficult, since our editor must read what's on the screen in order to save it in a file. Fortunately, `curses` allows you to determine the character displayed at a particular position on the screen with the `inch` and `mvinch` functions. The code

```
move (10, 10);
c = inch ();
```

or

```
c = mvinch (10, 10);
```

returns the character displayed at screen location 10,10 and stores it into `c`.

Our editor has been modified to read lines from the file specified on the command line when it starts up and to write the screen to the file and quit when the `w` command is entered.

The `getfile` routine reads the specified file:

```
/*
** file input routine:
** opens file, copies up to LINES - 1 lines to screen
*/

void getfile (name)
char *name;
{
    int    line;
    char   linebuf[512];
    FILE   *infile;

    /* open file for reading */

    if ( (infile = fopen (name, "r")) == (FILE *) NULL ) {
        mvprintw (LINES - 1, 0, "cannot read %s", name);
        refresh ();
        return;
    }

    /* read up to LINES - 1 lines from input file */

    for ( line = 0; line < LINES - 1  &&  fgets (linebuf,
            COLS + 1, infile) != (char *) NULL; ++line )
        mvaddstr (line, 0, linebuf);    /* put line on screen */

    fclose (infile);
}
```

It opens the file for reading, reads a line from the file with `fgets`, and puts each line on the screen with `mvaddstr`. Up to LINES - 1 lines are read from the file.

The `putfile` routine writes out the screen to the specified file:

```
/*
** file output routine:
** opens file, copies screen to file
*/

void putfile (name)
char *name;
{
    int    line, col;
    FILE   *outfile;

    /* open file for writing */

    if ( (outfile = fopen (name, "w")) == (FILE *) NULL ) {
        mvprintw (LINES - 1, 0, "cannot write %s", name);
        refresh ();
        return;
    }

    /* output all lines but bottom one */

    for ( line = 0; line < LINES - 1; ++line ) {
        for ( col = 0; col < COLS; ++col )
            putc (mvinch (line, col), outfile);

        /* output NEWLINE at end of each line */
        putc ('\n', outfile);
    }

    fclose (outfile);
}
```

It opens the file for writing and outputs all lines on the screen with the exception of the bottom line. The outermost `for` processes each line, the innermost `for` scans across each line, and `putc (mvinch (line, col), outfile)` outputs the character in each column.

Except for the code to handle the file specified on the command line and to call `getfile` and `putfile`, the rest of the program remains unchanged:

Program 6-8

```
#include <curses.h>
#include <signal.h>

/* current line and column */
int curline = 0, curcol = 0;

main (argc, argv)
int argc;
char *argv[];
{
    void  finish (), getfile (), putfile ();
    int   in;

    if ( argc != 2 ) {
        fprintf (stderr, "%s: needs file\n", argv[0]);
        exit (1);
    }

    /* call finish() if user hits BREAK or DELETE */
    signal (SIGINT, finish);

    /* initial setup of curses */
    initscr ();
    cbreak ();
    noecho ();
    nonl ();

    /* set up screen by reading file */
    getfile (argv[1]);

    for (;;) {

        /* refresh screen */
        move (curline, curcol);
        refresh ();

        /* get command and process */
        in = getch ();
```

```
        switch (in) {
            . . .
            case 'w':          /* write file */
                putfile (argv[1]);
                finish ();
                break;
            case 'q':  /* quit */
                finish ();
                break;
        }
    }
}
```

```
$ cat testfile
this is a
test file for
the edit
program
$ a.out testfile
```

```
┌─────────────────────┐                  ┌─────────────────────┐
│▣his is a            │                  │this is a            │
│test file for        │                  │▣est file for        │
│the edit             │                  │the edit             │
│program              │        j         │program              │
│                     │      down        │                     │
│                     │      one         │                     │
│                     │      line        │                     │
│                     │                  │                     │
│                     │                  │                     │
└─────────────────────┘                  └─────────────────────┘
```

```
┌─────────────────────┐                  ┌─────────────────────┐
│this is a            │                  │this is a            │
│▣est file for        │                  │▣he edit             │
│the edit             │                  │program              │
│program              │        d         │                     │
│                     │      delete      │                     │
│                     │      line        │                     │
│                     │                  │                     │
│                     │                  │                     │
│                     │                  │                     │
└─────────────────────┘                  └─────────────────────┘
```

```
this is a
▢he edit
program
```

```
w
write
and
quit
```

```
this is a
▢he edit
program
```

```
$ ▢
```

```
$ cat testfile
this is a
the edit
program
```

```
$
```

Notice that the `testfile` has `LINES` lines in it. That's because `putfile` doesn't check to see if the lines at the end of the screen are empty or not. Also, the length of all lines is `COLS` now, since `putfile` writes out the full line, and lines are padded on the right with blanks by `curses`. The line length problem can be solved by looking for the first nonblank character on each line *from the right side of the screen* and writing out the characters from the first column up to that one. The file length problem can be solved by looking for the first nonblank line from the bottom of the screen and writing out lines to that one:

```
void putfile (name)
char *name;
{
    int   line, col, linelen, pagelen;
    FILE  *outfile;

    /* open file for writing */

    if ( (outfile = fopen (name, "w")) == (FILE *) NULL ) {
        mvprintw (LINES - 1, 0, "cannot write %s", name);
        refresh ();
        return;
    }
```

```
        pagelen = scrsize ();

        /* output screen */

        for ( line = 0; line < pagelen; ++line ) {

            /* get line length */
            linelen = len (line);

            for ( col = 0; col < linelen; ++col )
                putc (mvinch (line, col), outfile);

            putc ('\n', outfile);
        }

        fclose (outfile);
    }

/* len:  returns length of specified screen line */

int len (line)
int line;
{
    int  col;

    /* look for first nonblank from right side of screen */

    for ( col = COLS - 1; col >= 0 &&
            mvinch (line, col) == ' '; --col )
        ;

    return (col + 1);
}

/* scrsize:  returns number of lines on screen */

int scrsize ()
{
    int  line;

    /* look for first nonempty line from bottom */

    for ( line = LINES - 2; line >= 0 &&
            len (line) == 0; --line )
        ;

    return (line + 1);
}
```

The `len` routine returns the length of the specified line. It simply starts at the last column on the screen (`COLS - 1`) and scans to the left until it finds the first nonblank character:

```
for (col = COLS - 1; col >= 0 &&
        mvinch (line, col) == ' '; --col)
    ;
```

It then returns that column number plus 1 as the length of the line.

The `scrsize` routine work similarly, except that it looks for the first nonempty (length > 0) line starting at the bottom of the screen, going up.

Let's see if we can write a file properly now:

$ a.out testfile

```
This is a
the edit
program




```

   w

```
This is a
the edit
program




$ □
```

```
$ cat testfile
this is a
the edit
program
$ ls -l testfile
-rw-r--r--    1 phw        phw             31 May 22 12:17 testfile
$
```

Notice that there are no extra lines at the end of `testfile` and that the file's size (31 bytes) shows there are no blanks at the end of each line (but if you count up the number of characters, remember that there's a *NEWLINE* at the end of each line).

Other Useful curses Routines

In order to implement all the features of a good screen editor, you have to use many different `curses` routines. In fact, the initial set of terminal independent cursor manipulation routines that became `curses` was a part of the `vi` editor.

We're going to mention some other useful screen manipulation routines here, and we'll discuss how they might be used in the screen editor.

The `insertln` routine inserts a blank line above the current line. The current line and all lines following it are moved down one line, and the new line becomes the current line. This routine could be used to implement the `o` and `o` `vi` functions.   `o` "opens" a line below the current one by shifting all lines below down by one, moving the cursor to the beginning of the line, and going into input mode; `o` does the same thing above the cursor.

```
case 'o':              /* open line below current line */

    /* move down a line unless at bottom */
    if (curline != LINES - 2)
        ++curline;
    else
        break;

    curcol = 0;                 /* move cursor to      */
    move (curline, curcol);  /* start of next line */
    insertln ();                /* insert new line    */
    refresh ();                 /* show it            */
    add ();                     /* enter input mode   */
    break;
case 'O':          /* open line above current line */
    insertln ();                /* insert new line    */
    curcol = 0;                 /* move cursor to      */
    move (curline, curcol);  /* start of it        */
    refresh ();                 /* show it            */
    add ();                     /* enter input mode   */
    break;
```

Note that `o` and `o` merely open up one line; if you type in more than one line, `add` will simply overwrite subsequent lines. Also, if text is pushed off the screen with `o` or `O`, it is lost.

The `insch` routine inserts a character before the character under the cursor. All characters to the right of the cursor are moved one column to the right, and the character (if any) in column `COL - 1` is lost. If used instead of `addch` in the editor's `add` routine, `insch` would cause text to be inserted instead of overwriting what's already there (making it more like the `i` command in `vi`).

The `delch` routine deletes the character under the cursor, moving all characters to the right of the cursor left one column. This can be used to implement the `x` command in `vi`, which deletes a single character:

```
case 'x': /* delete character under cursor */
    delch ();
    break;
```

The `clrtoeol` and `clrtobot` routines erase from the current cursor position to the end of the line or bottom of the screen, respectively. `clrtoeol` can be used to implement the `D` command in `vi`, which deletes characters from the current position to the end of the line:

```
case 'D':
    clrtoeol ();
    break;
```

The following table summarizes the routines discussed in this section.

TABLE 6-3. More Advanced curses Routines

Routine	Description
deleteln	Deletes line at curent cursor position
insertln	Inserts line above current cursor postion
getyx	Gets cursor position
inch	Gets character at current cursor postion
mvinch	Combination of move and inch
insch	Inserts character at current cursor position
mvinsch	Combination of move and insch
delch	Deletes character at current cursor position
mvdelch	Combination of move and delch
clrtoeol	Clears line from current cursor position to end
clrtobot	Clears screen from current cursor position to bottom

One thing to keep in mind with this editor is that it's more of a tool for learning about `curses` than about editors. Most editors can work on files longer than 24 lines; they must keep track of all the lines, not just the ones on the screen, and manage them as the editor scrolls through the file. `vi` does a lot of work to keep track of what's going on with the file; we've cheated by letting `curses` do the data management for us.

· Handling Multiple Windows ·

A *window* in `curses` is a data structure that maps onto a portion of the terminal screen. It contains an image of what a section of the terminal screen looks like (or will look like after refreshing the window to the terminal screen). There are always at least two windows in existence when a `curses` program runs: `stdscr` and `curscr`. `stdscr` is the window that all the routines you've learned about so far perform output to. It buffers your output until a `refresh` is performed, causing modifications to the window to be sent to the terminal. `curscr` is the window that contains what is actually on the terminal.

After a `refresh`, `stdscr` and `curscr` contain the same screen image. When changes are made to `stdscr` and `refresh` is called, `curses` compares `stdscr` and `curscr` to determine what has to be changed on the screen to make it look like `stdscr`.

`curses` allows you to create other windows that overlap part or all of `stdscr`. You can perform output to these windows and then output the changes to the terminal with `wrefresh`. You can even create several overlapping windows, shuffling them on the screen as if they were a pile of papers.

Creating Windows

The `newwin` routine creates a new window. It is called with four arguments: the number of lines and columns in the new window, and the location (on the screen) of the upper left hand corner of the new window. It returns a pointer to a structure of type `WINDOW`, that may be used to perform I/O on that window.

```
WINDOW *win1, *win2;

win1 = newwin (10, 10, 0, 0);
win2 = newwin (15, 20, 5, 10);
```

`win1` is a 10 by 10 window located in the upper left hand corner of the screen. `win2` is a 15 by 20 window with its upper left hand corner at screen coordinates 5, 10.

`newwin` will allocate memory for the new window's data area.

`delwin` may be called to delete a window and its associated data, and `mvwin` may be called to move a window. `mvwin` is called with the window to move, and the coordinates for the new upper left hand corner. It is an error to create or move a window where any part of it is not on the screen.

Window Manipulation Routines

`curses` has many routines that deal with windows. Most of the routines that you've already seen have variants that can be used to operate on a given window. Just put a `w` in front of the routine's name and you'll have the window version (e.g., `winch`, `wprintw`). If the routine starts with `mv`, then put the `w` after the `mv` (e.g., `mvwprintw`, `mvwinch`, `mvwaddch`). For all of these routines, the window is specified as the first argument, and the rest of the arguments are specified as in the nonwindow routines:

```
wmove (win1, 10, 10);
waddch (win1, 'x');
wprintw (win1, "%s", str);
mvwaddch (win1, 0, 0, 'x');
wrefresh (win1);
```

In fact, routines that deal with stdscr are mostly macros defined in <curses.h> that map into a call to the respective window routine with stdscr as an argument:

```
#define refresh()           (wrefresh (stdscr))
#define move(y, x)          (wmove (stdscr, y, x))
#define mvaddch(y, x, c)    (mvwaddch (stdscr, y, x, c))
```

These are the window versions of all the routines you've learned up to now:

```
waddch          wgetch          winch
mvwaddch        mvwgetch        mvwinch
waddstr         wgetstr         wdelch
mvwaddstr       mvwgetstr       mvwdelch
wprintw         wscanw          winsch
mvwprintw       mvwscanw        mvwinsch
wmove           wrefresh        wclear
wclrtoeol       wclrtobot       wdeleteln
```

Windows can be used in various ways: they can be nonoverlapping, for example, two windows for editing two files at the same time; or they can be overlapping, for example, a "desktop" system where several windows are used to run several applications, or where windows "pop up" with information useful at some point in an application (e.g., help or error information).

The following program uses a single window (errwin) to display an error if the user types in any character but q (to quit):

Program 6-9

```
#include <curses.h>
#include <signal.h>

main ()
{
    void    finish ();
    int     in, i;
    WINDOW  *errwin;

    /* call finish if user hits BREAK or DELETE */
    signal (SIGINT, finish);

    /* initial setup of curses */
    initscr ();
    cbreak ();
    noecho ();
    nonl ();
```

```
          /* set up error window */
          errwin = newwin (6, 30, LINES / 2 - 3, COLS / 2 - 15);
          box (errwin, '|', '-');
          mvwprintw (errwin, 2, 6, "Error in user input");
          mvwprintw (errwin, 3, 4, "Hit any key to continue");

          /* set up stdscr */
          for ( i = 0; i < LINES; ++i )
              mvprintw (i, i, "This is just junk on line %d", i);

          for (;;) {
              refresh ();

              /* get command and process */

              in = getch ();

              switch (in) {
                  case 'q':  /* quit */
                      finish ();
                  default:
                      touchwin (errwin);
                      wrefresh (errwin);
                      getch ();
                      touchwin (stdscr);
                      break;
              }
          }
      }


      /* cleanup routine: call endwin and exit */

      void finish ()
      {
          endwin ();
          exit (0);
      }
```

box is a curses routine that draws a box around a window. The three arguments are the window to box, and vertical and horizontal drawing characters. (We've used | and - as our boxing characters.) Note that the box characters use up two columns and two rows of the window (i.e., the box is drawn *inside* the window, not outside).

Notice the use of `touchwin` on both `errwin` and `stdscr`. `touchwin` addresses every location on the specified window and "touches" them so that (w)`refresh` thinks the characters have been modified and need to be output to the terminal screen. We must do this because the windows aren't written to after their initial setup, so after refreshing `stdscr` and `errwin` once each, the screen will simply remain unchanged. `touchwin` is usually used when dealing with overlapping windows, where one window may need to be "on top of" another even if it hasn't been modified since the last `wrefresh` on it. `curses` is still smart enough when doing the refresh to output only to those portions of the screen that are different due to the `touchwin` and `wrefresh`, and not to redo the entire screen.

We used a `switch` in the program instead of an `if` because this code would usually be part of a larger program that reads commands and processes them (like Program 6-8).

```
This is just junk on line 0
 This is just junk on line 1
  This is just junk on line 2
   This is just junk on line 3
    This is just junk on line 4
     This is just junk on line 5
      This is just junk on line 6
       This is just junk on line 7
        This is just junk on line 8
         This is just junk on line 9
          This is just junk on line 10
           This is just junk on line 11
            This is just junk on line 12
             This is just junk on line 13
```

Hit `x`:

```
This is just junk on line 0
 This is just junk on line 1
  This is just junk on line 2
   This is just junk on line 3
    This |---------------------------|
     This|                           |
      Thi|      Error in user input  |
       Th|   Hit any key to continue |
        T |                          |
          |---------------------------|
          This is just junk on line 10
           This is just junk on line 11
            This is just junk on line 12
             This is just junk on line 13
```

Hit `x`:

```
This is just junk on line 0
 This is just junk on line 1
  This is just junk on line 2
   This is just junk on line 3
    This is just junk on line 4
     This is just junk on line 5
      This is just junk on line 6
       This is just junk on line 7
        This is just junk on line 8
         This is just junk on line 9
          This is just junk on line 10
           This is just junk on line 11
            This is just junk on line 12
             This is just junk on line 13
```

Hit `q`:

```
This is just junk on line 0
 This is just junk on line 1
  This is just junk on line 2
   This is just junk on line 3
    This is just junk on line 4
     This is just junk on line 5
      This is just junk on line 6
       This is just junk on line 7
        This is just junk on line 8
         This is just junk on line 9
          This is just junk on line 10
           This is just junk on line 11
            This is just junk on line 12
$            This is just junk on line 13
```

Scrolling

One of the attributes of a window is whether it will scroll when a *NEWLINE* is output on the last line of the window or when a character is placed in the bottom right hand corner. If scrolling is enabled, all the lines in the window are moved up one line (with the top line disappearing) and a new line is created at the bottom of the window. By default, scrolling is not enabled.

`scrollok` is called to turn scrolling on or off for a window. Its two arguments are a window and a flag specifying whether scrolling is to be turned on or off. The predefined `curses` flags `TRUE` and `FALSE` may be used as the second argument to turn scrolling on or off, respectively. The following lines turn scrolling on for `stdscr` and off for `win1`:

```
scrollok (stdscr, TRUE);
scrollok (win1, FALSE);
```

The following program illustrates scrolling. It sets up a small window in the middle of the screen, turns scrolling on in it, and proceeds to write lines into the window (at the rate of one line per second), forcing it to scroll:

Program 6-10

```
#include <curses.h>
#include <signal.h>

main ()
{
    void    finish ();
    int     i;
    WINDOW  *scrwin;

    /* call finish if user hits BREAK or DELETE */
    signal (SIGINT, finish);

    /* initial setup of curses */
    initscr ();
    nonl ();

    /* set up scroll window */
    scrwin = newwin (6, 30, LINES / 2 - 3, COLS / 2 - 15);
    scrollok (scrwin, TRUE);

    /* set up stdscr */
    for ( i = 0; i < LINES; ++i )
        mvprintw (i, i, "This is just junk on line %d", i);

    /* refresh stdscr to terminal screen */
    refresh ();

    for ( i = 0 ; ; ++i ) {
        wprintw (scrwin, " Test line %d \n", i);
        touchwin (scrwin);
        wrefresh (scrwin);
        sleep (1);
    }
}
```

```
/* cleanup routine: call endwin and exit */

void finish ()
{
    endwin ();
    exit (0);
}
```

After four seconds:

```
This is just junk on line 0
 This is just junk on line 1
  This is just junk on line 2
   This is just junk on line 3
    This    Test line 0
    This    Test line 1
     Thi    Test line 2
      Th    Test line 3
       T    Test line 4


         This is just junk on line 10
          This is just junk on line 11
           This is just junk on line 12
            This is just junk on line 13
```

One second later:

```
This is just junk on line 0
 This is just junk on line 1
  This is just junk on line 2
   This is just junk on line 3
    This    Test line 1
     This    Test line 2
      Thi    Test line 3
       Th    Test line 4
        T    Test line 5


         This is just junk on line 10
          This is just junk on line 11
           This is just junk on line 12
            This is just junk on line 13
```

One second later:

```
This is just junk on line 0
 This is just junk on line 1
  This is just junk on line 2
   This is just junk on line 3
    This    Test line 2
     This    Test line 3
      Thi    Test line 4
       Th    Test line 5
        T    Test line 6


        This is just junk on line 10
         This is just junk on line 11
          This is just junk on line 12
           This is just junk on line 13
```

Notice how the scrolling window covers the text in the standard window; also note that when a line is output on the last line of the window, the `\n` that ends it scrolls the screen, and so the last line is left empty while the program sleeps.

If you want to draw a box around the window, you'll find that it's not as easy as just calling `box`. Scrolling affects everything in a window, including the border drawn by `box`. There are two ways around this:[†] the first is to redraw the box every time the screen is scrolled. You'll also have to remove the box before the screen is scrolled; otherwise, parts of it will scroll up on the screen:

```
for ( i = 0 ; ; ++i ) {
    box (scrwin, ' ', ' ');
    wprintw (scrwin, "  Test line %d  \n", i);
    box (scrwin, '|', '-');
    . . .
```

Here we remove the box by drawing a border of blanks around the window.

The second way of drawing a box around a scrolling window is to create a new window that's one column wider on each side and one line larger on the top and bottom:

---

† There is really a third way that involves defining a *sub-window*, but that's beyond the scope of this introduction to `curses`.

```
main ()
{
    . . .
    WINDOW *scrwin, *boxwin;
    . . .
    boxwin = newwin (8, 32, LINES / 2 - 4, COLS / 2 - 16);
    scrwin = newwin (6, 30, LINES / 2 - 3, COLS / 2 - 15);
    box (boxwin, '|', '-');
    . . .
    refresh ();
    wrefresh (boxwin);
    . . .
```

Note that `boxwin` is refreshed *after* `stdscr`, to prevent the box from being overwritten.

```
This is just junk on line 0
 This is just junk on line 1
  This is just junk on line 2
   This |---------------------------|
    This|  Test line 0              |
    Thi|  Test line 1              |
     Th|  Test line 2              |
      T|  Test line 3              |
       |  Test line 4              |
       |                           |
       |---------------------------|
            This is just junk on line 11
             This is just junk on line 12
              This is just junk on line 13
```

One second later:

```
This is just junk on line 0
 This is just junk on line 1
  This is just junk on line 2
   This |---------------------------|
    This|  Test line 1              |
    Thi|  Test line 2              |
     Th|  Test line 3              |
      T|  Test line 4              |
       |  Test line 5              |
       |                           |
       |---------------------------|
            This is just junk on line 11
             This is just junk on line 12
              This is just junk on line 13
```

▪ A Multiple Window Editor ▪

Now that you know something about windows, we're going to discuss the program in Appendix C, a version of the editor program that edits two files at the same time. The screen is divided down the middle into two windows. This program is run from the shell with two arguments—the two files to edit. Note that most of the program hasn't changed; however, the calls to various curses routines have been changed to the window versions, and operate on the current window. The length of the lines is now COLS / 2 - 1. A few extra calls to getyx, wmove, and wrefresh have been added to keep the cursor in the right place when switching windows. The s command has been added to switch between the two windows, and getfile, putfile, len, scrsize, and add now take a WINDOW as their first argument.

Two windows are created with calls to newwin (lines 46 and 47):

```
ed[0] = newwin (LINES - 1, COLS / 2 - 1, 0, 0);
ed[1] = newwin (LINES - 1, COLS / 2 - 1, 0, COLS / 2 + 1);
```

The length of each window is the length of the screen – 1, and the width of each window is one half the width of the screen – 1. The first window's origin is the upper left corner, and the other window's origin is the middle of the first line.

Two vertical lines are drawn with vline to separate the two windows visually, and the two files specified on the command line are read into the two windows.

The s command is used to switch between windows, and is implemented by simply changing from window zero to one or one to zero (lines 70–74):

```
case 's':     /* switch windows */
    curwin = ed[1 - icurwin];
    icurwin = 1 - icurwin;
    getyx (curwin, curline, curcol);
    break;
```

getyx gets the current cursor position in the other window, so the subsequent calls to wmove and wrefresh at the beginning of the for loop (lines 65 and 66) move the cursor on the screen to that position in the other window.

```
$ cat test1
This is a test file
for the window editor
line 3
line 4 4 4 4 4

line 6
```

```
$ cat test2
This is another test
file for the window
editor....




    line 10
    line 11
    line 12
    line 13
$ a.out test1 test2
```

```
┌─────────────────────────────────────────────────────┐
│This is a test file   ||This is another test          │
│for the window editor ||file for the window            │
│line 3                ||editor....                     │
│line 4 4 4 4 4        ||                               │
│                      ||                               │
│line 6                ||                               │
│                      ||                               │
│                      ||                               │
│                      ||                               │
│                      ||line 10                        │
│                      ||line 11                        │
│                      ||line 12                        │
│                      ||line 13                        │
│                                                       │
│                                                       │
└─────────────────────────────────────────────────────┘
```

Hit s: *switch windows*

```
┌─────────────────────────────────────────────────────┐
│This is a test file   ||This is another test          │
│for the window editor ||file for the window            │
│line 3                ||editor....                     │
│line 4 4 4 4 4        ||                               │
│                      ||                               │
│line 6                ||                               │
│                      ||                               │
│                      ||                               │
│                      ||                               │
│                      ||line 10                        │
│                      ||line 11                        │
│                      ||line 12                        │
│                      ||line 13                        │
│                                                       │
│                                                       │
└─────────────────────────────────────────────────────┘
```

Hit jj: *down two lines*

```
This is a test file     ||This is another test
for the window editor   ||file for the window
line 3                  ||▣ditor....
line 4  4  4  4  4       ||
                        ||
line 6                  ||
                        ||
                        ||
                        ||
                        ||line 10
                        ||line 11
                        ||line 12
                        ||line 13
```

Hit d: *delete line*

```
This is a test file     ||This is another test
for the window editor   ||file for the window
line 3                  |□
line 4  4  4  4  4       ||
                        ||
line 6                  ||
                        ||
                        ||
                        ||line 10
                        ||line 11
                        ||line 12
                        ||line 13
                        ||
```

Hit s: *switch windows*

```
▣his is a test file     ||This is another test
for the window editor   ||file for the window
line 3                  ||
line 4  4  4  4  4       ||
                        ||
line 6                  ||
                        ||
                        ||
                        ||line 10
                        ||line 11
                        ||line 12
                        ||line 13
                        ||
```

Hit `jjj`:   *down three lines*

```
This is a test file      ||This is another test
for the window editor     ||file for the window
line 3                    | |
▯ine 4 4 4 4              | |
                          | |
line 6                    | |
                          | |
                          | |
                          ||line 10
                          ||line 11
                          ||line 12
                          ||line 13
                          | |
```

Hit `atestESC`:   *add "test"*

```
This is a test file      ||This is another test
for the window editor     ||file for the window
line 3                    | |
tes▯ 4 4 4 4              | |
                          | |
line 6                    | |
                          | |
                          | |
                          ||line 10
                          ||line 11
                          ||line 12
                          ||line 13
                          | |
```

Hit `w`:   *write files and quit*

```
This is a test file      ||This is another test
for the window editor     ||file for the window
line 3                    | |
test 4 4 4 4              | |
                          | |
line 6                    | |
                          | |
                          | |
                          ||line 10
                          ||line 11
                          ||line 12
                          ||line 13
                          | |
$ ▯
```

```
$ cat test1
This is a test file
for the window editor
line 3
test 4 4 4 4 4

line 6
$ cat test2
This is another test
file for the window




line 10
line 11
line 12
line 13
$
```

The following table summarizes the window routines covered so far.

TABLE 6-4. Window Routines

Routine	Description
newwin	Creates new window
delwin	Deletes window
mvwin	Moves window
scrollok	Allows/Disallows scrolling in specified window
getyx	Gets current cursor position in specified window
touchwin	"Touches" every location in window to force output of entire window on next wrefresh
box	Draws box around window
wrefresh	Outputs specified window to terminal
wmove	Moves cursor in specified window to new position
wclear	Clears specified window
wgetch	Inputs character from terminal associated with specified window
mvwgetch	Combination of wmove and wgetch
wgetstr	Inputs line from terminal associated with specified window
mvwgetstr	Combination of wmove and wgetstr
wscanw	Inputs line from terminal associated with specified window using scanf style formatting
mvwscanw	Combination of wmove and wscanw
waddch	Adds a character to current cursor location in specified window
mvwaddch	Combination of wmove and waddch
waddstr	Adds a string to current cursor position in specified window
mvwaddstr	Combination of wmove and waddstr
wprintw	Adds a string to current cursor position in specified window using printf style formatting
mvwprintw	Combination of wmove and printw
wdeleteln	Deletes line at curent cursor position in specified window
winsertln	Inserts line above current cursor postion in specified window
winch	Gets character at current cursor postion in specified window
mvwinch	Combination of wmove and inch
winsch	Inserts character at current cursor position in specified window
mvwinsch	Combination of wmove and insch
wdelch	Deletes character at current cursor position in specified window
mvwdelch	Combination of wmove and delch
wclrtoeol	Clears line from current cursor position to end in specified window
wclrtobot	Clears screen from current cursor position to bottom in specified window

▪ Advanced and Miscellaneous Features ▪

Erasing and Clearing the Screen

The erase routine erases stdscr by copying blanks to all locations on the window. If a refresh is performed right after an erase, the terminal screen will be blank. Note that erase is still subject to cursor optimization. If you fill stdscr with x's, call refresh to get the x's out to the terminal screen, call erase, and then fill stdscr with x's again, the next call to refresh will do nothing, since there is no net effect on stdscr between the two refreshes.

The clear routine also erases stdscr, but it also sets a flag that forces refresh to clear the screen with a hardware clearing operation before redrawing it. Of course, this defeats the cursor optimization of refresh, but sometimes you'll want to do that. For example, suppose a burst of static on the telephone line causes garbage to show up on your screen. Now, the terminal's screen is no longer consistent with curses idea of it, and refresh will not be able to set it right. In vi, the *CTRL-l* command can used to redraw the screen when your screen gets garbled; let's consider for a moment how that might be done.

Calling erase, writing everything back to stdscr, and then calling refresh will not work, since refresh will think the screen hasn't changed at all. Calling clear, writing everything back to stdscr, and calling refresh will work, since clear forces the terminal to be cleared before redrawing it.

Instead of clearing stdscr and putting everything back into it, if you simply want to force the terminal screen to be redrawn with the present contents of stdscr, you can set the clear flag by calling the clearok routine. This flag is used by refresh to determine if the terminal screen should be cleared when refresh is called. Calling clearok doesn't erase data the window, it merely means that the next time refresh (or wrefresh) is called it will clear the screen and redraw everything.   clearok takes two arguments, a WINDOW pointer and a flag (TRUE or FALSE):

```
/* redraw screen */
clearok (stdscr, TRUE);
refresh ();
```

The terminal is cleared when wrefresh is called on the window specified to clearok or when stdscr is specified to clearok and refresh is called (as in the above case).

The werase and wclear routines are like erase and clear and perform their respective operations on the specified window.

An Outstanding Screen

The `standout` and `wstandout` routines turn on what's referred to as *standout mode* on the terminal. This is the most conspicuous form of output the terminal can produce, and is usually reserved for error messages and "eye catching" information. On some terminals, standout mode may simply be underlined or bold characters; on others, it can be inverse-video and blinking. All output to a window after calling `wstandout` on it is displayed in standout mode. `standout ()` is equivalent to `wstandout (stdscr)`. Standout mode is turned off by calling `wstandend` with the window that has standout mode turned on. `standend ()` is equivalent to `wstandend (stdscr)`.

This prints an error message in standout mode on the last line of the screen:

```
standout ();
mvprintw (LINES - 1, 0, "Cannot open %s", argv[1]);
standend ();
refresh ();
```

Standout mode is one of many attributes associated with each character; when a character is moved (e.g., by `deleteln` or `insch`), its attributes move with it. So once a character is displayed in standout mode, it continues to be displayed in that mode until it is removed from the screen.

Nodelay Mode

(Note: This feature is not available in all versions of `curses`.) The `nodelay` routine turns *nodelay mode* on or off for the specified window. Nodelay mode is simply the polling mode we discussed in Chapter 5, where `read` (which `getch` and all other `curses` input routines ultimately call) returns if no characters have been typed in at the terminal. `nodelay` is called with a `WINDOW` pointer and a flag (`TRUE` or `FALSE`). With nodelay mode on, `getch` will return –1 if no character is available.

Pads

(Note: This feature is not available in all versions of `curses`.) A *pad* is like a window with a few exceptions: a pad may be of arbitrary size (e.g., larger than the screen) and has no fixed origin on the screen. Pads are useful for programs that must display large amounts of data (i.e., more than can fit on the screen at a time). The program fills the pad with the data, and interprets various commands to scroll (or pan) the pad both vertically and horizontally.

Pads are created by calling `newpad`. It takes two arguments: the number of lines and columns in the pad. It returns a `WINDOW` pointer. All standard window routines (e.g., `wprintw`, `wmove`, `wstandout`) except `wrefresh` may be called on a pad. Since a pad has no origin on the screen, the mapping of the pad's coordinates and the screen's coordinates is done by a special routine, `prefresh`. `prefresh` is called with a pointer to a pad, the line and column in the pad that will be the upper left corner of the data displayed, and the line and column of the upper left and lower right corners of the area on the screen (the rectangle) where the pad will be displayed:

```
prefresh (pad, pad-start-line, pad-start-col, screen-start-line, screen-start-col,
    screen-end-line, screen-end-col)
```

So the statement

```
prefresh (pad1, 5, 10, 12, 0, 21, 60);
```

causes data in pad1 to be displayed on the screen starting at line 12, column 0, through to line 21, column 60. The data is taken starting at line 5, column 10 from the pad pad1, so that the character at location 5, 10 in pad1 is placed at 12, 0 on the screen, and the character at 5, 11 in pad1 is placed at 12, 1 on the screen, etc. See Fig. 6-2.

traceon and traceoff

(Note: This feature is not available in all versions of curses.) The traceon and traceoff routines allow you to get debugging information from the curses package. When you call traceon, debugging is turned on, and when you call traceoff, debugging is turned off.

Keypads

(Note: This feature is not available in all versions of curses.) The keypad routine lets you to write programs that allow the the use of special keys on a terminal (e.g., the arrow keys, page forward and back keys, insert and delete keys, the home key). Like nodelay and scrollok, keypad takes a WINDOW pointer and a flag (TRUE or FALSE) to turn this feature on or off.

   Once keypads is turned on, when a user presses a special key, curses maps this action into a special, non-ASCII character returned by getch. These characters are defined in curses.h and all start with the letters KEY_. The most commonly used are KEY_UP, KEY_DOWN, KEY_LEFT, KEY_RIGHT, and KEY_HOME, which are for the up arrow, down arrow, left arrow, right arrow, and home keys, respectively. For example, if you wanted to change the screen editor to accept the arrow keys as well as h, j, k, and l for cursor motion, you simply put

```
keypad (stdscr, TRUE);
```

in with the other initialization routines (initscr, etc.) and change the case statements for h, j, k, and l:

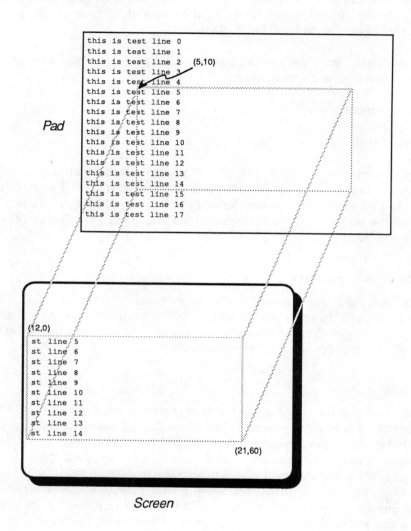

Fig. 6-2. Placing a pad on the screen

```
case 'j':  /* down */
case KEY_DOWN:
   if (curline != LINES - 2)
      ++curline;
   break;
case 'k':  /* up */
case KEY_UP:
   if (curline != 0)
      --curline;
   break;
```

```
case 'h':  /* left */
case KEY_LEFT:
   if (curcol != 0)
      --curcol;
   break;
case 'l':  /* right */
case KEY_RIGHT:
   if (curcol != COLS - 1)
      ++curcol;
   break;
```

One thing you should keep in mind when using keypads is that `getch` will be returning values greater than 255 when a special key is pressed, so it should always be assigned to an `int`.

minicurses

(Note: This feature is not available in all versions of `curses`.) The `minicurses` package is a subset of the `curses` library that doesn't allow multiple windows (`stdscr` is the only one available). If you compile your programs with the `cc` option `-DMINICURSES`, the `minicurses` package will be loaded in, making your program smaller and faster than it would be with `curses`.

```
$ cc -DMINICURSES miniprog.c -lcurses
```

The routines that are part of `minicurses` are marked with a * in Appendix B.

▪ References ▪

[1]   *AT&T 3B2 Computer UNIX System V Release 2.0 Terminal Information Utilities Guide.* Select Code 305-424, Comcode 403778392, AT&T Technologies, Inc., October 1984.

[2]   K. Arnold, "Screen Updating and Cursor Movement Optimization: A Library Package," *UNIX Programmer's Manual 4.2 BSD User Document*, Computer Science Division, Department of EECS, University of California, Berkeley, CA.

[3]   J. Strang, *Programming with Curses*, O'Reilly and Associates, Inc., Newton, MA, 1985.

[4]   J. Strang, *Reading and Writing Termcap Entries*, O'Reilly and Associates, Inc., Newton, MA, 1985.

E   X   E   R   C   I   S   E   S

1. Modify Program 6-5 so that it handles lines that cross page bounaries.

2. Modify the editor so that it handles files longer than LINES lines. Your program should scroll the file if the user attempts to move past the bottom or top of the screen.

3. Modify the editor so that the message "Input Mode" is displayed on the last line of the screen whenever the user is in input mode. Remove the message as soon as the user presses the ESC key to leave input mode.

4. Add an r command to the editor that allows the user to read a new file, effectively changing the file being edited.

5. Modify the w command so that the editor doesn't exit after writing the file.

6. Implement the error messages from the r and w commands as pop-up windows.

7. Use pads to implement horizontal scrolling in the editor.

8. Add all of the above extensions to the two-window editor.

9. Modify the two-window editor so the screen is divided horizontally instead of vertically.

10. Modify the two-window editor to handle an arbitrary number of windows stacked on top of each other. All the windows should be LINES by COLS in size.

11. Modify the two-window editor to handle an arbitrary number of windows of arbitrary size that can be created, resized, and moved about by the user.

12. Implement the tput command distributed in UNIX System V Release 2.

GENERATING PROGRAMS WITH make

This chapter is about a command called make. make maintains programming systems by issuing the commands needed to produce an executable program from source files. The version of make described here is the System V Release 2.0 version, which is the same as the one distributed with Berkeley UNIX.

· How make Works ·

make works by producing a list of *dependencies*. A dependency describes the relationship of one file to another in terms of a programming environment. For example, if the file cat.c exists, then the object module file cat.o can be produced by the command

```
$ cc -c cat.c
```

which says "compile the file cat.c but don't link edit it; instead, place the object code for cat.c in cat.o." This means that the file cat.o *depends upon* the file cat.c, because changes to the file cat.c will require that it be recompiled in order to produce a new cat.o.

Similarly, if the file who.c exists, then the program who can be created from the file who.c (assuming the entire program is in the file who.c) by the command

```
$ cc -o who who.c
```

which says "compile the file who.c, link edit it with the Standard C Library, and place the program in the executable file who." Here the file who depends upon the file who.c, and any time who.c is changed, who has to be remade by recompiling who.c.

make knows how to determine dependencies automatically; it makes use of file modification information (see stat in Chapter 5) to determine which files in a programming system have changed, and from that what has to be done to recreate the program.   make has several built-in dependencies; among them are the ones described above: *file*.o depends upon *file*.c, and *file* also depends upon *file*.c. Along with the built-in dependencies, make has commands associated with them that are executed to produce the *target* (the file that is being "made"). These commands are basically the same as those shown above.

So, if you have a file xyz.c and you want to use make to produce the target xyz.o, simply use the make command with xyz.o as a command line argument:

```
$ cat xyz.c
main ()
{
    printf ("hello world\n");
}
$ make xyz.o
        cc -O -c xyz.c
```

The command cc -O -c xyz.c is issued by make and printed on the terminal so that you know what it's doing. (The -O option to the cc command tells it to invoke the object code optimizer after compiling the file. The optimizer attempts to improve the object code by removing redundant instructions, making better use of registers, etc.)

Similarly, if you want to produce the executable program who from who.c, simply specify who to make:

```
$ make who
        cc -O -o who who.c
$ make who
'who' is up to date.
```

Here, make issues the command cc -O -o who who.c the first time it is run. When run a second time, make doesn't recompile who.c because it isn't newer than who: since no changes have been made to the source file since the last time it was compiled (i.e., who is newer than who.c), the target is "up to date" and does not need to be remade. This is a key feature of make and one of the things that makes it so useful: it only performs work when necessary, saving you from using unnecessary CPU time recompiling programs that haven't changed or doing ls -l all the time to see whether the source file is newer than the object or executable program. The value of this capability will become even more apparent when we show you how well it works with large programs consisting of numerous files.

So, to summarize, make uses dependencies to produce files. Dependencies are simply the relationship of one file to another based on the file name (for example, x is dependent upon x.c). If the files that the specified target depends upon are newer than the target, make issues the commands necessary to recreate the target; otherwise, make produces the message "'*target*' is up to date."

• The makefile •

When make starts up, it looks for a file in the current directory named makefile or Makefile (in that order) and reads it, if found. This file may be used to override and augment the built-in dependencies and commands that make uses. Let's say that the program xyz.c includes the file global.h in the current directory:

```
$ cat xyz.c
#include "global.h"

main ()
{
    . . .
}
```

The xyz.o and xyz files are actually a combination of the compilation of both xyz.c *and* global.h, since inclusion of a file causes the file to be read in at that point. This means that xyz.o and xyz both depend upon two files: xyz.c and global.h, since a change to either file will require recompiling. make doesn't have the smarts to handle this all by itself. It doesn't know what's included in a program, so it has to be told. This is where the makefile comes in handy: you can specify to make via the makefile the dependencies of programs on included files. The typical dependency line in a makefile looks like this:

```
xyz: xyz.c global.h
```

which states that the file (target) xyz depends upon xyz.c and global.h. Typically, a dependency line has one or more commands associated with it that are to be executed when the target is out-of-date and must be remade:

```
xyz: xyz.c global.h; cc -O -o xyz xyz.c
```

Here the command is specified by separating it from the rest of the line with a semicolon.

In general, a dependency line has the following format:

target(s): *depend(s)*; *command(s)*

Where *target(s)* is a blank-separated list of files that depend upon the files (blank-separated) specified after the colon, *depend(s)*; and *command(s)* is any UNIX shell command or sequence of commands separated by semicolons. *depend(s)* or *command(s)* may be omitted. We'll soon discuss what happens if you omit them.

For convenience, any lines after a dependency line that begin with a tab are considered to be commands that are executed when creating the target:

```
xyz: xyz.c global.h
        cc -O -o xyz xyz.c
```

is the same as

```
xyz: xyz.c global.h; cc -O -o xyz xyz.c
```

The first form (using the tab) is the preferred format, as it is easier to read when maintaining a large `makefile`.

The `makefile` that is used to produce `xyz` from `xyz.c` and `global.h` is simply the above dependency line:

```
$ cat makefile
xyz: xyz.c global.h
        cc -O -o xyz xyz.c
$ ls -l
total 3
-rw-r--r--    1 phw        phw              420 May 30 10:41 global.h
-rw-r--r--    1 phw        phw               40 May 30 10:45 makefile
-rw-r--r--    1 phw        phw              131 May 30 10:40 xyz.c
$ make xyz
        cc -O -o xyz xyz.c
$ make xyz
'xyz' is up to date.
$ touch global.h                    Change last modification to now
$ ls -l
total 5
-rw-r--r--    1 phw        phw              420 May 30 10:52 global.h
-rw-r--r--    1 phw        phw               40 May 30 10:45 makefile
-rw-r--r--    1 phw        phw              131 May 30 10:40 xyz.c
-rwxr-xr-x    1 phw        phw             1750 May 30 10:51 xyz
$ make xyz
        cc -O -o xyz xyz.c
```

When make starts, it looks up the target xyz (taken from the command line) in the makefile and finds the dependency line

```
xyz: xyz.c global.h
```

which states that xyz is to be remade only if it is older than xyz.c or global.h. Since xyz doesn't exist the first time make is run, make issues the command

```
        cc -O -o xyz xyz.c
```

to make xyz.

The touch command simply changes the last modification time of the specified file(s) to the time that touch is run (i.e., it "touches" the file, making it look like it was modified). After "modifying" global.h, make realizes that xyz is no longer up to date and recompiles it.

Comments may be placed in a makefile by simply putting a # before the comment. An entire line may be a comment.

```
$ cat makefile
# this is a comment
xyz: xyz.c global.h     # this is also a comment
        cc -O -o xyz xyz.c
```

Multiple-File Programs

One useful feature of make is its ability to handle multiple-file programs, i.e., programs that consist of more than one .c file. make will keep track of large programming projects for you, so that once the dependencies between the various files have been placed in a makefile, you no longer have to worry about which files need to be recompiled and which don't.

When a program comprises many .c files, the usual approach is to keep the corresponding .o files around and produce the executable program from them. Thus, when a few .c files have changed, you only have to recompile those files, producing the corresponding .o files. You can then link all the .o files together to produce the executable program.

The way to handle multiple files with make is to specify a separate dependency line in the makefile for each .c file of the program and a dependency line for the final target:

```
$ cat makefile
#
# makefile for grep
#
grep: main.o match.o output.o
        cc main.o match.o output.o -o grep

main.o: main.c pattern.h
        cc -O -c main.c
match.o: match.c pattern.h
        cc -O -c match.c
output.o: output.c io.h
        cc -O -c output.c
```

(Remember that each cc command line in the makefile must begin with a tab.) This makefile specifies a three file program (also with two header files) called grep that depends upon main.o, match.o, and output.o. main.o and match.o depend upon their respective .c files and the pattern.h header file. output.o depends upon output.c and io.h. When make starts up, it reads the makefile and builds a dependency hierarchy, or tree, that details all the dependencies (see Fig. 7-1).

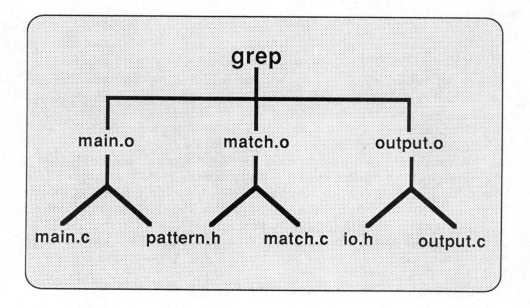

Fig. 7-1. Dependencies for grep

```
$ ls -l
total 9
-rw-r--r--    1 phw        phw         580 May 30 11:30 io.h
-rw-r--r--    1 phw        phw         521 May 30 11:34 main.c
-rw-r--r--    1 phw        phw        2344 May 30 11:35 match.c
-rw-r--r--    1 phw        phw         197 May 30 11:31 makefile
-rw-r--r--    1 phw        phw        1131 May 30 11:30 pattern.h
-rw-r--r--    1 phw        phw         734 May 30 11:34 output.c
$ make grep
        cc -O -c main.c
        cc -O -c match.c
        cc -O -c output.c
        cc main.o match.o output.o -o grep
$ touch main.c
$ make grep
        cc -O -c main.c
        cc main.o match.o output.o -o grep
$ touch pattern.h
$ make grep
        cc -O -c main.c
        cc -O -c match.c
        cc main.o match.o output.o -o grep
$ touch io.h
$ make output.o
        cc -O -c output.c
```

Typing in `make grep` causes `make` to scan the `makefile` for the dependency line for the target `grep`:

```
grep: main.o match.o output.o
```

This line says that before `grep` can be made, the files `main.o`, `match.o`, and `output.o` must be up to date.   `make` determines whether `main.o` must be remade by checking the corresponding dependency:

```
main.o: main.c pattern.h
```

If `main.o` doesn't exist or is older than `main.c` or `pattern.h`, the command

```
        cc -O -c main.c
```

is issued. This process is repeated for the two other `.o` files. Finally, `make` is ready to make the target `grep`, so it issues the command

```
        cc main.o match.o output.o -o grep
```

to create it.

By changing the modification time on `pattern.h`, we forced `make` to recompile both `main.c` and `match.c` because both `main.o` and `match.o` depend upon `pattern.h`.

Notice the last use of make:

```
$ make output.o
      cc -O -c output.c
```

Here we specified that `output.o`, not `grep`, was the target. This caused `make` to determine the dependency of `output.o` (on `output.c` and `io.h`) and remake it. Any target specified on a dependency line in the `makefile` or any target from one of `make`'s built-in dependencies may be specified on the `make` command line.

One of the features of `make` is the built-in dependencies we mentioned before. Recall that `make` already has built into it the necessary commands and dependencies to create `.o` files from `.c` files. All that really need be done to specify the above dependencies for `grep` is to list the include file dependencies and the final target dependency for the file `grep`:

```
$ cat makefile
#
# makefile for grep -- version 2
#      makes use of built-in dependencies
#
grep: main.o match.o output.o
      cc main.o match.o output.o -o grep

main.o match.o: pattern.h
output.o: io.h
```

This `makefile` is equivalent to the larger one shown previously. It specifies that `main.o` and `match.o` are dependent upon `pattern.h` and that `output.o` is dependent upon `io.h`. The built-in dependencies take care of the relationship between the `.o` files and the respective `.c` files. Also, the built-in commands for producing `.o` from `.c` files are the same as the ones we specified previously (e.g., `cc -O -c output.c`), so there is no reason to specify them in the `makefile`.

```
$ ls -l
total 9
-rw-r--r--    1 phw        phw         580 May 30 11:30 io.h
-rw-r--r--    1 phw        phw         521 May 30 11:34 main.c
-rw-r--r--    1 phw        phw        2344 May 30 11:35 match.c
-rw-r--r--    1 phw        phw         108 May 30 11:31 makefile
-rw-r--r--    1 phw        phw        1131 May 30 11:30 pattern.h
-rw-r--r--    1 phw        phw         734 May 30 11:34 output.c
```

```
$ make grep
        cc -O -c main.c
        cc -O -c match.c
        cc -O -c output.c
        cc main.o match.o output.o -o grep
$ touch main.c
$ make grep
        cc -O -c main.c
        cc main.o match.o output.o -o grep
$ make grep
'grep' is up to date.
$ touch pattern.h
$ make
        cc -O -c main.c
        cc -O -c match.c
        cc main.o match.o output.o -o grep
```

Note the last use of make. If a target isn't specified to make on the command line, it simply makes the first target found in the makefile, in this case, grep.

If a line in a makefile gets too long, you can continue it on the next line by simply putting a \ at the end of the line you want to continue:

```
uucp: uucp.h parms.h cico.o conn.o callers.o dialers.o ulockf.o \
anlwrk.o uucpdefs.o gwd.o
        cc cico.o conn.o callers.o dialers.o ulockf.o \
anlwrk.o uucpdefs.o gwd.o -o uucp
```

You can even put tabs or blanks at the beginning of the continuation line, since the continuation is not considered to be a new line, but is merely appended to the previous one:

```
uucp: uucp.h parms.h cico.o conn.o callers.o dialers.o ulockf.o \
        anlwrk.o uucpdefs.o gwd.o
        cc cico.o conn.o callers.o dialers.o ulockf.o \
        anlwrk.o uucpdefs.o gwd.o -o uucp
```

▪ make Variables ▪

make allows you to assign strings to variables and later recall their contents. (make variables are sometimes called *macros*.) A make variable is assigned a value by using the variable name on the left-hand side of an equal sign (=):

variable = value

variable may consist of any character except those with special meaning to `make`, e.g., `#`, `:`, `;`, `=`, blank, tab, *NEWLINE*. In general, you should not use any characters other than alphanumerics, since `make` has its own built-in variables that it sets internally (such as `?` and `@`). *value* may be any string of characters up to a `#` (comment) or a *NEWLINE* that isn't preceded by a `\` (continuation). Spaces around the `=` are optional. The following are all valid `make` variable assignments:

```
FILES = abc.c def.c ghi.c
OBJ = main.o
a=this is a test
123 = variable name may start with a number
C = this variable is going to be continued \
        on the next line
OFILES = abc.o \
        def.o \
        ghi.o
```

You access `make` variables by enclosing them in parentheses and preceding them with a dollar sign. This causes the contents of the variable to be substituted at that point:

```
$ cat makefile
TESTVAR = this is a test

test: test.c
        echo $(TESTVAR)
        cc -o test test.c
```

Here we have a `make` variable `TESTVAR`. It is assigned the value `this is a test`. `echo $(TESTVAR)` becomes `echo this is a test` and is executed whenever `test` is made:

```
$ make test
        echo this is a test
this is a test
        cc -o test test.c
```

As you can see, `$(TESTVAR)` is replaced by `this is a test` before the `echo` command is executed. One thing to note about `make` variables: variables with single character names do not have to be enclosed in parentheses, so the following uses of the `make` variable `x` are equivalent:

```
echo $(x)
echo $x
```

When make starts up, it copies all exported shell variables from the environment into make variables of the same name. For example, you can access the name of your HOME directory within a makefile by simply using $(HOME):

```
$ cat makefile
grep: main.o match.o output.o
        cc main.o match.o output.o -o grep

main.o match.o: pattern.h
output.o: io.h

install: grep
        cp grep $(HOME)/bin
$ make install
        cp grep /u1/phw/bin
```

Here the command cp grep $(HOME)/bin is executed whenever the target install is specified to make (after make gets grep up to date).

Built-in make Variables

make has certain predefined variables. For C programmers, the variables that come into play are CC and CFLAGS. CC is normally set to the string cc, the C compiler command. make uses $(CC) in its built-in dependencies as the command to produce .o and executable files from .c files. It also uses $(CFLAGS) as the flags given to the C compiler (usually set to -O). By changing these variables, you can tailor make to your liking.

For example, let's say you're working on a C program for a microcomputer in your office. The microcomputer doesn't have a C compiler (it doesn't even have a disk drive), so you write the program on your UNIX system and send the compiled program to the microcomputer over a communication line (e.g., a terminal line). Since the microcomputer doesn't have the same microprocessor as your UNIX system, you have to use a C compiler different from the standard cc command you're used to running:

```
$ dmdcc -O -o prog prog.c
```

Here dmdcc is used to compile prog.c. It produces an executable module for a type of microcomputer called a "dmd." (Yes, this is a real machine; it's an intelligent terminal manufactured by Teletype that you can load programs into.)

If you want, you can let make handle the compilation:

```
$ cat makefile
CC = dmdcc
$ make prog
        dmdcc -O prog.c -o prog
```

Well, that's probably the shortest makefile you're likely to see! All we did was set CC to dmdcc and let the built-in dependencies and commands do the rest. Of course if you have a large programming project for the microcomputer, you can expand the makefile to contain the correct dependencies and commands for the program:

```
$ cat makefile
CC = dmdcc

draw: main.o ctrl.o line.o circle.o spline.o
        $(CC) -o draw main.o ctrl.o line.o circle.o spline.o

main.o ctrl.o line.o circle.o spline.o: global.h
```

draw is composed of five .o files: main.o, ctrl.o, line.o, circle.o, and spline.o; and each of the .o files depends upon global.h and the corresponding .c files. dmdcc is used to both compile the .c files (using the built-in commands) and to link edit the .o files ($(CC) -o draw main.o ctrl.o ...). Note that this makefile can be rewritten to make better use of variables:

```
$ cat makefile
CC = dmdcc
OBJS = main.o ctrl.o line.o circle.o spline.o

draw: $(OBJS)
        $(CC) -o draw $(OBJS)

$(OBJS): global.h
```

By setting OBJS to the list of object files, we've not only simplified the makefile, but made it easier to maintain: if you expand the program and add another file, only one line needs to be changed to update the makefile (the assignment to OBJS).

make sets up all its variables when it starts up. It actually scans the makefile for variable assignments and does them all at once, so a make variable can actually be used before its assignment in the makefile. If a variable is assigned more than once, the last assignment is used.

The way make handles variables has some drawbacks; for example, you cannot use a variable on both the left and right side of an equal sign; so

```
OBJS = $(OBJS) new.o
```

is an error.   make will scan the line forever attempting to resolve the assignment. (Actually, the System V Release 2 version of make will detect this problem and issue an error message. Older versions of make usually produce a core
dump.) You can't get around this problem by multiple assignments; for example,

```
SAVEOBJS = $(OBJS)
OBJS = $(SAVEOBJS) new.o
```

is also illegal.
      Of course, it's all right to use different make variables in an assignment,
such as

```
NOBJS = $(OBJS1) $(OBJS2) new.o
```

Internal make Variables

make also maintains several special variables that contain information about the
internal settings of make. The contents of these variables change from target to
target. For example, the variable $? is set to the list of files that the current tar-
get depends upon that are newer than the target. So if you add

```
print: *.h *.c
        pr $? | lp
        touch print
```

to a makefile, you add the ability to print just those files that have changed
since the last time you printed files using make. Let's see how this works: the
file print depends upon all the .h and .c files in the current directory (yes,
the * works in make the same as in the shell—it is expanded into matching file
names). If any of the files are newer than print, the command pr $? | lp is
executed, with the $? replaced with those files newer than print, causing the
files to be printed on a line printer. The file print is then touched, making it
newer than all the program files. Thus, the next time make print is run, only
those files that have been modified are printed, as they will be newer than
print:

```
$ ls
circle.c
circle.o
ctrl.c
ctrl.o
draw
global.h
line.c
line.o
main.c
main.o
makefile
spline.c
spline.o
$ make print
        pr global.h circle.c ctrl.c line.c main.c spline.c | lp
request-id is laser-2103 (6 files)
        touch print
$ touch circle.c main.c     Update modification times on circle.c and main.c
$ make print
        pr circle.c main.c | lp
request-id is laser-2104 (2 files)
        touch print
```

Note that the file `print` is only used for its modification time; it doesn't contain any useful data.

One thing you should know about the `$?` variable is that it cannot be used in dependencies; it can be used only on command lines.

The special variables `$@` and `$$@` are set to the current target, where `$@` is used only on command lines and `$$@` is used only on dependency lines. These can be helpful if you're maintaining a lot of single-file programs in one directory (and therefore need to put dependency lines for all of them in the `makefile`). For example, if the programs `a.c`, `b.c`, `c.c`, and `d.c` include `io.h`, and you want to maintain the programs with a `makefile`, you could use

```
a: a.c io.h
        cc -O -o a a.c
b: b.c io.h
        cc -O -o b b.c
c: c.c io.h
        cc -O -o c c.c
d: d.c io.h
        cc -O -o d d.c
```

However, this can get to be tedious when there are a lot of files around, so you can use `$@` and `$$@` to reduce the size of the `makefile`:

```
a b c d: $$@.c io.h
        cc -O -o $@ $@.c
```

This makefile says that whenever one of the targets `a`, `b`, `c`, or `d` is being made, it depends upon `io.h` and `$$@.c`, which is simply that target's name with `.c` appended as a suffix. If the target is out of date, then it is remade with the command

```
        cc -O -o $@ $@.c
```

which says to place the executable program file in `$@` (the target) and to use `$@.c` as input. So typing in

```
$ make a
```

causes `make` to interpret the lines

```
a b c d: $$@.c io.h
        cc -O -o $@ $@.c
```

as

```
a: a.c io.h
        cc -O -o a a.c
```

Typing in

```
$ make a b c
```

causes `make` to create each target, one at a time, interpreting the dependency and command lines differently for each target.

You'll see more of these internal variables in the next section when we discuss how `make` handles its built-in dependencies.

· **Suffix Rules** ·

A *suffix rule* is a dependency that describes how a file ending with one set of characters (e.g., `.o`) depends upon the corresponding file ending with another set of characters (e.g., `.c`). Suffix rules are used to define `make`'s built-in dependencies. The typical suffix rule looks like

    .suffix1 .suffix2:
        command(s)

where files ending in *.suffix2* depend upon the corresponding file name ending in *.suffix1*, for example,

```
.c.o:
        . . .
```

which describes the rules for producing .o files from. .c files. The command
used with suffix rules usually makes use of some of make's internal variables as
well as built-in variables like CC and CFLAGS. For example, the standard
.c.o: suffix rule looks like this:

```
.c.o:
        $(CC) $(CFLAGS) -c $<
```

CC and CFLAGS you've seen before, but $< is a new one. It is set to the file that
is causing the target to be remade (in this case, the .c file). $< is similar to $?,
except that it has meaning only in suffix rules, and it always contains only one
file name.

Another internal variable set by make in suffix rules is $*, which refers to
the target name stripped of its suffix. For example, if you wanted to rewrite the
previous suffix rule so that a .x file is created at the same time as the .o file,
you can write

```
.c.o:
        $(CC) $(CFLAGS) -c $<
        widgit $@ > $*.x
```

(The widgit command is an imaginary one that does something useful to the
.o file.) $@ is simply the current target (the .o file). The output of widgit is
redirected to $*.x which is interpreted by make as the target without the .o
and with .x appended to the end.

```
$ make abc.o
        cc -O -c abc.c
        widgit abc.o > abc.x
```

The Null Suffix

The *null suffix* is a special suffix rule that lists only one suffix, i.e.,

```
.suffix:
        command(s)
```

This type of suffix rule is used to make the target whose name is that of the
depended on file stripped of the suffix. For example, the following makefile

```
.c:
        $(CC) $(CFLAGS) $(LDFLAGS) $< -o $@
```

states that to create a program file from a .c file, the $(CC) command is to be executed with the flags $(CFLAGS) and $(LDFLAGS) ("loader" flags, usually unset). The source file is $< (the file the target depends upon), and the output of the link editor goes to the file $@ (the name of the current target). This suffix rule is the one that's actually built into make for producing programs from .c files.

```
$ ls
abc.c
makefile
$ make abc
        cc -O  abc.c -o abc
```

Making Your Own Suffix Rules

Let's say you want to add a suffix rule for creating .x files from .o files (using the widgit command, of course). The suffix rule is fairly simple:

```
.o.x:
        widgit $< > $@
```

which says that to produce a .x file from the corresponding .o, run widgit on $<, the file the target depends upon (the .o file), and redirect the output to the file $@ (the target).

There is one other matter that has to be attended to before this suffix rule will work. You have to tell make that .x is a valid suffix. make has a default set of suffixes it recognizes (e.g., .c, .o, .h, .l (lex file), .f (FORTRAN file)). The method of informing make about a new suffix is simple: you use the special target .SUFFIXES: followed by the new suffix(es) you want make to recognize:

```
.SUFFIXES: .x
```

This tells make that .x is a new valid suffix (it doesn't delete any of the old built-in suffixes). Using .SUFFIXES: without any dependencies causes the current suffix list to be deleted:

```
.SUFFIXES:
```

Normally, this is something you won't want to do.

Getting back to our .x suffix, the following makefile will convert our .o files to .x files:

```
$ cat makefile
.SUFFIXES: .x

.o.x:
        widgit $< > $@
$ ls
abc.c
def.c
ghi.c
makefile
$ make abc.x
Make:  Don't know how to make abc.x.  Stop.
```

Well, that's an interesting message. make is telling us that it doesn't have any idea how to make the file abc.x. That's because we've told make how to create .x files from .o files, *not* .c *files*! Let's make the .o file and then see what happens when we try to make the .x file:

```
$ make abc.o
        cc -O -c abc.c
$ make abc.x
        widgit abc.o > abc.x
```

That's better.

This brings up an interesting and sometimes frustrating problem in make: it uses only one suffix rule at a time. Even though the .c to .o conversion is built into make, it won't use that suffix rule when creating .x files, even though .x files depend upon .o files, which can be created from .c files. So, for every suffix conversion you want to implement with make, you must specify a suffix rule.

We can modify this makefile so that make will know how to create .x files directly from .c files, by adding a new suffix rule for .c to .x conversion:

```
$ cat makefile
.SUFFIXES: .x

.c.x:
        echo using .c.x rule
        $(CC) $(CFLAGS) -c $<
        widgit $*.o > $@

.o.x:
        echo using .o.x rule
        widgit $< > $@
```

(The `echo` commands are here just to show what rules `make` uses in the examples that follow.) Here we simply compile the `.c` file (`$<`) and then run `widgit` on the `.o` file (the target stripped of its suffix, `$*`, with `.o` appended to it) with the output going to the target (`$@`):

```
$ rm abc.o abc.x
$ make abc.x
        echo using .c.x rule
using .c.x rule
        cc -O -c abc.c
        widgit abc.o > abc.x
```

So if the `.o` file doesn't exist, `make` uses the `.c.x` rule to produce the `.x` file.

Now that the `abc.o` file exists, let's see what happens if we "modify" `abc.c` and then try to make `abc.x`:

```
$ rm abc.x
$ touch abc.c
$ make abc.x
        cc -O -c abc.c
        echo using .o.x rule
using .o.x rule
        widgit abc.o > abc.x
$ make abc.x
'abc.x' is up to date.
```

When a `.c` file *and* a `.o` file exist, `make` uses the `.o.x` rule to create the `.x` file.[†] In this case, `make` will first invoke its builtin `.c.o` rule to ensure that the `.o` file is up to date.

Suffix rules can be combined with other dependencies to create a `makefile` for a specific project. For example, the previous dmd application's `makefile` could read

```
CC = dmdcc
OBJS = main.o ctrl.o line.o circle.o spline.o
MAPFILES = main.map ctrl.map line.map circle.map spline.map

.SUFFIXES: .map

.c.map:
                $(CC) $(CFLAGS) -c $<
                objmap $*.o > $@


.o.map:
                objmap $< > $@
```

---

† That's because the the `.o` suffix appears *before* the `.c` suffix in `make`'s built-in suffix list. Use the `-p` option to make to get a list of these suffixes (see page 424).

```
draw: $(OBJS)
        $(CC) -o draw $(OBJS)

map: $(MAPFILES)
        sort -o map $(MAPFILES)

$(OBJS): global.h

print: *.h *.c
        pr $? | lp
        touch print
```

Here we create object map files with the `objmap` program, and create a map of the program by sorting the maps (assume that `objmap` can't map a linked file). Note that the `.map` suffix rule doesn't affect the original workings of the `makefile`—it still uses `dmdcc` to produce the `draw` program that is loaded into the microcomputer. Setting `CC` to `dmdcc` does have an interesting side effect: `.o` files are now created with `dmdcc` in the `.c.map` suffix rule (as they should be) since we used `$(CC)` in that rule.

The last internal `make` variable is `$%`. Since this variable is used when maintaining program libraries, we cover it in the next section.

The following table summarizes `make`'s internal variables.

TABLE 7-1. Internal make Variables

Variable	Description
$@	The current target
$$@	The current target (like $@, but used only on dependency lines)
$?	The list of files "out of date" with respect to the current target
$*	The current target without its suffix (only set within suffix rules)
$<	The file that is "out of date" with respect to the current target (only set within suffix rules)
$%	If the target is a library member, $% is set to member name, and $@ is set to library name

▪ make and Program Libraries ▪

A library is simply a collection of object modules that have been grouped into one file with the ar command. The link editor ld knows how to read library files maintained by ar. Libraries such as Standard C and curses are simply large ar files containing many routines.

The usefulness of libraries comes from the way they are handled by the link editor: when a library is specified to ld, either as a file on the command line or as an option with −l, all external references that have not been resolved (i.e., all routines that have been used but haven't appeared in any of the files linked so far) are sought from the library. If the routine is there, it is linked into the program. If the routine isn't there, it is simply left as unresolved (hopefully, to be resolved later). This is good from an efficiency standpoint, since only those routines that you use are actually copied to your program from a library. In other words, if you use the scanf routine, only scanf and those routines that scanf calls are linked in; printf, gets, fopen, etc., aren't copied into your program as well, saving you a lot of memory when your program runs.

When you link in a .o file, its contents are copied into the program, *whether you call the routines in it or not*. So if the standard C and standard I/O libraries were simply in one big .o file, every time you produced an executable program with it you'd be linking in a *lot* of object code.

This "dynamic" linking of files out of a library does have some disadvantages: the libraries usually must be specified last on the ld or cc command line, e.g.,

```
cc window.o −lcurses
```

That's because the linker only resolves those references that are unresolved at the point the library is read in, meaning that

```
cc −lcurses window.o
```

causes curses to be linked before window.o is reached, so *nothing* from curses is copied into the a.out file. When ld then attempts to resolve the references to the curses routines in window.o it will fail.

Creating Your Own Program Libraries

It's fairly simple to create your own library. Simply use the ar command with the rv options, followed by the library name and the .o files you wish to place in the library:†

```
ar rv library file1.o file2.o    . . .
```

---

† On Seventh Edition UNIX, Berkeley UNIX, and XENIX systems, you'll also have to use the following command after creating the library:
```
ranlib library
```
and on System III, you'll have to create the library like this:
```
ar rv library `lorder *.o | tsort`
```

Assume you want to create a library called `mine` from all of the `.o` files in the current directory:

```
$ ls *.o
abc.o
def.o
ghi.o
$ ar rv mine *.o
ar: creating mine
a - abc.o
a - def.o
a - ghi.o
```

That's it! `ar` printed out a few messages (the `v` in `rv` requests that `ar` be "verbose" in its diagnostics) that simply tells you `mine` is being created and `abc.o`, `def.o`, and `ghi.o` are being added to the `mine` library (the `a` in the first column).

You now have a program library called `mine` that can be linked in by simply listing it on the `cc` or `ld` command line (note that the library comes last):

```
$ cc main.c io.c mine
```

If you want to replace a file in the archive, simply use `ar` with the name of the file to replace:

```
$ cc -O -c abc.c
$ ar rv mine abc.o
r - abc.o
```

Here, `ar` tells us that `abc.o` is being replaced and not added (an `r` in the first column instead of an `a`).

If, for some reason, you wish to delete a file from a library, simply use `dv` instead of `rv`:

```
$ ar dv mine abc.o
d - abc.o
```

`abc.o` is deleted from the `mine` archive (`d` in first column).

Note that when linking your own library with `cc`, only those routines that are called by the program are linked, just like when linking standard libraries with the `-l` option.

Maintaining Program Libraries with make

Considering the work involved in maintaining large program libraries (think of trying to keep track of all the standard C routines), they seem ripe for maintenance with make. A target or dependency of the form *name* (*file*) refers to the member *file* in the library *name*, e.g.,

```
library: mine(abc.o) mine(def.o) mine(ghi.o)
```

This line says that abc.o, def.o, and ghi.o are all members of the library archive mine. The target library doesn't exist as a file, but it is specified as a target to make when the library mine is to be remade. The three .o files will be created using the default suffix rules if nothing else is specified in the makefile:

```
$ cat makefile
library: mine(abc.o) mine(def.o) mine(ghi.o)
$ rm *.o
$ ls
abc.c
def.c
ghi.c
global.h
io.c
libs.h
main.c
makefile
$ make library
        cc -c -O abc.c
        ar rv mine abc.o
ar: creating mine
a - abc.o
        rm -f abc.o
        cc -c -O def.c
        ar rv mine def.o
a - def.o
        rm -f def.o
        cc -c -O ghi.c
        ar rv mine ghi.o
a - ghi.o
        rm -f ghi.o
```

Well, make compiled each file, archiving the resulting .o file and then removing it—once the file is in the library, it's redundant to keep it around.

Let's see what happens when we change one of the .c files:

```
$ touch abc.c
$ make library
        cc -c -O abc.c
        ar rv mine abc.o
r - abc.o
        rm -f abc.o
```

As we'd expect, the file abc.o is remade and replaced in the library.

Suppose a program called prog consists of two object files called main.o and io.o, and the three routines from the mine library: abc, def, and ghi. Also suppose that the three library routines depend upon the header file libs.h and that main.o and io.o depend upon the header file global.h. Here is a makefile to handle this setup:

```
$ cat makefile
OBJS    = main.o io.o
LIBOBJS = mine(abc.o) mine(def.o) mine(ghi.o)

prog: $(OBJS)  $(LIBOBJS)
        cc $(OBJS) mine -o prog

$(OBJS): global.h

$(LIBOBJS): libs.h
```

Here we're telling make that main.o and io.o depend upon global.h (as well as on the respective .c files), and that all the library members depend upon libs.h.

Let's give this new makefile a workout:

```
$ make prog
        cc -O -c main.c
        cc -O -c io.c
        cc main.o io.o mine -o prog
$ touch abc.c
$ make prog
        cc -c -O abc.c
        ar rv mine abc.o
r - abc.o
        rm -f abc.o
        cc main.o io.o mine -o prog
$ touch libs.h
$ make prog
        cc -c -O abc.c
        ar rv mine abc.o
r - abc.o
        rm -f abc.o
```

```
        cc -c -O def.c
        ar rv mine def.o
r - def.o
        rm -f def.o
        cc -c -O ghi.c
        ar rv mine ghi.o
r - ghi.o
        rm -f ghi.o
        cc main.o io.o mine -o prog
```

Maintaining Libraries in Subdirectories

Often, especially with large programming projects, you may want to put your libraries in one or more separate subdirectories of the current one. There are several ways to handle this with make. The most straightforward way is to put a separate makefile in each of the subdirectories (see Fig. 7-2).

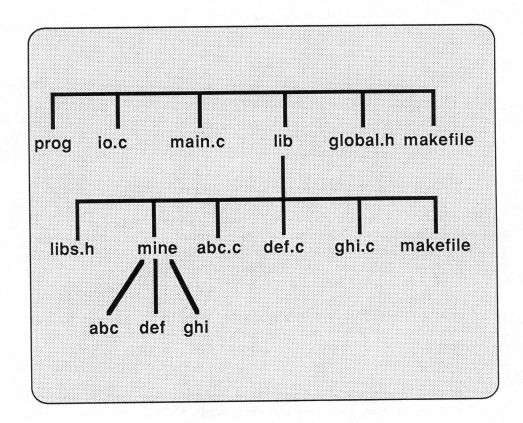

Fig. 7-2. Directory hierarchy for prog

Now you simply run a separate `make` in each directory:

```
$ ls lib                                    The lib subdirectory
abc.c
def.c
ghi.c
libs.h
makefile
$ ls                                        The main program directory
global.h
io.c
lib
main.c
makefile
$ cat makefile
OBJS = main.o io.o

prog: $(OBJS) library
        cc $(OBJS) lib/mine -o prog

$(OBJS): global.h

library:
        cd lib; make library
$ cat lib/makefile
LIBOBJS = mine(abc.o) mine(def.o) mine(ghi.o)

$(LIBOBJS): libs.h

library: $(LIBOBJS)
```

We have simplified the `makefile` in the main directory by removing all the files and dependencies of the library from it, replacing them with the target `library`. All the library information has been moved to the `makefile` in the `lib` subdirectory. Note that when a target depends on nothing and doesn't exist as a file (like `library`), it is always considered out of date; therefore, whenever `make prog` is run, the `library` target will be out of date. The command `cd lib; make library` will therefore be run every time `prog` is remade, whether the library needs it or not. This causes a separate invocation of `make` to be run in the `lib` subdirectory (sometimes called a *recursive make*). If the library doesn't need to be remade, the `make` in `lib` will simply exit without a message.

The `cd lib` and `make library` have been placed on one line (separated by a ;) due to the way `make` executes commands; we'll discuss this in more detail in the next section.

Let's see what happens when we try to make the library:

```
$ make library                                    In main directory
        cd lib; make library
        cc -c -O abc.c
        ar rv mine abc.o
ar: creating mine
a - abc.o
        rm -f abc.o
        cc -c -O def.c
        ar rv mine def.o
a - def.o
        rm -f def.o
        cc -c -O ghi.c
        ar rv mine ghi.o
a - ghi.o
        rm -f ghi.o
$ make library
        cd lib; make library
```

Well, so far, so good. Let's try making `prog`:

```
$ make prog
        cc -O -c main.c
        cc -O -c io.c
        cd lib; make library
        cc main.o io.o lib/mine -o prog
```

That seems to work well, too. Let's get rid of all the intermediate files and start over:

```
$ rm lib/mine
$ rm *.o prog
$ make prog
        cc -O -c main.c
        cc -O -c io.c
        cd lib; make library
        cc -c -O abc.c
        ar rv mine abc.o
ar: creating mine
a - abc.o
        rm -f abc.o
        cc -c -O def.c
        ar rv mine def.o
a - def.o
        rm -f def.o
```

```
        cc -c -O ghi.c
        ar rv mine ghi.o
a - ghi.o
        rm -f ghi.o
        cc main.o io.o lib/mine -o prog
```

That went smoothly. There's only one other thing we need to try—we'll attempt to remake prog, even though it's up to date:

```
$ make prog
        cd lib; make library
        cc main.o io.o lib/mine -o prog
```

We told you that since library is always out of date, the make in lib will always be run. But why was prog relinked? If you go back to the makefile, you'll see that prog depends upon main.o, io.o, and library:

```
prog: $(OBJS) library
```

Since library is always considered out of date, and since prog depends upon it, prog is also always considered out of date!

We can rewrite the makefile slightly to fix this:

```
$ cat makefile
OBJS = main.o io.o

all: library prog

prog: $(OBJS) lib/mine
        cc $(OBJS) lib/mine -o prog

$(OBJS): global.h

library:
        cd lib; make library
$ make all
        cd lib; make library
$ rm prog
$ make all
        cd lib; make library
        cc main.o io.o lib/mine -o prog
$ touch lib/abc.c
$ make all
        cd lib; make library
        cc -c -O abc.c
        ar rv mine abc.o
r - abc.o
        rm -f abc.o
        cc main.o io.o lib/mine -o prog
```

As you can see, we've added a new target, all. Now when we type in make all, make will attempt to create library (as before) and will then attempt to make prog. This time, however, prog depends upon lib/mine, which exists, instead of library, which doesn't. If lib/mine is modified by the cd lib; make library, then prog is out of date, and make recreates it.

The only problem that arises here is that prog can no longer be used reliably as a target:

```
$ touch lib/abc.c
$ make prog
'prog' is up to date.
```

prog doesn't depend upon library anymore, so make won't attempt to remake it if one of the library's source files changes.

Even though this method has a potential problem, you'll see it used often in makefiles for large programming systems—it improves the makefile's structure and readability, and in systems where several programs are maintained by the same makefile, it aids installation, since all the user has to do is type in make all (or something similar, like make install) to create everything.

One thing to keep in mind is that there can't be a file or directory named library; otherwise, the library target will *always* be up to date (after all, it doesn't depend upon anything), and mine will never be remade.

Suffix Rules for Libraries

make has a special suffix rule for libraries:

```
.c.a:
```

This suffix rule is special in that the .a file doesn't actually exist; instead, the .a suffix refers to files that have the form *name (file)* (i.e., library members) *as if they had a .a as a suffix*. So the commands associated with the .c.a suffix rule are executed to remake a library member. The commands normally associated with the .c.a rule are

```
.c.a:
        $(CC) -c $(CFLAGS) $<
        ar rv $@ $*.o
        rm -f $*.o
```

The $(CC) -c $(CFLAGS) $< is as we've discussed before: it compiles the .c file. The ar command uses $@ as the library name and $*.o as the member name. $@ and $* have special meaning in a library context: $@ is the name of the library, and $* is the name of the member with the suffix stripped. So ar rv $@ $*.o archives the .o file into the library.

The internal variable $\%$ has meaning *only* in a library context: it is the member name.[†] So the above lines could be rewritten as

```
.c.a:
        $(CC) -c $(CFLAGS) $<
        ar rv $@ $%
        rm -f $%
```

▪ Using make with the Shell ▪

make and the shell are very closely tied together. Exported shell variables are read into make on startup, and the shell is often called upon by make to execute a command associated with one of its dependencies. Any command in the makefile that contains a special shell character (`;`, `|`, and `*` are special shell characters, to name a few), and any command that is continued on another line with the `\` are passed to the shell as is. Anything else is handled by make directly.[‡] This accounts for the perplexing error message when a command that is built into the shell is placed in a makefile:

```
$ cat makefile
test:
        cd /tmp
$ make test
        cd /tmp
Make: Cannot load cd.  Stop.
*** Error code 1

Stop.
```

make simply couldn't find the command cd.

The error goes away as soon as you use something that causes make to run the shell on the command:

```
$ cat makefile
test:
        cd \
                /tmp
$ make test
        cd \
                /tmp
```

[†] Older versions of make don't implement $\%$, thus the $*.o construct in .c.a suffix rules.

[‡] By default, make will search your PATH for the command to execute. Then it will fork/exec the command with the appropriate arguments; if the exec fails because the file is not a binary (a.out) program, then the shell will be invoked on the command. This is more efficient than running the shell directly on every command that make executes.

Since `make` passes commands separated with a semicolon (`;`) to the shell, you can do things like

```
library:
        cd lib; make library
```

as we saw in the previous section.

Note that each line that doesn't end with a `\` is executed individually; a new shell is started for each one, so the two following `make`s are executed in different directories:

```
        cd lib; make library
        make print
```

The `make library` is executed in the subdirectory `lib`; whereas the `make print` is executed *in `lib`'s parent*, the original directory.

You can also get a little more complicated with the shell and do things differently depending upon certain conditions on the system. For example, suppose you have a program that will be used on both the Seventh Edition and System V. For the most part, if written properly, the program will not need to be changed when going from one to the other; however, there are some things that are different between the two versions, and sometimes you have to use nonportable features (e.g., `ioctl`). The best way to solve the problem is to write the program with code for *both* versions included. `#ifdef` may be used to test a preprocessor constant that tells the preprocessor whether to include the code for the Seventh Edition or System V:

```
$ cat seterase.c
/* set erase character to CTRL-h
   uses ioctl in nonportable fashion */
#ifdef V7    /* Seventh Edition UNIX */

#include <sgtty.h>
#define CTRLBACK      (tty.sg_erase)
#define TCGETA        (TIOCGETP)
#define TCSETA        (TIOCSETP)
struct sgttyb tty;

#else       /* System V */

#include <termio.h>
#define CTRLBACK      (tty.c_cc[VERASE])
struct termio tty;

#endif
```

```
      seterase ()
      {
          if (ioctl (0, TCGETA, &tty) == -1) {
              perror ("TCGETA failed");
              exit (1);
          }

          CTRLBACK = '\010';

          if (ioctl (0, TCSETA, &tty) == -1) {
              perror ("TCSETA failed");
              exit (1);
          }
      }
```

If V7 is defined (e.g., by running the command `cc -c -DV7 seterase.c`), then CTRLBACK is set to `tty.sg_erase`, the Seventh Edition's equivalent to `c_cc[VERASE]`; TCGETA and TCSETA are defined to be TIOCGETP and TIOCSETP (the Seventh Edition equivalents); and an `sgttyb` structure called `tty` is declared. The resulting program looks like this:

```
      /* set erase character to CTRL-h
         uses ioctl in nonportable fashion */

      #include <sgtty.h>
      struct sgttyb tty;

      seterase ()
      {
          if (ioctl (0, TIOCGETP, &tty) == -1) {
              perror ("TCGETA failed");
              exit (1);
          }

          tty.sg_erase = '\010';

          if (ioctl (0, TIOCSETP, &tty) == -1) {
              perror ("TCSETA failed");
              exit (1);
          }
      }
```

If V7 isn't defined, then CTRLBACK is set to the System V backspace character, `c_cc[VERASE]`, and the `termio` structure `tty` is declared. The resulting program for System V looks like this:

```
/* set erase character to CTRL-h
   uses ioctl in nonportable fashion */

#include <termio.h>
struct termio tty;

seterase ()
{
    if (ioctl (0, TCGETA, &tty) == -1) {
        perror ("TCGETA failed");
        exit (1);
    }

    tty.c_cc[VERASE] = '\010';

    if (ioctl (0, TCSETA, &tty) == -1) {
        perror ("TCSETA failed");
        exit (1);
    }
}
```

Now we need to hook all this into `make`. The simplest way is to let `make` figure out which version of UNIX is running by simply testing for the existence of a file with the shell:

```
$ cat makefile
seterase.o: seterase.c
        if [ -f /etc/ttys ]; \
        then \
            cc -c $(CFLAGS) -DV7 seterase.c; \
        else \
            cc -c $(CFLAGS) -UV7 seterase.c; \
        fi
```

This `makefile` is fairly simple once you understand how the shell is involved here. The `seterase.o: seterase.c` line simply defines the dependency of `seterase.o` on `seterase.c`. If `seterase.o` needs to be remade, the `if` statement is given to the shell. We don't have the space here to go into detail about what the shell is doing; however, we can give you a general overview. The shell tests for existence of the file `/etc/ttys`, which exists on Seventh Edition and Berkeley UNIX systems but is absent from System V. (System V has the file `/etc/inittab` instead.) If the file exists, then the command

```
cc -c -O -DV7 seterase.c
```

is executed; otherwise,

```
cc -c -O -UV7 seterase.c
```

is executed. Due to the shell's syntax, the semicolons have to appear after the
`if` and after every command, but not after `then` or `else`. Backslashes are
required after every line but the last, since the whole construct must be passed to
one invocation of shell.

Note that the `-U` option is interpreted by the C preprocessor to *undefine*
`V7`, just as `-D` is used to define `V7`.

Maintaining Programs on Different Versions of UNIX

As you can see from the previous example, `make` may be used to maintain programs that will be compiled on different machines and different versions of
UNIX. By testing for existence of certain files and by running certain commands,
`make` (well, actually the shell) can determine which version of UNIX is being run
on what machine and define preprocessor names accordingly.

Several commands were added to System V that allow you to determine
what type of machine you are running on. Among them are `pdp11`, `u3b`,
`u3b5`, and `vax`. The command that describes the machine it's on exits with a
zero status; all others exit with nonzero status. Commands for other types of
machines (like `u3b2`) may exist, but since all manufacturers of UNIX systems
don't adhere to this convention, there is no guarantee that your system will have
the appropriate command. Also, non-System V UNIX systems usually don't
have any of these commands.

The following shell program determines what type of machine it's running
on using the above commands, and determines whether it's running on the
Seventh Edition or System V using the test for `/etc/ttys`. It then prints out
the version and machine type, each preceded by a `-D` for use by the preprocessor:

```
$ cat version
# version -- determine UNIX version and machine type

# default machine and version
MACHINE=VAX
VERSION=SV

if [ -x /bin/pdp11 ] && /bin/pdp11
then
    MACHINE=PDP11
elif [ -x /bin/u3b ] && /bin/u3b
then
    MACHINE=U3B
elif [ -x /bin/U3B5 ] && /bin/u3b5
then
    MACHINE=U3B5
fi
```

```
if [ -f /etc/ttys ]
then
    VERSION=V7
fi

echo "-DVERSION=$VERSION -DMACHINE=$MACHINE"
$ version                              Assume a Seventh Edition VAX
-DVERSION=V7 -DMACHINE=VAX
```

This program can be used in a `makefile` to help `make` handle different versions and machines:

```
seterase.o: seterase.c
        cc -c $(CFLAGS) `version` seterase.c
```

This `makefile` is fairly simple once you understand how the shell is involved here. If `seterase.o` needs to be remade, the `version` command is executed. The shell replaces the `version` with the output of the `version` program, say, -DVERSION=V7 -DMACHINE=VAX; then `cc` is executed with these arguments, for instance,

```
        cc -c -O -DVERSION=V7 -DMACHINE=VAX seterase.c
```

The `version` program can be modified to handle more machine types and other versions of UNIX. For example, Berkeley UNIX systems have the file /vmunix, so you can distinguish between Seventh Edition and Berkeley systems by testing for existence of this file. Similarly, XENIX systems have the /xenix file, Venix systems have the /venix file, and so on. Practically every version of UNIX has at least one file that no other version has; you just have to determe what that file is.

• Command Line Options •

`make` takes several command line options:

-b   Turn on compatibility for old `makefiles`.

-d   Turn on debug mode. List detailed information about file modification times and internal settings.

-e   Let shell environment variables override variable assignments in the `makefile`.

-f   Use the following argument instead of `makefile`.

-i   Ignore exit codes returned by commands.

-k   Don't stop if a command returns a nonzero exit status. Continue work on other targets.

-n   Don't execute commands. The commands that would be executed to create the target(s) are listed but not run.

-p   Print out the complete set of variable assignments, suffix rules, and `makefile` dependencies.

-q   Test the target to see if it's up to date. If it is, return a zero exit status; otherwise, return a nonzero exit status.

-r   Do not use built-in suffix rules.

-s   Turn on silent mode. `make` will not list the commands as they are executed.

-t   Touch the target(s) instead of making them, so they appear to be up to date.

The –e Option

There is a certain precedence of variable assignments in `make` (from highest to lowest):

1. Assignments in `make`'s command-line arguments.

2. `makefile` assignments.

3. Shell environment variables.

4. Built-in definitions.

Using the –e option switches the precedence of the middle two in the above list, so that environment variables override `makefile` assignments.

For example, the following `makefile` simply prints the value of the variable `test`:

```
$ cat makefile
test = inside makefile
echo:
        echo $(test)
$ make echo                                 Use value set in makfile
        echo inside makefile
inside makefile
$ make test="command line" echo             Use value set on command line
        echo command line
command line
```

```
$ test=environment; export test
$ make echo                          Use value set in makefile
        echo inside makefile
inside makefile
$ make -e echo                       Use value set in environment
        echo environment
environment
```

Error Handling

When make runs a command that returns a nonzero exit status, it quits. There are a few ways to tell it to ignore nonzero exit codes. The -i option causes make to totally ignore the exit codes of the commands it runs. This can be dangerous, since many commands require that the previous ones complete successfully (e.g., archiving a library member after compiling the .c file). Placing the dummy target .IGNORE: anywhere in the makefile has the same effect as the -i option.

By placing a dash (-) in front of any command in the makefile, you can force make to ignore the exit status *of just that command*. This can be very useful if you need to run a command that doesn't call exit to finish, so the exit status is undefined (and usually nonzero):

```
$ cat makefile
print: *.h *.c
        pr $? | laser
        touch print
$ make print
        pr global.h circle.c ctrl.c line.c main.c spline.c | laser
Print job phw.23 scheduled for LaserWriter
*** Error code 255

Stop.
```

Here the laser program returns a nonzero exit code (presumably because it doesn't call exit (0) when it's done), and make terminates before touching print. So every time make print is run, every file is printed regardless of whether or not it's been modified since the last printing. This problem is fixed by placing a - in front of the pr $? | laser:

```
$ cat makefile
print: *.h *.c
        -pr $? | laser
        touch print
$ make print
        pr global.h circle.c ctrl.c line.c main.c spline.c | laser
Print job phw.24 scheduled for LaserWriter
*** Error code 255 (ignored)
        touch print
$ make print
'print' is up to date.
```

The −k option causes make to handle error codes intelligently. If a command exits with a nonzero status, make abandons work on the current target. It continues to work on other targets as if the previous one finished properly; however, when it comes to a point that needs the target that couldn't be made, it stops. This feature is particularly useful when running make unattended, e.g., overnight or at lunch time. If you run make on a programming system with 100 source files, go to lunch, and find out when you return that make died because there was an error in the third file, you'll probably be more than a little annoyed. Running make −k forces make to continue on the other files in the system.

If you hit *BREAK* or *DELETE* while make is running, it removes the current target (if it exists). Normally, this is what you want make to do, since a partially completed target would be considered up to date the next time make was run. Sometimes, however, you'll want make to save the target when it is interrupted. In that case, you have to explicitly tell make what targets are "precious." This is done by placing these targets on a dependency line beginning with the dummy target .PRECIOUS:.

```
$ cat makefile
.PRECIOUS: print

print: *.h *.c
        pr $? | laser
        touch print
```

Here, the file print is considered "precious" and will not be removed by make when you hit *BREAK* or *DELETE*. Without making print precious, when you interrupt make while it's printing something, print will be removed. Since print is only used for its modification time, you don't want it removed (then the next printing will be of everything, which could be a lot).

The −n Option

The −n option causes make to process your makefile and print the commands it would run without actually executing them.

```
$ cat makefile
CC = dmdcc
OBJS = main.o ctrl.o line.o circle.o spline.o

draw: $(OBJS)
        $(CC) -o draw $(OBJS)


$(OBJS): global.h
$ make -n draw
        cc -O -c main.c
        cc -O -c circle.c
        cc -O -c spline.c
        cc -o draw main.o ctrl.o line.o circle.o spline.o
```

This tells you that if you run make again without the −n option, it will compile main.c, circle.c, and spline.c and will relink all of the objects.

Recall the mine library. When it was placed in the lib subdirectory, it was maintained by simply changing to that directory and running make in there:

```
library:
        cd lib; make library
```

Guess what happens when you try to see what make will do when you use the −n option on library.

```
$ rm lib/mine
$ make -n library
        cd lib; make library
```

Not too exciting. The problem here is that make isn't executing the commands, merely listing them, so the second make isn't even run! There is a remedy for this: when the special variable MAKE is used on a command line in the makefile, make will execute that line *even when −n is used*. MAKE is set to the string make by default.

```
$ cat makefile
OBJS  =  main.o io.o

all: library prog

prog: $(OBJS) lib/mine
        cc $(OBJS) lib/mine -o prog

$(OBJS): global.h

library:
        cd lib; $(MAKE) library
$ make -n library
        cd lib; make library
        cc -c -O abc.c
        ar rv mine abc.o
        rm -f abc.o
        cc -c -O def.c
        ar rv mine def.o
        rm -f def.o
        cc -c -O ghi.c
        ar rv mine ghi.o
        rm -f ghi.o
```

Note that when the make in lib is run, it doesn't execute any of the commands listed; in other words, it too is run with the -n option. make does this by placing a variable called MAKEFLAGS that contains all the command line options into the environment before running cd lib; $(MAKE) library. The second make reads this environment variable and sets its options accordingly. So when make is run with the -n option, it is passed on to any other make that is run. Others options, such as -i and -k are also passed in MAKEFLAGS. (The -f, -p, and -r options are not passed in MAKEFLAGS.)

As you can see, the -n option is useful for tracing execution of your makefile (without actually executing any commands) and also as a quick way to determine which of your targets are out of date.

The -s Option

The -s option tells make to be "silent" about the commands it is running. No commands are listed. This can also be done on a per-command basis by preceding any command with an at sign (@). The @ is most useful on commands that you don't want listed when they are run (e.g., echo, which simply prints out its arguments):

```
$ cat makefile
print1:
        echo this is a test message
print2:
        @echo this is a test message, too
$ make print1
        echo this is a test message
this is a test message
$ make print2
this is a test message, too
```

The @ reduces redundant and confusing information when used properly. Placing the dummy target .SILENT: anywhere in the makefile has the same effect as the -s option.

When you use the -n option, make will list *all* commands that would be executed, even those that have an @ in front of them, unless -s or .SILENT: has been specified (i.e., -s and .SILENT take precedence over -n).

The -t Option

The -t option is both useful and dangerous. It causes make to touch all of the specified targets and intermediate targets *without actually remaking them*. It's useful if you wish to make one or more targets up to date without going to the trouble of remaking them all. This is obviously something you don't want to do if you really *do* need to remake something; however, if you make a change that has no effect on the executable code, like fixing a misspelled comment in one of your include files, you certainly can use make -t to update everything without performing a multitude of compiles. Just remember that although trivial changes to statements may seem innocuous at times, they can potentially cause major problems later on if simply touched and not remade. Unless you're *absolutely sure* your changes don't require recompiling, it's not a good idea to use -t.

▪ Miscellaneous Features ▪

More on make Variables

There are two *modifiers* that may be used with the internal make variables $@, $$@, $<, $*, and $%. These are D and F, which allow you to access different portions of these variables if their contents begin with a slash (/). They allow you to access the directory and file parts of a full path name.

The constructs $(@D), $$(@D), $(<D), $(*D), and $(%D) access the directory part of the $@, $$@, $<, $*, and $% variables, respectively. Similarly, the constructs $(@F), $$(@F), $(<F), $(*F), and $(%F) access the file name part of the $@, $$@, $<, $*, and $% variables, respectively.

For example, if the current target is /usr/bin/cc, then $@ will be /usr/bin/cc, $(@D) will be /usr/bin, and $(@F) will be cc. This can be useful with makefiles that must support lots of targets in several different directories:

```
$ cat makefile
OBJS = /usr/src/cc/c1.o \
       /usr/src/cc/c2.o \
       /usr/src/opt/c3.o

/usr/bin/cc:  $(OBJS)
        cc $(OBJS) -o /usr/bin/cc


.c.o:
        cd $(@D); $(MAKE) $(@F)
$ make /usr/bin/cc
        cd /usr/src/cc; make c1.o
        cc -O -c c1.c
        cd /usr/src/cc; make c2.o
        cc -O -c c2.c
        cd /usr/src/opt; make c3.o
        cc -O -c c3.c
        cc /usr/src/cc/c1.o /usr/src/cc/c2.o /usr/src/opt/c3.o
-o /usr/bin/cc
```

If the internal variable doesn't begin with a / (e.g., not a full path name), then the D modifier produces a dot (.), meaning the current directory, and the F modifier produces the entire contents of the internal variable.

Pseudo-Targets

A *pseudo-target* is a target like .SUFFIXES: and .PRECIOUS:. You've seen all but one of the pseudo-targets that make recognizes—.DEFAULT:. .DEFAULT: is used to specify commands that are to be executed when make can't figure out how to make a target using the built-in rules and the dependencies in the makefile. It is simply followed by whatever commands you want executed to remake the target:

```
$ cat makefile
.DEFAULT:
        cp default $@
```

Here, if the specified target ($@) doesn't exist and can't be made from any of the built-in or makefile dependencies, the file default is copied to it.

```
$ make anything
        cp default anything
```

The following table summarizes all of make's pseudo-targets.

TABLE 7-2. Pseudo-Targets

Pseudo-target	Description
.DEFAULT:	Commands listed with this pseudo-target are executed if a target must be made and no built-in or makefile dependencies can be found for it
.IGNORE:	Nonzero exit codes are ignored
.PRECIOUS:	Targets listed as dependencies with this pseudo-target are not removed by make when interrupted
.SILENT:	Commands are not listed before execution
.SUFFIXES:	Targets listed as dependencies with this pseudo-target are added to the list of valid suffixes; if no targets are listed, the list of valid suffixes is cleared

make and SCCS

SCCS stands for the *Source Code Control System*. It's used to maintain different versions of programming projects. It has several useful features, including the ability to prevent more than one user from modifying a source file at the same time. A source code file is kept by SCCS in a file whose name begins with the *prefix* "s.". This file is manipulated by various SCCS commands to get the actual source file from it, update the SCCS file based on changes made to the source file, add revision information to the SCCS file, etc. Covering SCCS in detail is beyond the scope of this chapter; however, if you are interested in learning more about SCCS, you can look at the manual descriptions for admin, get, delta, and prs in the *UNIX User Reference Manual*, and in [1], and [2].

make has several suffix rules built into it that handle SCCS files properly. If you keep your .c files under SCCS, when you attempt to create a .o file using the default suffix rules, make will issue the proper commands to extract the .c file from the SCCS file and will then compile the .c file, creating the .o file. For example, if you have the SCCS files s.abc.c and s.def.c, then you can create the .o files simply by using the default suffix rules *without a makefile*:

```
$ make abc.o def.o
        get  -p s.abc.c > abc.c
        cc -O -c abc.c
        rm -f abc.c
        get  -p s.def.c > def.c
        cc -O -c def.c
        rm -f def.c
```

Note that make removes the .c file after compiling it. make knows that SCCS is to have complete control over the source file, so it considers the source file extracted from the SCCS file temporary and removes it.

If you need to use a makefile, you can still use the built-in suffix rules by simply augmenting them with whatever information is needed:

```
$ cat makefile
CC = dmdcc
OBJS = main.o ctrl.o line.o circle.o spline.o

draw: $(OBJS)
        $(CC) -o draw $(OBJS)

$(OBJS): global.h
$ ls
makefile
s.circle.c
s.ctrl.c
s.global.h
s.line.c
s.main.c
s.spline.c
$ make draw
        get  -p s.global.h > global.h
        get  -p s.main.c > main.c
        cc -O -c main.c
        rm -f main.c
        get  -p s.ctrl.c > ctrl.c
        cc -O -c ctrl.c
        rm -f ctrl.c
        get  -p s.line.c > line.c
        cc -O -c line.c
        rm -f line.c
        get  -p s.circle.c > circle.c
        cc -O -c circle.c
        rm -f circle.c
        get  -p s.spline.c > spline.c
        cc -O -c spline.c
        rm -f spline.c
        cc -o draw main.o ctrl.o line.o circle.o spline.o
```

Note that `make` knew how to extract the `global.h` file from `s.global.h`, but didn't remove `global.h` after it was finished with it. Unfortunately, there is no way presently available in `make` to remedy this—if `global.h` were removed, it would be extracted on the next `make` and would be newer than all the `.o` files, forcing everything to be recompiled.

You can even put your `makefile` under SCCS (`s.makefile`), and `make` will extract it if `makefile` doesn't exist.

`make` also knows about single-file programs under SCCS. For example, if the file `s.cat.c` contains the SCCS copy of the entire `cat` program, then you can simply issue the command `make cat` to create the executable file:

```
$ make cat
        get  -p s.cat.c > cat.c
        cc -O cat.c -o cat
        rm -f cat.c
```

If you're interested in messing around with the suffix rules for SCCS files, it's not too difficult. Any suffix in a suffix rule with a tilde (~) following it is considered to be an SCCS file:

```
.c~.o:
        get $(GFLAGS) -p $< > $*.c
        $(CC) $(CFLAGS) -c $*.c
        rm -f $*.c
```

This is the standard built-in suffix rule for converting `s.`*file*`.c` files to *file*`.o` files. The `.c~` means "any file name beginning with `s.` and ending with `.c`." The SCCS `get` command is issued with `$(GFLAGS)` and `-p` as options (`GFLAGS` is null by default); `$<` is the `s.` file, and `$*.c` is the intermediate `.c` file. The `$(CC)` command is run on the intermediate `.c` file, and then the `.c` file is removed.

Similar suffix rules exist for `.c~.c`, `.c~.a`, `.c~`, `.h~.h`, and others for other programming languages supported by `make`, such as FORTRAN 77, RAT-FOR, `lex`, and `yacc`. The following table summarizes the built-in `make` variables.

TABLE 7-3. Built-in make Variables

Variable	Default	Description value
AS	as	Assembler used to produce .o files from .s files
ASFLAGS		Flags for $(AS)
CC	cc	C compiler used to produce .o files from .c files
CFLAGS	-O	Flags for $(CC)
FC	f77	Fortran compiler used to produce .o files from .f files
FFLAGS		Flags for $(FC)
GET	get	SCCS command to get regular files from SCCS files
GFLAGS		Flags for $(GET)
LD	ld	Loader used to link edit .o files
LDFLAGS		Flags for $(LD)
LEX	lex	Command used to produce .c files from .l files
LFLAGS		Flags for $(LEX)
MAKE	make	The make command
MAKEFLAGS	b	Flags for $(MAKE)
YACC	yacc	Command used to produce .c files from .y files
YFLAGS		Flags for $(YACC)

• Tying it All Together •

The following makefiles maintain the grep program that we've discussed throughout this chapter. There are library files in the directory lib, a version dependent routine seterase, and several targets for creating, installing, printing, and shipping the program and documentation.

The install target makes grep and then copies it to $(INSDIR), which has been set to /usr/bin. The workings of the all, library, and print targets have been discussed earlier. The docs target runs nroff on the documentation files grep.guide and grep.1, respectively. The tar target creates a tar archive of the program files and the makefile, which can be shipped to other systems. The clean and clobber targets remove all the targets so we can start make with a clean slate.

```
$ cat makefile
INSDIR = /usr/bin
OBJS   = main.o match.o

install: all
        cp grep $(INSDIR)
        strip $(INSDIR)/grep

all: library grep

grep: $(OBJS) lib/mine
        cc main.o match.o lib/mine -o grep

$(OBJS): pattern.h

library:
        cd lib; $(MAKE) library

print: *.h *.c lib/*.c
        pr $? | lp
        touch print

docs:
        nroff -mm grep.guide | lp
        nroff -man grep.1 | lp

tar:
        tar cf - makefile *.h *.c lib/*.c > grep.tar

clean:
        -rm  $(OBJS) lib/mine grep print

clobber: clean
        -rm $(INSDIR)/grep
$ cat lib/makefile
library: mine(output.o) mine(seterase.o)
```

```
$ make all
        cd lib; make library
        cc -c -O output.c
        ar rv mine output.o
ar: creating mine
a - output.o
        rm -f output.o
        cc -c -O seterase.c
        ar rv mine seterase.o
a - seterase.o
        rm -f seterase.o
        cc -O -c main.c
        cc -O -c match.c
        cc main.o match.o lib/mine -o grep
$ make install
        cd lib; make library
        cp grep /usr/bin
$ make print
        pr pattern.h match.c main.c lib/output.c lib/seterase.c | lp
request id is PS-1414 (standard input)
        touch print
$ make tar
        tar cf - makefile *.h *.c lib/*.c > grep.tar
$ make docs
        nroff -mm grep.guide | lp
request id is PS-1416 (standard input)
        nroff -man grep.1 | lp
request id is PS-1418 (standard input)
$ touch main.c
$ make all
        cd lib; make library
        cc -O -c main.c
        cc main.o match.o lib/mine -o grep
$ make print
        pr main.c | lp
request id is PS-1419 (standard input)
        touch print
$ make clean
        rm main.o match.o lib/mine grep print
$ make clobber
        rm main.o match.o lib/mine grep print
rm: main.o non-existent
rm: match.o non-existent
rm: lib/mine non-existent
rm: grep non-existent
rm: print non-existent
*** Error code 2 (ignored)
        rm /usr/bin/grep
```

▪ The New make ▪

Over the past few years, an effort to improve on some of make's deficiencies resulted in a new make. The new make (sometimes called the *fourth generation make* or *aug-make*) has many improvements over the current make:

1. It supports source and targets in multiple directories, vastly improving the way libraries and programming projects with many programmers can be managed.

2. It improves the way files in object libraries are specified and maintained.

3. It supports an improved interface to the shell. All commands are given to the same shell, and multiple commands can be run in the background to produce targets concurrently. Also, backslashes and semicolons are not required in blocks of shell code.

4. It provides support for maintaining programs across various machines and versions of UNIX.

5. It uses compiled makefiles to improve startup time.

6. It makes use of an enhanced C preprocessor when compiling makefiles, allowing for conditional compilation *of the makefile*.

7. It supports a completely new method of describing default dependencies.

8. It supports a pattern matching syntax in variable substitution.

9. It can automatically generate dependencies based on #include statements in the source code.

10. It has several new built-in rules for printing, archiving, linting, installing, and removing files.

11. It provides an improved interface to SCCS.

12. It is two to five times faster than the current make, and its makefiles are five to ten times smaller.

For more information on the new make, see [5]. The new make is currently available from the AT&T UNIX Toolchest.

▪ References ▪

[1]   L. E. Bonanni and C. A. Salemi, "Source Code Control System User's Guide," *System V Programmer's Manual*, AT&T Bell Laboratories.

[2]   M. J. Rochkind, "The Source Code Control System," IEEE Transactions on Software Engineering, SE-1 (December 1975).

[3]   S. I. Feldman, "Make—A Program for Maintaining Computer Programs," Software — Practice and Experience, Vol. 9 No. 4, April 1979.

[4]   S. Talbot, *Managing Projects with Make*, O'Reilly and Associates, Inc., Newton, MA, 1985.

[5]   "Augmented Version of Make," *UNIX System V Release 2.0 Support Tools Guide*, April 1984.

E X E R C I S E S

1. Define the following terms:

   a. Dependency

   b. Target

   c. Suffix rule

2. Assume the following file dependencies for a program called dact:

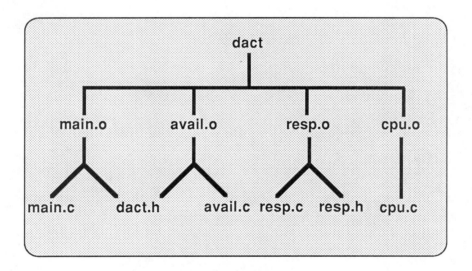

Fig. 7-3. File dependencies for dact

   Write a makefile that can be used to manage the dact program.

3. Split the routines in the window editor in Appendix C into separate files and write a makefile to manage them.

4. Move all of the files from Exercise 2, except main.c, into a subdirectory. Write a makefile for the subdirectory and rewrite the makefile for the main directory.

5. Place all of the executable objects from the subdirectory created in Exercise 4 into a library. Rewrite the makefiles to maintain it.

6. Add print, tar, clean, and clobber targets to the makefiles. (See the makefile at the end of this chapter.)

7. Write a makefile for the pre3.c program in Chapter 8. Make sure you add a provision for compiling in/out the debugging code.

8. Add a suffix rule that produces .to files from .tbl files with the following command:

```
tbl name.tbl > name.to
```

C H A P T E R
8

DEBUGGING C PROGRAMS

There are many useful methods and tools that can be employed to help debug C programs in the UNIX environment. We'll cover several of them in this chapter:

1. `lint`

2. The C preprocessor

3. `ctrace`

4. `sdb`

▪ `lint` ▪

The `lint` program checks for constructs in C programs that may be erroneous, nonportable, or simply wasteful. It finds problems that the C compiler doesn't detect. (It picks the "lint" from your programs.) It does a very good job of finding

- Nonportable usage of code, particularly problems with `chars` that should be `ints`.

- Wasteful code, such as unused variables and functions.

- Inconsistent use of function arguments and return values.

- Inconsistent use of types and type casting.

- Use of automatic variables before assignment.

- Inconsistent or incorrect use of library functions.

`lint` performs two passes over the specified file(s). The first pass lists problems found within each routine. The second pass lists the *inter-routine* inconsistencies, or the problems between the various routines in the program and between those routines and library routines that they call (e.g., incorrect type or number of function arguments).

lint is invoked like the C compiler, with the name of the program to scan.

```
$ lint junk.c
```

Let's give lint an erroneous program and see what it tells us:

```
$ cat lint1.c
main ()
{
    char c;
}
$ lint lint1.c

lint1.c
===============
(3)   warning: c unused in function main
```

This is a very simple program—it does nothing, but lint does give us a simple message about it. The variable c is declared but not used.   lint considers this to be wasteful, since space must be created for it. The message also tells you which line it considers incorrect; here it's line 3, where c is declared.[†]

Here's a slightly longer program that copies standard input to standard output. It has a nonportable problem: the variable c is declared to be a char, which on some machines is unsigned.   EOF is defined to be –1 in stdio.h, and the comparison of c to EOF will *never be true* on those machines where chars are always unsigned, since a non-negative value is compared against –1:

```
$ cat lint2.c
#include <stdio.h>

main ()
{
    char c;

    while ((c = getchar ()) != EOF)
        putchar (c);
}
```

---

† On some systems, lint may also complain that "main returns a random value to invocation environment." You can ignore this message.

```
$ lint lint2.c

lint2.c
==============
(7)  warning: nonportable character comparison



==============
function returns value which is always ignored
    putchar
```

Here, lint is trying to tell you two things. First, it's telling you about a character comparison that may be nonportable. If you check the line numbers, you'll
see that indeed it's the line where c is being compared against EOF.

The second message from lint comes from the inter-routine checks
(printed after the second ==============) and is also interesting; it says that
putchar returns a value and you're always ignoring it. Well, looking at your
UNIX Programmer Reference Manual shows you that putchar returns its argument if successful and –1 if unsuccessful. lint is picky about types, return
values, and the like; note that this is good, since programmers often do not pay
attention to these details.

In order to get lint to consider the statement correct, either assign the
return value from putchar to something or cast it to the type void:

```
$ cat lint3.c
#include <stdio.h>

main ()
{
    int c;

    while ((c = getchar ()) != EOF)
        (void) putchar (c);
}
$ lint lint3.c
$
```

lint is now satisfied with the program. The void typecast tells lint that
you're well aware that putchar returns a value but that you're choosing to
ignore it (by "throwing it away").

As you can see from the two previous examples, lint knows about the
putchar routine. In fact, lint knows about the Standard C and Standard I/O
Libraries and the UNIX interface routines, so it checks all usages of these routines against the information it has about them, e.g., number of arguments, argument type, and return value type.

If you have a program that uses another library, simply specify the library to `lint` in the same manner you would specify it to the `cc` command:

```
$ cat lint4.c
main ()
{
    int i;

    (void) scanf ("%d", &i);
    (void) printf ("%f\n", sqrt (i));
}
$ lint lint4.c -lm


==============
value type used inconsistently
    sqrt          llib-lm(20) :: lint4.c(6)
value type declared inconsistently
    sqrt          llib-lm(20) :: lint4.c(6)
function argument ( number ) used inconsistently
    sqrt( arg 1 )          llib-lm(20) :: lint4.c(6)
```

We told `lint` to scan the file `lint4.c` and to read in the math library (the `-lm` option), as well as the Standard C Library (which is read in by default). `lint` found some problems with the `sqrt` routine.

The first message, "`value type used inconsistently`," means that `lint` knows `sqrt` is supposed to return a `double` value, and we're using it as an `int` here (because we haven't declared it otherwise).

The second message, "`value type declared inconsistently`," means again that `lint` knows `sqrt` returns a `double`, and since `sqrt` hasn't been formally declared, the C compiler will assume it returns an `int`. The first and second messages usually come together. When you get rid of one (by declaring the function properly), the other is fixed as well.

The last message says that the argument to `sqrt` is used inconsistently. The message

```
function argument ( number ) used inconsistently
```

tells you that one of the arguments to `sqrt` is not correct. (`number`) tells you how to interpret the next line:

```
sqrt( arg 1 )          llib-lm(20) :: lint4.c(6)
```

The function is `sqrt`, and the first argument is not correct (`arg 1`). Looking at `sqrt`'s entry in the manual, you'll see that its argument should be of type `double`, not `int`.

All of the messages told you that the problem occurs on line 6 of `lint4.c`; the `llib-lm(20)` gives you the cross-reference of the `sqrt` routine in the `lint` library `llib-lm` (more on libraries later). You can get rid of these messages by simply declaring the types correctly:

```
$ cat lint5.c
main ()
{
    double i;
    double sqrt ();

    (void) scanf ("%lf", &i);
    (void) printf ("%f\n", sqrt (i));
}
$ lint lint5.c -lm
$
```

or, better yet, by including the `math.h` header file which contains return type declarations for all math library routines:

```
$ cat lint5.c
#include <math.h>

main ()
{
    double i;

    (void) scanf ("%lf", &i);
    (void) printf ("%f\n", sqrt (i));
}
$ lint lint5.c -lm
```

`lint` will often catch some of the most difficult-to-find bugs in a program. Take a look at the following function to see if you can figure out what's wrong with it:

```
$ cat lint6.c
process (array)
int array[];
{
    int i;

    for (i = 0; array[i] & 0377 != 0; ++i)
        (void) putchar (array[i] & 0377);
}
$ lint lint6.c

lint6.c
==============
(6)  warning: constant in conditional context


==============
name defined but never used
    process     lint6.c(3)
```

Take a close look at the `for` statement. There's a problem with the precedence of one of expressions in it:

```
array[i] & 0377 != 0
```

Since `!=` has higher precedence than `&`, this expression is evaluated as

```
array[i] & (0377 != 0)
```

which is the same as

```
array[i] & 1
```

Therefore, the `for` loop will continue as long as the low-order bit of `array[i]` is on, or in other words, as long as `array[i]` is odd.

   `lint` will catch this problem, even if its warning message is a little odd: "`constant in conditional context`." It's saying that the expression

```
0377 != 0
```

is the comparison of two constants, which it feels is strange (and it is). The message that `process` is `defined but never used` comes from the fact that we ran `lint` on a portion of the program, and `lint` can't find the place where `process` is called.

Another problem that lint finds has to do with the evaluation order of certain statements. Most of the time, the order of evaluation in C is regulated by precedence and associativity; however, there are some instances where order of evaluation is left up to the implementation of the compiler. For example, consider the following program and lint output:

```
$ cat lint7.c
main ()
{
    int i = 0;
    char buf[80];

    (void) gets (buf);
    while (buf[i])
        (void) printf ("%d: %c\n", i, buf[i++]);
}
$ lint lint7.c

lint7.c
===============
(8)  warning: i evaluation order undefined
```

Line 8

```
(void) printf ("%d: %c\n", i, buf[i++]);
```

does something that will not necessarily be evaluated the same by all C compilers: it uses i and i++ in the same statement, and the value of the first i can be evaluated either before or after the increment in buf[i++]. The order of evaluation is left up to the compiler, so if buf[i++] is evaluated first, then the value of i when printed out will be one larger than normally expected. If the evaluation is reversed, everything will be all right, since the value of i that is printed will be evaluated before buf[i++]. In other words, compilers reserve the right to evaluate function arguments in any order.

The ++ and -- operators can cause other problems, as in

```
buf[i++] = i;
```

Here, the value assigned to buf[i] may be the value of i either before or after incrementing it by one; there is no way to know which way a compiler will evaluate the expression without trying it out. The thing to remember here is that even if your compiler produces the code you want now, *there is no guarantee that other compilers will or even that new versions of your compiler will continue to do so.*

The following program has several bugs in it. See if you can find everything that lint does.

```
$ cat lint8.c
main ()
{
    int i = 0, j;

    (void) printf ("%f\n", process (i, j));
}

int process (i)
float i;
{
    if (i > 100)
        return (-i);
    else if (i < 0)
        return (i);
}
$ lint lint8.c

lint8.c
==============
(5)   warning: j may be used before set
(15)   warning: function process has return(e); and return;


==============
function argument ( number ) used inconsistently
    process( arg 1 )    lint8.c(10) :: lint8.c(5)
function called with variable number of arguments
    process       lint8.c(10) :: lint8.c(5)
```

Let's see what lint found here. On line 5, it says that "j may be used before set"; sure enough, we didn't initialize it like we did i. On line 15, lint says "function process has return(e); and return;". This strange message says that process uses return in two fashions: sometimes it returns a value or expression (return(e);), and sometimes it simply returns without a value. Looking at the routine, all you can see are two returns that both return expressions, so what's lint all upset about? Note that both returns are inside conditional blocks. What if i is between 0 and 100? Neither return will be executed, and process will simply return without a value (actually, a random value is returned). If you count down to line number 15 in lint8.c, you will see that it is the last line in the file, the closing } in process, so lint recognized that there is an implied return there.

lint also tells you that the first argument to process is used inconsistently: in main it's an int, and in process it's declared float. Also, it says that process is called with a "variable number of arguments": in main process is called with two arguments, but process declares only one.

Notice that `lint` *doesn't* mention that the format string to `printf` is inconsistent, i.e., that the string says to print a `float` and that `process` returns an `int`. `lint` does check argument types, but as far it's concerned, the first argument to `printf` must be a string, and the rest can be anything. `lint` doesn't "look inside" the format string to see what other types are expected by `printf`.

There are only two other `lint` messages we want to cover for now. The first has to do with wasteful constructs such as

```
while (*from) {
    *to = *from;
    *to++;
    *from++;
}
```

`*to++` and `*from++` are better written as `to++` and `from++`, since the `*` in this instance is unused. (The `++` increments the pointer, not what it points to, and nothing uses the pointed-to value.) Some compilers may be smart enough to optimize the indirection out of the actual code, but many will not. `lint` will catch this and display the message "`null effect`" along with the lines it is flagging.

Another message `lint` produces is "`warning: unsigned comparison with 0?`". This is produced whenever an unsigned variable is compared against zero:

```
unsigned int x;
  . . .
if (x > 0) {
  . . .
}
```

`lint` feels that this is a little weird, so it flags the comparison.

lint Options

The following command line options are recognized by `lint`. Those marked with a † are new to System V Release 2:

- `-a`   Suppress warnings about possible truncation of `longs` assigned to `ints` (not used on machines where `ints` are the same size as `longs`).

- `-b`   Suppress warnings about `break` statements that can't be reached (a condition often produced by `lex` and `yacc`).

-c[†]   For each `.c` file specified, create a `.ln` file that contains the output of `lint`'s first pass. These files may be given to `lint` at a later time to produce the list of inter-routine inconsistencies. `-c` is useful in creating a local `lint` library or for use with `make` where only files that change are run through the first pass of `lint`. (Note: Previous versions of `lint` interpret the `-c` option differently.)

-D*var*[†]   Define preprocessor variable *var*, optionally assigning it a value. Same as for the `cc` command.

-g[†]   Ignored. Implemented for compatibility with the `cc` command.

-h   Suppress warnings about wasteful constructs and possible bugs (e.g., comparison of two constants).

-I*dir*[†]   Search *dir* for include files before `/usr/include`. Same as for the `cc` command.

-l*lib*   Use the library *lib* as well as the Standard C Library.

-n   Do not check file(s) against the Standard C Library or the portable `lint` library.

-o*lib*[†]   Ignored. Implemented for compatibility with the `cc` command.

-o*lib*[†]   Create a file in `/usr/lib` named `llib-l`*lib*`.ln`. The same as the `-c` option, but causes output file to go to `/usr/lib`. This option requires write permission on the directory `/usr/lib`. (`lint` libraries are covered in the next section.)

-p   Check portability of program to other operating systems. All nonexternal names are truncated to eight characters, and all external names are truncated to six characters and converted to one case. Also, instead of using the Standard C `lint` library, the portable `lint` library is used. (The portable `lint` library contains a portable subset of standard I/O and standard C functions.)

-U*var*[†]   Undefine preprocessor variable *var*. Same as for the `cc` command.

-u   Suppress warnings about functions and external variables that are defined but not used or used but not defined. Typically used when checking a few files from a large programming system.

-v   Suppress warnings about unused arguments in functions.

-x   Suppress warnings about unused external variables. Useful if include files declare lots of externals that don't get used.

When `lint` runs, it defines the preprocessor variable `lint`. This may be used by `#ifdef`'s in the program to change or remove code that would otherwise cause `lint` to print a warning message. Also, certain C comments are recognized by `lint`:

`/*NOTREACHED*/`	Causes `lint` to assume that the following statement(s) is never executed (and consequently `lint` suppresses warnings about it). It is placed before code that cannot be reached; `lint` doesn't know about `exit`, `exec`, `longjmp`, and other routines that do not return.
`/*VARARGSn*/`	Informs `lint` that the following function declaration may be called with a variable number of arguments, like `printf`. `lint` will perform type checking of the first n arguments. If n is not specified, it is assumed to be zero.
`/*ARGSUSED*/`	Causes `lint` to suppress warnings about unused arguments in the following function (turns on `-v` option for just this function).
`/*LINTLIBRARY*/`	When placed at beginning of the file, it is the same as using `-v` and `-x` options. Used in `lint` libraries to suppress messages about unused functions and function arguments.

Some versions of `lint` differ in which warning messages you will get by default. The differences have to do with portability issues that won't affect you on that system. For example, assigning a `long` to an `int` may cause loss of information if `int`s are smaller than `long`s on your system. Therefore, on systems where `int`s are smaller than `long`s, (e.g., IBM-PCs and PDP-11s) `lint` will produce a warning, and on systems where the two are the same size (e.g., VAX and 3B20), `lint` will be silent. The `-p` option to `lint` forces it to be pickier about such things:

```
$ cat port.c
main ()
{
    long L1 = 0;
    int i1 = 0;

    i1 = L1;
}
$ lint port.c
$ lint -p port.c

port.c
===============
warning: conversion from long may lose accuracy
    (6)
```

The -p option also forces lint to check the program against the portable C library, not the Standard C and Standard I/O Libraries. The routines in the portable C library are a subset of Standard C and Standard I/O. The following routines are in the portable C library:

calloc	exit	fclose	fdopen	fflush	fgetc
fgets	fopen	fprintf	fputc	fputs	fread
free	freopen	fscanf	fwrite	malloc	mktemp
printf	realloc	rewind	scanf	setbuf	signal
sprintf	sscanf	strcat	strchr	strcmp	strcpy
strcspn	strlen	strncat	strncmp	strncpy	strpbrk
strrchr	strspn	strtok	time	ungetc	

Creating Your Own lint Library

A lint library is simply a file used by lint that contains declarations and information about routines in a C library. For example, consider the routine putchar. In the Standard I/O Library, it is declared to take an int argument and return an int. For the purposes of lint, the only information needed about this routine (which we assume is completely debugged, so lint doesn't have to be run on the whole thing) is the following:

```
int putchar (c)
int c;
{
    return (0);
}
```

This routine is only a skeleton of putchar; however, it's enough information for `lint` to perform the necessary type checking for argument type and return value. If you were to look at the `lint` library for standard C, you'd see similar information for all the standard I/O, standard C, and UNIX system routines.

Knowing this, you can create your own `lint` library:

```
$ cat mylib.c
/*LINTLIBRARY*/

int foo1 (x, y)
int x, y;
{
    return (0);
}


/*VARARGS2*/
void foo2 (x, y, z)
char *x;
int y, z;
{
}
$ lint -c mylib.c
$ cat testlib.c
main ()
{
    int j = 0;
    char c = 'a', *foo1 (), *cptr;

    cptr = foo1 (c, j);
    j = foo2 (j);
}
$ lint testlib.c mylib.ln

testlib.c
===============
(6)  warning: cptr set but not used in function main


===============
value type used inconsistently
    foo1     mylib.c(5) :: testlib.c(6)
value type declared inconsistently
    foo1     mylib.c(5) :: testlib.c(6)
function argument ( number ) used inconsistently
    foo2( arg 1 )      mylib.c(13) :: testlib.c(7)
function value is used, but none returned
    foo2
```

Note that the /*VARARGS2*/ tells lint that the foo2 function takes a variable number of arguments, but that there must be at least two, a character pointer and an integer; any other arguments are optional, and their types are not checked.

The lint -c mylib.c creates the file mylib.ln, which is a lint library and can be subsequently used when running lint on testlib.c or any other program that uses the functions in mylib.c.

lint tells us that foo1 is used and declared inconsistently: it's an int in the library and a char * in main. foo2 is called with an incorrect first argument: it's supposed to be a char *, not an int. foo2 is declared to be void, but a return value is assumed in main. Note that lint doesn't complain about calling foo1 with a char instead of an int. lint knows that chars are converted to ints in expressions, so foo1 is actually passed the value of c as an int.

If you wanted to install this library in the system's library directory, /usr/lib, simply use the -o option instead of -c. You must specify to the -o option the name you'd like to give the library. The library is installed in /usr/lib with the name llib-l*name*.ln (note that this requires that you have write permission on the /usr/lib directory):

```
# lint -omylib mylib.c
# ls -l /usr/lib/*.ln
-rw-r--r-- 1 bin   bin   8226 Jan  3 16:51 /usr/lib/llib-lc.ln
-rw-r--r-- 1 bin   bin   1038 Jan  3 16:51 /usr/lib/llib-lm.ln
-rw-r--r-- 1 root  root   232 Jun  1 10:23 /usr/lib/llib-lmylib.ln
-rw-r--r-- 1 bin   bin   1828 Jan  3 16:51 /usr/lib/llib-port.ln
```

Now mylib may be requested by simply specifying it with the -l option:

```
$ lint testlib.c -lmylib

testlib.c
==============
(6)  warning: cptr set but not used in function main


==============
value type used inconsistently
    foo1      mylib.c(5) :: testlib.c(6)
value type declared inconsistently
    foo1      mylib.c(5) :: testlib.c(6)
function argument ( number ) used inconsistently
    foo2( arg 1 )      mylib.c(13) :: testlib.c(7)
function value is used, but none returned
    foo2
```

To give you a flavor of what `lint` libraries look like, let's take a look at a few lines from the standard C `lint` library (`/usr/lib/llib-lc`):

```
        /*LINTLIBRARY*/
long    time(t) long *t; {return((long) 0);}
FILE    *fopen(path, typ) char *path, *typ; { return((FILE *) 0); }
int     getc(fp) FILE *fp; { return(0); }
int     getchar() { return(0); }
        /*VARARGS1*/
int     scanf(fmt) char *fmt; { return(0); }
        /*VARARGS2*/
int     fscanf(fp, fmt ) FILE *fp; char *fmt; { return(0); }
        /*VARARGS2*/
int     sscanf(s, fmt) char *s, *fmt; { return(0); }
char    *strcpy(s1, s2) char *s1, *s2; { return(s1); }
```

As is usual in standard `lint` libraries, each routine is defined on a single line.

As you have seen in this section, `lint` performs a lot of cross-checking between program files and libraries, something the C compiler doesn't do; it also performs cross-checking between multiple program files, checking argument types and return values. For more information on `lint`, refer to [1].

▪ Debugging with the C Preprocessor ▪

The C preprocessor may be used to insert debugging code into your program. By appropriate use of `#ifdef`, the debugging code can be enabled or disabled at your discretion. The following is a program (admittedly contrived) that reads in three integers and prints out their sum. Note that when the preprocessor identifier `DEBUG` is defined, the debugging code (which prints to `stderr`) is compiled with the rest of the program, and when `DEBUG` isn't defined, the debugging code is left out.

```
$ cat debug.c
#include <stdio.h>

#define DEBUG

main (argc, argv)
int argc;
char *argv[];
{
    int i, j, k, nread;

    nread = scanf ("%d %d %d", &i, &j, &k);

#ifdef DEBUG
    fprintf (stderr, "Number of integers read = %d\n", nread);
    fprintf (stderr, "i = %d, j = %d, k = %d\n", i, j, k);
#endif

    printf ("%d\n", process (i, j, k));
}

int process (i, j, k)
int i, j, k;
{
    return (i + j + k);
}
$ cc debug.c
$ a.out
1 2 3
Number of integers read = 3
i = 1, j = 2, k = 3
6
$ a.out 1 2 e
Number of integers read = 2
i = 1, j = 2, k = 0
3
```

The statements

```
#ifdef DEBUG
    fprintf (stderr, "Number of integers read = %d\n", nread);
    fprintf (stderr, "i = %d, j = %d, k = %d\n", i, j, k);
#endif
```

are analyzed by the preprocessor. If the identifier DEBUG has been previously defined (#ifdef DEBUG), the preprocessor sends the statements that follow up to the #endif (the two fprintfs), to the compiler to be compiled. If DEBUG hasn't been defined, the two fprintfs never make it to the compiler (they're removed from the program by the preprocessor). As you can see, the program prints out messages after it reads in the integers. The second time the program is run, an invalid character is entered (e). The debugging output informs you of the error. Note that to turn off the debugging code, all you have to do is remove the line

```
#define DEBUG
```

and the fprintfs won't be compiled with the rest of the program. Although this program is so short you may not feel it's worth the bother, consider how easy it is to turn debugging code on and off in a program several hundreds (or thousands) of lines long by simply changing one line.

You can even control the debugging from the command line when the program is compiled. The command

```
$ cc -DDEBUG debug.c
```

runs the C compiler on the file debug.c, *defining the preprocessor variable DEBUG for you.* So this is equivalent to putting the line

```
#define DEBUG
```

in the program.

Let's take a look at a slightly longer program. This program takes two options, -f and -g. Each of these options requires that an integer value follow it, and the value is assigned to the corresponding variable (f or g). The program reads an integer from standard input and calls the process routine, which returns the value read times f plus g. As you can see, when the DEBUG identifier is defined, various debugging messages are printed, and when it isn't defined, only the result is printed.

```
$ cat pre1.c
#include <stdio.h>

int f = 0, g = 0;

main (argc, argv)
int argc;
char *argv[];
{
    extern char *optarg;
    int a;
    char c;

    while ((c = getopt (argc, argv, "f:g:")) != EOF)
        switch (c) {
            case 'f':
                f = atoi (optarg);
                break;
            case 'g':
                g = atoi (optarg);
                break;
            case '?':
                exit (1);
        }

#ifdef DEBUG
    fprintf (stderr, "processed arguments\n");
    fprintf (stderr, "f = %d, g = %d\n", f, g);
#endif
    scanf ("%d", &a);
    printf ("%d\n", process (a));
}

int process (val)
int val;
{
#ifdef DEBUG
    fprintf (stderr, "process (%d)\n", val);
#endif
    val = val * f + g;
#ifdef DEBUG
    fprintf (stderr, "return (%d)\n", val);
#endif
    return (val);
}
```

```
$ cc -DDEBUG pre1.c                    Compile with DEBUG defined
$ a.out -f5 -g10
processed arguments
f = 5, g = 10
15
process (15)
return (85)
85
$ cc pre1.c                            Compile without DEBUG defined
$ a.out -f1 -g2
10
12
```

When the program is ready for distribution, the debugging statements may be left in the source without affecting the code, as long as DEBUG isn't defined. If a bug is found at some later time, the debugging code can be turned on and the output examined to see what's going on.

The above method is still rather clumsy, since the programs themselves tend to be difficult to read. One thing you can do about that is change the way the preprocessor is used. You can define a macro that produces debugging output:

```
#define DEBUG(fmt, arg)  fprintf (stderr, fmt, arg)
```

and use it instead of fprintf:

```
DEBUG ("process (%d)\n", val);
```

This gets evaluated as

```
fprintf (stderr, "process (%d)\n", val);
```

This macro can be used throughout a program, and the intent is quite clear:

```
$ cat pre2.c
#include <stdio.h>

#define DEBUG(fmt, arg)   fprintf (stderr, fmt, arg)

int f = 0, g = 0;

main (argc, argv)
int argc;
char *argv[];
{
    int a;
    extern char *optarg;
    char c;
```

```
        while ((c = getopt (argc, argv, "f:g:")) != EOF)
            switch (c) {
                case 'f':
                    f = atoi (optarg);
                    break;
                case 'g':
                    g = atoi (optarg);
                    break;
                case '?':
                    exit (1);
            }

        DEBUG ("processed arguments\n", NULL);
        DEBUG ("f = %d, ", f);
        DEBUG ("g = %d\n", g);
        scanf ("%d", &a);
        printf ("%d\n", process (a));
    }

    int process (val)
    int val;
    {
        DEBUG ("process (%d)\n", val);
        val = val * f + g;
        DEBUG ("return (%d)\n", val);
        return (val);
    }
$ cc pre2.c
$ a.out -f1 -g10
processed arguments
f = 1, g = 10
5
process (5)
return (15)
15
```

As you can see, the program is much more readable in this form. Of course, there are some drawbacks: only one variable can be printed out in a single DEBUG statement (macros can't be given a variable number of arguments),

```
    DEBUG ("f = %d, ", f);
    DEBUG ("g = %d\n", g);
```

and two arguments must be given to DEBUG when it's used, even if you're only printing out a simple message.

```
DEBUG ("processed arguments\n", NULL);
```

When you no longer need debugging output, simply define the macro to be nothing:

```
#define DEBUG(fmt, arg)
```

This tells the preprocessor to replace calls to the DEBUG macro with *nothing*, so all uses of DEBUG simply turn into null statements:

```
$ cat pre2.c
#include <stdio.h>

#define DEBUG(fmt, arg)

int f = 0, g = 0;
  . . .
$ cc pre2.c
$ a.out -f1 -g10
5
15
```

You can expand on the notion of the DEBUG macro a little further to allow for both compile-time and execution-time debugging control: Declare a global variable Debug that defines a debugging *level*. All DEBUG statements less than or equal to this level will produce output. DEBUG now takes three arguments, the first is the level:

```
DEBUG (1, "processed arguments\n", NULL);
DEBUG (3, "f = %d, ", f);
DEBUG (3, "g = %d\n", g);
```

If the debugging level is set to 1 or 2, only the first DEBUG statement produces output; if the debugging level is set to 3 or more, all the above DEBUG statements produce output. Usually, the debugging level is set via a command-line option:

```
a.out -d1 -f1 -g10          Set debugging level to 1
a.out -d3 -f1 -g10          Set debugging level to 3
```

The definition for DEBUG is fairly simple:

```
#define DEBUG(level, fmt, arg) \
    if (Debug >= level) \
        fprintf (stderr, fmt, arg)
```

So

```
DEBUG (3, "f = %d, ", f);
```

becomes

```
    if (Debug >= 3)
        fprintf (stderr, "f = %d", f);
```

Again, if DEBUG is defined to be nothing, the DEBUG calls become null statements.

The next program provides all the mentioned features, as well as the ability
to control the definition of DEBUG at compile time.

```
$ cat debug.h
int Debug = 0;

#ifdef DEBON
#   define DEBUG(level, fmt, arg) \
        if (Debug >= level) \
            fprintf (stderr, fmt, arg)
#else
#   define DEBUG(level, fmt, arg)
#endif
$ cat pre3.c
#include <stdio.h>
#include "debug.h"

int f = 0, g = 0;

main (argc, argv)
int argc;
char *argv[];
{
    int a;
    extern char *optarg;
    char c;

    while ((c = getopt (argc, argv, "d:f:g:")) != EOF)
        switch (c) {
            case 'd':   /* set debug level */
                Debug = atoi (optarg);
                break;
            case 'f':
                f = atoi (optarg);
                break;
            case 'g':
                g = atoi (optarg);
                break;
            case '?':
                exit (1);
        }
```

```
    DEBUG (1, "processed arguments\n", NULL);
    DEBUG (3, "f = %d, ", f);
    DEBUG (3, "g = %d\n", g);
    scanf ("%d", &a);
    printf ("%d\n", process (a));
}

int process (val)
int val;
{
    DEBUG (1, "process (%d)\n", val);
    val = val * f + g;
    DEBUG (2, "return (%d)\n", val);
    return (val);
}
```

`$ cc -DDEBON pre3.c`	*Compile with* DEBON *defined*
`$ a.out`	*Default action is no debugging output*
`10`	
`0`	
`$ a.out -d0`	*Debugging level zero also produces no output*
`10`	
`0`	
`$ a.out -d1 -f10`	*Debug level one*
`processed arguments`	
`10`	
`process (10)`	
`100`	
`$ a.out -d2 -f10 -g5`	*Debug level two*
`processed arguments`	
`5`	
`process (5)`	
`return (55)`	
`55`	
`$ a.out -d3 -f1 -g15`	*Debug level three*
`processed arguments`	
`f = 1, g = 15`	
`12`	
`process (12)`	
`return (27)`	
`27`	
`$ a.out -d3 -f5 -g5 2>debug.out`	*Debugging output to* debug.out
`25`	
`130`	
`$ cat debug.out`	
`processed arguments`	
`f = 5, g = 5`	
`process (25)`	
`return (130)`	

```
$ cc pre3.c                          Compile without DEBON defined
$ a.out -d3 -f1 -g15                 Debugging code was compiled out
12
27
```

Note that `a.out -d0` is equivalent to `a.out` in that the debugging level is zero in either case and no debugging output is generated even though the debugging code is still in there.

When `DEBON` is defined to the preprocessor, `DEBUG` is defined to be the proper statements for debugging output; when `DEBON` isn't defined, `DEBUG` is null. The debugging level, `Debug`, is set to zero by default, and is set from the command line with the `-d` option. This produces a two-tiered debugging scheme: debugging code can be compiled in/out of the code, and when compiled in, different debugging levels produce varying amounts of debugging output.

Placing the definition of `DEBUG` in the separate header file `debug.h` makes it available for use by other programs or by different routines in the same program that are kept in different files.

▪ ctrace ▪

`ctrace` was added to UNIX in System V Release 2. It allows you to observe the execution of your program. It inserts output statements throughout your program that print trace messages for each executable statement. `ctrace` is used as a preprocessor for your C program.

```
$ cat div0.c
main (argc, argv)
int argc;
char *argv[];
{
    int a, b, c;


    scanf ("%d %d %d", &a, &b, &c);
    printf ("%d\n", process (a, b, c));
}

int process (val, f, g)
int val, f, g;
{
    val = val / f + g;
    return (val);
}
```

The program reads three integers from standard input and then passes them to the `process` function. That function divides the first argument by the second, adds in the third, and returns the result, which is displayed with `printf`.

Here are two sample runs of the program:

```
$ cc div0.c
$ a.out
10 2 25
30
$ a.out
2 0 1
Illegal instruction -- core dumped
```

Let's use `ctrace` to help determine the cause of the abnormal termination in the second run.

```
$ ctrace div0.c > tr.c
$ cc tr.c
$ a.out
  1 main (argc, argv)
  8     scanf ("%d %d %d", &a, &b, &c); 2 0 1
  9     printf ("%d\n", process (a, b, c));
        /* a == 2 */
        /* b == 0 */
        /* c == 1 */
 12 process (val, f, g)
 15     val = val / f + g;
        /* val == 2 */
        /* f == 0 */
        /* g == 1 */
```

`ctrace` reads in `div0.c`, massages it, and writes the traced version to standard output, which is redirected to `tr.c` (remember that all C source files must end with `.c`). This file is then compiled and executed. As your program executes, each line that is executed is displayed, preceded by its line number from your source file. `ctrace` also shows variable assignments and function arguments as "comments". The trace output indicates that the program died at line 15. Closer examination shows that the statement

```
val = val / f + g;
```

results in a division by zero since the value of `f` is zero.

The following program runs in an infinite loop (take a close look at the `for` statement):

```
$ cat loop.c
main ()
{
    int i;

    for (i = 1000; i > 0; i++) {
        process ();
    }
}

process ()
{
    /* dummy routine */
}
$ ctrace loop.c > trloop.c
$ cc trloop.c
$ a.out
  1 main ()
  5     for (i = 1000; i > 0; i++)
        /* i == 1000 */ {
  6         process ();
 10 process ()
    /* return */
  7     }
  5     for (i = 1000; i > 0; i++)
        /* i == 1001 */ {
  6         process ();
 10 process ()
    /* return */
  7     }
    /* repeating */
    /* still repeating after 1000 times */
    /* still repeating after 2000 times */
    /* still repeating after 3000 times */
    /* still repeating after 4000 times */
    /* still repeating after 5000 times */
    /* still repeating after 6000 times */
    /* still repeating after 7000 times */
BREAK
$
```

Here, ctrace has shown us a problem with the loop.c program: it increments i instead of decrementing it (it's supposed to go from 1000 down to 0). If you look at the output, you see that i starts at 1000 (/* i == 1000 */), but the next time through the loop, i is incremented (/* i == 1001 */), not decremented. ctrace is smart enough not to inundate us with output—it turns off tracing inside loops as long as the same statements are being executed in the loop. Every 1000 times through the loop, ctrace informs us it's "still repeating."

Normally, all ctrace output goes to standard output; however, the -p option may be used to change the way output is produced. The default print statement is printf(. The argument following -p replaces this default, so

```
ctrace -p "fprintf(stderr," xyz.c > trxyz.c
```

will cause the trace output from trxyz.c to go to standard error.

ctrace has its disadvantages: it produces copious amounts of output, and it can't be used on large programs (on some systems "large" is only about 200 lines) because it creates huge C programs that are too big for some compilers. ctrace does have some options you can use to reduce the amount of output it produces. The -s option suppresses the trace output of simple assignment statements (like the ones shown above).

The -f option may be used to specify one or more functions to trace, so that ctrace will only affect those routines:

```
$ ctrace -f process loop.c > trloop.c
$ ctrace -f foo1 foo2 foo3 foo.c > trfoo.c
```

The first says to trace just the function process in loop.c. The second says to trace just the functions foo1, foo2, and foo3 in foo.c.

The -v option may be used to specify one or more functions **not** to trace:

```
$ ctrace -v process loop.c > trloop.c
$ ctrace -v foo1 foo2 foo3 foo.c > trfoo.c
```

Note that the -f and -v options use up all the command line arguments but the last one, which is assumed to be the program that will be traced. All other options must come **before** the -f or -v option. The following formats will not work:

```
$ ctrace -f "foo1 foo2 foo3" loop.c > trloop.c
$ ctrace -f foo1 -f foo2 -f foo3 loop.c > trloop.c
```

Note also that -f and -v are mutually exclusive.

ctrace also gives you the dynamic ability to turn tracing on and off by calling the routines ctron and ctroff within your program. ctrace defines the preprocessor variable CTRACE, which may be used with ctron and ctroff to turn tracing on and off at a particular debugging level:

```
$ cat pre4.c
#include <stdio.h>
#include "debug.h"

int f = 0, g = 0;

main (argc, argv)
int argc;
char *argv[];
{
    int a;
    extern char *optarg;
    char c;

#ifdef CTRACE
    ctroff ();
#endif

    while ((c = getopt (argc, argv, "d:f:g:")) != EOF)
        switch (c) {
            case 'd':
                Debug = atoi (optarg);
#ifdef CTRACE
                if (Debug >= 5)
                    ctron ();
#endif
                break;
            case 'f':
                f = atoi (optarg);
                break;
            case 'g':
                g = atoi (optarg);
                break;
            case '?':
                exit (1);
        }

    DEBUG (1, "processed arguments\n", NULL);
    DEBUG (3, "f = %d, ", f);
    DEBUG (3, "g = %d\n", g);
    scanf ("%d", &a);
    printf ("%d\n", process (a));
}
```

```
int process (val)
int val;
{
    DEBUG (1, "process (%d)\n", val);
    val = val * f + g;
    DEBUG (2, "return (%d)\n", val);
    return (val);
}
```

If `ctrace` is being used, `ctroff` is called to turn off tracing until the debugging level is determined:

```
#ifdef CTRACE
    ctroff ();
#endif
```

If the debugging level is 5 or more, tracing is turned back on:

```
#ifdef CTRACE
    if (Debug >= 5)
        ctron ();
#endif
```

If you have `ctrace` on your system, we urge you to try it out; however, be forewarned: any but the most trivial programs will produce enormous amounts of trace information. For tracing program execution, you may prefer to use `sdb`.

▪ sdb ▪

`sdb` is a *symbolic debugger*, meaning that it allows programs to be debugged using constructs in the C language, as opposed to debuggers that use assembly language constructs. `sdb` may be used to control the execution of C programs: it allows you to run your program, stop at a predetermined location, display and/or set variables, and continue execution. It allows you to trace your program's execution (like `ctrace`) and even execute it one line at a time. `sdb` also has a facility for determining where *core dumps* occur. A core dump occurs due to receipt of certain signals (see the **Signals** section in Chapter 5), resulting in the creation of a file named `core` that contains a snapshot of the contents of the process' memory at the time it terminated.

Your C program must be compiled with the `-g` option to make full use of `sdb`'s features. The `-g` option causes the C compiler to add extra information to the output file, including variable and structure types, source file names, and C statement to machine code mapping:

```
$ cc -g loop.c                          Infinite loop program from previous section
$ sdb
No core image
*
```

Up to three arguments may be given to sdb: the executable program (defaults to a.out), a core file (defaults to core), and the directory or directories where the source files for the program are located (defaults to the current directory). Here, sdb is run without any arguments, so a.out is used as the program to debug, and core is assumed to be the core file. Since it doesn't exist, sdb prints out a warning message when it starts. The current directory is assumed to contain the program file. When it's ready for user interaction, sdb prints a * as a prompt.

We'll try to debug this program with a few simple sdb commands. The r command is used to run the program being debugged. When typed in, the program runs to completion or until a signal (e.g., *BREAK* or *DELETE*) is received:

```
*r
a.out                                   Wait a few seconds
BREAK
Interrupt (2) (sig 2)
 at
main:5:for (i = 1000; i > 0; i++) {
*
```

sdb caught the interrupt from the keyboard and stopped the program at line 5 in main. We can now use the / command, along with a variable name, to list the contents of the variable i (note that the variable name is placed *before* the / command):

```
*i/
12793
*
```

i is obviously too big, so we've found the problem. We can check out the loop termination condition by setting i with the ! command and continue execution until completion with the c command:

```
*i!-1                                   Set i to -1
*i/                                     Verify that i is -1
-1
*c                                      Continue execution
Process terminated
*
```

This simple example shows a small part of the power and flexibility of sdb.

Note that sdb knows to print i as an integer. In general, it will print a variable according to its declared type: an integer variable in an integer format, a float and a double in a floating point format, a character pointer as a null-terminated string (starting from the location pointed to by the pointer), and so on.

Working with Variables

sdb has three basic commands that allow you to work with variables in your program. Two you've seen already, / and !. The third variable command is the = command, which prints out the address (in memory) of the variable; most of the time, you won't need to use this command, since sdb can usually be used without knowing or caring what the address of a variable or instruction is.

All three of these commands are preceded by a variable specification. The simplest specification is just the name of the variable (like i in the previous section):

```
*i/                                    Display contents of i
0
*i=                                    Display address of i
0x2068
*
```

A variable specified in this fashion must be accessible to the *current procedure*. sdb maintains an idea of a current line (like an editor), a current file (the source file of the program), and a current procedure. If sdb starts up without a core file, the current procedure is main, the current file is the one that contains main, and the current line is the first executable line in main; otherwise, the current line, file, and procedure are set to the location where the program aborted.

If a local variable with the specified name doesn't exist, sdb looks for an external variable of the same name. In the previous example, the current procedure after sdb caught the signal was main, and i was a variable local to main. If sdb were to stop the program in process, then i wouldn't be accessible and

```
*i/
```

would result in the error message:

```
process:i not found
```

A procedure may be specified as part of the variable name in the form

procedure : *variable*

to reference a variable local to a specific routine, e.g.,

```
*main:i/
0
*main:i!0
*
```
           Display contents of i *in* main

           Set value of i *in* main

Note that attempting to set a variable in an inactive routine (i.e., a routine that hasn't been called or has been called but has returned) is an error and results in the following message:

routine `not an active procedure`

Global variables may be specifically referenced as

: *variable*

This forces `sdb` to access an external variable and ignore any local variable of the same name in the current procedure.

     Array elements and structure members may be accessed using standard C syntax. For example, if `array` is an integer array, then `array[0]/` will print the first element of that array, and if `today` is a `date` structure, then `today.year/` will print the `year` member of the structure. If `strptr` is a pointer to a `date` structure, then `strptr->year/` will print the `year` member of the structure pointed to by `strptr`.

     Referencing an array or structure name without an element or member causes the contents of the entire array or structure to be displayed. We'll show you some examples of this soon.

     `sdb` displays variables using information placed in the executable module when `cc -g` is used. This information includes the type of each variable; so `sdb` can distinguish between strings, integers, floats, arrays, structures, etc., and display them properly. You can force `sdb` to display a variable in a different format, say hexadecimal, by following the `/` command with a letter that specifies the format to use:

```
*i!35
*i/x
23
*
```
           Set i *to* 35
           Display i *in hexadecimal*

For a complete list of the formats you can specify to the `/` command, refer to Appendix D.

Attempting to reference the value of a variable with no active process (i.e., nothing executing) is an error, and results in the message

```
main not an active procedure
```

Source File Display

`sdb` provides several commands that give you access to the source files. This enables you to debug the program without having to reference a source listing.

As we mentioned before, `sdb` maintains an idea of what the current line and file are. You may display the area around the current line with the `w` command. `w` displays ten lines around the current line (a *window*). The `p` command simply displays the current line.

If you want, you may change the current line by simply typing in a new line number, which sets the current line to that line in the file. If you precede the line number with a file or procedure name and a colon, e.g.,

`main:5`	*Set current line to line five in procedure* `main`
`loop.c:12`	*Set current line to line 12 in file* `loop.c`

the current line is set to that line in the file or in the file containing the procedure.

You may also change the current line by using the `/` or `?` commands, followed by a regular expression (a pattern). These commands are interpreted in the same manner as the editor `ed`.

`/for`	*Set current line to next one containing "for"*
`?^int`	*Set current line to previous one beginning with "int"*

Typing the `+` command causes the next line in your source file to be displayed and set to the current line, and typing `–` does the same for the previous line.

You may simply change the current file by using the `e` command followed by the file or procedure name that you'd like to make current:

`e main`	*Change current file to one containing* `main`
`e loop.c`	*Change current file to* `loop.c`

If you use `e` without an argument, the current file and procedure names are listed.

Controlling Program Execution

Changing the current line doesn't modify the way a program is executed. You must use other commands for that. You've seen two commands that control the execution of a program in `sdb`: `r`, which runs the program and `c`, which continues the program after a signal is caught.

The r command may be followed with arguments and/or redirection (< or >), and sdb will handle them properly. Subsequent use of the r command without any arguments will reuse the previous arguments and redirection. The R command runs the program without arguments.

The b command may be used to set a *breakpoint* at any line in your program by simply specifying a line number followed by b. When your program runs, sdb will stop it right before the line containing the breakpoint. If you don't specify a line number, the breakpoint is set on the current line; if you specify a line number but no procedure or file name, the breakpoint is set on that line in the current file; if you specify a procedure name without a line number, the breakpoint is set on the first executable line in that procedure:

`*b`	*Set breakpoint on current line*
`*12b`	*Set breakpoint on line 12 in current file*
`*main:12b`	*Set breakpoint on line 12 in* main
`*main:b`	*Set breakpoint on first executable line in* main

When a breakpoint is encountered, sdb suspends execution of your program, returns control to you, and prints out a * prompt. You may do anything you want at this point, display or set variables, set or unset breakpoints, etc. To resume execution of the program, simply use the c command to continue.

Another command you may use to control program execution is the s command. This command *single steps* your program, meaning that *one* line of C code in your program is executed for each s command you enter. If you follow the s command with a number, then that many lines will be executed. Note that a *line* may contain several C *statements*; however, sdb is line oriented, and will execute all statements on a line as a single step. If a statement spans several lines, then single-stepping the first line of the statement will cause all the lines of the statement to be executed. You may single step your program at any time that a continue (c) is appropriate (after a signal or breakpoint).

Let's try out some of sdb's features:

```
$ cat sdbtest.c
struct date {
    int month;
    int day;
    int year;
};

main ()
{
    static struct date today = {10, 11, 1987};
    static int array[5] = {1, 2, 3, 4, 5};
    struct date *newdate, foo ();
    char *string = "test string";
    int i = 3;

    newdate = (struct date *) malloc (sizeof (struct date));

    newdate->month = 11;
    newdate->day = 15;
    newdate->year = 1987;

    today =  foo (today);
}

struct date foo (x)
struct date x;
{
    ++x.day;

    return (x);
}
$ cc -g sdbtest.c
$ sdb a.out
No core image
```

```
*p                          Print current line
7: main () {
*main:b                     Set breakpoint at first executable line in main
main:12 b
*r
a.out
Breakpoint at
main:12:  char *string = "test string";
*s                          Execute line 12
main:13:  int i = 3;
*string/                    Display string
test string
```

```
*array/                              Display array
array[0]/ 1
array[1]/ 2
array[2]/ 3
array[3]/ 4
array[4]/ 5
*array[3]/                           Display array[3]
4
*string[2]/                          Display string[2]
s
*today/                              Display today
today.month/ 10
today.day/ 11
today.year/ 1987
*today.month/                        Display today.month
10
*i/                                  Display i
0                                    i isn't set yet
*s                                   Execute line 13
main:15:  newdate = (struct date *) malloc (sizeof (struct date));
*i/
3
*s 3                                 Single step 3 lines
main:19:  newdate->year = 1987;
*newdate->month/                     Print member month
11
*newdate->year/                      Print member year
0                                    Not set yet
*foo:b                               Set breakpoint at start of foo
0x8e (foo: 25+0xa) b
*c                                   Continue execution
Breakpoint at
0x8e in foo:25: {
*x/                                  Display argument
x.month/ 10
x.day/ 11
x.year/ 1987
*today/                              Display today
foo:today not found
*main:today/                         Display today in main
today.month/ 10
today.day/ 11
today.year/1897
*
```

Note one feature of sdb: it always lists the line that *will be executed* when it begins execution again, not the last executed line.[†] That's why i was still zero the first time it was displayed. Single stepping one line caused it to be initialized. Also note that declarations that initialize automatic variables are considered executable lines (they actually do cause the compiler to produce executable code).

The $m command is preceded by a variable; it causes your program to single step *until the specified variable is modified*. Although this command is very useful, it is also quite expensive in terms of processing time because sdb must execute each line one at a time, checking after each one to see if the specified variable has changed. An example follows the next paragraph.

The v command is very useful when single stepping a program. It controls how much information sdb displays when it's single stepping more than one line at a time. 1v turns on first level verbose mode: each C line is displayed before it is executed. 2v turns on second level verbose mode; each C line and assembly statement is displayed before it is executed. Using v without a level when verbose mode is off turns on the default verbose mode; the current procedure and file name is displayed when it changes. Using v without a level when verbose mode is on turns it off.

```
$ sdb a.out
No core image
*main:b                        Set breakpoint at first executable line in main
main:12 b
*r
a.out
Breakpoint at
main:12:  char *string = "test string";
*1v                            Turn on verbosity level 1
*newdate$m                     Single step until newdate changes
[sdbtest.c]
main:12:  char *string = "test string";
main:13:  int i = 3;
main:15:  newdate = (struct date *) malloc (sizeof (struct date));
Prev stmt changed loc 0xc0200 [main:newdate]
                  from 0(0) to 131680(0x20260).
main:17:  newdate->month = 11;
*newdate->year$m
[sdbtest.c]
main:17:  newdate->month = 11;
main:18:  newdate->day = 15;
main:19:  newdate->year = 1987;
Prev stmt changed loc 0x20268 [newdate->year]
                  from 0(0) to 1987(0x7c3).
main:21:  today = foo (today);
*
```

[†] sdb's l command can be used at any time to list the next line it will execute. This is often useful after you've been examining different portions of your program and you want to verify where sdb will resume execution when you type a c or s command.

A breakpoint is set at the first executable statement of main, and the program is started. When the breakpoint is reached, verbose mode 1 is turned on and the program is single stepped until newdate changes. Each line is displayed before being executed, and when the assignment to newdate is reached, sdb prints the message that the line changed main:newdate. The program is continued, this time until newdate->year is modified.

Once set, breakpoints remain in a program until sdb exits or until you delete them. The B command lists all breakpoints, and the D command deletes *all* breakpoints. The d command may be preceded with a line number, and the breakpoint at that line is deleted. If no line number is specified, each breakpoint will be listed and a line read from the terminal; if the line begins with a y or a d, then that breakpoint will be deleted.

```
*B                              List breakpoints
main:12
0x8e (foo: 25+0xa)
*d                              Delete breakpoints
main:12 ?RETURN                 Don't delete
0x8e (foo: 25+0xa) ?y           Delete
*B                              See what's left
main:12
*
```

When setting breakpoints, one or more sdb commands can follow the b command, in which case those commands will get executed whenever the breakpoint is reached:

```
*15b i/
```

This says to display the value of i whenever line 15 is to be executed. Note that with this form of the b command, control does not go back to you when the breakpoint is reached; sdb simply executes the command and then resumes execution of the program. Multiple commands can be specified by delimiting them with semicolons:

```
*foo:b x/;i!0
```

This says to display the value of x and to set the variable i to zero whenever the function foo is entered.

If you're finished with a program that is stopped due to a signal or breakpoint, you may kill it with the k command. You exit sdb with the q command:

```
$ sdb a.out
No core image
*main:b                         Set breakpoint at first line in main
```

```
main:12 b
*r
a.out
Breakpoint at
main:12:  char *string = "test string";
*s 5
main:19:  newdate->year = 1987;
*array/
array[0]/ 1
array[1]/ 2
array[2]/ 3
array[3]/ 4
array[4]/ 5
*today/
today.month/ 10
today.day/ 11
today.year/ 1987
*k
17945: Killed
*q
$
```

Producing a Stack Trace

As we mentioned earlier, sdb is useful in determining where a program aborted and produced a core dump. The t command produces a "stack trace" from the core file, showing you the routine where the error occurred, all the routines called to get there, and all of the values the routines were called with.

Recall the div0.c program:

```
$ cat div0.c
main (argc, argv)
int argc;
char *argv[];
{
    int a, b, c;


    scanf ("%d %d %d", &a, &b, &c);
    printf ("%d\n", process (a, b, c));
}
```

```
int process (val, f, g)
int val, f, g;
{
    val = val / f + g;
    return (val);
}
$ cc -g div0.c
$ a.out
11 x2 33
Illegal instruction - core dumped
$ sdb
process:15:   val = val / f * g;
*t
process(val=11,f=0,g=0)    [div0.c:15]
main(1,786680,786688)    [div0.c:9]
*
```

After the core file is created, sdb is run. It tells you that the error occurred on line 15 (now the current line). The t command shows you that process was called with f and g equal to zero. Looking back at the input to the program, you'll see that the second value was x2, which caused scanf to return without assigning anything to b or c.

This ability to determine where a program aborted and what the arguments to routines along the way are is extremely useful in debugging large programs where the flow of execution through various routines isn't obvious.

Other Features of sdb

sdb intercepts all signals, whether they're generated from the keyboard (e.g., the *DELETE* key is pressed), or from your program (e.g., an alarm signal due to a sleep finishing).   sdb's action is to suspend execution of your program, list the signal that was received at the terminal, and turn control over to you to enter sdb commands.

Normally, when you're ready to continue execution of the suspended program, you'll use the c command. This causes the program to continue *without* passing the signal to the program.

Sometimes, you may want to see how the program handles signals; in that case, you can use the C command, which will cause the program to continue with the signal that stopped it. For example, suppose a program calls sleep to suspend itself for a while. When the alarm interrupt that sleep schedules is received, control returns to sdb. Restarting this program with c will cause it to continue *without* receiving the alarm signal, causing it to stay asleep indefinitely. Restarting it with C will cause the program to receive the signal, return from sleep, and continue execution as was intended.

You can call any routine in your program from `sdb` simply by entering a call to the routine, e.g.,

```
*process (a, b, 100)
*
```

Arguments to the routine may be any integer, character, or string constant, or any variable accessible from the current procedure. If the call is followed by a /, the return value of the routine is displayed in integer format:

```
*process (a, b, 100)/
121
*
```

If the / is followed by a format specification, the return value is displayed according to that format. Refer to Appendix D for more information on the formats `sdb` supports.

Table 8-1 lists the `sdb` commands covered in this chapter.

There are some applications that `sdb` isn't good at debugging. Real-time applications like video controllers often have events that take place too quickly for `sdb` to control; programs that use screen manipulation routines like `curses` leave the screen in a strange state when interrupted, and usually don't refresh the screen when restarted; child processes can't be controlled with `sdb`, so programs that call `fork` usually can't be handled. In all of these cases, there are other ways of following the execution of the programs, either with `ctrace` or with debugging statements embedded in the code. Even a `curses` program can write debugging messages to a file (never to the screen!); or you can use `ctrace -p 'fprintf(stderr,'` to have the tracing messages sent to standard error, and then you simply redirect standard error to a file.

There are other debugging tools available on most UNIX systems: `adb` is like `sdb` in many ways, except that it debugs programs at the machine language level. It's useful, but only as a last resort if you don't have `sdb`. `dbx` is a symbolic debugger with the same capabilities as `sdb`. It has a more verbose (and perhaps easier to understand) user interface; however, it is only available on BSD 4.2 and later versions of Berkeley UNIX. For more information on `dbx`, refer to [2] and [3]. `cflow` produces a subroutine calling graph, printing a list of routines, and the routines they call, etc. It can be useful in determining the structure of an unfamiliar program. The `pi` debugger allows you to debug programs using multiple windows on an AT&T 5620 or BLIT terminal. It allows you to execute the program in one window, control it from another, and look at the source and machine code in other windows. Unfortunately, the `pi` debugger is only available on the Eighth Edition UNIX System, and some in-house AT&T System V Release 2 versions of UNIX; in time, however, `pi` should find its way into the commercial marketplace. For more information on `pi`, refer to [4]. For more information on `sdb`, refer to [2], [3], and [5].

TABLE 8-1. Common sdb commands

Command	Meaning
var / *fmt*	Display contents of *var* using format *fmt*, where *var* may be of the form *variable-name*, *procedure* : *variable-name*, or : *variable-name*; default format is taken from type of variable being displayed
var ! *val*	Assign *val* to *var*
var=	Display address of *var*
num	Display line number *num*
proc : *num*	Display line number *num* in the file containing procedure *proc*
file : *num*	Display line number *num* in *file*
/ *string*	Display the next line containing *string*
?*string*	Display the previous line containing *string*
+	Display the next line
–	Display the previous line
p	Display the current line
l	Display the next line to be executed
w	Display 10 lines around the current line
r *args*	Run program with (optional) *args* as arguments; if no *args* given, run with previous arguments (if any); redirection (with < and >) is also allowed
R	Run program without arguments
c	Continue program without signal that stopped program
C	Continue program with signal that stopped program
*line*b*cmd(s)*	Set breakpoint at *line*, where *line* may be of the form *line-number*, *file* : *line-number*, *procedure* : *line-number*, *file* : , or *procedure* : If *cmd(s)* is supplied, then execute *cmd(s)* when breakpoint is reached (and don't return control to user).
B	List all breakpoints
D	Delete all breakpoints
*line*d	Delete breakpoint at *line*; if *line* isn't specified, interactively delete breakpoints
s *num*	Single step *num* lines; default is one
var$m	Single step until *var* changes
*level*v	Set single step debugging print level to *level*; if no *level* specified, toggles debugging on/off
t	Print stack trace
k	Kill currently running process
function (*args*)	Call *function* with *args* as parameters.
function (*args*) / *fmt*	Call *function* with *args* as parameters; print returned value using *fmt* as format; default format is integer
q	Quit sdb

Most people develop schemes for debugging programs, usually something like this:

1. Once the program passes the C compiler, run it through `lint`.

2. Use the preprocessor to insert debugging code; some people like to make this (1) so that the debugging code is in the program from the start.

3. Use `ctrace` for small programs or for one or two functions.

4. Use `sdb` as your main debugging tool; it's the most powerful debugging tool generally available on UNIX.

5. On systems without `sdb`, use `adb` as a last restort.

As you become more experienced at debugging your programs, you'll learn which debugging methods are best suited for various situations.

▪ References ▪

[1]   S. C. Johnson, "Lint: a C Program Checker," *System V Programmer's Manual,* AT&T Bell Laboratories.

[2]   B. Tuthill, "Debuggers: Part 1," *UNIX World,* Vol. 4 No. 1, January 1987, pp. 69-73.

[3]   B. Tuthill, "Debuggers: Part 2," *UNIX World,* Vol. 4 No. 2, February 1987, pp. 83-86.

[4]   T. Cargill, "Debugging C Programs with the Blit," *AT&T Bell Laboratories Technical Journal,* Vol 63 No.8, Part 2, October 1984, pp. 1633-1647.

[5]   H. Katseff, "Sdb: A Symbolic Debugger," *UNIX Programmer's Manual 4.2 BSD User Document,* Computer Science Division, Department of EECS, University of California, Berkeley, CA.

E X E R C I S E S

1. Run the following program through `lint` and explain the results.

    ```
    main ()
    {
        int number, j;

        scanf ("%d", &number);

        if (number & 1 == 0)
            printf ("%d is even\n", number);
        else
            printf ("%d is odd\n", number);
    }
    ```

2. Run the above program through `ctrace`. Explain why `ctrace` doesn't find the problem.

3. The preprocessor recognizes two special names: `_ _LINE_ _` and `_ _FILE_ _`. These are defined as the current source file line number, and the current source file name, respectively. Extend the `DEBUG` macro on page 461 so that it writes the name of the source file and the line number to standard error. Use this new version of `DEBUG` with program `pre3.c` (pp. 462-463).

4. Run `ctrace` and `sdb` on `pre3.c` (pp. 462-463). Single step the program in `sdb` and examine the output.

5. Run some of the other programs in this book through `lint`. Don't forget to use `-lcurses` (and `-ltermcap` if you're not running AT&T's `curses`) for the programs in Chapter 6.

6. Run one of your own programs through `lint`, `ctrace`, and `sdb`. Set breakpoints at various locations, print variable values, and single step the program a few lines. Also, include `debug.h` and add calls to the `DEBUG` macro as appropriate. Now check the various levels of debugging.

A

`ioctl` MODES

The following tables list the various fields in the `termio` structure used by `ioctl`:

TABLE A-1. `c_cc` array elements

Flag	Subscript	Meaning
INTR	0	Interrupt character
QUIT	1	Quit character
ERASE	2	Erase character
KILL	3	Line kill character
EOF	4	End of file character
EOL	5	End of line character
SWTCH	7	Process suspend character, used to switch between layers
MIN	4	Minimum number of characters that must be input before `read` returns (raw mode only)
TIME	5	Maximum time in tenths of a second to wait before `read` returns (raw mode only)

TABLE A-2. `c_lflag` fields

Flag	Value	Meaning
ISIG	01	Enable signals
ICANON	02	Turn on canonical input processing
XCASE	04	Convert uppercase char to \char
ECHO	010	Echo characters
ECHOE	020	Echo erase character as backspace-space-backspace
ECHOK	040	Echo *NEWLINE* after line kill character
ECHONL	0100	Echo *NEWLINE* even if ECHO is off
NOFLSH	0200	Don't flush input and output on receipt of quit, interrupt, or switch

TABLE A-3. `c_iflag` fields

Flag	Value	Meaning
IGNBRK	01	Ignore *BREAK*
BRKINT	02	Allow *BREAK* to cause interrupt signal
IGNPAR	04	Ignore parity errors
PARMRK	010	Mark parity errors
INPCK	020	Check parity on input
ISTRIP	040	Strip input characters to seven bits
INLCR	0100	Map *NEWLINE* (\n) to *RETURN* (\r) on input
IGNCR	0200	Ignore *RETURN* on input
ICRNL	0400	Map *RETURN* to *NEWLINE* on input
IUCLC	01000	Map uppercase to lowercase on input
IXON	02000	Enable stopping (*CTRL-s*) and restarting (*CTRL-q*) of output
IXANY	04000	Allow any character to restart output
IXOFF	010000	Send *CTRL-s* and *CTRL-q* to control input

TABLE A-4. c_oflag fields

Flag	Value	Meaning
OPOST	01	Postprocess output—if not set, all other c_oflag flags are ignored
OLCUC	02	Map lowercase to uppercase on output
ONLCR	04	Map *NEWLINE* to *RETURN-NEWLINE* on output
OCRNL	010	Map *RETURN* to *NEWLINE* on output
ONOCR	020	Don't *RETURN* in column zero
ONLRET	040	Assume *NEWLINE* forces *RETURN* on output device
OFILL	0100	Send fill characters to perform delay
OFDEL	0200	Set fill character to *DELETE*, otherwise null
NLDLY	0400	Define bits used for *NEWLINE* delay
NL0	0	Don't delay after *NEWLINE*
NL1	0400	Delay approximately .1 seconds after *NEWLINE*
CRDLY	03000	Define bits used for *RETURN* delay
CR0	0	Don't delay after *RETURN*
CR1	01000	Delay after *RETURN* (amount depends upon current column)
CR2	02000	Delay approximately .1 seconds after *RETURN*
CR3	03000	Delay approximately .15 seconds after *RETURN*
TABDLY	014000	Define bits used for tab delay
TAB0	0	Don't delay after tabs
TAB1	04000	Delay after tab (amount depends upon current column)
TAB2	010000	Delay approximately .1 seconds after tab
TAB3	014000	Expand tabs to blanks
BSDLY	020000	Define bits used for backspace delay
BS0	0	Don't delay after backspace
BS1	020000	Delay approximately .05 seconds after backspace
VTDLY	040000	Define bits used for vertical tab delay
VT0	0	Don't delay after vertical tab
VT1	040000	Delay approximately 2 seconds after vertical tab
FFDLY	0100000	Define bits used for form-feed delay
FF0	0	Don't delay after form-feed
FF1	0100000	Delay approximately 2 seconds after form-feed

TABLE A-5. `c_cflag` fields

Flag	Value	Meaning
CBAUD	017	Define bits used for baud rate
B0	0	Hang up
B50	01	Set 50 baud
B75	02	Set 75 baud
B110	03	Set 110 baud
B134	04	Set 134 baud
B150	05	Set 150 baud
B200	06	Set 200 baud
B300	07	Set 300 baud
B600	010	Set 600 baud
B1200	011	Set 1200 baud
B1800	011	Set 1800 baud
B2400	013	Set 2400 baud
B4800	014	Set 4800 baud
B9600	015	Set 9600 baud
EXTA	016	Set external A baud rate
EXTB	017	Set external B baud rate
CSIZE	060	Define bits used for character size
C5	0	Set character size to five bits
C6	020	Set character size to six bits
C7	040	Set character size to seven bits
C8	060	Set character size to eight bits
CSTOPB	0100	Set number of stop bits to two; otherwise, one
CREAD	0200	Enable receiver; if not set, no characters are read
PARENB	0400	Enable parity generation
PARODD	01000	Enable odd parity; otherwise, even
HUPCL	02000	Hang up on last close
CLOCAL	04000	Assume line is local with no modem
LOBLK	010000	Block process output when not in current layer

B

curses ROUTINES

The following summarizes the routines in the AT&T release of curses as of System V Release 2. All routines require the inclusion of curses.h. All routines that return ints return the constant ERR upon error, and routines that return WINDOW pointers return NULL upon error. Routines marked with † may be called when using minicurses, i.e., when compiling with –DMINICURSES. The following variable naming conventions are used:

win, win1, win2	WINDOW pointers
sp	SCREEN pointer
fp	FILE pointer
y, x, y1, x1, y2, x2, y3, x3, ny, nx	ints describing row and column positions
attr	int describing a set of terminal attributes
flag	int that is either **TRUE** or **FALSE**
fd	int file descriptor
c, c1, c2	chars
str	string (char *)
fmt	printf or scanf type format string
arg1, arg2, ...	arguments of any type

`int        addch (c)`[†]
Equivalent to `waddch (stdscr, c)`.

`int        addstr (str)`[†]
Equivalent to `waddstr (stdscr, str)`.

`void       attroff (i)`[†]
Equivalent to `wattroff (stdscr, i)`.

`void       attron (i)`[†]
Equivalent to `wattron (stdscr, i)`.

`void       attrset (i)`[†]
Equivalent to `wattrset (stdscr, i)`.

`int        baudrate ()`[†]
Returns the baud rate of the terminal.

`void       beep ()`[†]
Sounds a beep (ASCII 7) on the terminal.

`void       box (win, c1, c2)`
Draws a box around the window `win` using `c1` as the vertical drawing character and `c2` as the horizontal drawing character. If `c1` and/or `c2` is zero, `box` substitutes ' | ' and ' - ', respectively.

`void       cbreak ()`[†]
Turns on *cbreak* mode; all characters are available as they are typed in (no line buffering on input).

`int        clear ()`
Equivalent to `wclear (stdscr)`.

`void       clearok (win, flag)`
Forces the screen to clear and be redrawn on the next `wrefresh` of `win`.

`void       clrtobot ()`
Equivalent to `wclrtobot (stdscr)`.

`void       clrtoeol ()`
Equivalent to `wclrtoeol (stdscr)`.

`void       delch ()`
Equivalent to `wdelch (stdscr)`.

`void       deleteln ()`
Equivalent to `wdeleteln (stdscr)`.

`void       delwin (win)`
Deletes the window `win`.

`void       doupdate ()`
Performs low level screen refresh; called by `wrefresh`.

void   echo () [†]
Turns on character echo on input.

void   endwin () [†]
Cleans up and exits `curses` window mode.

void   erase ()
Equivalent to `werase (stdscr)`.

int   erasechar ()
Returns the user's erase character.

void   fixterm ()
Places terminal back into `curses` state; used after call to `resetterm`.

void   flash ()
Flashes the screen; if flashing isn't possible, beeps.

void   flushinp () [†]
Flushes input character queue.

int   getch () [†]
Equivalent to `wgetch (stdscr)`.

int   getstr (str)
Equivalent to `wgetstr (stdscr, str)`.

int   gettmode ()
Returns terminal stats; called by `initscr`.

void   getyx (win, y, x)
Puts row and column coordinates of cursor in `win` into `y` and `x`.

int   has_ic ()
Returns TRUE if terminal can insert characters.

int   has_il ()
Returns TRUE if terminal can insert lines.

void   idlok (win, flag) [†]
Allows use of the terminal's delete line capability when redrawing `win` if `flag` is TRUE.

int   inch ()
Equivalent to `winch (stdscr)`.

void   initscr () [†]
Initializes `curses` window mode.

void   insch (c)
Equivalent to `winsch (stdscr, c)`.

void   insertln ()
Equivalent to `winsertln (stdscr)`.

```
void      intrflush (win, flag)
```
Allows interrupts to flush the output queue if `flag` is TRUE.

```
void      keypad (win, flag)
```
Allows keypad input if `flag` is TRUE.

```
int       killchar ()
```
Returns user's line kill character.

```
void      leaveok (win, flag)
```
Allows cursor to be left at arbitrary position after refresh of `win` if `flag` is TRUE.

```
char *    longname ()
```
Returns long name of terminal from `terminfo` data base.

```
void      meta (win, flag)
```
[†]
Allows meta (eight-bit) characters on input if `flag` is TRUE.

```
int       move (y, x)
```
[†]
Equivalent to `wmove (stdscr, y, x)`.

```
int       mvaddch (y, x, c)
```
Equivalent to combining `wmove (stdscr, y, x)` and `waddch (stdscr, c)`.

```
int       mvaddstr (y, x, str)
```
Equivalent to combining `wmove (stdscr, y, x)` and `waddstr (stdscr, str)`.

```
int       mvdelch (y, x)
```
Equivalent to combining `wmove (stdscr, y, x)` and `wdelch (stdscr)`.

```
int       mvgetch (y, x)
```
Equivalent to combining `wmove (stdscr, y, x)` and `wgetch (stdscr)`.

```
int       mvgetstr (y, x, str)
```
Equivalent to combining `wmove (stdscr, y, x)` and `wgetch (stdscr, str)`.

```
int       mvinch (y, x)
```
Equivalent to combining `wmove (stdscr, y, x)` and `winch (stdscr)`.

```
int       mvinsch (y, x, c)
```
Equivalent to combining `wmove (stdscr, y, x)` and `winsch (stdscr, c)`.

```
int       mvprintw (y, x, fmt, arg1, arg2, ...)
```
Equivalent to combining `wmove (stdscr, y, x)` and `wprintw (stdscr, fmt, arg1, arg2, ...)`.

```
int       mvscanw (y, x, fmt, arg1, arg2, ...)
```
Equivalent to combining `wmove (stdscr, y, x)` and `wscanw (stdscr, fmt, arg1, arg2, ...)`.

int   mvwaddch (win, y, x, c)
Equivalent to combining wmove (win, y, x) and waddch (win, c).

int   mvwaddstr (win, y, x, str)
Equivalent to combining wmove (win, y, x) and waddstr (win, str).

int   mvwdelch (win, y, x)
Equivalent to combining wmove (win, y, x) and wdelch (win).

int   mvwgetch (win, y, x)
Equivalent to combining wmove (win, y, x) and wgetch (win).

int   mvwgetstr (win, y, x, str)
Equivalent to combining wmove (win, y, x) and wgetch (win, str).

int   mvwin (win, y, x)
Moves window win so that its origin (upperleft corner) is at y, x.

int   mvwinch (win, y, x)
Equivalent to combining wmove (win, y, x) and winch (win).

int   mvwinsch (win, y, x, c)
Equivalent to combining wmove (win, y, x) and winsch (win, c).

int   mvwprintw (win, y, x, fmt, arg1, arg2, ...)
Equivalent to combining wmove (win, y, x) and wprintw (win, fmt, arg1, arg2, ...).

int   mvwscanw (win, y, x, fmt, arg1, arg2, ...)
Equivalent to combining wmove (win, y, x) and wscanw (win, fmt, arg1, arg2, ...).

WINDOW * newpad (ny, nx)
Creates a pad of size ny rows by nx columns.

SCREEN * newterm (str, fp)
Initializes curses for use on terminal of type str associated with the FILE pointer fp. Used in multiterminal curses applications.

WINDOW * newwin (ny, nx, y, x)
Creates a window of size ny rows by nx columns with its origin at y, x.

void   nl ()[†]
Turns on newline mapping on input and output.

void   nocbreak ()[†]
Turns off cbreak mode.

void   nodelay (win, flag)
Turns on nodelay mode if flag is TRUE. wgetch no longer waits if there is no input (allows polling).

void   noecho () [†]
Turns off character echo on input.

void   nonl () [†]
Turns off newline mapping on input and output.

void   noraw () [†]
Turns off raw mode.

void   overlay (win1, win2)
Copies `win1` onto `win2`; blanks in `win1` do not overwrite characters in `win2`.

void   overwrite (win1, win2)
Copies `win1` onto `win2`; blanks in `win1` overwrite characters in `win2`.

void   pnoutrefresh (win, y1, x1, y2, x2, y3, x3)
Performs low level copy of the pad `win` to `curscr`; called by `prefresh`. Arguments are the same as for `prefresh`.

void   prefresh (win, y1, x1, y2, x2, y3, x3)
Refreshes the pad `win` to the screen. `y1`, `x1` specify the upperleft corner of a rectangle *in the pad* that is to be copied to the screen; `y2`, `x2` specify the upperleft corner of the *screen* where the rectangle is to be copied; and `y3`, `x3` specify the lowerright corner of the *screen* where the rectangle is to be copied.

int   printw (fmt, arg1, arg2, ...)
Equivalent to `wprintw (stdscr, fmt, arg1, arg2, ...)`.

void   raw () [†]
Turns on raw mode; all characters are available as they are typed in (no line buffering on input). Different from `cbreak` in that the interrupt and quit characters are ignored, and eight-bit input and output are enabled.

int   refresh () [†]
Equivalent to `wrefresh (stdscr)`.

void   resetterm () [†]
Takes terminal out of `curses` state.

void   resetty () [†]
Resets terminal's state to values saved by `savetty`; called by `endwin`.

void   saveterm () [†]
Saves current `curses` state.

void   savetty () [†]
Saves terminal's state; called by `initscr`.

int   scanw (fmt, arg1, arg2, ...)
Equivalent to `wscanw (stdscr, fmt, arg1, arg2, ...)`.

int   scroll (win)
Scrolls window `win` one line.

void   scrollok (win, flag)
Allows scrolling in win if flag is TRUE.

void   setscrreg (y1, y2)
Equivalent to wsetscrreg (win, y1, y2).

void   set_term (sp)
Changes current terminal to one associated with the SCREEN pointer sp. Used in multiterminal curses applications.

void   setterm (str)
Initializes curses for use with terminal defined in str; called by initscr.

char *   standend () [†]
Equivalent to wstandend (stdscr).

char *   standout () [†]
Equivalent to wstandout (stdscr).

WINDOW * subwin (win, ny, nx, y, x)
Returns a subwindow of win ny rows by nx columns located at y, x on the screen.

void   touchwin (win)
"Touches" every character in win so that it is redrawn when wrefreshed.

void   traceoff ()
Turns off debugging output.

void   traceon ()
Turns on debugging output.

void   typeahead (fd)
Causes curses to perform operations on input queue associated with fd (e.g., flushinp).

char *   unctrl (c) [†]
Returns a printable version of c. Control characters are printed as *^char*; all others are unchanged.

int   waddch (win, c)
Adds character c to the current position in win, overwriting whatever was there. The current position is moved right by one column; if the character is put at the right margin, the current position is moved to the left margin of the next line; if scrolling is enabled, and the character is put at the lowerright corner of the window or a *newline* is output at the bottom of the window, the screen is scrolled one line.

int   waddstr (win, str)
Adds the string str to the current position in win. Equivalent to a series of calls to waddch, one for each character in str.

void   wattroff (win, i)
Turns off terminal attributes specified by i in window win. Attributes include underlining, blinking, inverse-video, bold, and dim.

void   wattron (win, i)
Turns on terminal attributes specified by i in window win.

void   wattrset (win, i)
Sets terminal attributes in window win to i.

int   wclear (win)
Sets the window win to all blanks. If win is stdscr or curscr, the terminal will be cleared before redrawing on the next refresh.

void   wclrtobot (win)
Clears from the current position in win to the bottom of the window. All lines after the current line are cleared, and the current line is cleared from the current column to the end of the line.

void   wclrtoeol (win)
Clears from the current position in win to the end of the line.

void   wdelch (win)
Deletes the character at the current position in win. Each character after it on the line is shifted to the left, and the character at the right margin becomes blank.

void   wdeleteln (win)
Deletes the line at the current position in win. Each line below it in the window is moved up, and the bottom line becomes blank.

void   werase (win)
Sets the window win to all blanks.

int   wgetch (win)
Reads a character. If character echo is turned on, it takes place at the current position in win.

int   wgetstr (win, str)
Reads characters up to a *newline*, placing them in str. Equivalent to a series of calls to wgetch.

int   winch (win)
Returns the character at the current position in win.

void   winsch (win, c)
Inserts the character c at the current position in win. The current character and all characters to the right of the current column are shifted to the right. The character at the right margin is lost.

void   winsertln (win)
Inserts a blank line above the current line. The current line and all lines below it are shifted down. The bottom line is lost.

int   wmove (win, y, x)
Changes the current position in win to y, x.

int   wnoutrefresh (win)
Performs low level copy of win to curscr; called by wrefresh.

int   wprintw (win, fmt, arg1, arg2, ...)
Outputs like printf at current position in win. fmt and arg1, arg2, ... are
treated the same as with printf. waddch is used to output the resulting
characters.

int   wrefresh (win)
Refreshes the window win to the terminal's screen. All portions of win that
have changed since the last refresh are written to the terminal.

int   wscanw (win, fmt, arg1, arg2, ...)
Inputs like gets combined with sscanf. fmt and arg1, arg2, ... are
treated the same as with sscanf. wgetstr is used to read a line of input,
which is passed to wscanf for parsing.

void   wsetscrreg (win, y1, y2)
Sets scrolling region in win, starting at line y1 and ending at line y2. When
this region is set and scrolling is enabled via scrollok, an attempt to scroll off
the bottom of the region (waddch off the end of the bottom line) causes the lines
in the region to be scrolled.

void   wstandend (win)
Ends standout mode in win.

void   wstandout (win)
Starts standout mode in win. All subsequent output to win is done in a distinc-
tive fashion, typically bold or inverse-video.

THE WINDOW EDITOR

```
1    /*******************************************************
2     *                                                     *
3     *                 window editor program               *
4     *                 edits two files in two              *
5     *                 windows; uses curses                *
6     *                                                     *
7     *******************************************************/


8    #include <curses.h>
9    #include <signal.h>

10   /* current line and column */
11   int      curline = 0, curcol = 0;

12   /* current window index */
13   int      icurwin;

14   WINDOW  *ed[2], *curwin;

15   /* files for two windows */
16   char    *file1, *file2;

17   main (argc, argv)
18   int argc;
19   char *argv[];
20   {
21           void  finish ();

22           init (argc, argv);
23           process ();
24           finish ();
25   }
```

```
26    init (argc, argv)
27    int argc;
28    char *argv[];
29    {
30          void finish ();

31          /* needs 2 file names as arguments */
32          if (argc != 3) {
33                  fprintf (stderr, "%s: needs two files\n", argv[0]);
34                  exit (1);
35          }

36          file1 = argv[1];
37          file2 = argv[2];

38          /* call finish if user hits BREAK or DELETE */
39          signal (SIGINT, finish);

40          /* initial setup of curses */
41          initscr ();
42          cbreak ();
43          noecho ();
44          nonl ();

45          /* set up two windows (same size) */
46          ed[0] = newwin (LINES - 1, COLS / 2 - 1, 0, 0);
47          ed[1] = newwin (LINES - 1, COLS / 2 - 1, 0, COLS / 2 + 1);

48          /* draw lines between windows */
49          vline (COLS / 2 - 1);
50          vline (COLS / 2);

51          /* set up screen with files */
52          icurwin = 0;
53          getfile (ed[icurwin], file1);
54          icurwin = 1;
55          getfile (ed[icurwin], file2);

56          /* start with left window current */
57          icurwin = 0;
58          curwin = ed[icurwin];
59    }

60    process ()
61    {
62          int  in;

63          for (;;) {

64                  /* refresh screen */
65                  wmove (curwin, curline, curcol);
66                  wrefresh (curwin);

67                  /* get command and process */
68                  in = getch ();
```

```
69              switch ( in ) {
70                  case 's':           /* switch windows */
71                      curwin = ed[1 - icurwin];
72                      icurwin = 1 - icurwin;
73                      getyx (curwin, curline, curcol);
74                      break;
75                  case 'j':    /* down */
76                      if ( curline != LINES - 2 )
77                          ++curline;
78                      break;
79                  case 'k':    /* up */
80                      if ( curline != 0 )
81                          --curline;
82                      break;
83                  case 'h':     /* left */
84                      if ( curcol != 0 )
85                          --curcol;
86                      break;
87                  case 'l':     /* right */
88                      if ( curcol != COLS / 2 - 2 )
89                          ++curcol;
90                      break;
91                  case 'd':     /* delete line */
92                      wdeleteln (curwin);
93                      break;
94                  case 'a':     /* add chars */
95                      add (curwin);
96                      break;
97                  case 'o':    /* open line below current line */
98                      /* move down a line unless at bottom */
99                      if ( curline != LINES - 2 )
100                         ++curline;
101                     /* ignore 'o' command at bottom */
102                     else
103                         break;
104
105                     curcol = 0;
106                     wmove (curwin, curline, curcol);
107                     winsertln (curwin);
108                     wrefresh (curwin);
109                     add (curwin);
110                     break;
111                 case 'O':    /* open line above current line */
112                     winsertln (curwin);
113                     curcol = 0;
114                     wmove (curwin, curline, curcol);
115                     wrefresh (curwin);
116                     add (curwin);
117                     break;
118                 case 'x':    /* delete character under cursor */
119                     wdelch (curwin);
120                     break;
121                 case 'D':
122                     wclrtoeol (curwin);
123                     break;
```

```
124                         case 'w':        /* write file */
125                             icurwin = 0;
126                             putfile (ed[icurwin], file1);
127                             icurwin = 1;
128                             putfile (ed[icurwin], file2);
129                             return;
130                         case 'q':    /* quit */
131                             return;
132                 }
133             }
134     }

135     /* vertical line drawing routine:
136        draws line down screen at specified column */

137     vline (col)
138     int col;
139     {
140         int  i;

141         for ( i = 0; i < LINES - 1; ++i )
142                 mvaddch (i, col, '|');
143         refresh ();
144     }

145     /* file input routine:
146        opens file, copies up to LINES - 1 lines to specified window */

147     getfile (win, name)
148     WINDOW *win;
149     char *name;
150     {
151         int    line;
152         char   linebuf[512];
153         FILE   *infile;

154         if ( (infile = fopen (name, "r")) == (FILE *) NULL ) {
155                 /* put error message at bottom of stdscr */
156                 mvprintw (LINES - 1, icurwin * COLS / 2,
157                     "cannot read %s", name);
158             refresh ();
159             return;
160         }

161         /* read up to LINES - 1 lines from input file */
162         for ( line = 0; line < LINES - 1 &&
163                     fgets (linebuf, COLS / 2, infile) != (char *) NULL;
164                     ++line ) {

165             /* put line on screen */
166             mvwaddstr (win, line, 0, linebuf);
167         }

168         fclose (infile);
169         wmove (win, 0, 0);
170         wrefresh (win);
171     }
```

```
172    /* file output routine:
173        opens file, copies specified window to file */

174    putfile (win, name)
175    WINDOW *win;
176    char *name;
177    {
178            int   line, col;
179            int   linelen, pagelen;
180            FILE  *outfile;

181            if ( (outfile = fopen (name, "w")) == (FILE *) NULL ) {
182                    /* put error message at bottom of stdscr */
183                    mvprintw (LINES - 1, icurwin * COLS / 2,
184                            "cannot write %s", name);
185                    refresh ();
186                    return;
187            }

188            pagelen = scrsize (win);

189            for ( line = 0; line < pagelen; ++line ) {
190                    linelen = len (win, line);

191                    for ( col = 0; col < linelen; ++col ) {
192                            putc (mvwinch (win, line, col), outfile);
193                    }

194                    putc ('\n', outfile);
195            }
196            fclose (outfile);
197    }

198    /* line length routine:
199        returns length of specified window's line */

200    int len (win, line)
201    WINDOW *win;
202    int line;
203    {
204            int  col;

205            for ( col = COLS / 2 - 2; col >= 0 &&
206                        mvwinch (win, line, col) == ' '; --col )
207                    ;

208            return (col + 1);
209    }
```

```
210    /* window size routine: returns number of lines in window */
211    int scrsize (win)
212    WINDOW *win;
213    {
214          int line;

215          for ( line = LINES - 2; line >= 0 &&
216                      len (win, line) == 0; --line )
217                  ;

218          return (line + 1);
219    }

220    /* character add routine:
221       reads characters from terminal and puts in window
222       handles line wraparound and bottom of screen condition */

223    add (win)
224    WINDOW *win;
225    {
226          int in;

227          /* read in characters until ESC */
228          while ( (in = getch()) != '\033' ) {

229                  /* output character and get new location */
230                  waddch (win, in);
231                  getyx (win, curline, curcol);

232                  /* if RETURN and not bottom, go to next line */
233                  if ( in == '\r' && curline != LINES - 2 )
234                          ++curline;

235                  wmove (win, curline, curcol);
236                  wrefresh (win);
237          }
238    }

239    /* cleanup routine: call endwin and exit */

240    void finish ()
241    {
242          endwin ();
243          exit ();
244    }
```

APPENDIX

D

sdb SUMMARY

This appendix summarizes sdb's commands and syntax.

sdb is invoked as follows:

sdb *options executable corefile dir1 : dir2 : . . .*

The *options* are −w, which says that sdb may modify the executable program it is debugging; and −W, which says that sdb is not to display warning messages if the source files that created the executable program cannot be found or if they are newer than the program.

executable is the name of the executable program that is to be debugged; the default is a.out.

corefile is the name of the file containing the program's core dump; the default is core; if − is specified, it forces sdb to ignore any existing core file.

dir1 : dir2 : . . . is a colon-separated list of directories used to locate the source files that created the executable program; the default is the current directory.

• sdb Command Summary •

The following conventions are used in the sdb command summary: *[any]* means that *any* is optional; *var* specifies a variable in the program; *line* specifies a line number; *proc* specifies a procedure's name.

addr specifies an address in memory; *RE* specifies a *regular expression* (as in ed); *c* specifies an integer count or number of repetitions; and *fmt* specifies a format. Unless otherwise specified, the default for *line* is the current line.

Displaying Values

var ! val	Assign *val* to *var*
var / [fmt]	Display contents of *var* using format *fmt*
var=[fmt]	Display address of *var* using format *fmt*
line=[fmt]	Display address of *line* using format *fmt*
number=[fmt]	Display *number* using format *fmt*
line?[fmt]	Display instruction at *line* using format *fmt*
x	Display machine registers and current machine instruction
X	Display machine instruction

Changing the Current Line and Current File

line	Make *line* the current line
/ *RE*	Make the next line containing *RE* the current line
? *RE*	Make the previous line containing *RE* the current line
p	Display current line
w	Display 10 lines around current line
z	Display current line and next nine lines; set current line to last line displayed
c+	Add *c* to current line and print new current line
c−	Subtract *c* from current line and print new current line
RETURN	Print the next line or memory location depending upon which was printed last
e *proc*	Set current file to file containing *proc*
e *file*	Set current file to *file*
e *dir*	Set source file directory to *dir*
e *dir file*	Set source file directory to *dir* and current file to *file*

Controlling the Program

*[c]*r *[args]*	Run program with *args* as arguments; if no *args* given, run with previous arguments (if any); redirection using < and > is also allowed; *c* specifies the number of breakpoints to ignore
*[c]*R	Run program without arguments; *c* specifies the number of breakpoints to ignore
*[line]*c *[c]*	Continue program without signal; *line* specifies a temporary breakpoint on *line*; *c* specifies the number of breakpoints to ignore

*[line]*C *[c]*	Continue program with signal; *line* specifies a temporary breakpoint on *line*; *c* specifies the number of breakpoints to ignore
*line*g *[c]*	Continue program execution starting at *line*; *c* specifies the number of breakpoints to ignore
*[line]*b *[commands]*	Set breakpoint at *line*; when breakpoint is encountered, if no sdb *commands* were given, control returns to the user; otherwise, *commands* are executed and execution continues; multiple *commands* are separated with semicolons
B	List all breakpoints
D	Delete all breakpoints
*[line]*d	Delete breakpoint at *line*; if *line* isn't specified, interactively delete breakpoints, prompting user for each one
s *[c]*	Single step *c* lines; default is one line
S *[c]*	Single step *c* lines; default is one line; procedure calls count as one line
i	Single step one machine instruction without signal
I	Single step one machine instruction with signal
var$m *[c]*	Single step *c* lines or until *var* changes; default for *c* is infinity
addr:m *[c]*	Single step *c* lines or until *addr* changes; default for *c* is infinity
*level*v	Set single step debugging print level to *level*; if no *level* specified, toggles debugging on/off
*[line]*a	If *line* is of the form *proc*:, this command is equivalent to *proc*:b T; otherwise, it is equivalent to b l.
l	Print the next line to execute
t	Print stack trace
T	Print top of stack
proc (*args*)	Call *proc* with *args* as parameters.
proc (*args*) /*fmt*	Call *proc* with *args* as parameters; print returned value according to *fmt*; default format is integer
k	Kill currently running process

Miscellaneous Commands

CTRL-d	Print the next ten lines of source or data depending upon which was printed last
< *file*	Execute commands from *file*
M	Display address maps
M? *vals*	Set text map to *vals*
M/ *vals*	Set data map to *vals*
"*string*	Display *string*
!*command*	Execute *command* with the shell
q	Quit sdb

Variables may be specified using one of the following forms:

variable	The *variable* in the current procedure. *variable* may be a regular variable, an array, or a structure.
:*variable*	The global *variable*. *variable* may be a regular variable, an array, or a structure.
procedure:*variable*	The *variable* in *procedure*. *variable* may be a regular variable, an array, or a structure.
variable, *n*	The *n*th instance on the stack of *variable* in the current procedure. *variable* may be a regular variable, an array, or a structure.
procedure:*variable*, *n*	The *n*th instance on the stack of *variable* in *procedure* (for recursive procedures).

In all of the above, *variable* may be a regular variable, an array, or a structure, and the shell's pattern matching characters ? (which matches one character) and * (which matches zero or more characters) can be used in variable and procedure names.

Array elements may be referenced using the following forms:

array	All elements of *array*.
array[*sub*]	The element *sub* in *array*.
array[*sub*][*sub*] ...	An element in a multidimensional *array*.

sub may be of the form

number	The subscript *number*.
number1;*number2*	The subscripts from *number1* to *number2*.
*	All valid subscripts.

A final subscript (i.e., [*number*]) that is omitted is equivalent to [*]. To access the value a pointer points to, you must use *pointer*[0], and not **pointer*.

Structure members may be referenced using the following forms:

structure	All members of *structure*.
structure.*member*	The *member* in *structure*.
address.*member*	The *member* in the structure at *address*; the template for the most previously referenced structure is used to evaluate *member*.
structptr->*member*	The *member* in the structure pointed to by *structptr*.

Array and structure specifications may be combined to reference arrays of structures and structures of arrays, e.g.,

```
array[0].member
array[0;10].member
structure.array[0][10]
```

Some commands print a variable's value; normally, the value is printed in a
format suitable for the variable's type as declared in the program. The variable's
size may be specified using the following letters:

b   one byte

h   two bytes

l   four bytes

and the format may be specified using the following letters:

c   character

d   decimal

u   unsigned

o   octal

x   hexadecimal

f   32-bit floating point

g   64-bit floating point

s   string

a   characters starting at the variable's address

p   pointer to procedure

i   machine language with addresses printed symbolically and numerically

l   machine language with addresses printed numerically

The size specifier may be used with the c, d, u, o, and x formats, e.g., cb—a
one-byte character, oh—a two-byte octal value, and lu—a four-byte unsigned
value.

The character . (period) refers to the last specified variable.

Line numbers may be referenced using the following forms:

number	The line *number* in the current file.
file : *number*	The line *number* in *file*.
procedure : *number*	The line *number* in the file containing *procedure*.
file :	The first executable line in *file*.
procedure :	The first executable line in *procedure*.

INDEX